Materialist Philosophy of History

Materialist Philosophy of History

A Realist Antidote to Postmodernism

Branko Mitrović

LEXINGTON BOOKS
Lanham • Boulder • New York • London

Published by Lexington Books
An imprint of The Rowman & Littlefield Publishing Group, Inc.
4501 Forbes Boulevard, Suite 200, Lanham, Maryland 20706
www.rowman.com

6 Tinworth Street, London SE11 5AL, United Kingdom

Copyright © 2020 by The Rowman & Littlefield Publishing Group, Inc.

All rights reserved. No part of this book may be reproduced in any form or by any electronic or mechanical means, including information storage and retrieval systems, without written permission from the publisher, except by a reviewer who may quote passages in a review.

British Library Cataloguing in Publication Information Available

Library of Congress Cataloging-in-Publication Data
The hardback edition of this book was previously cataloged by the Library of Congress as follows:

Names: Mitrovic, Branko, author.
Title: Materialist philosophy of history : a realist antidote to postmodernism / Branko Mitrović.
Description: Lanham : Lexington Books, 2020. | Includes bibliographical references and index. | Summary: "This book examines the wide-ranging implications for historical research of the view that everything is physical and that no immaterial entities, forces, or phenomena exist. It presents the consequences of materialism for our understanding of the historical past, including the rejection of postmodernist perspectives on history"-- Provided by publisher.
Subjects: LCSH: Materialism. | History--Philosophy.
Classification: LCC B825 .M58 2020 (print) | LCC B825 (ebook) | DDC 901--dc23
LC record available at https://lccn.loc.gov/2020010393
LC ebook record available at https://lccn.loc.gov/2020010394

ISBN 978-1-7936-2000-2 (cloth : alk. paper)
ISBN 978-1-7936-2002-6 (pbk. : alk. paper)
ISBN 978-1-7936-2001-9 (electronic)

Phoebe fave . . .

Contents

Preface	ix
Acknowledgments	xi
Introduction	1
1 Realism	29
2 Individualism	47
3 Free Will	65
4 Thoughts and Contents	83
5 Language	105
6 Essentialism	127
7 Contexts and Rationality	143
8 Understanding, Interpretation and Translation	173
9 Transparency	189
Conclusion: Materialism and Humanist Values, Or: How Is Idealism Possible?	209
Appendix: On Not Seeing-As	219
Bibliography	233
Index	249
About the Author	259

Preface

Almost twenty years ago, without thinking that these interests would eventually result in a book, I started to analyze in a systematic way the methodological problems and dilemmas that I encountered in my historical work and in works of my colleagues. Originally, I thought of this interest as an interest in the methodology of historical research, and only after some time I realized that these problems were, in fact, genuine philosophical problems that belong properly in the field of the philosophy of history. I owe this insight to my doctoral adviser in philosophy, Christopher Martin—as he put it when I described the topic: "You are proposing to do more philosophy, not less." The choice of methodological problems that interested me seemed spontaneous at the time. The approach, it soon turned out, had to be bi-disciplinary, pertaining to the philosophical treatment of methodological problems on the one hand and their position in the history of historiography on the other. Over a decade, its result was two series of papers that came out mostly in *History and Theory* and the *Journal of Art Historiography*. I owe huge gratitude to the editors of these two journals, Brian Fay and Richard Woodfield for their interest in my work, encouragement and theoretical feedback regarding numerous issues and dilemmas that I faced while working on these articles. When it comes to the philosophical papers and ultimately the material that makes up this book, I also need to express my gratitude to Nick Zangwill, Barry Smith, Ian Verstegen and Robert Nola for extensive philosophical help, advice and support, as well as to my proof-editors Karen Wise and Julie Perkins for their help with written English.

The papers pertaining to the history of the methodological problems that interested me, mostly originally published in the *Journal of Art Historiography*, gradually came to present a coherent picture about the rise of collectivist ideologies in German (art) historiography and became my book *Rage and*

Denials, published by the Penn State University Press in 2015. By that time I also knew that my philosophical work on the methodology of historical research constituted material for a book. Nevertheless, the awareness about the nature of this project developed in phases. Originally, I thought that the book was about the philosophy of intellectual history, because most of my work up to that time pertained to problems of interpretation. However, methodological problems of interpretation are not limited to intellectual history; all historians face them and it took me some time to accept that the implications of the book necessarily pertained to a wider picture. It took another, later, insight to realize that my methodological concerns, that stimulated my interests in the philosophy of history from the beginning, were consistently motivated by my unwillingness to accept the expansion of ontology beyond the physical world. The very choice of the methodological dilemmas that I sought to resolve in my earlier work was not spontaneous as I originally thought; rather, it was motivated by my rejection of (what I perceived as) the widespread ontological laxity in the historical works that I read. My tendency to see hidden (often political) agendas behind inflationary ontologies only strengthened my motivation through the years in which I worked on these problems.

From the very beginning of my work in the philosophy of history I have been aware that my views and assumptions were incompatible with and opposed to the postmodernist perspectives that were dominant in the final decades of the twentieth century and whose influence is still sometimes strongly felt. My original intention was, nevertheless, to avoid the discussion of postmodernism in this book, and I am therefore grateful to the anonymous reviewer of the manuscript for emphasizing the need to describe explicitly the incompatibility of materialism with anti-realist, anti-foundationalist and social-constructionist paradigms. I have no doubt that postmodernist perspectives have had poisonous effects on the intellectual life and the political culture of English-speaking countries for the past half a century. In the philosophy of history they have led the discipline into a dead end and resulted in its reduction into desperate and unproductive efforts to prove that the past did not happen. The introduction of questions pertaining to the methodology of historical research and to the compatibility of our understanding of the past with the materialist, physicalist worldview should, I hope, help break the deadlock.

Philadelphia, December 2019.

Acknowledgments

I should like to express my gratitude to *History and Theory* and *Journal of Art Historiography* for the permission to reproduce parts of the following articles:

Mitrović, Branko. "Intellectual History, Inconceivability and Methodological Holism." *History and Theory* 46 (2007): 29–47.

Mitrović, Branko. "Intentionalism, Intentionality and Reporting Beliefs." *History and Theory* 48 (2009): 180–198.

Mitrović, Branko. "Atribution of Concepts and Problems with Anachronism." *History and Theory* 50 (2011): 303–327.

Mitrović, Branko. "Opacity and Transparency in Historical Representations. Frank Ankersmit: *Meaning, Truth and Reference in Historical Representation* by Frank Ankersmit. Ithaca: Cornell University Press, 2012." [Book review.] *History and Theory* 53 (2014): 277–294.

Mitrović, Branko. "Historical Understanding and Historical Interpretation as Contextualization." *History and Theory* 54 (2015): 311–332.

Mitrović, Branko. "'Without thinkers . . . no theories of the world.' Tim Crane: *Aspects of Psychologism*, Cambridge, Mass.: Harvard University Press, 2014 and *The Objects of Thought*, Oxford: Oxford University Press, 2013." [Book review.] *History and Theory* 55 (2016), 141–153.

Mitrović, Branko. "A Panofskian Meditation on Free Will and the Social World: Is Humanist (Art) Historiography Still Credible?" *Journal of Art Historiography* 15 (2016): BM2

Mitrović, Branko. "A Refutation of (Post-) Narrativism, or: Why Postmodernists Love Austro-Hungary. Jouni-Matti Kuukkanen, *Postnarrativist Philosophy of Historiography*, Houndmills: Palgrave Macmillan, 2015." [Book review.] *Journal of Art Historiography* 15 (2016): BM1.

Introduction

In some German train stations, one can read the announcement: "Es besteht Rauchverbot" ("There exists a prohibition of smoking"). Presumably, this does not suggest that the prohibition of smoking, *Rauchverbot*, is an entity that can be found in the train station in addition to trains, passengers, shops, and so on. Nor is it a property of the objects that exist in the train station. Rather, the announcement means that a person who smokes will be involved in specific types of interactions with security guards, such as paying fines. What actually exists is the guards instructed to fine everyone who tries to smoke. It is a common practice in many languages, and the German bureaucratic style often requires that situations that involve only material entities (including human beings) be described using sentences about imaginary immaterial entities. Taken literally, such sentences are false because they attribute existence to fictional objects—nevertheless, they convey their message and describe metaphorically a situation that really obtains. The tendency to describe real events by talking about imaginary or abstract objects differs from one language to another. Latin is, in this sense, possibly on the opposite end of the spectrum from German: good Latin style precludes the possibility that an abstract noun could be the subject of an active verb.[1] Students who learn to write Latin are, for instance, told that the English sentence "The replacement of the emperor changed everything" cannot be literally translated into Latin because "the replacement of the emperor" is not really a thing and cannot act or change anything. Rather, one is advised to write the equivalent of "The emperor having been replaced, everything changed"—even though, it may be argued, this does not mean quite the same thing. Similar dilemmas result from standard English phrases as well. A statement such as "people are obligated to act" easily becomes "there exists an obligation to act." Should this allow us to assume that such obligations are real things, on equal footing with dogs and electricity? On the one hand, one is tempted to say that they are not, that words such as "obligation" merely refer to widespread types of human relations and interactions. On the other hand, they do make people act in certain ways, and if we admit that they cause events to happen, it is difficult to say that they are mere fictions.

Quandaries of this kind are unavoidable in historical research. Dilemmas about the nature and the causal capacities of historical entities such as states or armies, phenomena or periods such Baroque or Antiquity, or events such as wars or revolutions underlie every attempt to understand and explain what happened in history. Was the Renaissance or the French Revolution an immaterial force over and above participating individuals and their interactions—or are these words merely joint names for these individuals and (or) their interactions? Did the Renaissance and the French Revolution actually have causal powers on their own, and did they cause the interactions of participating individuals—or should a historian assume that their causal powers merely resulted from these individuals' actions and interactions? Were the Renaissance or the French Revolution identical with the actions and interactions of participating individuals, or were they something more? In order to describe or explain an event, a historian necessarily makes assumptions about the nature of the forces and the protagonists involved; these assumptions determine the possible frameworks of the descriptions and the credibility of the explanations a historian can provide.

MATERIALISM AND THE PHILOSOPHY OF HISTORY: AN OLD DILEMMA

These introductory observations bring us to the topic of this book. Let me use the term "materialism" for the view that things that are not describable within the worldview of modern natural sciences do not exist and have never existed.[2] (Some people prefer words "physicalism" or "naturalism.") A straightforward way to describe this position, which certainly requires further philosophical elaboration, is to say that everything is physical. Human mental states and their contents, on this account, are biological phenomena, human beings are biological creatures, and chemistry that underlies human biology ultimately results from the physics of particles. The assumption is not that everything should be studied using physical methods, but that all that there is, is physically constituted. The aim of this book is to describe and analyze the implications of this worldview for historical research. What does it mean to approach historical research and history-writing with the assumption that materialism is true? What kinds of constraints on the assumptions that a historian can make and what kinds of implications for the methodology of historical research arise from the adoption of a materialist ontology—an ontology that precludes entities, forces or phenomena that are not physical? What kind of understanding of historical events results from the refusal to include spiritual, abstract, or immaterial forces, entities, events or phenomena in historical descriptions and explanations? Considering the wide and pervasive influence of the materialist worldview today, for anyone interested in history, it is certainly important to know about the constraints that materialism imposes on historical research and our understanding of the past. Quite probably many, maybe the majority, of the readers of this book endorse the materialist worldview in some form. The same applies to the majority of historians I know. This widespread private endorsement of materialism, however, stands in sharp contrast with idealist ideologies and theoretical approaches such as postmodernism, anti-realism, cultural constructionism or anti-foundationalism that have dominated the humanities for the past fifty years—and that often cannot be reconciled with the materialist understanding of the world and its physical constitution. The same applies, we shall see, to various idealist positions in analytic philosophy.

The implications of materialism for historical research and the understanding of history penetrate very deep into a historian's work and have wide-ranging consequences. My motivation for writing this book came precisely from the awareness that these consequences are neither always clear nor obvious to many historians or even philosophers of history. A historian may, for instance, reject the validity of historical explanations that rely on spiritual or divine forces and rely on culture or social context instead, but attribute to cultures or social contexts causal powers that make them different from spiritual forces only by their name. Materialism imposes constraints on historical research that have significant consequences when it comes to a wide range of methodological dilemmas pertaining to, for instance, historical causation, the nature of historical contexts, the contents of the mental states of historical figures, reporting the beliefs of historical figures, the nature of languages, the translation of historical documents, and many others. The purpose of this book is to survey these consequences. Materialism in historical research makes it impossible for a historian to rely on abstract and immaterial entities and forces in understanding, describing, or explaining historical events or phenomena. Hardly any historians today will explicitly state that the Renaissance was a spiritual force in its own right that determined the actions of individuals during the *quattro-* and *cinquecento*—but insofar as they describe and explain the actions of Renaissance individuals, they will have to decide whether they will, or will not, attribute explanatory and causal capacities to the period taken on its own, over and above the actions and interactions of biological individuals. Similarly, a historian who attributes free will to historical figures is bound to provide different explanations for their actions from a historian who assumes that these actions were predetermined by Providence or the social-historical context—and it is important to discuss whether and in what form free will can be compatible with an understanding of historical figures as biological creatures. The assumption that the contents of the mental states of historical figures result from their neurobiology and do not have abstract, immaterial existence on their own has a wide range of consequences for the understanding and interpretation of historical documents. Additional complexities arise from the fact that historians also live in historical contexts and that, consequently, the assumptions that materialism makes about the contents of mental states, reasoning capacities, free will, the use of language and so on, apply not only to the historical figures they research about but to these historians as well.

The materialist perspective on history is not a novel one. Obviously, ancient historians could not have shared our modern materialist worldview nor did they differentiate between things that can and cannot have physical descriptions the way we do. Nevertheless, Tacitus discussed, though he did not endorse, the equivalent view that historical events are exclusively predetermined by natural causes.[3] Thucydides's and Polybius's avoidance of spiritual forces in historical descriptions and explanations was arguably motivated by ontological concerns that are quite similar to those that motivate the materialist perspective that this book seeks to analyze. Thucydides famously warned about the absence of fabulous events in his narration, and Polybius recommended that wherever one can specify other causes of events, one should not have recourse to gods.[4] An example of a different approach is Herodotus's explanation of the fact that, during the battle of Platea, many Persian soldiers died around the temple of Demeter as the revenge of the goddess for the destruction of her temple in Eleusine.[5] Historical explanations that explicitly rely on divine intervention were still common among nineteenth-century historians: Leopold Ranke thus claimed that God's intervention caused the failure of Maximilian I's plans to create a universal monarchy.[6] One of the turning points in the rejection of divine intervention in historical explanations was the 1890s *Methodenstreit* and Karl Lamprecht's attacks on the Rankean tradition.[7] However, Lamprecht replaced Providence with supra-natural determinism exercised by the collectives to which individuals belong, and the idea of cultural history that he promoted anticipated the supra-individual immaterial forces that marked Oswald Spengler's *Decline of the West*.[8] About the same time, Alois Riegl introduced into art historiography the concept of *Kunstwollen*, a self-propelled, immaterial artistic force that belongs to the community and has the capacity to causally affect the work of individual artists.[9] In other words, one may cease to use words such as "God" or "Providence" in history-writing, but as long as one relies on immaterial causation, one will have to postulate immaterial causes. As Erwin Panofsky suggested, such a methodology of historical research often merely rearticulates in new words theological positions from centuries ago.[10] A historian who introduces Culture or Discourse as forces on their own that explain actions of individuals and their interactions, that determine or delimit everything individuals think and know, and even construct their reality, is relying on a concept that is not unlike Luther's conception of a Deity that created reality and predetermines everything, including human actions and thoughts.[11] Old-fashioned metaphysics can thus easily sneak in, disguised by new words. Consider the implications for the history of literature of Roland Barthes's thesis about "the death of the author." This is the view that the author does not contribute to the content of a literary work, that he or she is a mere "scriptor" (*scripteur*).[12] Barthes explicitly rejected the possibility that authors' actions (writing) may result from their free will and insisted that it is *language itself* that writes through authors.[13] It is consequently not clear that (or in what sense) the underlying ontology of his theory of literary creativity is different from the one presented by Plato in the *Ion*. Plato says there that poets do not work by their own skill (τέχνῃ) but are driven by a Divine force (θείᾳ δυνάμει), and God uses them as laborers (ὑπηρέταις).[14] One way to look at what Barthes was saying is that he merely replaced what Plato called "God" and "laborers" with "language" and "scriptors." However credible such a view may have been in Plato's time, today one would be expected to take into account, at least as a possibility, that these "scriptors" are biological creatures that can be affected only by something that can have a physical description. A history of literature based on Barthes's perspective would need to explain the ontology of what Barthes calls "language" and the nature of its causal capacities. If it is an immaterial force, then one needs to explain how it can affect biological creatures such as "scriptors"; alternatively, if it has material causal capacities, then one needs to explain what they might be.

Postmodernist historiography provides numerous similar examples of ontological expansions that introduce immaterial historical forces, such as epistemes or discourses, and attribute to them genuine causal properties.[15] In a 1985 polemic well known to art historians, Norman Bryson criticized Ernst Gombrich for the view that styles of representation change through history, while the natural world that painters strive to represent remains unchanged.[16] He claimed instead that nature and physical reality themselves are products of History. History in this case becomes a force that (not unlike God in Protestant traditions) generates both the physical world and the human mental lives.[17] Another example of similar reasoning one finds in the work of the architectural historian Alberto Pérez-Gómez. Pérez-Gómez explicitly states that the objective world is an illusion and that it does not exist.[18] The reality of the modern world, he claims, "is not independent of our consciousness."[19] This leads him to infer that forces such as language construct the physical reality and human interactions with it. He thus states that "[t]he verb 'to see' was reciprocal in Greek; whoever saw was seen, and the blind were invisible."[20] The claim assumes that language parcels, structures and organizes human reality. If one did not attribute such causal capacities to ancient Greek language, one simply could not say that "whoever saw was seen, and the blind were invisible" merely because of the claim that the verb "to see" does not differentiate between active and passive forms.[21]

Cultural, linguistic or historical constructionism of this kind is not particular to postmodernism; rather, postmodernism shares it with the idealist tradition to which it belongs. Bryson's claims, for instance, are very similar to a research program described in 1927 by the Viennese art historian Hans Sedlmayr, who claimed that the natural world that artists imitate depends on the *Geist* of the community.[22] For both Bryson and Sedlmayr communal forces (history, the spirit of the community) construct the physical world itself. It is therefore not surprising that the implications of materialism—a position traditionally opposed to idealist worldview—systematically turn out to be incompatible with the core tenets of postmodernist, constructionist, anti-realist, anti-foundationalist agendas, highly influential for the past half a century. Materialism cannot be reconciled, for instance, with the popular views that social phenomena such as culture or language exist over and above human individuals and their interactions, that theory-free perception (and concept formation) is impossible or that language determines the cognitive and mental capacities of historical subjects. The same applies to the idea, promoted by some postmodernist philosophers of history, that colligatory concepts (such as "the Renaissance" of "the French Revolution") have no reference. At the same time, it is not easy for postmodernists to reject physicalism the way idealist philosophers of the past traditionally rejected materialist positions. The claim that human history, languages or beliefs construct the physical reality cannot be simply asserted (the way postmodernist authors often do)—if it is to be credible, one needs to support it with a comprehensive metaphysical elaboration showing that most of our modern science is false.

Throughout the book, I will be thus obliged to point out when the implications of materialism run against popular postmodernist positions. However, the aim of the book is not a polemic against postmodernism. Its aim is also not to prove or to refute the validity of materialism (physicalism). The aim is to provide a comprehensive survey of the consequences of materialism for the philosophy of history and its implications for historical research. I hope, for instance, that a religious reader, who believes that God sometimes intervenes in history and sometimes not, will still endorse the description of historical research presented here as valid insofar as one leaves aside God's immaterial interventions in history. Similarly, I hope that the readers who believe that social institutions or languages are something over and above human individuals and their interactions, or the readers who believe that mental states are something other than brain states, will still agree that the perspective on historical research presented here is accurate, insofar as these non-materialist assumptions are bracketed. Possibly, they may even use the conclusions of the book in order to argue that materialism is not compatible with a sound methodology of historical research, as they conceive of it. Postmodernists may also try to do the same. It is therefore appropriate to criticize the book if and insofar as it fails to describe accurately the implications of materialism for historical research—but insofar as some readers disagree with these implications as valid approaches to historical research, and think that historical research should proceed differently and consequently in ways that require one to rely on immaterialist assumptions, then this is not really a criticism of this book. Rather, I can only hope that this book will contribute to their project of defining what these immaterialist assumptions need to be. And I can also offer advice: if such project is going to yield credible results, it will need to rely on comprehensive metaphysics, capable of supplanting the materialist worldview. Materialism is a metaphysical position like any other, and since a rejection of a metaphysical position necessarily entails the formulation of an alternative metaphysical position, this alternative position will remain unconvincing as long as it is not appropriately elaborated.

MATERIALISM, PHYSICALISM AND NATURALISM, DEFINITIONS, HEMPEL'S DILEMMA

Throughout the book, I use the term "materialist" for the kind of worldview that many philosophers also refer to as "physicalist" or "naturalist." I considered using one of these two terms instead, but eventually decided that the phrases "physicalist philosophy of history" or "naturalist philosophy of history" sound too unusual. It is generally accepted that the terms "materialism," "naturalism," and "physicalism" are broadly interchangeable; John Searle, on whose views I rely extensively throughout this book, uses the term "materialism."[23] (Some authors suggest that physicalism should be taken to be the modern successor of materialism, materialism that is informed by modern developments in physics.[24] Such a distinction in terminology could be made, but it is also not clear that it would have much relevance for research in history.) I am also aware that for some readers, the use of the term "materialist" in relation to history may invoke associations with the works of Karl Marx and Friedrich Engels. In one way this is appropriate. I consider their youthful *German Ideology* and *Holy Family* masterpieces of the materialist philosophy of history of their time—though I am skeptical that their later theories about dialectics, class struggle, or revolution are compatible with materialism. These early works certainly have a venerable position in the history of the materialist philosophy of history—a position similar to that of Epicurus's or Lucretius's writings in the general history of materialism—but their concerns, and the arguments they made, are very dated from the perspective of modern materialism. They have very little to say about the topics discussed in this book. At the same time, it is also not clear why the Marxist tradition should hold exclusive rights to the term "materialism" in relation to history.

It is important to specify here in more detail the assumptions the book makes about the materialist worldview. There exists an extensive philosophical literature about materialism (physicalism). Most of this literature concentrates on the questions of whether materialism is (can be) true, what the arguments are in favor of or against it, how they can be responded to, whether materialism is true necessarily or contingently (if it is true at all), whether our knowledge that it is true or false is a priori or a posteriori, and so on. Instead of discussing such questions, the book examines the implications for historical research of the assumption that materialism is true. In the philosophical literature, there is also an extensive debate about the possible definitions of materialism. Different definitions that have been proposed describe broadly the same position. It is not clear that some of them are more suitable for our discussion here than others. Rather than choosing between them, through this Introduction I will try to survey the physicalist assumptions that are likely to affect historical research. I will start with two common ways of defining materialism and then proceed by analyzing various assumptions that are normally associated with it.

The first way to describe materialism has already been mentioned: this is the view that the world in which we live and in which the historical past happened ultimately consists of particles, forces, fields, entities and phenomena that physics describes, and nothing else. Things that we encounter in the world, on this account, consist of particles and their aggregates that behave in accordance with the laws of physics. Chemical phenomena are understood to be ultimately physical, and biological phenomena are chemical and therefore physical phenomena. Human beings, including historical figures and the historians who write about them, are biological creatures. Their mental capacities and mental states together with mental contents result from their neurobiology.[25] This does not mean that materialism should be understood as rabid reductionism—although this might seem to be the case. Since it is assumed that historical items (entities, events, phenomena) are interactions among biological organisms, that human mental states are or are caused by biological states of the brain, that biological states are ultimately chemical states, and that chemical states are ultimately physical, it may indeed seem that materialism in the historical humanities requires that all historical descriptions and explanations be stated in terms of physical subatomic processes. There is no reason why this should be the case.[26] Neither biology nor chemistry abandons the materialist paradigm when they describe chemical and biological phenomena without talking about them in terms of physical subatomic processes. Rather, when a chemist or a biologist talks about phenomena from their disciplines using terminologies of their disciplines, they are talking about the way physical phenomena manifest themselves in their disciplines, in terms of their disciplines. They are using a language that is appropriate for their disciplines to describe these phenomena. Reducibility does not imply elimination: water is H_2O but this does not mean that water does not exist nor does it mean that chemical laws do not apply to it; it still freezes at 0°C. The same applies to historians. When materialist historians describe a medieval battle, from their point of view, all the items they refer to are assumed to be physical items anyway, and the description would not get any more physical if we replaced it with a description that would directly list the movement of all subatomic particles involved. (Even if one could actually list all the movements of all participating particles within a workable time, a description that talks about soldiers and horses would certainly be preferable because it would be shorter and easier to comprehend.) The important consequence of physicalism is, however, that it precludes the assumption that non-physical forces could have participated in historical events or could be relevant for historical explanations—the way it precludes their role in explanations of chemical or biological phenomena.

It may also be pointed out that the reducibility of everything to physical phenomena is problematic because of multiple realizability and Jerry Fodor's thesis about the disunity of science.[27] This is the argument that some types of mental states can be realized in a great variety of neuro-systems in different ways—for instance, octopuses may be able to feel pain like humans, although their neuro-system is quite different. Multiple realizability does not, however, suggest the need to expand ontology and rely on abstract, immaterial or spiritual substances. The fact that pain is differently realized in different biological systems does not mean that it is not biological. Also, the multiple realizability argument pertains to types of events, situations or properties, whereas historians are mainly interested in their individual (token) events, situations and properties. A historian who believes that stomach pain affected Napoleon's capacity to command a battle may be interested in the specific biological condition that caused it, but hardly in its similarity with the pain that an octopus may feel. Finally, it should be mentioned that the multiple realizability argument is not applicable to complex social structures—it cannot be used to argue, for instance, that armies or governments are instantiated in such a variety of ways that they cannot be reduced to biological individuals and their interactions.[28]

There are various other ways to define physicalism.[29] Here is an approach that avoids associations with reductionism.[30] Imagine that there is another world that is an exact copy of our world in all its physical elements (such as particles, forces, fields, causation, laws of nature, and so on) but nothing else. Let me call such a world "a purely material world." In such a world, chemical and biological substances would be the same as in our world, and, insofar as we argue that mental states are biological—ultimately physical—they would be replicated too. The materialist assumption is then going to be that our world and the purely material world necessarily have the same history. In other words, even if our world contains non-physical items (communal spirits, discourses, immaterial cultural contexts, and so on), the materialist assumption is that they do not participate in history. The question that this book addresses is then: what does it mean for historical research to make this assumption? We shall see throughout this book that the implications are numerous. Two observations should be made here. First, the idea that a world that replicates the physical elements of our world would repeat the same human history suggests a determinist perspective—that the necessity of natural laws fully determined the way human history evolved and historical events happened. In fact, we shall see later that, precisely because of such determinism, materialism in historical research requires historians to make assumptions that are equivalent to the attribution of free will to historical figures in the explanation of their decisions and actions. Second, our assumption will be that indeterminacy at the quantum level of particles does not interfere with human-level history.

The use of the term "physical" in these descriptions of materialism can be questioned. What kind of physics do materialists have in mind? This dilemma, formulated by Carl Hempel, is often cited as an argument against materialism (physicalism).[31] Presumably, someone who is talking about adjusting the worldview of the modern humanities to that of science is not talking about medieval science. But then, should we mean our contemporary scientific worldview, which is recognized to be imperfect in many ways, or some ideal scientific worldview of the future that has achieved ultimate truths about our physical world? If one wants to have views that are consistent with the future worldview of science that has achieved ultimate truths, it is fair to point out that we do not know what such a science would be like, nor what these truths might be. But if we rely on the positions endorsed by our contemporary science, then many of them are likely to be proven to be false in the future. The substantial discussion about this dilemma that exists in the literature about physicalism is, however, hardly relevant for us here. Although we certainly know nothing about the discoveries natural sciences will make in the future, it is nevertheless important to be aware of the implications of the contemporary scientific worldview for research in the historical humanities. We are thus certainly talking about our contemporary physics and contemporary natural sciences. In this sense, historical research does not differ from research in other fields. The fact that biochemistry may make new discoveries in the future does not make it irrelevant for biologists to interpret the results of their research in relation to contemporary biochemistry. This also answers Noam Chomsky's variation of Hempel's argument.[32] Should it happen, Chomsky pointed out in relation to the physicalist approach to the study of the mind, that there exist separate forces that make the mind function and that are independent of physical forces as we conceive of them today, then the conception of physics will be expended to include them as well—the way it happened with electric phenomena, magnetic fields, and so on, none of which are in the mechanical conception of physics inherited from Newton. One can certainly agree with this. Nevertheless, we do not know what such future discoveries will be like, while it is interesting to know what it means for historical research to assume that the world in which historical events occurred is the one that our contemporary natural sciences describe. It should also be mentioned that discussions presented in this book pertain to the implications of very general aspects of the materialist worldview for historical research—such as causation or the rejection of immaterial, abstract, or spiritual items. Arguably, these elements are unlikely to change with the advancements of science that one can expect in the future. At the same time, since sciences make new discoveries and abandon old views, it is important to be cautious about situations in which well-established positions in historiography and the philosophy of history depend on such abandoned scientific positions. For instance, we shall see that some influential views of Arthur Danto and Thomas Kuhn depend on the 1950s' theories of perception that were abandoned by psychologists decades ago.

ASSUMPTIONS ABOUT CAUSATION

Assumptions about causation play the core role when it comes to the implications of materialism in historical research.

Throughout the book I will use the term "physical items" for physical things, their properties, physical events as well as physical objects such as particles, their conglomerates, fields, forces, their movements and changes, and so on. In other words: various things, events, phenomena can be described and identified (conceptualized, as we shall see in Chapter Four) in various ways. They count as "physical items" or "can be physically describable" if it is possible, in principle, to state a description that identifies them in physical terms. "In principle" means that the description needs to be possible, but need not be available (for instance, we may lack the information necessary to do that). Also, I will use the term *historical items* for the historical entities, events, phenomena, and so on, that historians write about.

I will rely on the following assumptions or postulates about causation:

(a) Physical or historical items or their properties typically have more than one cause. (For instance, the outcome of a medieval battle may have resulted from the late arrival of auxiliary troops, the better equipment of the victorious army, internal dissension in the defeated army, circumstances such as the fact that the earth exercised gravity on the participants, that water freezes at

0°C, so that the cavalry was able to charge over a frozen river, and so on.) When providing a historical explanation, we typically presuppose many causes that we do not state. In the third chapter, I will discuss the way historians choose which causes to state in historical explanations.

(b) The causes of physical or historical items precede their effects in time. (In some cases, causes can also continue to obtain during and after events they caused, but they cannot cause them if they do not precede them.)

(c) During human history, no physical or historical items came about or were changed without a cause. In the case of historical and physical items and their changes, *at least some* of their causes must have been actually existing items and their properties. (This point needs to be made because historians sometimes discuss *causation-by-omission*. For instance, it may be argued that an event would not have happened had some other event failed to happen. The non-occurrence of this latter event is then said to have caused the occurrence of the former. But even in such cases, no event could have happened whose only causes were causes-by-omission. Some real events had to happen as well in order to cause it.)

There is nothing particularly materialist about these three postulates. They are formulated to pertain to physical and historical items and could be applied even if these were two different kinds of items. Materialism is introduced with the assumption of causal closure:

(d) Only physical items (items that can have a physical description) can be causes or effects.[33]

Causal closure is a stronger thesis than the statement that non-physical items are non-existent and therefore cannot cause anything. Rather, it is asserted that even if they existed, non-physical items would be causally inert and would have no capacity to affect causally physical items nor could they be affected by them. Herodotus's explanation of the numerous deaths of Persian soldiers in the vicinity of the temple of Demeter thus has to be dismissed not merely because ancient Greek gods did not exist and could not have caused anything, but because such deities, as immaterial items that could not have a physical description, would have to be inert in the sense of causation and could not have caused biological events such as deaths of Persian soldiers.

Non-existing physical items can still be *imagined* to have existed and to have caused something. The assumption that even if they existed, non-physical items could not causally affect physical items is important because historians often discuss the possible causal impact of the non-happening of certain events. An extensive philosophical literature exists about such causation by omission.[34] For instance, one of the causes that contributed to the successful assassination of Franz Ferdinand in Sarajevo on 28 June 1914 was the failure of Austro-Hungarian officials to inform his driver about their decision to change the route for security reasons. As a result, the driver drove down the wrong street, and this is where the assassination took place. Had the driver been informed about the change of the route, the assassination would not have happened. It may therefore be said that the non-existence of an event—the communication between the officials and the driver—was one of the causes of the assassination. From this point of view, non-existent items can be causes—which may suggest the view that nothing can cause something. It can be responded that this concern is unnecessary, since we are merely talking here about counterfactual dependence that carries no ontological commitments.[35] Alternatively, one may postulate "negative events" and respond that the actual event that did happen, and that was one of the actual causes that contributed to the assassination, was precisely the non-communication between the officials and the driver.[36]

In relation to such causation-by-omission, causal closure merely states that non-physical items could not have caused anything. A conversation between officials and the driver of Franz Ferdinand would have been a physical event, and it is perfectly legitimate to say that had it happened, the assassination could have been prevented. Imaginary physical events can be legitimately imagined to have imaginary physical effects. But it is quite different if we say that "Had angels removed to iceberg from the course of Titanic, the disaster would not have happened." Angels are not physical entities and they cannot move icebergs. The important point is thus not to argue that non-physical items could not have existed and therefore could not have had causal capacities. (It is assumed that they could not have existed anyway.) Rather, the point is to deny them even hypothetical causal capacities: even if they had existed, such items would have been causally inert in the sense that they would have been unable to produce a causal impact. Physical items cannot be affected by non-physical items, regardless of whether the latter exist or not. (But also note that the statement "had angels removed the iceberg, Titanic would not have sunk" is still true, even if we accept causal closure. What is false is the belief that angels could have removed the iceberg from its course.)

CAUSATION AND EXPLANATION

Some further clarifications about causation are necessary here in order to complete the picture. In contemporary philosophical literature, causation is typically understood in two ways.[37] One view is that when we talk about causation, we must rely on some kind of regularity that ensures that an event of a certain kind is always followed by an event of another kind. David Lewis, in the 1980s, developed an alternative, counterfactuals-based approach.[38] This approach seeks to explain causal dependence in terms of counterfactual dependence—in general, the idea is that an event is the cause of another if the latter would not have occurred had the former not occurred. Regularity-based conceptions of causation are usually not helpful for historians because it is difficult to state the general rules that would underwrite historians' claims about causal relationships between historical events. Also, historians are more concerned with causal relationships between particular events and not general law-like regularities anyway. Alexander Maar has therefore convincingly argued that counterfactuals-based conceptions of causation are more applicable in historical research.[39] In any case, the above assumptions about causation are compatible with both regularity-based and counterfactuals-based approaches.

In the natural and experimental sciences, one often establishes causal laws on the basis of generalization from a large number of instances. In principle, experiments should be infinitely repeatable, and one can construct various experimental situations in order to confirm or disconfirm a hypothesis about a general causal law. In historical research, as well as in some sciences such as astronomy or geology, one typically deals with a limited number of instances. It is therefore often possible to state a general rule that applies to all cases, because their number is limited, but such a rule need not pertain to actual causes.[40] All Caesars who were named Caius died by the dagger, Suetonius observed.[41] It is not quite clear that this claim is true, but even if it were true, we would not say that the person's name is the cause of death. Full coincidence of a type of event with other events need not indicate a *causal* regularity. More generally, one should bear in mind that coincidence does not always indicate causation.

Questions pertaining to causation also arise in relation to historical explanations. There is the view that in order to state an explanation, one needs to state information about causes. The alternative view is that explanation merely requires explanatory information that need not always pertain to causes.[42] There is no need to enter this debate here—information about causes certainly plays an important role in many (or most) historical explanations, even if someone may deny that this is always true. Different approaches to the dilemma should nevertheless make us careful about different intuitions that people may have about the use of words such as "cause," "effect," "event," or the like. During the battle of Stalingrad, in the final days preceding the Red Army counteroffensive, the Soviet units in the city itself fought with their backs to the Volga River, in order to avoid encirclement. One could therefore say that the position of the river (partly) *explains* the position of the Soviet units at that time. But should we say that the position of the river (partly) *caused* the disposition of the Soviet units? Or should one say that such geographical facts are explanatory circumstances or conditions, but not causes? Different people can have different intuitions about the use of the word "cause" in similar dilemmas. Something similar applies to the claim that only events can be causes. One may argue that geographical facts about an area are not events and that therefore the position of the river could not have *caused* the disposition of the Red Army units. This would be equivalent to saying that the presence of oxygen should not count as a contributing cause of a forest fire, because it is not an event. It may be responded that "geography" in the case of the Battle of Stalingrad results from the geological events that determined the position of the river many thousands of years ago, so these events should count among the causes of the position of Soviet military units. "The presence of oxygen that enabled a forest fire" then stands for the events in the history of our planet that provided it with an atmosphere with a high level of oxygen. Alternatively, one may turn the argument in the opposite direction and respond that the position of the Volga should count as an event precisely because it caused the Soviet units to take the positions that they did, and only events can be causes. Some authors propose simply stretching the use of the term "event" so that it can include the presence of oxygen when explaining a forest fire.[43] An additional complication results from the common assumption that causation is transitive, in the sense that the cause of a cause of an item also counts as that item's cause.[44] Sometimes transitivity contradicts our intuitions about the use of the word "cause"—for instance, in the case of very remote events or when our value systems make it hard for us to say that an event that we regard as good caused something bad. A doctor may save the life of a patient who dies some years later in a car crash. Had the patient not been alive, he or she could not have died in the car crash, but it is awkward to say that by saving the life of the patient, the doctor caused him or her to die in the car crash. One might propose using a different word in order to refer to such causes—for instance, one may call them "contributing factors" or the like—but this would merely re-name and not change the actual scheme of events that produced an effect. Throughout the book I will simply assume that causation is transitive and, more generally, try to avoid unproductive discussions that are based on different intuitions about terminology. I will also assume that contributing circumstances that enable an item (for instance, the presence of oxygen in the case of forest fire) count among its causes.

ASSUMPTIONS ABOUT THE MENTAL STATES OF HISTORICAL FIGURES

The existing literature about materialism (physicalism) is dominated by questions that pertain to the mind-body problem. The rejection of the expansion of ontology beyond the physical world implies the rejection of immaterial and spiritual conceptions of the mental capacities of historical figures (such as Cartesian dualism and some versions of emergentism), and this has a wide range of consequences for positions that can be taken in historical research. For instance, an approach to historical research that precludes cultural or historical contexts having affected historical figures independently of any material interaction with them is likely to deliver different results than an approach that assumes that this could have happened.

There are a number of different materialist positions in the philosophy of mind. The core assumption of materialism in regard to the minds of historical figures has to be that, in order to be in a certain mental state, historical figures had to be biological organisms and were in that state in virtue of having certain physical (biological) properties and nothing else. Depending on the kind of materialist position in the philosophy of mind that one endorses, it may then be argued that these physical properties caused the mental state, or that they were identical with the mental state, or that the mental state is reducible to the possession of physical properties, or that it was realized by these physical properties, or that it supervened on them—various other formulations are also possible.[45] It is certainly preferable for discussions in this book to avoid commitments to any of these specific views and to remain as general as possible. The rejection of Cartesian dualism is arguably sufficient for our discussion here. A correlated assumption is that if two historical figures were in different mental states, they must have been in different biological states. However, it does not follow necessarily that if they share the same mental state they had to be in the same biological state. Also, their intrinsic[46] mental states such as beliefs and pains could not have changed without some change of their biological states. Finally, causal closure implies that mental states can only be causally affected and their changes caused by physical (neurobiological) states. It should also be mentioned, for readers less acquainted with the contemporary philosophy of mind, that none of this suggests that historical figures did not have mental states such as beliefs, motives, or pains or that they were mechanical automata. They certainly did have such mental states—otherwise, the materialist claim that these states are, or are reducible to, or are caused (and so on) by biological states would be pointless. Readers may find John Searle's view—that mental states are caused by the biological states of the human nervous system, but that the subjective nature of human experiences (pain, thoughts) makes it impossible to reduce the way we experience them to the biology that causes them—particularly well-suited for our discussion.[47]

The principle of causal closure also provides a way to specify the materialist view on emergentist positions. It is sometimes argued that in the case of complex systems (such as the human brain or social entities), the organization of their parts results in the emergence of macro properties that are irreducible to parts and their interactions. Since the nineteenth century, emergentist positions have been particularly widespread in the philosophy of mind and the social sciences. The idea is that the organization of parts (such as molecules or human individuals) into highly complex systems can result in the emergence of new properties that are not reducible to the parts of the system that generate them and their interactions. The notorious problem is that it is not clear what "emergence" might be, or how to define "reduction." Here, too, a distinction made by Searle is going to be helpful.[48] Searle differentiates between two concepts of emergence. "Emergence 1" is the view that complex structures emerge from the parts of the system as a result of causal interactions among parts. From this point of view, the brain and the mind have different properties, but the presence of mental properties (such as consciousness, mental states, the capacity to make decisions) can be deduced or established from the state of neurons and their causal interactions. Similarly, a social institution can have different properties than its participating individuals, but its properties can be deduced, in principle, from the properties of individuals and their interactions. Emergence 1 is unproblematic from the materialist point of view, since it merely describes a result of causal interactions. "Emergence 2" involves a much stronger claim: a certain complex structure is emergent 2 if it has causal powers that cannot be explained by interactions among its constitutive parts. In other words, it comes about in a way that such interactions are not sufficient to explain. If the mind or social institutions were emergent 2, then they would have causal powers that could not be explained by the causal behavior of the elements of the nervous system or interactions among individuals that participate in a social institution. As Searle put it in the case of consciousness, the idea is that "consciousness gets squirted out by the behavior of the neurons in the brain, but once it has been squirted out, it then has a life of its own."[49] If a mental state is emergent 2 on the nervous system or a social institution is emergent 2 on the participating individuals and their interactions, this means that the causality of the material world cannot explain their existence. Saying that it is emergent 2 means saying that its causation is something over and above material causation. In order to explain their existence, it is necessary to expand ontology beyond the assumptions of the materialist worldview. This is precisely the kind of position that materialism rejects.[50]

Because of the variety of possible materialist positions in the philosophy of mind, I have struggled to find terminology that is appropriately inclusive.

The term that I have found very useful in order to deal with these difficulties is "to describe." Throughout the book I often talk about the possibility of describing mental states in physical (biological) terms, and this technical term is meant to cover the possibility of giving a materialist account of the relationship between the mind and the body in general. It avoids commitments to specific materialist theories about the body-mind relationship. It is also necessary to take into account that modern science does not actually know how the functioning of the mind relates to the functioning of the brain. This is why I use the potential form "describable." When I say that it is assumed that mental states are "describable" in physical terms, I mean that the assumption is that although the information necessary to state such a description may not be available (mental states cannot be "described"), such a description should be possible in principle. In other words, the assumption is that Cartesian dualism is false and that in order to explain mental phenomena one does not need to rely on non-physical items. In situations unrelated to the mind-body problem, I use the phrase "physically describable" to say that if the necessary information were available, something could be described in purely physical terms without reference to non-physical phenomena. I also use the term "describable" in relation to historical and social entities, events, and phenomena: I say that they are describable as sets of individuals and their interactions in situations when the necessary information is not available, but if it were available, it should be possible, in principle, to describe these entities, events, and phenomena as individuals and their interactions. For instance, we do not have lists of all soldiers who participated in Napoleon's invasion of Russia, but if we had it, we would be able to describe it as a set of individuals.

APPROACH

Describing and analyzing the materialist perspective on history and historical research does not mean advocating it. Some readers may believe that the assumptions about the materialist worldview I have described here are true and that they indeed state how the world works. Others may think that some or all of them are false. This disagreement is something that this book cannot address. Rather, the question is, what does it mean for historical research to endorse the materialist worldview? Readers may also disagree about the validity of various historiographical models that the book describes. Some readers may believe that the book shows that materialism is in line with standard and established approaches to historical research, or even that historical methodology can be valid only insofar as it is in line with the materialist worldview. Others may think that some implications of materialism that I describe are so out of tune with standard and established approaches to historical research that my description constitutes a *reductio ad absurdum* of the materialist view of history. My intention here is not, nor could it be, to prove that materialism is true, or to argue that abstract, immaterial, spiritual, divine, or similar forces do not exist and did not intervene in history. I am even not sure how such arguments could be made. (In these matters a historian is in the same situation as a natural scientist who assumes, but cannot prove, that spiritual forces do not systematically interfere in experiments.) Similarly, the book cannot be expected to refute the existence of abstract and immaterial entities or Platonic Forms, or to show that languages are not immaterial ahistorical entities, or that historical epochs or cultures are not immaterial forces that exist over and above individuals and their interactions. Rather, the aim is to analyze and to describe what it means for historical research to assume that this is so. It will also be necessary to analyze how arguments in favor of various kinds of ontological expansion beyond the world of physical items can be responded to from the materialist point of view. In order to give a fair account of the materialist perspective on historical research, it is important to see how it can be criticized and defended. One of my major efforts throughout the book is to present possible responses to arguments that suggest the need to postulate abstract and immaterial entities, forces or phenomena. Since the discussion pertains to materialism in historical research, it will also be important to see when ontological expansion beyond the material world leads to ahistorical or anachronistic perspectives on the past.

The discussion analyzes arguments from a wide range of philosophical disciplines. This very emphasis on arguments, as well as the fact that many of them derive from works written by analytic philosophers, is likely to make many readers classify the book as a work in the analytic philosophy of history. I have made the effort to ensure that discussions related to problems in analytic philosophy are up to date. A number of the positions on which I rely may be novel to readers who have knowledge of more traditional positions in analytic philosophy (for instance, I endorse the impenetrability of vision in the philosophy of perception and metalinguistic descriptivism in the theory of names, I reject externalism about mental contents, and so on)—and I believe that when it comes to the philosophy of history, there are good reasons to move away from the traditionally established views. At the same time, I have included a range of examples from historiography, and this wider perspective results in a style that may be unusual for readers used to reading works in analytic philosophy. The examples I have chosen come largely from ancient historians, the fields of historical research in which I have formal training (histories of architecture and philosophy), fields in which I have worked (history of art), or topics that interest me (the July 1914 crisis)—and I hope that examples will help with the reception of the book among scholars in the historical humanities.

In general, I assume that many (maybe the majority of) readers are not necessarily acquainted with arguments and debates in analytic philosophy discussed here. The major challenge is to present these arguments and debates in a way that is clear without sacrificing intellectual complexity in those aspects that are relevant for problems of the philosophy of history. In particular, I have endeavored to ensure that readers with a general philosophical education but without specialist training in analytic philosophy can follow the arguments that I present. (For instance, I assume that such readers understand terms such as "ontology" but not necessarily "supervenience"; terms more specific to analytic philosophy had to be explained or avoided.) Attention to technical rigor typical of works in analytic philosophy really becomes important in the consideration of arguments and debates that directly pertain to the philosophy of history. In these matters, I had to struggle between a technically accurate presentation and one that would be clear and accessible, and I can only hope that I have found the right balance.

There is, also, an important caveat regarding the relationship between the materialist perspective on history presented here and some mainstream positions in analytic philosophy. The analytic philosophers whose views I discuss throughout the book are not necessarily materialists. Also, it is not uncommon that well-established positions in analytic philosophy imply ahistorical or highly counterintuitive perspectives on history or historical research. In many details, the materialist positions discussed here are opposed to views that are dominant, or were dominant among analytic philosophers. Analytic philosophers are sometimes as susceptible to idealism as postmodernists. For instance, forty years ago, the view that all thinking is verbal was absolutely dominant among analytic philosophers; similarly, many analytic philosophers today still seem to subscribe to externalism about mental contents. As we shall see, applied to historical research, the former position results in unbridgeable difficulties for a historian who wants to report the beliefs of historical figures who used languages different from the one in which the historian is writing; the latter view can easily lead to anachronistic attributions of beliefs to historical figures. A philosophy of history needs to approach the challenges and arguments formulated in other philosophical disciplines from the point of view of its own topic, history, and in a way that is informed by what happens in historical research, its practice and methodology. Morton White once protested against the idea that philosophers of history should become methodological consultants—but it is also fair to be skeptical about the actual relevance of a work in the philosophy of history that does not engage with actual historical research and the methodological dilemmas that require philosophical treatment.[51]

The implications of materialism for historical research that the book describes tend to correlate *grosso modo* to the views of some contemporary philosophers of history, such as Aviezer Tucker, C. Behan McCullagh, or

Tor Egil Førland. Obviously, this does not suggest that any of these philosophers of history conceive of their views as materialist—they may or they may not, and in various details their views certainly differ, but my point here is rather that materialism can be seen compatible with or even supporting (many of) their positions. Also, there are authors whose assumptions are quite far from being materialist, but on whose important theoretical contributions I have been able to rely. Throughout the book, I have relied extensively on Mark Bevir's theory of understanding and interpretation that, because of Bevir's principle of "procedural individualism," avoids the need to expand ontology and introduce abstract, immaterial meanings—even though, more generally, the assumptions of Bevir's approach are quite far from the materialist perspective that this book sets out to analyze.[52]

In the book I discuss the implications of materialism for historical research, rather than for historiography or history-writing. In the final decades of the twentieth century, the influence of narrativism in the philosophy of history produced the tendency to emphasize history-writing over other things historians do. It is, however, fair to say that some of these things, such as archival work, the interpretation of documents, the analysis of physical artifacts, the study of alternative interpretations in the work of other historians, and so on, are much more central to a historian's work. The emphasis on history-writing has produced the tendency to blur the distinction between artistic literary pursuits and history as a discipline of research and inquiry. Arguably, for most historians, the actual activity of reporting the results of their investigations—that is, writing for publication—is secondary to actual historical research. Otherwise there would be nothing to write about. It is true that history-writing itself is not reducible to the mere reporting of research results and that it is often difficult to separate it from the interpretation of these results. While writing, the historian often creates new concepts and formulates new questions that shed further light on the research results that history-writing articulates. But this does not mean that historical research is part of history-writing—or even more radically, that history-writing is like other literary pursuits and that, since other fields of literature, such as fiction of poetry, are not constrained by reality, historical works have no relationship to historical reality. Rather, it means that history-writing itself is part of historical research and one of its tools.

CONTENTS

The aim of the book—to provide a comprehensive survey of the consequences of materialism for historical research and the philosophy of history—implies that it has to analyze a wide set of philosophical topics, debates, arguments and dilemmas. Some of these topics have strong ties to other topics, some do not, and some almost stand on their own. The diversity of topics is reflected in the order of the book's nine chapters and their relationships. It has also made the book exceptionally hard to compose.

The first three chapters of the book are reasonably independent of each other and in principle they could be read in any order. They describe general aspects of the materialist philosophy of history and frame the discussions that follow, but later chapters do not depend on them for technical details. In a way, these chapters stand as essays on their own. *Chapter One* addresses the debate about historical reality and analyzes the view that historical past is constructed by historians, for instance, as a coherent account of historical evidence. I argue that the necessary causal connection between historical events and evidence about them makes such anti-realism slightly credible. The past has to have happened in order to cause the existence of evidence. *Chapter Two* discusses the dilemma about the nature of historical (social) entities, forces, events and phenomena, such as armies, governments, crises, wars and so on. Can they be understood as sums of individuals and (or) their interactions—or is it necessary to assume that they are something more and attribute to them abstract and immaterial existence in order to understand how they happen or function? The dilemma is debated much more vehemently among philosophers of the social sciences than among philosophers of history, but it has significant importance for the topic of this book: if one could successfully argue that social and historical entities, forces, events or phenomena have immaterial, abstract existence, then materialism in the philosophy of history would be hard to defend. The second chapter therefore surveys the debate and the arguments that have been proposed in the social sciences in order to show that they do not successfully demonstrate the need to expand ontology beyond the material world. *Chapter Three* addresses a cluster of dilemmas pertaining to historical explanations and causation in history. There exists a long-standing debate about the nature of historical explanations and in how far they need to provide causal information. On the one hand, Hempel's thesis about general laws in history is known to face problems when it has to explain decisions and actions of individual historical figures. On the other, it is not clear whether and how Erwin Panofsky's conception of humanist historiography, that attributes free will to historical figures, can be squared with materialism. The third chapter develops a theory of *quomodo* explanations that resolves these dilemmas in a way that relies on the compatibilist understanding of free will and is aligned with materialist assumptions in the philosophy of history.

Chapter Four is in many ways the central chapter of the book. It introduces a series of philosophical distinctions that play a core role through the rest of the book. Its main topic is the attribution of mental contents (concepts, propositions, consequently beliefs, knowledge and so on) to historical figures. The aim of the discussion is to establish how this can be done without postulating such contents as abstract and immaterial entities. The chapter provides the basis for the analysis of the materialist understanding of language presented in Chapters Five and Six, and the subsequent discussion of historical interpretation developed in the final chapters of the book. At the same time, in combination with the discussion of concept-free perception in the Appendix, it provides the basis for the rejection of anti-foundationalism. *Chapter Five* then expands this discussion on problems of language and seeks to show that it is unnecessary to postulate linguistic meanings as abstract, immaterial entities, independent of the mental states of historical figures. (Obviously, should such expansion of ontology be necessary, this could seriously affect the possibility of a materialist philosophy of history.) The rejection of the understanding of meanings as abstract and immaterial entities makes it necessary to discuss a number of well-established philosophical arguments pertaining to externalism about mental states, such as Hilary Putnam's "Twin Earth" and Tyler Burge's argument about arthritis. *Chapter Six* addresses the problem of essentialism—that is, the assumption that among various concepts that identify the same item one pertains to its essence, its true nature, that what the item really is. The idea that things have essences is problematic from the materialist point of view, and it also results in anachronistic attributions of beliefs to historical figures. Historians thus have good reasons to avoid essentialism, although it is often implied in historical writings (especially, for instance, in the history of science).

Taken together, these three chapters whose contents I have just described, Four, Five and Six, provide philosophical analyses of a series of methodological problems well-established in historical research, that are hardly ever addressed in the contemporary philosophy of history. They should be thus particularly interesting to practicing historians. At the same time, they are also philosophically the most demanding and technical parts of the book. On the one hand, these chapters deal with problems of language while methodological problems of historians' work often derive from the fact that historical research is predominantly a language-based activity. On the other, my efforts are largely directed towards showing that it is possible to account for linguistic phenomena relevant to historical research without postulating meanings and reference as immaterial, abstract, physically unexplainable entities or relationships. This latter aim obviously results in significant philosophical technicalities. The situation is further aggravated by the fact that the analytic philosophy of language has dealt only marginally with the dilemmas that result from differences between languages, such as those that pertain to translation. At the same time, many methodological problems of historical research originate precisely from these dilemmas. Providing the proper balance between the necessary philosophical technicalities and the need to make the text accessible to non-philosophers has been a particularly difficult task when it comes to these three chapters.

The last three chapters deal with problems of interpretation. *Chapter Seven* addresses the relationship between historical, social and linguistic contexts on the one hand and the contents of the mental states of historical figures and historians. One important problem pertains to situations in which certain views, ideas or beliefs were inconceivable for individuals from certain contexts. The validity of such claims is an important methodological dilemma for a historian. Another problem derives from the view (widespread in the humanities of the final decades of the twentieth century) that all thinking is verbal and thus constrained by the limits of the linguistic community that the historical figure or the historian belongs to. I will argue that this view results in irresolvable difficulties when it comes to the translation of historical documents. Finally, important problems arise from the fact that historians are historical figures too, and if historical-social contexts affect the mental states of historical figures, they also affect the capacity of historians to grasp these mental states and report about them. This is the well-known "reflexive argument" in historical research that presented an insurmountable difficulty for the German historicist tradition. A significant advantage of the materialist philosophy of history, I will argue, is that it can avoid it. *Chapter Eight* deals with the distinction between meaning and interpretation in historical works, problems of translation, and the situations in which a historian has to report beliefs of historical figures who expressed them in languages different from the one in which the historian is writing. *Chapter Nine* addresses the problem of the meaning and reference of historical works taken as wholes. It presents a transparent alternative to the narrativist view, advocated by Frank Ankersmit and Jouni-Matti Kuukkanen, that historical works are opaque and do not refer to the historical past.

NOTES

1. Colebourn, *Latin Sentence*, 56.
2. For a history of materialism in modern times see Papineau, "The Rise."
3. Tacitus, *Annales*, 6.22, described an equivalent of the materialist position but did not endorse it. Rather, he extensively relied on astrological predictions (ibid., 6.21), supra-natural apparitions (ibid., 11.21), and described the terrible prodigies announcing Nero's rise to power (ibid., 12.43, 12.64).
4. Thucydides, *Peloponnesian War*, 1.22. Polybius, *The Histories*, 36.17.1. See also ibid., 2.38.4–5.
5. Herodotus, *The Persian Wars*, 9.65.
6. Ranke, *Geschichten*, 131.
7. See Mitrović, *Rage and Denials*, 25–44. See also Schleier, "Der Kulturhistoriker," Srbik, *Geist und Geschichte*, vol. 2, 227–235 and Chickering, *Lamprecht*, 175–253. For descriptions of Lamprecht's wider influence see Seeba, "Ansätze," Spreizer, "The Old Guard," and Brush, "The Cultural Historian." A comprehensive survey of Lamprecht's polemics is Seifert, *Der Streit*.
8. Lamprecht, "Kulturgeschichte." Lamprecht, *Einführung*. Spengler, *Untergang*.
9. See Mitrović, *Rage and Denials*, 38–41.
10. Panofsky, "History of Art." He presents the individualism-collectivism debate in art history as a variation of the debate about free will between Erasmus and Luther. For an analysis of Panofsky's views see Mitrović, "Humanist Art History."
11. Luther, *De servo*, 615.
12. Barthes, "La mort."
13. The origin of scriptor's actions is language itself ("le langage lui-même"), ibid., 64. He attributes to Mallarmé the view, with which he agrees, that it is language who speaks, not the author. Ibid., 62.
14. Plato, *Ion*, 534C.
15. The well-known problem in the case of Michel Foucault's writings is the source of the causal capacities that he attributes to "discourses." In *Archaeology of Knowledge*, 49, 122, he attributes to them the capacity to form the objects of which they speak, and states that the source of this causal capacity does not belong to the mental states of individuals or a communal opinion. It remains unclear what this source might be. Dreyfus and Rabinow, *Michel Foucault*, xxiv admit that "the causal power attributed to the rules governing discursive systems is unintelligible." The causal capacities of discourse thus do not have a possible physical, materialist explanation. (See also the discussion in Elder-Vass, *Reality*, 143–158.) In any case, one should not think that the idea of discourses as immaterial, non-mental forces with causal capacities is present only in Foucault's writings. Another good example is, for instance, to be found in Burr, *Constructionism*, 63–67. The tendency to postulate immaterial historical forces is a commonplace in idealist perspectives on history. There are, for instance, important parallels between Foucault's discourses and Oswald Spengler's cultures and Spengler faces similar problems as Foucault when he has to explain their causal capacities.
16. Bryson, *Vision and Painting*, 13.
17. See the analysis in Mitrović, "A Defence of Light."
18. Pérez-Gómez, "Abstraction," 50.
19. Pérez-Gómez, "Place," 134.
20. Pérez-Gómez, "Myth," 11.
21. This latter claim, with regard to Greek grammar, is actually false. The verb ὁράω ("I see") has different active and passive forms in various tenses. For instance, in aorist active εἶδον and passive ὤφθην; perfect active ἑόρακα or ἑώρακα and passive ἑώραμαι or ὦμμαι.
22. Sedlmayr, "Quintessenz."
23. For an analysis of terminology, see Stoljar, "Physicalism" and Stoljar, *Physicalism*, 10–12.
24. See for instance Kim, *Philosophy of Mind*, 11, 32.
25. Throughout the book, I assume the compatibility of realism about consciousness and mental states with the materialist worldview. This is not a book about the philosophy of mind;

the positions on which I rely throughout the book when it comes to consciousness, mental states, and so on, are *grosso modo* aligned with the views of philosophers such as John Searle. (See Searle, *The Rediscovery of Mind*.)

26. See Kim, *Physicalism*, 55 and 160 for a discussion of this argument.

27. For a general discussion see Cat, "The Unity of Science." See also Fodor, "Special Sciences or: the Disunity of Science" and Fodor, "Special Sciences: Still Autonomous."

28. Some sociologists such as Keith Sawyer and Harold Kincaid have unsuccessfully tried to apply the multiple realizability argument to social structures. See the discussion in Mitrović, "Multiple Realizability."

29. For instance, Loewer, "Physics," 37: "Physicalism claims that all facts obtain *in virtue of* the distribution of the fundamental entities and properties—whatever they turn out to be—of completed *fundamental physics*." Witmer, "Sufficiency Claims," 69: "Every law of nature and every particular fact is either physical or to be explained by the physical in such a way as to imply that the nonphysical facts are nothing over and above the physical facts, where the physical facts include the actual distribution of physical properties and the laws of physics." For Otto Neurath and Rudolf Carnap physicalism was the thesis that every meaningful sentence could be translated into physical language. See Gates, "Physicalism," 251.

30. See Witmer, "Sufficiency Claims" for a detailed elaboration of various possible formulations of physicalism on the basis of replication of physical properties of our world.

31. Hempel, "Comments." See also the summary of the discussion in Nay, "Defining Physicalism" and Stoljar, *Physicalism*, 93–108.

32. Chomsky, "Internalist Explorations," 262.

33. There are various ways to formulate the principle of causal closure. Typically, authors insist that causes have to be physical. See Papineau, "The Rise," 8: "all physical effects are fully determined by law by prior physical occurrences." Kim, *Physicalism*, 50: "Any cause of a physical event is itself a physical event—that is, no nonphysical event can be a cause of a physical event." Since I am here assuming that everything is physical, then effects cannot be non-physical anyhow. This corresponds to the traditional formulation that goes back to Lucretius, *De natura*, 1.304: "Tangere enim et tangi, nisi corpus, nulla potest res."

34. For a survey of arguments about causation by omission see Paul and Hall, *Causation*, 173–214.

35. That is, we are merely talking about statements that "if the event A occurred then . . ." and "if . . . , then the event B would have occurred." See Paul and Hall, *Causation*, 227–276, esp. 254.

36. See Lewis, "Causation."

37. See the survey of approaches in Paul and Hall, *Causation*, 7–24.

38. See especially Lewis, "Causation." For counterfactuals-based understanding of historical causation see Issue 3 of the 2016 volume of the *Journal of the Philosophy of History* that was guest-edited by Aviezer Tucker and dedicated to counterfactuals in historiography. See especially the analysis by Maar, "Applying" in the same volume.

39. Maar, "Applying."

40. See especially the discussion by Cohen, "Causation," 18–19.

41. Suetonius, "Caligula," LX.

42. For the former view, see Lewis, "Causal Explanation." For the latter view, see Railton, *Explaining Explanation*. For a discussion of the later view in relation to historical research, see Førland, *Values*, 113–134.

43. See for instance Paul and Hall, *Causation*, 225–276, esp. 227.

44. For a discussion see Paul and Hall, *Causation*, 225–276. Some authors, such as McCullagh, *Truth in History*, 177, reject transitivity.

45. For a survey of possible positions see Kim, *Philosophy of Mind*.

46. I say "intrinsic" in order to exclude those mental states that can be affected by changes in the external environment without any physical change in the organism itself. For instance, I know that China is the most populous country in the world, but this knowledge will become a false belief if India becomes more populous. By comparison, it is assumed that beliefs or pains cannot cease to be beliefs or pains without some physical change in the organism itself.

47. See Searle, *Rediscovery*, esp. 111–126.

48. Ibid., 112.
49. Ibid., 112.
50. In other words, in a world that (as described earlier) would fully replicate all physical elements (particles, fields, forces, time-space and so on), items that are emerging 1 according to Searle would be reproduced, but those that are emerging 2 would not.
51. White, *Foundations*, 2.
52. The differences in assumptions between Bevir's *Logic* and the materialist perspective that this book seeks to analyze are extensive. Bevir explicitly rejected physicalism (Bevir, *Logic*, 29, 92). Also, he assumes that observation is inseparable from theory, whereas my assumption here, in line with contemporary psychology of perception, is that perception is largely independent of and impenetrable for the conceptual contents associated with it. (See the Appendix; it should be mentioned that Bevir was writing before Pylyshyn opened the debate about the impenetrability of the visual perception.) Similarly, following Quine, Bevir assumes that "we can continue to believe in a proposition despite evidence to the contrary simply by adjusting our background theories." Ibid., 94. The materialist worldview that I analyze in this book assumes serious constraints on such adjustments in historical research. Also, Bevir actually defines facts as "something the members of a community accept as a fundamental proposition" (ibid., 99)—and in Chapter One I analyze the problems that this kind of view entails. Nevertheless, when it comes to the understanding and the interpretation of texts, the principle of procedural individualism that he formulates in his book is of fundamental importance for my discussion here because it coincides with the materialist perspective. (It is actually not clear that the principle of procedural individualism is compatible with anti-foundationalism. Bevir obviously introduces it as the foundation of his discussion of interpretation and, as can be seen from his formulation cited in Chapter Two, the principle postulates the existence of "specific individuals.") One should also remember that Bevir was writing in the 1990s, during the heyday of anti-foundationalism. It may not be quite true that at the time, as Tom Rockmore claimed, "everyone, or almost everyone, has switched to anti-foundationalism"—counter-examples such as Searle are not hard to think of—but anti-foundationalism was certainly a very widespread view during the period. (Rockmore, "Introduction," 1.) For a rejection of anti-foundationalism that was published in the same year as Bevir's book see BonJour, "Dialectic." See also Elgin, "Non-Foundationalist Epistemology" and Cleve "Why Coherence is not Enough."

Chapter One

Realism

In a short and cryptic paragraph in his *Anabasis of Alexander*, Arrian described the views of the historian Callisthenes, a disciple of Aristotle and a follower of Alexander. Callisthenes, Arrian reported, declared that Alexander's exploits, deeds, and achievements were actually dependent on the history he would write about them.[1] Insofar as the report is accurate, it suggests that Callisthenes was (possibly) the first to assert that historians do not merely describe, but actually constitute historical reality through their work.[2] His views in that case would have been equivalent to the views of those modern philosophers of history who deny that historical events happened or that historians' descriptions about them can be reliable, and who then infer that historians actually construct events, rather than merely describe what happened. In a similar way, according to Arrian, Callisthenes denied that the memories of Alexander's mother about his divine birth were reliable and claimed that the factual divinity of Alexander depended on what he would write about it.

The view that historians construct historical reality has been exceptionally widely debated in English-speaking philosophy of history for the past fifty years. It seems almost necessary to start the discussions in this book by positioning them in relation to the dilemma. The dilemma goes like this.[3] On the one hand is the realist view that the historical past (including, for instance, historical events such as battles, and phenomena such as the Renaissance or periods such as Antiquity) did happen and that historians describe it. On the other is the constructionist (or anti-realist) view that the historical past is inaccessible (because it is nonexistent or simply cannot be known) and that historians construct it through their work: for instance, on the basis of evidence, available documents, physical remains, and so on. According to the former view, historians discover what happened, and their descriptions are true insofar as they correspond to the historical past. According to the latter view, they construct accounts of past events; for instance, it may be asserted that they merely strive to make coherent accounts of the available evidence. (Let me call this particular brand of constructionism "coherentism.") The realist assumes that on the basis of evidence it is possible to acquire knowledge of a realm of past events that happened independently of the historian; for the anti-realist, the past is either not there or it is inaccessible. To use Carlo Ginzburg's metaphor, for the realists, evidence is like a window that enables one to look at the past; for anti-realists, it is a wall: one can see the wall but not what is behind, and possibly there is nothing there at all.[4]

Constructionism is sometimes associated with the rise of postmodernism, but its predecessors are by no means limited to Callisthenes. Similar views are firmly rooted in the idealist tradition of the philosophy of history and closely relate to the assumption that the discipline of history does not deal with material reality.[5] In Benedetto Croce's work, the claim that there are no things outside spirit and thought leads directly to the view that the mind constructs facts and history by thinking.[6] Similarly, Michael Oakeshott wrote that there are no facts that are not ideas; insofar as history is a world of facts, it is a world of ideas, and historians do not discover, recapture, or interpret, but create and construct.[7] As one can expect, the materialist perspective that this book is intended to analyze stands in complex opposition to such idealist positions.

In what follows I will use the words "anti-realism" and "constructionism" interchangeably in order to refer to the same cluster of views. I will use the former term when I am talking about its aspects that pertain to the view that the past did not happen or cannot be known, and the latter term for the idea that it is constructed by the historian.[8] Other positions come close to anti-realism, but they will be discussed later in the book. Some authors do not deny the reality of the historical past and agree that individual statements about the past can be true on the basis of correspondence to that past. However, they deny that this applies to the complex clusters of such statements that historians produce ("narratives") or statements that rely on so-called colligatory concepts. These views will be discussed in Chapter Nine.

REALISM AND MATERIALISM

Materialism is a metaphysical thesis about the nature of reality—in the Introduction, I described it as the view that reality does not contain items that cannot have physical descriptions. Realism can be the ontological thesis that reality, including historical reality, exists (has existed) independently of human mental states. Alternatively, it can be understood as the epistemological thesis that (parts of) reality, including historical reality, can be known. One way or another, realism does not necessarily entail the materialist worldview. Throughout the history of historiography, many historians have endorsed realism in both senses and combined it with beliefs in immaterial forces and causation. At the same time, it is much harder to see how a materialist historian or a philosopher of history could reject realism. It seems pointless to claim that all historical items (events, phenomena, forces, causation, and so on) must be physically describable if one asserts at the same time that there were no such items in the past or that nothing can be known about them. Nevertheless, the incompatibility of materialism with constructionism may be only apparent. As mentioned, constructionism may have the form of the view that historians construct coherent accounts of the available historical evidence. In that case, materialism may be compatible with the coherentist version of constructionism if the resulting historical construct is required to be coherent with the materialist worldview and that all items it relies on can have a physical description.

The dilemma between realism and anti-realism is best described if we consider some well-known arguments in favor of these two opposing positions, and how they can be responded to. It is useful to ward off the most common misconceptions formulated in the debate. Both sides, realism and anti-realism, have a long history of being exposed to straw-man refutations. In the case of the realist position, this is aggravated by the fact that it appears commonsensical to many authors, and probably for this reason it is regarded as more vulnerable to various skeptical arguments. There actually exists the view that skeptical arguments can be directed only against the realist position, whereas anti-realist positions are immune to such attacks.[9] In fact, there is no reason that skeptical arguments could not go in both directions; arguably, there are stronger reasons to doubt the existence of the *present* than the existence of the past. Every object we perceive, by the time the light rays from the object reach our eyes and the brain processes the reflection of the object on the retina, is necessarily perceived in the past. In the case of stars, that past may be millions of years ago; I perceive the desk in front of me the way it was an infinitesimal part of a second ago. One way or another, things that I can see and experience can *only* be in the past. Every thought one can have is always already in the past by the time one consciously formulates it. Louis Mink's complaint against realism that the "past is inaccessible to any direct inspection" is thus plainly false.[10] As Peter Kosso pointed out, only past things can be available for direct inspection.[11] In fact, since inspection itself is a mental process, that very act of "inspection" is always already in the past by the time it is completed and one has thought it through. It may be in the very recent past, but it cannot be in the present.

The best-known argument against realism pertains to the non-observability of historical items. The argument consists in pointing out that historical items cannot be observed in the present, and therefore statements about them cannot be verified.[12] From the realist point of view, the argument merely misses the point: many historical events or phenomena would have been unobservable at the time they occurred, but the realist historian will claim anyhow that they happened. A historian may, for instance, want to say that many people died of radiation poisoning after the nuclear bombing of Hiroshima and Nagasaki and assume that the radiation that resulted from the bombing was real. But radiation itself is not, and could not have been, observable.[13] Similarly, a historian may describe a long series of events, such as the evolution of Roman republican institutions, that no single person could have lived long enough to observe. Also, a single observer can rarely observe the full course of a battle; individual observers' reports usually provide only partial descriptions of various actions that occurred as parts of a battle. It has been repeatedly pointed out by authors such as C. Behan McCullagh and Peter Kosso that sciences normally study unobservable objects whose descriptions are arrived at by inference from observations.[14] When a physicist refers to subatomic phenomena, these subatomic phenomena are not observable. What is observable is the evidence of their existence, much as is the case with past events. If the argument about observability were valid, it would seriously affect results in the natural sciences in general, insofar as they infer the existence of unobservable objects such as forces, fields, gravity, subatomic particles, and so on. Michael Dummett analyzed the kinds of observations that need to be taken into account if observability is going to play a role in the formulation of the realist position about the past.[15] Observability, he pointed out, cannot be taken to mean that the historian must be able to witness past events in person. Those who argue that the past is not a region we can travel to, overlook that in order to know what happens at another place one need not travel there; one can rely on reports from people who are there.[16] An observer can transmit his or her observations to others, and their possession of information will be based on testimony. This is precisely how old written records convey information about the past. It can be added, as Murray Murphey pointed out, observation is not necessarily the only procedure that provides knowledge: Hitler shot himself in his bunker on 30 April 1945; this was a real event on Dummett's account because it was observable in principle, but we do not know about it because someone observed it.[17] In this case someone observed other things that enabled him or her to infer what happened. In general, it is the interpretation of evidence and not observation that decides the realist historian's claims about past events. Only some past events were directly observed at the time they happened, and reports about such observations are only one kind of evidence.

At the same time, the critics of anti-realism often overlook that the position of their opponents may be much stronger than it appears, especially if the latter systematically replace the assumption that statements about the past are true because they correspond to what happened with the assumption that they are true because they are coherent with other statements that can be inferred from the evidence. The replacement of the correspondence-based theory of truth with a coherence-based one provides constructionists with a response to the most common criticism of anti-realism: that it abolishes the distinction between historiography and fiction. This is the criticism that if there was no past, or the past is unknown, then there was nothing that historical works could be about, and they are no different from literary works. A constructionist can, however, respond that historical research consists in establishing a coherent understanding of historical evidence. From this point of view, realist historians who believe that they are reporting the actual historical past are also not doing anything more than providing a coherent interpretation of the available evidence. Thus formulated, the response is cogent; its strong side is that it reduces the number of entities that need to be postulated in order to explain what historians are doing. It becomes unnecessary to postulate the past. The position may not be invincible, but the proper way to attack it is to find those aspects of historical research that it cannot account for; by attacking it as a free-for-all position, one is merely attacking a straw man.

Consistent anti-realism should not be confused with the claim that *some* events did not happen, whereas some other events happened (including the non-happening of the events that did not happen, since such a non-happening can still be regarded as an event).[18] Saying that *some* events did not happen still makes it possible to make statements about the past that are true on the basis of their correspondence with past events. Taken on its own, partial anti-realism of this kind is not sufficient to justify constructionism, and it cannot support the claim that the past is constructed by the historian. One can say that the non-happening of past events still happened and that denials of past events can be true on the basis of their correspondence with the past.

The opponents of constructionism often overlook the implications that the rejection of correspondence-based theories of truth for statements about the past can have when it comes to the consistent formulation of anti-realist perspectives on history. This easily leads to the formulation of unproductive arguments. Ontological anti-realism may seem to translate easily into claims that specific historical events did not happen, but it is important to note that such translations are not quite accurate, insofar as they still assume the attribution of truth or falsity to statements on the basis of their correspondence to the past. The proponents of ontological anti-realism have thus been accused, for instance, of Holocaust denial—but it is hard to say that their position enables them to deny anything about the past, because a denial is already a statement whose truth depends on correspondence with the past. By denying anything about the past, they would already be making a statement that could be true or false because of the way it corresponds to the past events, and this would defeat their aim to provide an anti-realist account of history.[19]

ADVANTAGES OF COHERENTISM

Among various versions of anti-realism and constructionism, coherentism is particularly important for the argument that needs to be discussed here. Even the alternative versions of constructionism, which do not state the coherent understanding of evidence as the main aim of historical research, must still assume that historical research provides coherent (non-self-contradictory) accounts of historical evidence. The realist position must assume this too. A theory of historical research that assumes or allows for contradictions in the understanding of historical evidence is simply not a candidate for a credible theory of historical research. The dilemma to be addressed here is whether the claim that historians construct historical reality by providing a coherent account of the existing evidence can be made compatible with materialism. It may be argued, as mentioned, that this can be the case if coherentism is further combined with the requirement that such accounts must also be coherent with (must not contradict) the assumptions of materialism such as those presented in the Introduction. The question is whether materialist constraints can be combined with the coherentist position in a way that is not incompatible with constructionism (and ontological or epistemic anti-realism on which it relies). If such a combination is incoherent with other tenets of constructionism (anti-realism), then this has to affect constructionism under any formulation. Since other versions of constructionism still have to assume a coherent account of evidence as a necessary aim of historical research, then if coherent historical accounts become impossible once they are combined with the assumptions of materialism, it will follow that constructionism (anti-realism) in general cannot be compatible with the materialist worldview.

In comparison to coherentism, other, non-coherentist versions of constructionism do suffer from considerable weaknesses. It is useful to summarize here briefly the well-known objections to the two best-known alternatives in order to see the latter's advantages. One of them is Leon Goldstein's position that the truth of historical statements results merely from agreement within the community of historians.[20] In Goldstein's view, the agreement of scholars is the ultimate reason that certain historical claims are true or false.[21] This agreement is not to be conceived of as justified on some independent criteria on their own (such as coherent interpretation of evidence or correspondence to the past) but, he says:

> For whatever reasons, some historical constructions will seem to the community of scholars better than others that have been proposed, and these latter will simply be dropped from consideration.[22]

Similarly, in cases where historians introduce new methodologies, what matters is not whether they are successful in providing new historical knowledge, but "... whether the community of ... historians will actually find the methods [they] propose [ ] are suited to their tasks."[23]

The major problem with this view is that it becomes unclear how the views of the majority of historians can ever be false, although they may decide to agree, as Goldstein puts it, "for whatever reasons." Admittedly, consensus can indeed be indicative of historical knowledge.[24] However, Goldstein suggests that a historian who makes claims contrary to the views of the majority of his or her colleagues can never be right; there are no other truth criteria apart from the consensus of one's peers. The most fundamental methodological principle of historical research in that case is to produce texts that other historians will agree with—and presumably, these other historians count as historians because they agree with each other. However, the majority need not be always right. The scholarly community may be controlled by a totalitarian political system, or permeated by ideological prejudices or rabid nationalism, or the majority of historians may be government employees and their jobs and livelihoods may depend on fabricating texts that justify their government's policies or legitimate the establishment.[25] A long time ago Tacitus warned that historians' desire to agree, *libido adsentandi* as he put it, can be seriously detrimental for their work.[26] Contrary to this view, the coherentist view that historical statements are true insofar as they provide a coherent account of the available evidence allows for an individual historian being right against the majority—insofar as his or her views constitute a more coherent account of the available evidence.

An alternative version of constructionism assumes that historical statements are true when they are generated from historical evidence, using established historical procedures and methodologies.[27] From this point of view, a historical statement would be true or false insofar as it conforms to established methodological principles and results from methodologically appropriate procedures. (This is quite different from the realist account, which sees methodology as a set of tools that enable the historian to make statements that are true because of the way they relate to past events.) Complications consequently arise when one considers the justification for the methodology and how its procedures could be formulated. How can one decide which methodological rules and procedures are the right ones? Also: how can one introduce and justify new methodological procedures? One line of response would be that the methodologies (including new ones) that are approved by the majority of scholars in a given field are the correct ones. This brings us back to the problems equivalent to the those of Goldstein's position discussed above. Alternatively, one may say that correct methodologies are empirically established by studying successful historical works. The problem is then to identify which works count as successful historical works—and in the absence of other criteria, such as the coherent understanding of evidence or correspondence to the past, the only response that seems possible is circular: one has to say that these are the works that exhibit good methodology. Here too, the coherentist perspective resolves the problem by saying that methodologies and procedures are appropriate for historical research insofar as they enable coherent accounts of historical evidence.

CAUSATION, CONSTRUCTIONISM, AND MATERIALISM

There are thus clear advantages to the coherentist approach for constructionist perspectives on the historical past. However, the answer that has to be givent to the dilemma about the compatibility of coherentism with the materialist worldview has to be negative. Problems related to causation make a coherent materialist account of historical evidence impossible if the existence of the past, with its causal powers, is not included in the account.

As stated in the Introduction, one of the core assumptions of materialism is that there are no items (events, objects, or their properties and so on) in human history that have no causes. An item (for instance, an event) could not cause another if it did not really happen and it must have happened before its effect. Although some causes of historical items or objects that constitute historical evidence may be hypothetical causes-by-omission, it is impossible to have an item caused only by omissions. Omission means precisely that something else happened.

From the constructionist perspective, causes, effects, and their causal relationships are all imaginary constructs that a historian introduces in order to have a coherent understanding of historical evidence. From this point of view, the assassination of the Austro-Hungarian heir apparent Franz Ferdinand by Gavrilo Princip in Sarajevo on 28 June 1914 did not really happen,[28] or if it did happen nothing can be known about it as a past event—but it is a highly useful construct, since it enables historians to achieve the coherent understanding of a large number of documents pertaining to another, larger (also constructed) event, World War I. The same applies to information about the past in scientific fields such as astronomy, geology, or evolutionary biology: such information does not pertain to past events that happened, but merely states the constructs that are necessary in order to provide a coherent account of evidence in those sciences. In other words, the evolution of species did not really happen, but it is a useful construct in order to explain fossils, for instance. A good example of this kind of approach is Frank Ankersmit's denial of the Renaissance.[29] "The Renaissance" is a term that "has no counterpart in the past itself," he says, but rather, its "primary task is to organize our knowledge of the past (as expressed in descriptively true sentences) into a coherent and consistent whole."[30] Nevertheless, according to Ankersmit, the term is not meaningless, arbitrary, or mere speculation, but "indispensable for rational discussion of history," "it enriches our understanding of the past," and discussions about notions such as "the Renaissance" are "a most rational and valuable enterprise."[31]

For a constructionist historian, causation is a relationship that a historian constructs between certain types of constructed events, classified as causes and effects. Causation, in the form that materialism postulates it, does, however, become a problem when one has to deal with present objects and the present properties of objects that have their causes in the historical past—and historical evidence typically consists of such objects. In the case of the Sarajevo assassination, the blood-stained shirt of Franz Ferdinand can be seen on display in a museum in Vienna; a real, not constructed, imaginary or hypothetical, assassination had to have occurred for it to have these bloodstains. A past event that is merely a historian's construct and did not happen could not have caused the objects and their properties that exist today. Similarly, if past events (or other historical items in the past) cannot be known in principle, then one cannot say why evidence that we encounter today has the properties that it has. A historian's work with objects and their properties that constitute evidence often consists in establishing the causes that made these objects and their properties come about. It is often the causal relationship of these objects and properties with past items that makes them into evidence of past items: a manuscript has certain properties (a disposition of letters that make it into a text) because it was made so by its author or by a scribe, a building has a certain type of Ionic entablature because this was a decision of the architect, a shirt is stained with blood because someone was shot while wearing it. Consider, for instance, Murray Murphey's comparison of George Washington with an electron.[32] The former is unobservable today, the latter is never observable, and the existence of both is postulated on the basis of evidence—more precisely, on the basis of the causal impact they exercise (or exercised) on the evidence. In the case of electrons, we say that they exist because the theories that postulate them are confirmed by observable evidence; in the case of Washington, our statements ("theory") about his actions are also confirmed by observable evidence. However, if electrons did not exist and if Washington had not existed—if they were mere theoretical constructs constituted in order to provide coherent understanding of evidence, and consequently causally inert—then it is unclear how there could be any evidence for their existence at all.

In many cases the properties of evidence from which we infer that an event happened are indeed caused by the event. This point was emphasized by Leon Pompa, in whose view historical inference reconstructs such direct causation.[33] Pompa's point was that mere coherence of an explanation of historical evidence with other evidence is not enough to establish that the event in question occurred. As he put it, the fact that a hypothetical event explains other things that we are independently inclined to believe is not enough to establish its non-hypothetical character.[34] To establish this, one needs causal relationships between the event hypothesized and our evidence for it. Historical analysis of evidence, from this point of view, is then an analysis of evidence as effects. When the belief that Caesar was assassinated is endorsed because it offers the best explanation of evidence, "what it explains are the standard causal consequences which such an event would have."[35] As he put it:

> Causal inferences are thus indispensable for knowledge about what occurred and only such present phenomena as can be subsumed under the relevant causal concepts and thus be taken to be effects of the past, can count as evidence for what occurred in the past.[36]

It may be, however, doubted that the relationship between evidence and the event it is evidence for must *always* be a direct relationship between an effect and its cause. Tucker, in his discussion of Pompa's views, appropriately observed that "most research in historiography is . . . about the processes that connect events with evidence."[37] Tucker's choice of the phrase "processes that connect" is significant. The relationship between historical events (historical items, more generally) and the properties of evidence from which we infer that these events (items) happened has to be necessary if the historian is going to infer that the event happened on the basis of evidence. But for Pompa's claim that this relationship is *always* the one between the cause and its effect to be true, one would have to identify (define) such necessity with (as) causation. It is not clear that this is always the case or how one could show that this is always the case. Nevertheless, it is certainly obvious that it is often the case—for instance, a written historical document is always evidence that it was written in the past. Such examples are sufficient to establish that mere coherence is not enough to explain how they came about and that one has to postulate that they were created in the real past.

COHERENCE AND CAUSATION

The problem with the coherentist perspective is that it is impossible to provide a coherent account of the relationship between different pieces of historical evidence if one does not consider the causes that generated the objects and the properties that count as that evidence. The relationship between a historical item and the evidence that it happened need not always be a relationship between a cause and its effect, but in many cases, it will be. In any case, causal relationships require causes, and causes have to precede effects. A coherent account of evidence in such situations requires the existence of real events (items) in the past, events (items) that happened that could have caused the objects that count as evidence. Also, if these causing events cannot be known in principle, historians cannot use them in order to establish relationships among diverse, mutually connected causes of different pieces of evidence—and ultimately a coherent account of the relationship between different pieces of evidence becomes impossible. It is hard to imagine a coherent account of the relationship between two artworks by the same painter, or two coins from the same mint, that fails to state that they share the same cause (the artist or the mint)—whereas if causation is included in the account, then one has to postulate real events in the historical past.

Further complications, also related to causation, are going to arise in relation to the identification of historical evidence itself. If all things that exist are of the same age (if there is no past), or if their age is unknown (if their past cannot be known), then it is unclear what it means for a document or an artifact to be authentic or a forgery. It cannot be responded that the age of documents and their authenticity are constructed on the bases of the properties of the document, such as those established by the chemical analysis of paper, ink, thermoluminescence dating, and so on, because such procedures are introduced precisely because of their capacity to discover causal relationships. They use material causation precisely in order to establish the age of documents. In art history, for instance, it becomes impossible to define the concept of the original artwork if the causal relationship between the author and the object including its properties is negated.

In his polemic against Goldstein, Patrick Horace Nowell-Smith described a similar problem. His argument pertained to the situations in which some human individuals, discussed in historical works, may still be alive. If their past (historical) existence and actions are not real but merely constructed, then they cannot be identified with their past behavior and responsibilities, Nowell-Smith pointed out. Why should we praise or blame living politicians if they are not identical with themselves ten years ago when they performed certain actions that are praise- or blameworthy? In other words, if past historical figures are mere constructs, then they cannot be identical with living human beings, and the latter cannot be responsible for what they did in the past. Nowell-Smith limited his argument to historical figures who are still alive, but the same argument can be expanded to apply to various material artifacts. It applies to the physical objects to which we attribute participation in historical events. We do identify a certain building that exists today as the one that was built by a specific architect centuries ago. A certain existing site can be identified as the place where a historical event happened: the specific, definite physical properties of the site that still exist, for instance, may have decided the outcome of a battle. They are actual, physical features of the site and not mere historiographical constructs. A coherent interpretation of historical documents may tell us that a river prevented the charge of cavalry, or that a painter made a certain painting, or that an architect designed a specific building, but since these are real, still-existing physical objects, they cannot be mere historiographical constructs—and the same applies to the events that caused them to be the way they are.

It is thus fair to conclude that the attempt to combine anti-realist coherentism with the materialist worldview must fail because anti-realism cannot account for causation, and without causation it is impossible to imagine how a description of past events that is coherent with the materialist worldview could be given. Obviously, pointing out that constructionism is incompatible with the concept of causation, and ultimately the materialist worldview, is not necessarily a refutation of constructionism. Advocates of coherentism may reject causation and assume that past events produce no causal impact on the objects that we can presently inspect. This assumption would pertain to everything present today and not only to historical evidence; past events from this point of view are either utterly unknown and cannot explain the world as it is today, or have not happened at all. The guiding principle of such a worldview has to be *omnia ex nihilo*—that everything currently present has come out of nothing. Possibly some kind of philosophy of history can be formulated along those lines, but it will certainly not be compatible with the materialist worldview, which constitutionally relies on the concept of causation.

The credibility of anti-realism in general is not our topic here, but merely its compatibility with materialism. Nevertheless, it needs to be observed that the implications of the view that historical evidence (and present things in general) is not caused by past events by far exceed the field of the philosophy of history. It amounts to a major metaphysical claim. Similarly, the thesis that the past events that caused present things cannot be known in principle is a major epistemological claim. It is thus fair to point out that providing an account of historical causation (or somehow explaining it away) would be a necessity for a credible anti-realist philosophy of history. In the chapters that follow, I will follow the realist line of thinking and assume that historians describe things that happened, τὰ γενόμενα, as Aristotle put it. (This still does not mean that they describe the way things *actually* happened, *wie es eigentlich gewesen*—Ranke's *eigentlich*, "actually," stands for an essentialist perspective, that, I will argue in Chapters Six and Nine is incompatible with materialism.) Repeatedly, the book will discuss various philosophical positions, in favor of or against materialism, and their compatibility with historical research—understood as the effort to discover what happened in the past. The aim to analyze the materialist perspective on historical research also means analyzing the aspects of materialism that make historical research possible.

HOW RELIABLE IS HISTORICAL KNOWLEDGE?

This book is not intended to discuss the nature of historical knowledge. Nevertheless, it is useful to make some general comments here concerning the implications of realism about the historical past for historical knowledge, now that we have seen that it necessarily applies to the materialist perspective that the book is intended to analyze. In principle, historical knowledge consists of true beliefs based on evidence about past items (events, phenomena, and so on) or artifacts produced in the past (artworks, scientific theories, philosophical systems, and similar objects that are studied by historians of art, science, philosophy, and so on).

The definition of knowledge as a true belief that is based on evidence, a justified true belief, goes back to Plato. It has been widely debated by epistemologists ever since 1963, when Edmund Gettier published two counterexamples that were intended to show that such a definition results in counterintuitive attributions of knowledge.[38] Both counterexamples presented situations in which a person had a true belief with *some* justification, but the justification turned out to be invalid. The belief would have been false if some other event did not intervene, and turned the belief into a true one by sheer luck. The common intuition is that such situations should not count as knowledge, although they seem to present cases of justified true beliefs. The examples triggered an extensive epistemological debate about the *infallibility* versus the *fallibility* of evidence. Obviously, "justified" in "justified true belief" can hardly be taken to refer to the possession of fallible evidence. Nevertheless, in epistemology there exists an extensive debate about warrant fallibilism and the dilemma of whether it is possible that warrant does not entail truth.[39] This debate is, however, hardly relevant for historical research. A historian (or a researcher in some other field) is unlikely to have much use for *fallible* evidence, warrant, or a justification of a belief or a hypothesis—that is, evidence, warrant, or a justification that cannot be relied on in order to establish that a proposition, belief, or hypothesis is true. Methodological debates in history often pertain precisely to the dilemma of whether certain evidence, warrant, or justification is sufficient in order to assert that the belief is true. Interests of historians (or researchers in general) are thus quite different from those of epistemologists: they are trying to establish whether a belief or hypothesis is true or not, and evidence, warrant, or justification that is fallible, or inadequate, is simply not helpful for the purpose. This also answers the concern that in many cases it is easy to doubt the infallibility of evidence. Documents could have been forged, or their authors could have been dishonest when stating their views in a document, testimonies of witnesses are notoriously unreliable, and so on. However, these are not undefeatable skeptical arguments, but genuine methodological concerns that a conscientious historical researcher needs to take into account. Historians' debates are indeed often about the validity and the implications of evidence or about the evidence that has been overlooked. A historian may think that the available evidence is sufficient for his or her claim to be true; another historian may find reasons to deny it. The same happens with research in all fields, not only in history.

Like research in other fields, historical research cannot be presuppositionless. In geometry, it is true that the sum of all the internal angles of a triangle is 180° if one assumes the axioms of Euclidean geometry. With different assumptions, the sum may be different. This, however, does not mean that knowledge in geometry is impossible. It is equally unreasonable to expect assumption-free knowledge in history. The important difference is that, unlike in mathematics, historians' assumptions are often more numerous. Also, they are often not stated explicitly, and implicit assumptions are a particularly common source of disagreement. The assumptions that are obviously true to one historian are often a matter of debate to another, and they need not be necessarily endorsed by the general public. When we say that evidence is sufficient to prove that a certain belief is true, we are stating our own judgment about the evidence that supports it. That judgment relies on assumptions that are often unstated and can be rejected by a person who relies on a different set of assumptions. Typically, we reject interpretations of evidence that contradict our normal intuitions about how the world works—but it is often not clear how an architectural historian can refute, for instance, the claim that extra-terrestrials built the Egyptian pyramids. An evolutionary biologist will find it equally challenging to defend his results against people who reject fossils as evidence for the evolution of species and who argue that fossils could have been made by God and placed in the earth in order to test people's faith in the Bible. In these matters, a historian is not in a worse situation than a natural scientist. As Jaegwon Kim pointed out in his *Philosophy of Mind*, a brain scientist who discovers a phenomenon that is not explainable by currently known facts in neural science will simply not consider the possibility that the Cartesian immaterial mind may be interfering with neural processes.[40] Research in all fields depends on assumptions. The purpose of this book is precisely to study and analyze the implications of materialist assumptions in historical research. As mentioned in the Introduction, its aim is not (and cannot be) to prove their validity. It is not even clear how this could be done. Imagine that neurobiology indeed manages to explain how biological (brain) states generate mental states. Even then, a historian will only be able to assume, but not prove, that this was so in the past as well. It is simply not possible to prove, however improbable this may seem, that in the past demons did not actively participate in human history and that the mental states of some historical figures did not result from demonic possession. This has to be assumed.

The impossibility of presuppositionless perspectives on history is also the reason that skeptical arguments against the possibility of historical knowledge have an air of irrelevance, for a historian at least. Anyone interested in historical knowledge has to start from the assumption that many types of skeptical arguments are not valid. Consider the well-known argument that the world may have been created only recently, a couple of minutes ago, including all of us, with our memories and the evidence of past events that actually never happened.[41] In that case we would have false beliefs that the world existed before it was created, including beliefs about the past that actually never happened. The reasonable response that a historian can give to this argument is that the necessary assumption of historical research is that this was not the case—and the same response would be given by researchers in astronomy, geology, evolutionary biology, and so on. Materialism too can only be an assumption; for the proponents of (believers in) immaterial causation or those historians who assume that abstract, immaterial, or spiritual forces play a role in history, the materialist rejection of such substances is essentially a version of skepticism.

At the same time, it is also fair to insist that one should not expect research in history to be more resistant to skeptical arguments than is research in other fields. In the existing literature, skeptical arguments that are phrased to target historical knowledge often have much wider implications. If they were applied in other fields of science or humanities, they would undermine the possibility of research in those fields as well. They may be valid or not, but if their implications are not limited to historical research, then their credibility needs to be considered in that wider context. Consider, for instance, the argument, stated by Jack Meiland, that historians' research, judgments, and the beliefs that they acquire through their work are necessarily biased and that bias cannot be avoided in the acquisition of the beliefs that are regarded as historical knowledge.[42] He also argued that different value systems with which historians operate make them approach evidence with different biases. In fact, problems with bias plague research in all fields; there is no reason to assume that scientists working for the pharmaceutical industry are under less pressure to produce research results that are biased in accordance with the interests of their employers than is the case with historians. At the same time, if one is going to argue that bias prevents historians from reaching historical knowledge, one has to formulate such an argument in a very strong form in order to make it a valid argument in favor of historical anti-realism. Historians certainly struggle with biases, but in order to use this as an argument for the impossibility of knowledge about the past, one has to assume that biases affect human reasoning processes in ways that are irreparable and uncontrollable. This is a much stronger version of skepticism than the one that Descartes struggled with when he worried that an evil demon may be cheating him when it comes to perception. Descartes was concerned that his perceptions were inaccurate; skepticism about biases pertains to the very integrity of mental processes. If skepticism about biases were taken in a form that is necessary to justify the view that the past cannot be known, Descartes could never have been confident in the validity of the inference "I think therefore I am" because he could never be confident that his inference is not biased. If the skeptical argument about bias is going to be sufficiently strong to refute claims of historical knowledge, then arguments such as "human thinking is affected by biases, therefore the past has to be unknown" cannot be made either, because one can never know for any inference whether it may be biased. In other words, in order to make the argument work, one needs to postulate uncontrollable and irreparable bias, which then undermines the very possibility of any argument.[43]

NOTES

1. Arrian, *Anabasis*, 4.10.1.
2. The constructionist interpretation of the passage depends on how one understands "depend" ("... ὑφ' αὐτῷ ... εἶναι") and the claim that Alexander's divinity derives from (that it is "... ἐξ ὧν") the content of Callisthenes writings. Ibid., 4.10.1.
3. For a summary of the two positions see articles by Murphey, "Realism" and Pataut, "Anti-Realism."
4. Ginzburg, "Evidence," 83.
5. As Chris Lorenz put it, "The 'idealistic temptation' has always been based on the argument that history as a discipline—in contrast with the natural sciences—does not deal with a material objects and therefore this object must first be constituted in a mental (Collingwood) or linguistic (White, Anktersmit) manner and universe." Lorenz, "Historical Knowledge," 353.
6. Croce, *Teoria e storia*, 23, 83, 119.
7. Oakeshott, *Experience*, 93.
8. Obviously, anti-realism is also compatible with the denial of any difference between the work of a historian and a fiction writer—and from that position historians do not construct anything.
9. Meiland, *Scepticism*, 34: "The skeptic's position on the possibility of knowledge of past events does not apply to history when history is regarded as concerned with the present significance of documents, not with past events."
10. Louis Mink, "Speculative Philosophy," 153.
11. Kosso, "Observation."
12. This argument has had exceptionally wide circulation. For the classic formulation see Goldstein, *Historical Knowing*.
13. It may be pointed out that it would have been *detectable* using the Geiger counter, but then it can be responded that past events, such as firing a brick or a vase are detectable using thermoluminescence dating.
14. McCullagh, *Truth in History*, 44. Kosso, "Observation."
15. Dummett, *Truth*.
16. Ibid., 67.
17. Ibid., 18–22.
18. For instance, the statement "ancient Greeks failed to discover the printing press" can be true on the basis of the non-happening of a certain event (the ancient Greeks' discovery of the printing press). Similarly, the statement "the Renaissance did not happen" is not a universal anti-realist claim, but merely an anti-realist claim about the Renaissance, insofar as it is assumed to be true.
19. However, the rejection of bivalent logic in the case of statements about the past does not resolve the problems that arise in the case of those authors who deny truth to those statements about the past that rely on colligatory concepts. In their case, it remains unclear why some statements would rely on bivalent logic and others not. (For colligatory concepts see the last chapter.)
20. As he put it: "we are confident that we have arrived at a notable degree of historical truth when those members of the historical community engaged in research on the subject in question reach a level of agreement" and "the initial plausibility of the historical way of knowing comes from the fact that so many different scholars, by applying the techniques of the discipline to the body of so-called historical evidence ... are able to achieve as broad an agreement as they actually have." Goldstein, *Historical Knowing*, 199, 200.
21. Goldstein's views on the coherence theory of truth are unclear, see for instance the discussion of his views in Murphey, "Realism," 184.
22. Goldstein, "History," 42.
23. Goldstein, *Historical Knowing*, 90.
24. See Tucker, *Our knowledge*, 23–45, for an analysis of the conditions when this is the case.
25. For a comprehensive analysis of the problems that arise when the historical profession of a small country becomes dominated by a single ideology see Førland, *Objectivity*.

26. Tacitus, *Historiae*, 1.1.
27. Goldstein occasionally suggests this view, when he says that factuality lies "in virtue of the way they [facts] are established . . . in light of the evidence." Goldstein, *Historical Knowing*, 86.
28. For the reasons described earlier, it also did not *not* happen, since the truth of any of these statements would have to rely on correspondence with past events.
29. Ankersmit, *Meaning*, 145, does not deny the existence of past events in principle, but only some of them—and the Renaissance is the example he chose. See also the analysis in Mitrović, "Opacity."
30. Ankersmit, *Meaning*, 83.
31. Ibid., 83, 145.
32. Murphey, *Our Knowledge*, 15–16.
33. Pompa, "Truth and Fact," 180–186.
34. Ibid., 180.
35. Ibid., 181.
36. Ibid., 181.
37. Tucker, *Our Knowledge*, 94.
38. Plato, *Theaetetus*, 201C. Gettier, "Justified True Belief."
39. Evidence ("warrant") *infallibilism* is the assumption that only true beliefs can have warrants; *fallibilism* is the view that false beliefs can also be warranted. See for instance, Merricks, "Warrant" and idem, "More"; Howard-Snyder, "Infallibilism," Coffman, "Warrant," Moon, "Warrant." It is commonly accepted that warrant infallibilism, or the assumption that full justification is necessary for knowledge, precludes examples such as Gettier's. See for instance Zagzebski, "Inescapability," 72 and Sturgeon, "Gettier," 160.
40. Kim, *Philosophy of Mind*, 113.
41. Russell, *Analysis*, 159.
42. Meiland, *Scepticism*, 85–92.
43. Nagel, "Some Issues," 166, attempted to refute skepticism based on bias by arguing that (a) the claim that historical judgments are biased assumes that there is a distinction between biased and unbiased judgments; (b) it follows that bias can be identified; (c) consequently, bias can be eliminated. However, the problem is that it may be denied that bias can be always identified: we know that judgments can be biased, but that does not mean that we can always identify which ones are biased. Nagel's counter-argument does not prevent the possibility that some arguments can be biased even though we cannot recognize them. Also, we do not know whether errors in our reasoning that derive from bias may be uncontrollable and irreparable. It is possible that their number may effectively block the reliability of historical knowledge about the past. However, if bias is uncontrollable and irreparable, it is also not clear how to prove that the argument that bias prevents historical knowledge is not biased, and the argument about bias turns against the very possibility of formulating the skeptical argument, or any argument at all.

Chapter Two

Individualism

Theoretical positions in the philosophy of mind and the philosophy of the social sciences are among the most common sources of challenges, explicit or implicit, to materialist perspectives on history. Should the possibility of the materialist approach to historical research be refuted some day, it is reasonable to expect that this may happen through a breakthrough in one of those two fields. In the case of the philosophy of mind, modern science still does not know how processes in the brain generate mental states. If future scientific research demonstrates that dualism is true, that some immaterial, abstract or even spiritual forces need to be relied on in order to explain the relationship between the brain and the mind, this will obviously invalidate the materialist understanding of the mental states of historical figures as well as the explanations of their actions that materialism can provide. For the past half a century, potential challenges to materialism in historical research that came from positions related to the philosophy of mind mostly pertained to the contents of mental states and the nature of languages. They will be surveyed and discussed in Chapters Four, Five and Six.

This chapter deals with the challenges that are motivated by arguments originating from the philosophy of the social sciences. They pertain to the nature of social items (social entities, events or phenomena) that a historian has to describe or explain. The materialist perspective assumes that social items can result exclusively from physical items. Since human individuals necessarily play important roles in social items, and since the materialist thesis has to be that social items do not include non-physical items, the implications is that from the materialist point of view, social items cannot consist of something else but human individuals, their actions, interactions and their physical environment. It would amount to the refutation of the materialist approach to historical research if one could show that in order to understand historical-social events such as battles, institutions such as armies, or phenomena such as the Renaissance, one has to postulate immaterial, abstract or spiritual substances, over and above individuals, what they did and the physical environment in which they acted. Materialism in historical research is thus necessarily coupled with the individualist perspective on human society. The important dilemma is whether individualism is sufficient to describe and explain the historical and social items that a historian may need to describe or explain. The dilemma parallels an equivalent, but much more vehement, debate in the philosophy of the social sciences, where, for the past fifty years, one could witness a steady production of idealist arguments that have endeavored to refute individualism (and thus materialism, by trying to show the necessity to expand social ontology beyond the physical world). This intensity of the debate about social ontology in the social sciences is not replicated in the contemporary philosophy of history, where, as Aviezer Tucker observed, there exists a wide endorsement of the individualist ontology of social items, and it is also widely accepted that the pragmatics of history-writing often makes historical descriptions phrased in terms of social items preferable.[1] Nevertheless, if some arguments from the philosophy of the social sciences managed to show that in order to understand or explain social items one needs to rely on abstract or immaterial entities, forces or phenomena over and above human individuals, their interactions and the physical environment in which they act, this would amount to the refutation of the possibility of materialist approaches to historical research as well. The aim of this chapter is to show that this is not the case. The chapter surveys a series of arguments that have been formulated in the philosophy of the social sciences in order to show that they are not sufficient to establish that it is necessary to postulate immaterial or abstract forces, entities of phenomena when describing or explaining social items in historical research.[2]

MATERIALISM AND THE HISTORICAL-SOCIAL ENVIRONMENT

Historical figures cannot inhabit history without being parts of social environments; as a result, discussions about the nature of historical items are often also discussions about the nature of corresponding social items. The debate about the implications of materialism for the understanding of historical contexts and social environments pertains to the role that human individuals, their actions and interactions (including interactions with the physical environment) play in the constitution of historical and social items. The core dilemma is whether one can understand and explain historical and social items by relying *only* on human individuals, their actions, interactions, properties and their physical environments? Can one understand their historical and social context as consisting only of other individuals, their actions and interactions and the physical environment? Or, is it maybe necessary to expand ontology beyond the physical world—beyond individuals, what they do, their properties (including mental states) and their physical environment—in order to understand historical-social items, historical contexts and social environments and explain how they work?

Consider Saul Kripke's formulation of the problem.[3] There are true statements about individuals and true statements about nations, he says. The question is then, could a description of the world that contains all such statements about individuals (and other physically describable items), but omits all statements about nations, still be a complete description of the world, from which the facts about nations would follow? *Ontological* individualism is the view that social items through history consisted exclusively of individuals, their properties and interactions with each other and the physical environment. In other words, this is the view that individuals exhaust the social world. *Methodological* individualism is the view that social items are reducible to or explainable by sets of individuals and their properties, actions or interactions. The opposing views are referred to as ontological or methodological *holism*. In principle, if ontological individualism is false, methodological individualism cannot be true. If social items are not only individuals and their interactions, then they certainly cannot be reduced to or explained by individuals and their interactions only. Similarly, if methodological individualism is true, ontological individualism cannot be false. If social items are reducible to individuals and their interactions, they cannot be something else.

The concept of reducibility that defines methodological individualism can be understood in a number of ways. One way is to say that it should be always possible, in the case of all social items, to identify all participating individuals and their interactions that make up the item, and that there will be no un-identifiable residue. Obviously, since in many cases the necessary information is missing, methodological individualism thus understood is trivially false: Napoleon's *Grande armée* will be irreducible to a set of individuals since archival sources do not enable us to identify all its soldiers. Tor Egil Førland has inferred from this—and it is hard to object to his observation—that historical research therefore necessarily requires a historian to take a methodological holist position.[4] One could rephrase the definition of methodological individualism and say that reducibility, thus understood, should be possible in principle, if all the necessary information were available—but it is hard to deny that when it comes to actual historical research methodological individualism is simply not an option. There are also other ways to understand reducibility. Social scientists are often interested in discovering social laws. They may not be interested in identifying all the participating individuals, but, rather, a general type of a set of individuals and their interactions in which certain situations will happen. The question is then going to be, can statements about types of social items be reduced to statements about types of sets of individuals. In the philosophy of the social sciences there exists significant literature about the possibility of such reductions. It has been often argued they are impossible because social items are realized in a great variety of social situations ("multiple realizability").[5] Obviously, irreducibility understood in one of these days does not entail that social items are in some sense immaterial or contain immaterial parts. Also, since few historians today believe in the possibility of historical laws, they are unlikely to be interested in the reducibility of types of historical-social items. Unlike social scientists, historians are more interested in singular (token) historical-social items.

For our discussion here, it is ontological individualism, not methodological individualism, that matters. The threat for the materialist perspective on historical research comes from the claim that in order to understand, describe or explain social entities, one needs to expand ontology beyond material items and postulate some additional, immaterial items in addition to individuals, their actions, interactions and their physical environment. We are thus here interested in arguments that state that social items, in the form they occurred through history, were something else, or were not only, or were something more than, or over and above sets of individuals, their actions, interactions with other individuals and their physical environment. The philosophers of the social sciences who propose these arguments say typically little about the nature of the ontological expansion that they advocate—for instance, is it some kind of "emergence 2" in Searle's terminology, or merely an abstract force or an entity over and above individuals and their interactions and so on. Such clarification would also be of marginal interest for us here. Rather, we are interested here in the arguments that have been proposed in favor of the expansion of social ontology beyond the material world. The aim is to show that they do not manage to justify the rejection of the materialist approach to historical research.

HISTORIANS AND SOCIAL ONTOLOGY

In historical research, the individualism-holism dilemma is unavoidable as soon as a historian attempts to understand or explain historical-social items. Were the French Revolution, the battle of Borodino, or the Counterreformation merely very complex clusters of individuals', their actions and interactions? Were they more than that? In the case that they were indeed abstract entities that cannot be identified with individuals and what individuals did, could they cause events independently of what individuals did? Where did they derive their causal capacities from? Throughout this book, problems pertaining to social ontology will also recur in relation to topics that are only indirectly related to the understanding social structures themselves. They will also play an important role later in discussions about the meaning and interpretation of historical documents and historical works. One important dilemma will be whether these meanings are always instantiated in the minds of individuals or should they be attributed independent existence. Mark Bevir's principle of "procedural individualism," on which I will extensively rely in the discussion of the understanding and interpretation of texts, requires that meanings, as contents of mental states, can be instantiated only in individual minds. As Bevir puts it: "As a matter of principle, we must be able to translate any statement about a collective consciousness into a series of statements about specific individuals."[6] Historically, the identification of the materialist perspective on history with the individualist perspective on human society was first fully articulated in the early writings of Karl Marx and Friedrich Engels. The important question that they asked in their youthful anti-Hegelian polemics pertained to the kind of history one can write if one rejects what they mocked as the history of spirits and ghosts (*Geister- und Gespenstergeschichte*)?[7] They strongly insisted, though they may have abandoned that view later in their lives, that the result has to be an individualist perspective.[8] An abstract force, such as history, they point out in *Holy Family*

> does nothing, it "possesses no huge wealth," and it "fights no battles"! Rather it is the human being, the real, living human being, that does everything, possesses and fights; "history" does not use humans as means for its purposes—as if it were a person—rather, history is nothing but the activity of humans who follow their aims.[9]

One can find a comprehensive elaboration of the individualist perspective on history, derived from the materialist point of view, in the opening section of their *German Ideology*.[10] The students of Marx's and Engels's philosophy of history have spent much time discussing whether, when and how the founders of communism abandoned their early individualist perspectives, but the historical significance of their insight cannot be doubted.

Assumptions that historians make about the nature of social items can be, but need not be, reflected in the way they phrase historical descriptions and explanations. Historians who systematically rejected the materialist and individualist perspectives have sometimes endeavored to develop historiography that avoided any reference to individuals and their activities. Such approaches were particularly dominant in German historiography during Wilhelmine and Weimar eras.[11] A good example is Ernst Troeltsch's historical works. Troeltsch actually used the term "individuality" to refer to epochs, cultural tendencies, states, nations and so on;[12] "absolutism," "capitalism," "state," "modern science," "democracy" and so in his perspective become genuine historical forces (*Mächte*) that act and affect each other, and they are not to be conceived as resulting from interactions between individuals.[13] Similar perspectives have often been appealing to art historians who deal with anonymous artworks (early Christian or medieval art; Max Dvořák is a good example) or to art historians who do not think that interactions between individuals suffice for the explanation of the phenomenon of style and believe that an appropriate explanation requires the introduction of additional immaterial or spiritual forces. In opposition to such approaches is the history-writing that engages with individuals and their interactions. A good example is the historical works about the July 1914 crisis. There exists an extensive production of historical works about it—one can mention as older examples Luigi Albertini's *Le origini della guerra del 1914* or Fritz Fischer's *Griff nach der Weltmacht* or more recently T. G. Otte's *July Crisis*. Such studies strive to reconstruct, describe and explain the actions and the interactions of protagonists in the crisis, and these protagonists are all biological individuals. Another good example of a historical narrative that deals only with individuals is Howard Zinn's *A People's History of the United States*. Zinn's book aims to present the history of various forms of oppression in the United States through history and in his narrative he insists on presenting individual cases, situations, and (inter)actions. The implicit assumption is that there is no such thing as oppression in general, that it always consists of specific situations. It is important to emphasize that one should not necessarily identify these approaches to history-writing with positions on social ontology. A historian who endorses ontological individualism about social items may still decide to describe historical situations in terms of large-scape social items. As we have seen Tucker point out, such descriptions are generally regarded to be often more useful. As long as these social items are understood to be constituted by individuals and their interactions, they still belong under the individualist paradigm. Vice versa, a historian who endorses ontological holism may still emphasize the actions and interactions of individuals, assuming that the whole, as a genuine force, manifests itself through what individuals do.

INDIVIDUALISM-HOLISM DEBATE IN THE SOCIAL SCIENCES

Ontological individualism is often described as the standard or mainstream view in the contemporary social sciences, while it is said that the validity of methodological individualism is debated.[14] At the same time, attempts to refute ontological individualism also have significant presence in the literature and these attempts are the main topic of this chapter. (There also exists a debate about so-called "collective intentions," but it is not important for us here since its main protagonists subscribe to materialist and individualist views and formulate their positions accordingly.[15])

The debate between individualism and holism in the philosophy of the social sciences is often affected by extra-theoretical concerns. Ever since Margaret Thatcher stated that there is no society but only individuals, individualist perspectives have been commonly associated with libertarian political views and possibly with opposition to social programs.[16] One important response to this concern is that it confuses individualism in the philosophy of the social sciences with political libertarianism. There is no reason why someone who believes that governments should provide support for disadvantaged members of society should have to subscribe to social ontology that postulates immaterial entities. In fact, actual social programs (for instance, in education or healthcare) can be organized only insofar as their recipients are definable as sets of identifiable individuals. If a government wants to organize a social program for poor schoolchildren, these schoolchildren have to be identifiable as individuals. Otherwise it will be impossible to specify the individuals that program is going to engage. Social programs can never be formulated for a population *in abstracto*; they target sets of the individuals that need them. In other words, they need to specify the individuals who satisfy certain criteria. At the same time, it is reasonable to associate holism and the opposition to individualism with a defense of unrestrained rights of corporate elites: if corporations are understood as entities whose actions (and therefore responsibilities) are not reducible to the actions and responsibilities of individuals who actually make decisions (managements, CEOs) then the latter should also be exempted from criminal responsibility for illegal actions committed by the corporation. A company that engages in illegal activity in order to increase financial gain (for instance, produces cars that pollute more than it is allowed) may be sued, lose a lot of money and its employees may lose jobs, but if it is understood as more than a set of individuals and their interactions, then the CEO who decided that the company should engage in illegal or criminal activities cannot be held responsible. The opponents of the individualist perspective may, however, point out that this argument assumes that the responsibility for criminal actions of social entities (such as corporations) always belongs to individuals—which is indeed what they deny. If they are right, there would be precisely situations in which a corporation engages in a criminal activity, but no individual (or a set of individuals) is responsible. Obviously, for an individualist, this perspective is unacceptable.

Even if such political concerns and debates are bracketed, the approaches to the individualism-holism dilemma are bound to reflect the deep-seated assumptions people have about their social environment. They easily translate to the assumptions people make about historical entities, phenomena or events. Consider, for instance, W. H. Walsh's statement that

> There can be no question of reducing historical movements to complicated sets of human actions for the very good reason that individual human actions do not have the independence which is so often claimed of them: men's minds reflect their upbringing and human environment, and we should find it hard to say what was in them if we had to abstract from these.[17]

The response is going to be that it is not necessary to deny that human minds reflect upbringing and environment in order to assert the reducibility of historical movements to individuals' interactions. Insofar as it is assumed that historical-social environments themselves are nothing but individuals and their interactions, then their impact on individuals (such as upbringing) will itself be reducible to these individuals' interactions with other individuals. The individualist thesis is not that social environments do not exist, but that they are individuals and their interactions.

A good example of the way authors inadvertently introduce their assumptions in the debate about the individualist understanding of the social-historical world are the attempts to refute methodological individualism by stating that social entities and phenomena cannot be reduced to individuals and their (inter)actions because in the process of reduction one needs to refer to other social entities and phenomena. In the existing literature, this kind of argument has had substantial circulation.[18] For instance, it is pointed out that one cannot explain educational or penal systems without reference to teachers or inmates and one cannot explain teachers or inmates without mentioning schools or prisons, while schools and prisons are social entities. The obvious individualist response is going to be that these other social entities (such as schools or prisons) and phenomena are themselves reducible to sets of individuals and their interactions. The argument assumes that they are not—while this is something the argument is meant to prove. In other words, this refutation of individualism is a classic case of *petitio principii*.

INDIVIDUALS' INTERACTIONS AND HOW TO AVOID STRAW-MAN ARGUMENTS

Human individuals, including historical figures, participate in their historical-social environment through their actions and interactions with other individuals and the physical environment. Unsuccessful refutations of individualism (and consequently the materialist perspective on historical-social items) often derive from the misunderstanding of the role of interactions in social life. The role of individuals' interactions for the understanding of social items has been known at least since the early twentieth century when

Georg Simmel described it.[19] "Interactions" are here understood broadly, and they include the actions of individuals in their social and physical environment, the way individuals are affected by the environment as well as their reactions to the environment. Obviously, individuals' actions, interactions or affections are not separately existing entities—rather, they are something done by existing entities (other individuals or physical objects). Individuals can perform interactions in different ways; they can also be affected in various ways and consequently interactions can have properties. If we say that a squash game was fast-paced, this merely means that the players acted in a certain way, not that the squash game was a separately existing entity with the property of being fast-paced. Members of a set of individuals (bank employees, soldiers of a company), may interact with other members of that set or with entities outside the set. The entities outside the set with which they interact may be other human individuals, but they also may be any other elements of the physical environment. (Bank employees approve mortgages to bank customers, scientists study a volcano.)

Many historical-social items need to be understood as individuals *plus* their item-relevant interactions. "Relevant" here means that a bank, for instance, is individual employees plus those interactions that these individuals need to perform in order to constitute a bank. For instance, all employees of a bank may also be members of a squash club, whereby at the same time, the squash club does not have members who do not work in the bank. When they play squash or decide about the running of the club, this activity is not relevant for the functioning of the bank, but when they approve mortgages to other people, this is a bank-relevant activity, in the sense that this is one of the activities that banks perform and it makes it into a bank. Note also that the replacement of individuals who constitute a bank, hiring and discontinuation of employment, are also interactions that occur between employees (including, e.g., the management).

Individualism is easy to defeat if one omits interactions from consideration and imagines individuals as isolated units that do not interact with other individuals or their physical environments. One is then easily led to the assumption that ontological expansion beyond the material world is necessary in order to understand what happens in history or the social world. A battle is not a set of soldiers on the battlefield; it is what they do, the interactions in which these soldiers engage. One should certainly dismiss as unproductive the arguments of those authors who refute individualism by pointing out that individuals must interact in the social environment while (in their understanding) individualism postulates individuals that have no interaction with other individuals.[20] Such refutations merely target a straw man, especially since interactions are often explicitly mentioned in definitions of individualism in the social sciences.[21]

Another common type of a straw-man argument is generated by introducing the assumption that individuals' interactions can only be interactions with other individuals and that, insofar as individualism strives to explain social items as individuals and their interactions, it overlooks the impact of the physical environment on social relations.[22] It is hard to see why one should assume that individuals cannot interact with their physical environment or that the physical environment could affect social items without affecting a single individual. Once we take into account that individuals act in relation to the physical environment and are affected by it, this criticism ceases to be relevant.

Alternatively, one may "refute" individualism by assuming that the individualist understanding of social institutions as sets of individuals and their interactions is limited to the interactions within the set. One then finds situations in which the individuals who constitute the institution need to interact with external individuals or institutions (for instance, because these other individuals formulate the regulations of the given institution or help structure and schedule its activities) and declares this situation for an example that defeats individualism.[23] Here too, the argument fails to present a fair and accurate account of the individualist position; there is no reason why one should exclude interactions with individuals external to the institution.

Anti-individualist arguments about the continuity and the coincidental identity of institutions are also based on the failure of take into account the important role that individuals' interactions play in the constitution of institutions. The continuity argument starts from the observation that institutions (such as an orchestra or a soccer club) typically remain the same institutions when the participating individuals are replaced. It is then pointed out that the identification of institutions with sets of individuals cannot be true, because such replacements cannot occur in the case of sets: if we replace some elements of a set with new ones, a set becomes a new set. The well-known version of the arguments pertains to the U.S. Supreme Court: the justices of that court change with time, but the institution still remains one and the same.[24] The simple response to this argument is that saying that institutions are sets of individuals (taken together with their relevant interactions) does not entail that every institution is a *single* set of individuals (plus the relevant interactions). An institution (and this happens with the U.S. Supreme Court) can be a number of different sets of individuals whereby each set performs the relevant interactions at a given time. Whenever a justice is replaced with a new one, another set of justices counts as the Supreme Court, but this does not mean that the Court is something over and above these justices and their interactions. (Alternatively, one could conceive of the Supreme Court as the total set of all individuals who, for a period of their lives, interact, have interacted or will interact as Supreme Court justices, whereby there is always a subset of active justices in any given period who make the decisions for the Court.)

Arguments about coincidence pertain to the observation that one and the same set of individuals can be more than one institution.[25] Imagine that the U.S. Senate appoints all and only Supreme Court justices to a Committee on Judicial Ethics. The set of individuals serving as members of the Committee on Judicial Ethics will consequently be identical to the set of individuals serving as Supreme Court justices. Nevertheless, while the Supreme Court may be in session at a certain time, the Committee on Judicial Ethics need not be. It will be argued that if they are one and the same set of individuals, it is hard to see how this difference could be made. Similarly, if the Supreme Court and the Special Committee on Judicial Ethics are one and the same set of individuals, it seems to follow that the Committee on Judicial Ethics is identical with the Supreme Court. Since the Committee on Judicial Ethics is one of the committees assembled by the Senate, it will follow that the Supreme Court is one of the committees assembled by the Senate, which is false. Finally, imagine that the Committee on Judicial Ethics (as mentioned, the same set of individuals as the Supreme Court), but not the Supreme Court, joins the Committee of Ethics Committees. If membership in the Committee of Ethics Committees is merely a relation between a set and its elements, then we must conclude that there would be a time at which both the Supreme Court and Special Committee on Judicial Ethics are members of the Committee of Ethics Committees. And this, again, is an unacceptable conclusion.

The three versions of the coincidence argument are also easily responded to if one takes individuals' interactions into account. They all overlook the fact that the Supreme Court or the Committee on Judicial Ethics cannot be defined merely as sets of individuals, but as sets of individuals who interact in specific ways. When defining a historical-social item one is often not merely talking about sets of individuals, but about these individuals and what they do, the interactions they perform. The phrase "to be in session" refers to different types of interactions in the case of the two institutional bodies. If the Supreme Court is in session at a certain time, this means that the justices are doing one kind of job; if the Committee on Judicial Ethics is in session, they are performing another kind of job. If the Senate appoints the set of individuals to interact as (perform tasks that are expected of) members of the Committee for Judicial Ethics, this does not mean that the Senate appoints the set of individuals to interact as (perform tasks that are expected of) Supreme Court justices. Finally, when one says that the Committee on Judicial Ethics has joined the Committee of Ethics Committees, one is saying that the set of individuals who (occasionally) interact as members of the Committee on Judicial Ethics has joined the Committee of Ethics Committees. One is not saying that the set of individuals who (occasionally) interact as Supreme

Court justices has joined this latter committee—though this happens to be the case.

COULD BISMARCK HAVE BEEN A FRENCHMAN?

Philosophically probably the most intricate argument against individualism pertains to modal statements about collective entities.[26] The argument seeks to show that modal statements about historical-social items (such as countries) cannot be made within the materialist paradigm and that consequently in order to make them the historian must postulate immaterial abstract social entities. Since historians often rely on modal statements—for instance, statements about what could have happened—if the argument were valid, this would seriously affect the credibility of materialism when it comes to historical research. It is therefore important to describe here why this is not the case, especially because the argument is mentioned from time to time as a decisive refutation of individualism. Similarly to the arguments that we have just seen, this argument fails to take into account the role individuals' interactions play in the constitution of social entities.

Let set "A" be the set of all French persons. The argument strives to show that we cannot identify France with this set, because of some types of counterfactual statements that can be made about it. In particular, it is reasonable to say that France could have had one national more or less—a statement that makes no sense if we identify France with the set A, because the set A is identical to the set A, and one cannot say that it could have one member more or less. If it did, it would be another set. One possible response would be to say that "France might have had one national more or less than it does have" means

> There could have been (but is not) a set which would have had the same members as the set A has, and in addition one member more or less.

It is then argued that reformulation is to be dismissed on the basis for the following reason. Consider the possibility that a specific person could have been a French national. Imagine that Bismarck's mother was in France before his birth, but left for Germany some time before he was born. In that case Bismarck might have been a Frenchman had she stayed a little bit longer. How could one express this possibility as a statement about sets? On the account just proposed, the formulation would be:

> There might have been (but is not) a set just like the set A except that Bismarck was a member of it.

Individualism 59

However, this set actually exists: this is the set of all French persons plus Bismarck—and that set is not France.

In other words, historical-social items have modal properties that sets of individuals cannot have. Consequently, serious difficulties are bound to arise when one tries to make modal statements about historical social entities if the latter are to be understood materialistically, as sets of individuals and their interactions.

In fact, it is important to differentiate between "the set of all French citizens plus the non-citizen Bismarck" is not the same as "the set of all French citizens including the citizen Bismarck." The set of all French citizens is not merely a set of individuals, but a set of individuals plus their interactions that made them French citizens. In order to be a French citizen, Bismarck (and his parents) would have to have engaged in specific interactions with other French citizens: for instance, it might have been necessary for Bismarck to be listed in the register of French citizens by an appropriate state official. (Or it may have been necessary for him to be born in France, which is a form of interaction with the social and the physical environments.) This was not the case. The hypothetical situation in which Bismarck would have been a French citizen is not identical with the situation in which he was merely a member of a set that includes all French citizens (individuals who have been listed in the register of French citizens) plus Bismarck. Here too, we face the situation that a specific historical-social item (France) is not merely a set of individuals, but a set of individuals and their item-specific interactions. If we talk about sets:

> The set of all French citizens plus the set of the interactions they were involved in that made them French citizens, plus Bismarck

is not the same as:

> The set of all French citizens plus the set of the interactions they were involved in that made them French citizens, plus Bismarck plus the interactions in which Bismarck was involved that made him a French citizen

Therefore when we say

> France might have had one national more or less than it does have.

this indeed means

> There could have been (but is not) a set which would have had the same members as the set A has, and in addition one member more or less who engaged in the interactions necessary in order to be a French citizen.

Chapter 2

RULES, REGULATIONS, ROLES

The anti-materialist argument about social rules, regulations and roles takes into account the significance of interactions, but nevertheless comes to the conclusion that individualism is insufficient to explain the nature of the forces that sustain historical-social items. The argument aims to conclude that materialist ontology is not sufficient in order to explain the functioning of social items and that it needs to be expanded. It is claimed that in order to explain interactions of individuals in historical-social contexts, one needs to postulate the existence of social rules, regulations or roles that exist independently, over and above individuals and that regulate (or determine) how individuals act and interact. For instance, the justices of the U.S. Supreme Court are nominated by the president of that country and their appointment is confirmed by the Senate. These interactions occur according to certain rules whereby the participating individuals must act according to their roles that are specified by these rules. The obvious challenge is to explain the ontology of these rules and how they determine the acting of individuals. A well-known variation of this argument is based on the example of a person who cashes a check in a bank.[27] It is pointed out that such an event relies on a number of social relations (rights, regulations, obligations and so on) that need to be in place if the interaction is going to be successful. The dilemma is how to explain what these "relations" are and their ontology. In other words, it is argued that it is not enough to describe interactions between individuals in order to explain what happens when a person cashes a check in a bank; one needs to postulate rules, regulations, roles, rights, obligations and so on, that (the argument is meant to conclude) exist on their own, in addition to and independently of individuals and that what individuals do, and that enable the transaction.

However, this line of argument overlooks the importance of individuals' mental states (such as believing, deciding or desiring) for the functioning of social entities and phenomena. Mental states are certainly parts of individuals they belong to. The response to the argument is going to be that social rules, regulations or roles exist only as the contents of the mental states of individuals, such as widely shared beliefs about ways certain actions are or should be performed. It is not necessary to postulate that the rules according to which the president of the United States nominates and the Senate approves the appointments of the justices of the Supreme Court exist independently of the mental states of the individuals involved. In fact, if they existed independently of everyone's mind, it is not clear how they could be taken into account in the process of appointment. If everyone forgot about these rules or believed that they are for some reason not valid, they would cease to have any effect on historical-social events, even if they existed in some Platonic world. If the bank client and the teller did not have specific beliefs about social relations (about the procedure for cashing a check, how much money there is on the account, etc.) the check could not be cashed. Even if we assume that rights and regulations are abstract items whose existence is independent of individual minds, this does not explain why individuals act accordingly. Rules, regulations, roles and so on cannot be operational in social or historical contexts independently of individuals' mental processes: what makes individuals act in accordance with rules and regulations are the beliefs that these individuals have about rules and regulations—about the ways various actions need to be performed.

It may be responded that this explanation still relies on rules and regulations that the client's and the teller's beliefs are about. In other words, that since there are proper procedures to elect the members of the Supreme Court or to cash a check, such procedures must be a set of rules and consequently exist in some form independently of what individuals think. Otherwise we would not be able to say when individuals break the rules. For instance, if such rules did not exist independently on their own, we would not know that a teller made a mistake when he cashed a check on Sunday.

The response is that, if such a rule existed independently of individuals' mental states, they could be operational in the social context only as long as people knew about it. What makes individuals act according to rules are their beliefs about the proper ways to perform certain actions. It is not through the consultation with some abstract, supra-individual forces that we establish the right way to cash a check. Rather, we establish it by consulting the statements (oral or written) of the individuals who had the authority to prescribe how things need to be done. When nominating the justices of the Supreme Court, the president of the United States is acting according to the instructions stipulated in the U.S. Constitution, while the constitution itself was written by the individuals who had the authority to do it. (Both in the case of a bank and in the case of the U.S. Constitution, such authorities were established through further interactions with other individuals.) Acting according to or violating rules and regulations is then a form of interaction with these authorities. Biological organisms such as bank clients, tellers or presidents of the United States cannot interact with immaterial propositions (even though they may believe that they do) because immaterial rules or regulations, even if they existed, could not affect them. At the same time, documents, bank regulations, laws, constitutions, social rules, architects' designs according to which buildings are built, do not come about from nowhere; they are contents of mental states, conveyed and enforced through actions and interactions of individuals; they are promulgated and enforced through interactions between individuals and if this does not happen, they will not be operational in a social context.

It is important to bear in mind what arguments about ontological holism can and cannot achieve. It is impossible to prove that ontological holism is false and that there do not exist immaterial social entities, over and above individuals and their interactions, the way it is impossible to prove that Santa Claus or Pegasus do not exist. The burden of finding a decisive proof thus necessarily falls on ontological holists. The type of argument that they can make is to try to find social functions that cannot be materialistically explained as results of interactions between individuals and their environments—and so far, since the times of Ludwig Gumplowicz and Émil Durkheim, their opponents have always been able to point out that an individualist account is still possible. There is, of course, no reason to believe that holists may not eventually be successful in their efforts, and this would most likely have serious consequences for the credibility of the materialist philosophy of history. The outcome of the debate thus can be seen as uncertain, but one has to admit that the intensive debate has been going on for a century and a half and that a definite argument in favor of ontological holism has not been found.

NOTES

1. Tucker, *Our Knowledge*, 212.
2. I believe to have covered the important and the well-known arguments. There are certainly more, but they are either quite weak and not worth discussing, or variations of those discussed here.
3. Kripke, *Naming and Necessity*, 50.
4. Førland, *Values*, 140.
5. See for instance Kincaid, *Individualism*, Sawyer, "Nonreductive Individualism: Part I," Sawyer, "Nonreductive Individualism: Part II," Sawyer, *Social Emergence*. For an argument against multiple realizability see Mitrović, "Multiple Realizability."
6. Bevir, *Logic*, 62.
7. Marx and Engels, *Die deutsche Ideologie*, 113.
8. There exists a substantial debate about the individualist perspectives in the writings of the young Marx and Engels. See Elster, *Making Sense,* Elster, "A Case for Methodological Individualism," Israel, "Methodological Individualism," Dumont, *From Mandeville to Marx*, 113, 125, 136–137. The question plays an important role in the debate about analytic Marxism, see Weldes, "Marxism," Wolff, "Methodological Individualism," Tarrit, "A Brief History," Kumar, "A Pragmatist Spin," Levine, Wright and Sober, "Marxism."
9. Marx and Engels, *Die heilige Familie*, 98.
10. Marx and Engels, *Die deutsche Ideologie*. Marx, *Der 18te Brumaire*, 115.
11. For a survey see Mitrović, *Rage and Denials*.
12. Troeltsch, *Historismus*, 120. See the analysis in Mitrović, *Rage and Denials*, 49–58.
13. Troeltsch, "Das Wesen," 124–167.
14. Udehn, *Methodological Individualism*, 2. Epstein, "Ontological Individualism," 187. Sawyer, *Social Emergence*, 66.
15. For a general presentation of this discussion see Tollefsen "Collective Intentionality," Schweikard and Schmid "Collective Intentionality" and Chant, Hindriks and Preyer, "Introduction." Michael Bratmann and Raimo Tuomela are explicit about their individualist views. Bratman, "Cooperative Activity," 338 and Tuomela, "We-intentions Revisited," 342, start from individuals' intentions and then specify the conditions that need to be satisfied for these intentions to count as "shared cooperative activity" (Bratman) or "joint intention" (Tuomela). Searle, "Collective Intentions," 406, is also explicit of his individualist commitments though he rejects the possibility of an analysis of we-intentions such as proposed by Bratman or Tuomela. Margaret Gilbert's phrase "plural subject" is also to be understood individualistically. As she explained in Gilbert, "Shared Intention," 182: "In earlier writings I have labeled those who are jointly committed with one another in some way a 'plural subject.' This label should not be thought to have any ontological implications beyond those involved in the claim that certain persons are jointly committed in some way."
16. Kincaid, *Individualism*, 2. See similarly Elster, *Making Sense of Marx*, xiii–xv.
17. Walsh, "Colligatory Concepts," 135.
18. Lukes, "Methodological Individualism," 122. Weldes, "Marxism," 362. Kincaid, *Individualism*, 23, 34, 35, 51. Similarly Giddens *Central Problems* 94–95. Giddens is often unclear, but I assume that he relies on this argument when he says that social institutions "are the outcome of action only in so far as they are also involved recursively as the medium of its production." Ibid., 94–95.
19. Simmel, *Soziologie*, 3, says that historical phenomena are to be understood as consisting "aus dem Wechselwirken und dem Zusammenwirken der Einzelnen." Society comes into being when a number of individuals interact, he pointed out. Ibid., 4. In Simmel, *Individuum*, 12, 14–15, he stated that society is but a name for a group of individuals, and that it is better understood as an event than as a substance.
20. Some examples are Bunge, "Ten Modes," 394 and Hodgson, "Meanings," 220–221.
21. For instance, Elster, *Nuts and Bolts*, 13, Sawyer, *Social Emergence*, 6, List and Spiekermann, "Methodological Individualism," 629.
22. See the discussion in Watkins, "Methodological Individualism" and Epstein, "Ontological Individualism."

23. Here is an example formulated by Epstein, *Ant Trap*, 225–230. Let there be two committees, A and B, that consist of the same individuals and differ only by having different secretaries ("parliamentarians"). They are all, including the secretaries, appointed by the governor of Massachusetts. The secretaries do not count as members of these committees and cannot vote. The committees are charged with making decisions about different types of problems. Imagine that a meeting of committee A was scheduled for the same time when the parliamentarian of committee B called the meeting of B. As a result, the wrong committee met at the given time and made decisions they had no right to make, so the decisions they made are invalid. The example shows that group action may depend on non-members. It is therefore wrong, in Epstein's view, to believe that once you have fixed the actions of the members of a group, you have thereby fixed the actions of the group. The problem with the example is that it takes into account only the *internal* interactions between committee members, and not their *external* interactions with the respective parliamentarians. The actual set of individuals that make the decision *de facto* includes the secretaries who schedule the meetings. Even though they cannot vote, their acting can affect the decision. People do not have to be called "members of a committee" in order to affect the decisions made by the committee and be part of the set of individuals whose acting results in the decision. (Epstein actually considers this response but thinks that he can avoid it by saying that one could attribute to the governor the decision about timing—but this merely makes the governor a member of the set of individuals whose acting contributes to the final decision.)

24. See Uzquiano, "Supreme Court." Uzquiano endeavored to show that such identification cannot explain the functioning of the U.S. Supreme Court and that an additional kind of entity (that Uzquiano calls a "group") needs to be taken into consideration. Understood as a group, an institution such as the U.S. Supreme Court is a different entity from the set of its members; Uzquiano insisted that it exists as a "separate object from the set of its members."

25. See Uzquiano, "Supreme Court" for these arguments.

26. See Ruben, "Social Entities," for the elaboration of this argument.

27. Mandelbaum, "Societal Facts."

Chapter Three

Free Will

Historians and social scientists often differ significantly in their interests, in spite of the fact that, we have seen in Chapter Two, they may share very similar dilemmas. Social scientists often strive to discover law-like regularities in the social environment, whereas few historians nowadays believe in the existence of such regularities in history or society in general. Vice versa, social scientists are rarely interested in describing individuals and what they do, whereas much of a historian's work concentrates on historical figures, what they did, how and why. The impact of the social environment on specific, identifiable, individuals is rarely addressed in sociology or economics, whereas the analysis of the ways in which historical contexts influence historical figures is often a core topic of historical research. It is the forms of this influence, the relationship between the historical-social context and human individuals, that interests us in this chapter.

The starting assumption has to be that historical and social entities, forces, or phenomena that can causally affect individuals and explain their actions must be physically describable; non-physical items are causally inert. In other words, causes have to be other individuals, their interactions, or other elements of the physical world. (Causation by absence is also possible, as mentioned in the Introduction, but in order to have causal capacities, absent items must also be physically describable.) Immaterial, abstract, supra-natural, or spiritual forces, from this point of view, cannot play a causal role in historical explanations. Throughout the history of historiography, many historians have taken the opposite view. A historian or a philosopher of history who is a religious believer is unlikely to assume that the divinities that he or she believes in do not affect human lives and consequently do not intervene in history. The assumption of divine intervention was clearly made, for instance, by St. Augustine when, in his explanation of the fall of Rome in 410, he described the actions of Visigoths as caused by divine wrath.[1] Similarly, Tacitus attributed the rise of Aelius Seianus to the gods' anger against the Romans.[2] Assumptions about immaterial causation are similarly implied in ancient and Renaissance historians' explanations of events that rely on Τύχη or *Fortuna* as a real force that causes events, or in astrological explanations of historical events, such as those one can find in Ptolemy's *Tetrabiblos*.[3] Early in the twentieth century, many German-speaking historians and philosophers of history were vehemently opposed to the idea that only materialistically explainable causation should be allowed in historical explanations—a view that Max Dvořák dismissed as "the superstition of causation," Hans Sedlmayr as "coarse materialism," and Ernst Troeltsch opposed as "psychologistic-positivist historiography."[4] Hans Sedlmayr's 1927 program of art history that explained artistic creativity by self-propelled movements of the Spirit (*Geist*) is probably the most significant systematic theorization of immaterial spiritual causation in the philosophy of (art) history during the Weimar era.[5] As described in the Introduction, in recent decades, various authors have formulated historiographical approaches that attribute causal powers to forces such as Culture, History, or Language that are assumed to act on their own and to construct historical and social reality. Obviously, these are the positions that a consistently materialist approach to historical explanation has to reject.

QUOMODO EXPLANATIONS

Insofar as historical explanations provide information about causes, it is important to differentiate between *how* and *why* explanations.[6] The description of how an event came about, the circumstances that enabled it, has been given different names by different philosophers of history. Following Cicero's terminology from *De oratore*, I will name it "*quomodo*-explanation."[7] *Quomodo* explanations describe the environment, circumstances, contributing factors, and so on without which an event could not have happened, or would not have happened the way it did. They are not necessarily sufficient to say that the event had to happen, or that it had to happen the way it did. They describe, for instance, the context of an action of a historical figure, but they are not sufficient to say that the historical figure could not have acted differently in the given context. (McCullagh's "contrastive explanations" that "point to some event(s) or conditions(s) which made the occurrence of an event more probable" are similar to *quomodo* explanations.[8] However, *quomodo* explanations simply state what made a historical item possible, not necessarily probable.) The content of the description of the situation in which an event happened—that which historians need to include in *quomodo* explanations—depends largely on the public that the historians are writing for and necessarily reflects the historians' beliefs about their public. It is, for instance, beyond any doubt that earth's gravity had a significant effect on the activities of participants in a medieval battle, but this is not something that a historian is likely to find important to mention in a description of its course. It would be wrong, however, to think that when explaining an event, one describes the context (i.e., provides the *quomodo* explanation) and then, on top of such a description, states the causing event of the event to be explained. As mentioned in the Introduction, events have numerous causes, but only some of them are worth mentioning, and they are parts of the context as well. Historians will typically mention those that they believe their public is not aware of. It is tempting to conceive of historical explanations as descriptions of triggering events in a stable context; however, what counts as the triggering event and what counts as the stable context depends on the perspectives and the beliefs of the historians and their public. The "triggering" event is merely one contributing element in the context. Consider the question of whether the assassination of Franz Ferdinand by Gavrilo Princip in Sarajevo on 28 June 1914 triggered World War I. (Because it has been so thoroughly studied by historians, the July Crisis of 1914 provides a wide range of suitable examples for the study of historical causation that I will discuss in this chapter.) Clayton Roberts, for instance, points out that assassinations, as well as international tensions, were common at the time.[9] They were thus the stable elements of the context on this account. He thinks that what was uncommon at the time was the state of mind of ministers in Vienna who seized on the assassination as the pretext for sending an ultimatum to Serbia. An alternative view would be that up to the assassination, there existed a system of stable international relations and that the assassination triggered the chain of events that led to the war. Other views are also possible. One may think that both international tensions and assassinations were normal at the time, but what triggered European-size conflagration was the decision of the Russian Tsar to side with Serbia and not to uphold monarchical principle and sympathize with the Austro-Hungarian ruling family. (This seems to have been the view of the German Kaiser.) In other words, saying that some events belong to the stable context, whereas others constitute the factor of change, depends on, and often says much about, the perspective of the person who tries to explain the past event.

Quomodo explanations list various contributing factors (causes), but this is typically not enough to say that an event had to happen the way it did. Only a full list of causes could provide such an explanation. It may also be argued that one needs a general rule, a system of laws that states that the given combination of causes had to produce the historical event that one is trying to explain. Without such a rule or a law, we are presented merely with two sets of events or phenomena and we have no reason to believe that one of these sets caused another or that the explanation is adequate. Famously, this point was made by Carl Hempel, and it triggered a decades-long debate about general laws in history.[10] According to Hempel, an explanation consists of a series of statements that assert the occurrence of certain events and a set of general laws on which the explanation is based. These laws explain why a specific event happened. If we have to explain the cracking of an automobile radiator during a cold night, we rely on physical laws that explain that water expands when it freezes, the (in)capacity of the steel radiator to sustain the pressure of expanding ice, and so on. Hempel's point was that when it comes to historical explanations, they are not different in structure from explanations in the natural sciences; as he put it,

> both can give an account of their subject-matter only in terms of general concepts, and history can "grasp the unique individuality" of its objects of study no more and no less than can physics or chemistry.[11]

At the same time, he was careful to point out that he was not advocating specifically historical laws, that his thesis did not imply a clear way to distinguish historical from sociological or other laws.[12] Rather, his point was that the general laws on which historians have to rely in their explanations have to be taken from various fields of scientific research and that "historical research has frequently to resort to general laws established in physics, chemistry and biology."[13] In subsequent debates, this last point was often overlooked by Hempel's critics, who seem to have understood him as advocating historical laws.[14] In fact, he did not go further than to admit that historical laws may "partly perhaps" play a role in historical explanations.[15] At the same time, when it comes to explaining the behavior and the actions of historical figures, historical laws are not easy to find. Consider the following argument that has been discussed by a number of authors.[16] When Henry VIII died, one of his titles was "the only supreme Head of the Church of England and Ireland." Elizabeth I subsequently replaced this formulation with "etc." Some historians have explained that the reason for the ambiguity was the need to avoid political complications. The explanation sounds convincing, but what kind of general rule could justify it? If one tries to formulate a general rule and states, for instance, that whenever someone in the position of great political power faces a politically difficult dilemma, such a person uses non-committal formulations in stating his or her policies, such a rule will be easy to refute by counterexamples. But if one tries to amend the rule by appropriate qualifications, once all qualifications are introduced, the rule is likely to end up applying only to a single person. Formulating historical laws becomes even harder when it comes to unique or extremely rare events such as papal abdications: what kind of rule, for instance, could explain *il gran rifiuto* (as Dante put it), the abdication of Celestine V?

A defender of Hempel's position could respond that attempts to explain the actions of historical figures merely on the basis of the context in which they acted can indeed only be futile. Rather, one needs to look deeper into the neurology of historical figures and the biological laws that ensure the functioning of their brains: "general laws established in physics, chemistry and biology," as we have seen Hempel stated. If individuals' decisions to act the way they did resulted from their mental processes, and these mental processes result from the neurology of their brains, then it is biological and not historical or social laws that can explain their actions. From this point of view, statistical generalizations about the ways people behave in specific circumstances—attempts to formulate social or historical laws—provide no better explanation than the attempts to predict movements of planets by relying on statistical observations without attempting a calculation that takes gravitation into account.

This kind of response is cogent as long as we assume—and the materialist position is expected to assume—that human decisions to act are indeed fully determined and explainable by facts pertaining to the human nervous system. Admittedly, modern science still cannot explain how a person's conscious decision to raise his or her left arm is formed and then converted into actual action—and if modern psychologists or neurologists cannot explain such a simple action, then it is unreasonable to expect historians to be able to explain Gavrilo Princip's action of pulling the trigger precisely when the Austro-Hungarian heir apparent's car stopped in front of him. However, if we assume that neurological explanations of human actions will be possible someday, then Hempel is arguably better understood if we take him to be asserting that biological, not historical, laws ultimately explain the actions of historical figures.

FREE WILL AND HISTORICAL EXPLANATIONS

Four years before Hempel's paper, Erwin Panofsky proposed a different view on historical explanations.[17] The program of what he called "humanist" (art) historiography attributed four characteristics to historical subjects: free will, rationality, frailty, and fallibility. Frailty and fallibility suggest that historical figures do not always manage to act in accordance with their free will or to grasp their options, but they do have the ability and possibly even tend to do so. Obviously, if historical figures can act in accordance with their free will, then no amount of causal analysis based on general rules or laws—historical, social, or neurological—can explain or fully state the causes of their decisions and actions. An implication of Panofsky's thesis is that even in those situations when the frailty of historical figures may block their free will, it is not certain that we can know that this was the case. It follows that one may be able to describe the conditions and circumstances that enabled their actions—that is, provide *quomodo* explanations—but not really say why they acted the way they did. A historian can describe the environment in which historical figures decided to act as they did, state the contributing factors, describe their possible motives, and so on, but this is never going to be enough to infer that they *had to* act the way they did. Free will means precisely that they could have decided to act differently. By introducing the problem of free will, Panofsky pointed out that discussions about historical explanations were more than mere methodological debates. Free will is one of the great problems in the history of philosophy. The claim that one can *explain* the actions of historical figures and state why they acted (or decided to act) the way they did ultimately implies the unconvincing claim that one has solved the problem of free will. The introduction of the dilemma about free will in the debate substantially delimits the claims that historians can make and suggests that historians can state only *quomodo* explanations but never prove that historical figures had to act the way they acted. Even a historian who merely admits that free will is an unresolved philosophical problem will find it impossible to state the sufficient causes of the actions of historical figures: if free will is an unresolved problem, then one cannot preclude the possibility that historical actors acted out of their free will and that the causes of their decisions cannot be stated.

Panofsky's views were formulated in reaction to and were meant to address a different intellectual context from the one Hempel, his opponents, and defenders had in mind. The debate about Hempel's thesis developed within the context of Anglo-American philosophy and historical scholarship; its participants hardly ever considered historical works that had not been written in English. An observation endorsed by all participants in the debate was that historians describe particular events and do not intentionally search for general laws; at most, the advocates of historical laws endeavored to show that historians nevertheless rely on general laws (at least implicitly) in their explanations.[18] Panofsky, however, wrote against the stream of historiography that dominated German scholarship at least since the *Methodenstreit* of the 1890s and that often concentrated on finding such laws. For the preceding half century—starting with the works of Karl Lamprecht and Alois Riegl—historiography, and especially art historiography, of the Wilhelmine and Weimar eras was marked by efforts to find and specify historical laws and especially general laws of artistic and intellectual production.[19] Typically, such studies used generalizations from a limited number of examples in order to argue that the common characteristics of these examples resulted from the shared *Geist* of a specific community or era.[20] Robert Hedicke's 1924 *Methodenlehre der Kunstgeschichte*—a methodology textbook for art history students—is a good example. Hedicke explained that objective *Geist* manifests itself in human cultures and that *Geistesgeschichte* studies the expressions and changes of this objective Spirit through history.[21] The study of the objective *Geist*, he says, consists of the study of analogies present in its manifestations. The method he advocated is thus equivalent to Spengler's approach based on analogies that enabled Spengler to claim, for instance, the existence of a deep common cause shared by the invention of perspective, book-printing, the credit system, and point-counterpoint in music, as important manifestations of western, "Faustian" culture.[22] The art historian Wilhelm Pinder made similar claims about similarities between Spinoza's philosophy and Vermeer's paintings, and Wilhelm Worringer claimed to see parallels between Scholastic philosophy and Gothic architecture.[23] Sedlmayr's 1927 program, mentioned above, was an explication of the theoretical assumptions of this historiographical production, marked by the claim that the spirit of the community determines the creativity of individuals. In addition to these spiritualist approaches during this era, there was also a long tradition that supplanted spiritualist determinism with racial. A good example is the writings of Dagobert Frey, who identified the source of human creativity with ethnic background and claimed to be able, for instance, to decide whether individual British artists had more Celtic or Germanic blood by the kinds of lines they used in their drawings.[24] Panofsky's essay about humanist (art) historiography thus targeted such a search for regularities in intellectual and artistic production.

The general implications of Panofsky's introduction of the dilemma about free will are, at the same time, profound. The attribution of free will to historical figures dramatically reduces space for the explanatory power of historical-social entities or the claim that they cause the individuals' decisions of act. The same applies to the possibility of historical laws. If individuals have free will, then there is no causation or laws—historical, social, or otherwise—that can explain why they decided to act the way they did. A collection of individuals or their properties that causes a certain social phenomenon on one occasion may not cause the same phenomenon on another occasion under identical circumstances, simply because the individuals involved may decide to act differently. Historical and social laws may be possible only insofar as individuals do not exercise their free will, for instance, in those situations when their actions result from their previous decisions to act with a certain aim. Laws of economics, for instance, function insofar as they are applied to individuals who are committed to financial gain and who have certain beliefs about the ways to achieve it. They are not applicable to a population that believes that financial gain is better avoided because it is detrimental for the salvation of the soul. Similar explanations can be given when it comes to the actions of individuals—these are the situations where we explain the actions of historical figures as consistent with some decisions they made previously. Collingwood thus observes:

> Suetonius tells me that Nero at one time intended to evacuate Britain. I reject his statement, not because any better authority flatly contradicts it, for of course none does; but because my reconstruction of Nero's policy based on Tacitus will not allow me to think that Suetonius is right.²⁵

This reasoning makes sense only if one assumes consistency in Nero's political actions. Such explanations are generally regarded as credible, although if free will is attributed to historical figures we cannot say that the historical figure could not have changed the way he or she acted. We can, however, say that a certain action is consistent with his or her previous actions.

RATIONALITY AND DECISIONS

The conception of human rationality that Panofsky introduced was also in strong contrast with that of the participants in the debate about Hempel's thesis, regardless of whether they agreed or disagreed with Hempel. Panofsky derived his understanding of rationality from Erasmus's concept of *libarum arbitrium*. It is a cognitive capacity, the unimpaired capacity to judge, that needs to be clearly differentiated from free will as the capacity to decide to act, or the capacity to act. The idea is that one needs an unimpaired capacity to understand one's situation and the possible results of one's actions before one can freely decide how to act. Understanding is not the same as deciding or acting. Rationality thus understood is a property of cognitive capacities: it prevents people, for instance, from having contradictory beliefs, but is not the same as the capacity to decide to act. At most, it provides a person with knowledge about the kind of decision that would be in line with one's aims. At the same time, the fallibility of historical figures means that rationality, understood as the capacity to understand one's options, is not necessarily always available to them; rather, it is there as a possibility. Frailty means that they may also fail to act in accordance with their free will.

For the participants in the debate triggered by Hempel's paper, however, rationality was inseparable from the capacity to decide and act; understanding meant deciding and even acting. William Dray thus proposed to analyze the explanation of an action of a historical figure as a set of statements: that the historical figure was in a certain situation, that in such a situation one should do X, and that consequently the historical figure did X.²⁶ Hempel corrected this version by adding that for the explanation to be valid one also needs to state that the historical figure was rational at the time, and that a rational agent in such a situation would perform X. Roberts, whose book provides a comprehensive summary of the entire debate, further rephrased their formulations by introducing general statements that all rational agents who perform X in such situations have the purpose Y, and that since the historical figure was a rational agent in the given situation, he or she had the purpose Y. Paul Churchland proposed an even more complex scheme, whereby if a person wants Ø, believes that doing A he or she will achieve Ø, does not believe that there are other preferable means, has no wishes that override wanting Ø, has the ability to perform A, then the person performs A.[27] In all these accounts, the awareness that a certain action is the right thing to do in a given context is assumed to trigger the action automatically. None of these analyses takes into account that, once (if) we attribute free will to historical figures, we have to assume that they could have decided not to perform the action. Panofsky's alternative perspective would be that rationality provides knowledge and awareness that a certain course of action would enable one to achieve one's aims, but this still does not guarantee that the person will actually follow this course of action. Even if the person decides to act accordingly, frailty may interfere and prevent the person from acting that way. At the same time, a person could have decided to act independently of his or her awareness of the consequences of the given action. Actions of historical figures may still be comprehensible and explainable although the person acted emotionally or irrationally.

An additional problem with accounts such as Dray's, Hempel's, Roberts's or Churchland's is that they explain people's actions by referring to their rationality, whereas we can know that they were rational only on the basis of their actions—that is, insofar as these actions can be interpreted as directed toward a certain aim. However, the fact that a certain action can be interpreted as rational does not mean that it was really so. Also, it may have been rational, but motivated by aims that are unknown to the historian or that may be different from those that the historian relies on. Finally, irrationality is certainly common when it comes to the actions of historical figures. It is also common that historians cannot say whether the action was rational or not (in the sense that it was performed in order to pursue some wider aim). Consider the decision of the Emperor Franz Joseph to declare war on Serbia in the aftermath of the Sarajevo assassination. Once war was declared, the existing system of alliances necessarily led to a European-scale war.[28] But the Sarajevo assassination did not necessarily entail declaring war, while all conceivable outcomes of the war were detrimental to Austro-Hungarian interests. This makes the decision to declare war one of the core mysteries of the July crisis. On the one hand, the risk of war with Russia was too great, and German help entailed a European-scale conflagration with an uncertain outcome. Even a favorable outcome of such a war would make Austro-Hungary subservient to Germany, with a substantial loss in the status of a European power. A defeat in such a war, one could predict, would seriously threaten its survival. On the other hand, even if Austro-Hungary could fight the war against Serbia without triggering Russian intervention, and won the war, it could not occupy the country or incorporate it, due to Hungarian politicians' opposition to a further increase in the Slavic population in the empire. As A. J. P. Taylor observed, "In 1914 Austro-Hungary was the only Great Power who could not conceivably gain anything from war; yet, of all the Great Powers, she alone was consciously bent on war. . . . [The Hungarian Prime Minister] Tisza's veto would have made the war pointless, had it had any purpose."[29] Although it is hard to conceive that such a major decision was made on emotional grounds, it is equally hard to see the actual rational reasoning behind the declaration of war.

The fact that it is often difficult to establish the motives of historical figures notoriously produces difficulties in actual historical research. Major historical events and major debates among historians are typically full of situations in which it is hard to estimate the reasons and motivations that would explain the actions of historical figures. Stating the reasons that *may have* led historical figures to perform certain actions does not mean stating the actual motivations that made them act the way they acted. The fact that a certain action was the rational thing to do for a historical figure in the given circumstances, and that he or she performed that action, does not mean that these rational reasons were the actual motivation. As McCullagh stated,

> The point is that historians are interested in the reasons which actually moved the agent. If they want to know why an action occurred, they evidently do not want to see that the action was rational, but to know what brought it about, the causes which led to its occurrence.[30]

Similarly, McCullagh pointed out, people may have reasons to act in a certain way, but not act on those reasons.[31] A description of possible reasons that may have motivated the actions of historical figures can even be helpful in order to describe the context in which they acted in a certain way—it can be an efficient way for a historian to provide a summary of a *quomodo* explanation—but it does not necessarily provide the motivation for the actions. One and the same action, that may appear as altruistic, could have been actually motivated by narcissistic gratification. Even knowing the moral code a person subscribes to does not allow us to infer simply and directly, in the situation when the person acts in accordance with that moral code, that he or she acted that way because of the moral code. Other motivations could have been involved. As Cristina Bicchieri put it, "Can we predict whether a person, who we know condemns corruption, will bribe a public officer when given a chance?"[32] In the case of complex historical events, actual motivations are especially hard to identify, and statements made by historical figures about their motives cannot be taken into account independently of the consideration of their motivation to make such statements. A historian may rely on additional assumptions, often derived from folk psychology, that in certain situations one should infer certain types of motivations—and such explanations are credible insofar as one regards such assumptions as credible.

Here is another example from the 1914 July Crisis. Consider two possible explanations for the decision of Serbian Black Hand officers to train a couple of young Bosnian Serbs, arm them, and send them to Sarajevo to assassinate the Austro-Hungarian heir apparent.

According to the first explanation, Black Hand officers were rabid nationalists who were outraged by the official visit of Franz Ferdinand to Sarajevo. In their view, Serbia had been humiliated in 1908 by the Austro-Hungarian annexation of Bosnia-Herzegovina. A public visit of the Austro-Hungarian heir apparent to Sarajevo on St. Vitus Day—the date of the catastrophic Serbian defeat in 1389 by the Ottoman Turks—following major military maneuvers intended to intimidate Serbia, was for them to add insult to injury. (Some British historians have compared the situation to an imaginary parade visit of the Prince of Wales to Belfast on St. Patrick's Day, following major military maneuvers held in Northern Ireland to intimidate the Republic of Ireland.) Black Hand officers thus decided to act, regardless of the fact that their actions may have had dire consequences for their country. In other words, their action was emotional and irrational. This does not mean that it was unexplainable: an explanation that states the cause of their action is possible, but that cause is irrational (emotional reaction to an insult).

According to the second explanation, the real aim of Black Hand officers was to topple the government of their arch-nemesis, the Serbian Prime Minister Nikola Pašić. The assassination in Sarajevo was only a collateral aspect of their efforts to force Pašić to resign, which they actually managed to achieve on 2 June, twenty-six days before the assassination.[33] (By that time Princip and other conspirators had left Serbia; they reached Sarajevo two days later.) Pašić's government was, however, saved by joint Russian-French diplomatic intervention, but the crisis escalated further, and on 24 June, four days before the Sarajevo assassination, the Serbian King was forced to abdicate. It is hard to imagine that Black Hand officers engaged in the assassination independently of their political aims and activities in Serbia itself. A major international crisis in which Pašić's government would appear weak and experience international humiliation would substantially reduce the government's credibility in the country and strengthen their own. They even provided Princip and his accomplices with cyanide that did not work, in order to ensure that they were caught alive and that the Austro-Hungarian investigation could make the link to Serbia. At the same time, some dire consequences for the country were hardly conceivable: relations with Austro-Hungary were already as bad as they could get, and no rational Austro-Hungarian government would dare declare war on Serbia because of the risk of a war with Russia and the resulting continental-scale conflagration. Showing that Austro-Hungary could not control Bosnia-Herzegovina, in spite of the 1908 annexation, would in that case be merely a collateral bonus; the very outcome of the assassination (most assassination attempts were unsuccessful in those days anyhow) was not of great importance for them. The actions of Black Hand officers from this point of view could be described as rational—if this is taken to mean that they were deducible from their wider political aims. Their only mistake was that they believed that whoever made decisions in Vienna would act rationally too.

Black Hand officers have left to historians a very limited number of actual written documents about their plans and deliberations. In principle, both explanations are credible, and one cannot say that the second one is more credible because it attributes rational acting to the protagonists. Further complications are also possible. Imagine that some historian actually finds notes from a Black Hand officers' meeting in which they state that the main motivation for the assassination of Franz Ferdinand was to topple the Serbian Prime Minister. Such a document may nevertheless merely reflect their need to rationalize the irrational decision that was motivated by their outrage. Or, conversely, a document that would record their moral outrage in relation to Franz Ferdinand's visit to Sarajevo may only be a record of how they justified in ethical terms their actions that they knew targeted the Prime Minister. This situation would not be unlike the one that leading British politicians had to ponder about a month after the Sarajevo assassination: they did not want to face a victorious Germany dominating Europe, let alone risk seeing the German fleet docked in Ostend, but these rational reasons for war could not be expressed openly, and they were articulated as moral outrage at the German invasion of Belgium. A sentence in Winston Churchill's *The World in Crisis* expresses this duplicity finely: "Believing as I did and do, that we could not, for our own safety and independence, allow France to be crushed as the result of aggressive action by Germany, I always from the earliest moment concentrated upon our obligations to Belgium, through which I was convinced the Germans must march to invade France."[34] In other words: for its own interest, Britain needed to save France from being crushed by Germany; the German army had to march through Belgium in order to crush France; Britain had earlier commitments to defend Belgium, and these commitments were to be used as a pretext for saving France.

The examination of *possible* motivations can provide substantial relevant information when explaining the action of historical figures. It can contribute to *quomodo* explanations. At the same time, it can be difficult to establish the *actual* motives of historical figures; what they say about their motivation is often likely to be influenced by other motives, and their actions may or may not be rational or rationally follow from the motives they had. All this substantially complicates the historian's ability to establish why they acted the way they did, whether their acting was irrational, emotional, or in line with their wider aims and interests. Explanations of actions of historical figures are often limited to *quomodo* explanations because one can describe the context, but it is much harder, though not necessarily impossible, to establish with reasonable certainty the motives for their acting.

FREE WILL AND MATERIALIST HISTORIOGRAPHY

In many situations, claims about historical necessity become very difficult to sustain once the free will of historical figures becomes a postulate in historical explanations. It becomes impossible to state the causes of actions of historical figures, and all a historian can provide are *quomodo* explanations—descriptions of how the context and the environment enabled some events or prevented others. At the same time, free will of historical figures may seem an irrelevant topic in the context of the materialist approach to historical research, since materialism assumes that human thinking and decisions result from the neurobiology of the central nervous system. Motives discussed in the preceding section, we should not forget, do not take their form independently of neurological states; they are caused by other neurological states and interactions with the physical environment. However, we shall see that when it comes to historical research, the determinist implications of materialism actually result in an approach to historical research that is equivalent to the attribution of free will to historical figures.

In spite of the exceptional complexity of the philosophical debate about free will, there are only three possible responses to the dilemma about the free will of historical figures.[35] The first is the libertarian view, according to which historical figures possessed free will. The second position is determinism: the view that decisions of historical figures ultimately result from mental processes in their brains that are neuro-biological and determined by natural laws. This view is aligned with the materialist perspective that assumes, as mentioned in the Introduction, that there can be no changes in mental states without some biological change. Compatibilism, the third possibility, endorses determinism, but does not take it to contradict free will because it relies on an understanding of free will that differs from the libertarian.[36] Both compatibilists and libertarians agree that people are free when they can choose between different courses of action. However, such freedom can be attributed to someone in absolute terms (the libertarian position) or only relative to the description of circumstances that abstracts from a certain type of information (the compatibilist position). The libertarian position assumes the capacity to choose freely when we take all relevant information into account, including the neurological and mental states of the person, circumstances, antecedent events, and so on. Compatibilists, however, agree with determinists that no person can have such freedom in an absolute sense—but they also point out that we can still describe the action of a person as free if we leave out some of this information, for instance, about the neurobiology of the brain. (This is not unlike saying that there are a number of ways an avalanche could have gone, if one disregards some relevant information about topography.) In that case, neurobiology makes historical figures decide how to act, but we do not know how neurobiology works, nor do we have information about their brain states. Consequently, our understanding of their decisions about how to act has to be more or less equivalent to the one we would have if we attributed to them libertarian-style free will.

Determinism in matters of free will rests on the assumption that individuals' decisions how to act result from their neurobiology. It is understood that given the state of the brain in a given moment, a certain type of input, and the laws of nature, a specific change of mental state must follow. (Obviously, these reactions are very complex, and internal mental states, although ultimately neurological, can exercise high levels of control; complex neurobiological states affect other neurobiological states.) Materialism, in principle, should entail such determinism. If nothing can change without cause, and if all causes are physical, then any mental process in the mind of a historical figure, including the decision to act in a certain way, has to result from his or her neurobiology and ultimately the laws of physics. (As described in the Introduction, some authors have tried to avoid this conclusion by arguing that, at a certain level of complexity, macro-properties emerge that are not to reducible micro-properties.[37] This would mean that some capacities of the human mind are not caused by processes in the brain. In that case it would be possible to make decisions independently of the causation that derives from the material structure of the brain. In other words, we could attribute full-blooded, libertarian free will to historical figures, and not merely compatibilist free will. However, in terms of Searle's analysis of emergence presented in the Introduction, this would mean relying on emergence 2, but the view that human beings have emergence 2-based free will is not available to a materialist historian as it falls outside the materialist paradigm.)

Paradoxically, however, in matters that are relevant for historical research, the implications of hard determinism, which assumes that human decisions are governed by human neurobiology, are equivalent to the position that attributes free will to historical figures. The important point here is not merely that modern science (still) cannot explain how the neurology of the nervous system generates mental states, nor is it able to say what kind of decision a person will make on the basis of his or her brain states. Much more importantly, *even if* modern science were able to determine a person's mental state, its content, and the decisions that a person will make on the basis of his or her brain states, this could not provide the historian with much information about the causes of the decisions made by historical figures. Simply put, their brain states are not available and cannot be studied. For a historian who wants to understand what was going on in Napoleon's mind when he ordered his army to cross the Nemen and invade Russia in 1812, hard determinism provides as much insight as the assumption that Napoleon acted from his free will: Napoleon's brain states at the moment before initiating his invasion of Russia are unknown. The same applies to all decisions of all historical figures in history. The neurobiological properties of historical figures that determined their thinking and decisions are simply not available to historians and will never be. *De facto*, the situation is the same as if we attributed them free will. The result is that materialist explanations of decisions and actions of historical figures necessarily assume compatibilist-style freedom. It is impossible to obtain the information about the brain states of historical figures that would be necessary in order to explain the actual causes of their decisions. Consequently it is impossible to go beyond the level of *quomodo* explanations that state the conditions, circumstances, and so on that enabled or prevented certain decisions and actions. "Compatibilism" here *de facto* means that, when it comes to explaining decisions of historical figures, religious historians, who postulate free will because of their religious beliefs, can be confident that their explanations will be in line with those of materialist historians.[38]

At the same time, materialist hard determinism and the assumption that human decisions result purely from biological processes in the brain eliminates the possibility of other types of determinist explanations, such as those based on historical or social determinism. It imposes serious limits on the causal capacity of historical and social contexts to determine the decisions of historical figures. They can contribute to these decisions, and it is certainly true that historical figures make their decisions and act in their historical and social contexts. Descriptions of historical and social contexts necessarily play important roles in *quomodo* explanations. However, insofar as the biology of the brain determines human thinking, deciding, and acting, there can be no place for social causation beyond biologically describable interactions with other individuals and the physical environment. Biology is always the biology of individuals; any interaction of individuals with their historical-social contexts has to be physical and will occur mostly through the senses. At the same time, the senses can be affected only by material objects, such as other individuals, artifacts that individuals produce, and so on. There can be no immaterial interaction between the mind and the society. Historical or social context can exercise influence on individuals only through their interaction with other individuals directly or via some other elements of the physical environment. But it cannot determine their thinking or decisions.

It is also important to bear in mind the wider picture at this point. This discussion of free will, hard determinism, compatibilism, neurobiology, and so on, pertains to specific types of historical problems and explanations—those in which decisions of historical figures matter. Insofar as it is assumed that decisions and actions of historical figures result from their neurobiology, no description of the environment, context, or circumstances in which decisions were made or actions performed alone will be sufficient in itself to explain fully these decisions or actions. *Taken on their own*, such descriptions will always be *quomodo* explanations, insufficient to infer that the historical figure had to act the way he or she did. This may seem insufficient in comparison with the common practice of historians to try to establish and describe motives and reasons that propelled historical figures to act the way they did. Are we to infer that materialism precludes, for instance, the use of folk psychology, psychoanalysis, or any discussion of motives when explaining decisions and actions of historical figures? The key to the response is in the above phrase "taken on their own." Consider, for instance, the situation when a historical figure acts in accordance with his or her financial interests. Insofar as there are no other, competing interpretations, it is reasonable for a historian to infer that financial gain motivated the action. In principle, this explanation would not contradict materialism, since such a motivation and the decision to act in accordance with one's financial interests can be conceived of as a mental, ultimately neurobiological process. However, since we can have no insight in the neurobiological processes in the brain of the historical figure, the materialist view of human mental processes in principle does not provide grounds to infer that the person had to decide to act the way he or she did. In order to infer this it is necessary to introduce the additional assumption that when a historical figure acts in accordance with his or her financial interests, and there is no alternative explanation of this action, then the historian may infer that the action was motivated by financial gain. (The same assumption would have to be introduced in order to explain actions of historical figures if we attributed them free will.) Such an additional assumption cannot be derived from materialism alone; it has to be introduced on its own. Some historians may oppose it, on methodological grounds, without opposing materialism. Materialism alone thus cannot be taken to provide grounds for the application, for instance, of folk psychology or psychoanalysis in explanations of actions of historical figures or to give some other rules for the interpretation of these actions or the attribution of motives. The validity of such interpretations and attributions of motives is a matter of methodological and interpretative principles that a historian may endorse or reject. A historian who wants to rely on them has to introduce them additionally, since materialism will not provide them—it merely precludes some of them, those that rely on and attribute causal capacities to non-material entities, forces and phenomena.

NOTES

1. Augustine, *De civitate*, 1.1–1.9.
2. Tacitus, *Annales*, 4.1.
3. For ancient historiography, see for instance Kurt von Fritz's discussion of Τύχη in Polybius, in Fritz, *Mixed Constitution*, 388–397. For a comprehensive Renaissance theorization of *fortuna* see for instance Pontano, *De fortuna*. Ptolemy, *Tetrabiblos*.
4. For Dvořák see Rosenauer, "Max Dvořák." Sedlmayr, "Quintessenz," 34. Troeltsch, *Historismus*, 37–38.
5. Sedlmayr, "Quintessenz," 46.
6. For the distinction between *why* and *how* histories see Grafton, "Preface," vii-xi.
7. Cicero, *De oratore*, 2.15. He says that a historian should describe what happened, how and state the cause, but he lists other things that a historian needs to describe as well. Similarly, Roberts, *Logic*, 17 lists a number of such terms: "a genetic explanation," "a sequential explanation," "the model of the continuous series," "a chain of causal explanations," "narrative explanations."
8. McCullagh, *Truth in History*, 173.
9. Roberts, *Logic*, 99.
10. Hempel, "General Laws."
11. Ibid., 35–36
12. Ibid., 47–48.
13. Ibid., 47–48.
14. The debate has been summarized by Roberts, *Logic*. For the collections of relevant articles see Gardiner, ed., *Theories of History*, 344–475 and Gardiner, ed., *The Philosophy of History*. See also Dray, *Laws*.
15. Hempel, "General Laws," 47–48.
16. Nagel, "Determinism," 200. See also Roberts, *Logic*, 62.
17. Panofsky, "The History of Art."
18. See for instance Hempel, "General Laws," 35, Nagel, "Some Issues," 164, Mandelbaum, "The Problem," 60.
19. See Mitrović, *Rage and Denials* for a survey of this type of scholarship.
20. See ibid., 63–81.
21. Hedicke, *Methodenlehre*, 3, 132.
22. Spengler, *Untergang*, 66.
23. Pinder, *Problem der Generation*, 134. Worringer, *Formprobleme*, 116.
24. For a survey of such theories see Mitrović, *Rage and Denials*, 63–81.
25. Collingwood, *Idea*, 244–245.
26. See the discussion in Hempel, "Reasons," 100. See also the summary of the debate by Roberts, *Logic*, 176–177.
27. Churchland, "The Logical Character." Churchland takes into account the possibility of ἀκρασία, that he understands as the incapacity to reach practical conclusions about the consequences of one's acting but he does not take into account the possibility that a person could choose to act differently although the person has grasped all the stages that he lists. Ibid., 223. See also the criticism in Martin, *Historical Explanation*, 158–184.
28. It is hard to imagine that, once the war was declared, the leading political figures in other countries could have not acted the way they did without being exposed to extreme pressures or removal from the position of power.
29. Taylor, *Habsburg Monarchy*, 231–232.
30. McCullagh, *Truth in History*, 175.
31. Ibid., 212.
32. Bicchieri, *Grammar*, 1.
33. For the struggle between Pašić and Black Hand officers that escalated precisely in the month of the Sarajevo assassination see Dedijer, *The Road to Sarajevo*, 386–400. The internal political crisis in Serbia in June 1914 is often overlooked in the histories of the Sarajevo assassination.
34. Churchill, *The World in Crisis*, 117.

35. For a popular survey of the debate about free will see Kane, *Introduction*. Comprehensive collections of papers are Kane, ed., *Oxford Handbook of Free Will* and Watson, ed., *Free Will*.

36. I summarize here the account by Bock, "Freedom."

37. For the elaboration of this position see O'Connor, "Agent Causation," 262–264.

38. Obviously, this pertains to explanations of decisions made by historical figures. In other cases, for instance when explaining events, religious historians may postulate immaterial and spiritual forces, or rely on divine intervention, and this will not be acceptable for a materialist.

Chapter Four

Thoughts and Contents

The discussion of rationality and free will in Chapter Three has introduced questions that pertain to the mental states of historical figures and their contents, and this topic will play an important role throughout the remaining chapters of the book. Arguably, the most elementary of these capacities is the ability to compare and differentiate between properties of things, to establish whether they are the same or different, and to classify the bearers of these properties accordingly. This capacity underwrites the ability of historical figures to think, make decisions and act, as well as a historian's own ability to describe and explain historical events and engage in historical research. It is indispensible in order to form and use concepts (and propositions that concepts constitute): classification always occurs according to specific classificatory criteria and, traditionally, "concept" is precisely the name for such sets of classificatory criteria. The so-called "classical theory" of concepts describes them as mental representations of sets of objects that list the necessary and sufficient criteria that something must satisfy in order to be classified as a member of that set.[1] For a materialist theory of historical research it is important to show what it means not to conceive, and to avoid the need to conceive, of such mental representations as abstract and immaterial entities. The understanding of concepts and propositions as purely mental entities and the assumption that they result from (ultimately biological) classificatory capacities is thus the main topic of this chapter. The assumption has exceptionally wide implications for a series of topics that are discussed in later chapters. Here belong, for instance, problems related to language, the interpretation and the translation of historical documents, essentialism and the meaning of historical works. The chapter also addresses a series of methodological dilemmas that result from problems related to the attribution of concepts to historical figures. In combination with the theories of perception discussed in the Appendix it provides the ground for the rejection of anti-foundationalism.

This and the next two chapters cover a substantial amount of material that belongs properly to the philosophies of mind and language, and that needs to be addressed in order to prevent the import of anti-materialist arguments from these fields into the philosophy of history. At the same time, this discussion prepares ground for the analysis of understanding and interpretation in historical research as well as the meaning of historical works in later chapters. These three chapters also present materialist analyses of a wide number of methodological dilemmas in historical research, in order to show that materialism is better aligned with the standard practices of historical research than its idealist alternatives.

CLASSIFICATIONS, CONCEPTS AND PROPOSITIONS

It is useful to start here with the introduction of some elementary notions and terminology. The classical theory of concepts understands concepts as mental representations that list the sufficient and necessary criteria that various items (i.e., anything that can be classified: things, properties, phenomena, events, and so on) satisfy or do not satisfy and consequently belong or do not belong under the same concept.[2] In other words, concepts on this understanding are conceived of as lists of classificatory criteria; if an item satisfies such a list, it is said that it can be "subsumed" under that concept.[3] To subsume an item under a concept means to establish that it shares, with other items that can be subsumed under that concept, the properties specified by the classificatory criteria of that concept. The extension of a concept is then all the items that satisfy its classificatory criteria. The concept is their identifying description. In the case of some concepts, their classificatory criteria are satisfied by many items, other concepts are satisfied by only one item, and some concepts are not satisfied by any item at all. Typically, it is possible to identify (i.e., describe and classify) an item with equal precision in many different ways—in other words, an item can satisfy the classificatory criteria of more than one concept. Bruno Latour, in his description of the debate between Louis Pasteur and Félix Alèxandre Pouchet, observed that both of them wrote to the Emperor Napoleon III, the former to ask for money for his research, the latter to ask him to take position in the debate in his favor.[4] Latour infers that they did not write to the same emperor because "one [emperor] is supposed to have an opinion and the other money." But this claim can only be taken as metaphorical. Certainly, there was only one physical person that satisfied both concepts "the Emperor to whom Pasteur wrote asking for money" and "the Emperor to whom Pouchet wrote asking to support him in the debate." If

Latour could show that France had two emperors at the time, this would be a ground-breaking discovery about France in the nineteenth century.

Strictly speaking, the ability to classify is necessary but not sufficient in order to attribute to a creature the capacity to operate with concepts. Concepts are also elements of propositions and a creature should be able to operate with propositions and make inferences in order to be said to be able to operate with concepts. A frog can identify and catch flies but one would not say that it operates with the concept of a fly. Our discussion here, however, will have to concentrate on the ability to classify, since numerous methodological problems in historical research are generated precisely by misunderstandings about this capacity. A good example is various debates about the anachronistic attribution of concepts. Insofar as concepts are conceived of as mental phenomena it is certainly anachronistic to attribute to historical figures the use of concepts that rely on classificatory criteria that they could not have known about in their time. It is, however, perfectly legitimate to use our modern concepts in order to classify past events according to the classificatory criteria that are available to us. (We could certainly not use the classificatory criteria that are not available to us.) Consider, for instance, the view that it is anachronistic to talk about "medieval aesthetic theories" because "aesthetics" is a modern concept that came about only in the eighteenth century. It may be pointed out that our modern concept of "aesthetics" would make no sense to medieval authors. However, medieval and Renaissance authors wrote on topics such as music, painting or beauty, and insofar as the content of these texts classify under the topic of aesthetics in our modern sense we can say that they wrote about aesthetics. Umberto Eco thus wrote about the aesthetic views of Thomas Aquinas. Similarly, we can say that Columbus discovered the American continent, although at the time of the discovery this landmass was still not conceptualized as such. But it would be quite wrong to attribute to Medieval or Renaissance authors beliefs that rely on our modern concept of aesthetics, the way it would be wrong to say that, for instance, Columbus sailed westward with the intention of discovering the American continent.

Insofar as concepts are understood to be mental representations, and propositions are their combinations, it is reasonable to say that propositions are mental representations too. Unlike concepts, propositions can be true or false: they have satisfaction conditions that describe the situation that must obtain if that proposition is to be true.[5] Propositions are thus that what historical figures or historians believe to be true or false. In the philosophy of logic there exists an extensive debate about the nature of propositions and ways to define them. For our discussion here, the relationship between propositions and the concepts that constitute them is particularly important. A simple proposition consists of two concepts and states that what is subsumable under one concept is also subsumable under another concept. The proposition specifies that this happens in all instances or in some instances or never (or now, in the past, future, possibly, necessarily, and so on). If that what satisfies the classificatory criteria of one concept satisfies the criteria of the other concept in accordance with such specification, the satisfaction conditions of the proposition are fulfilled.[6] It is assumed that the conditions that need to be satisfied for a certain proposition to be true depend fully and only on the classificatory criteria of the participating concepts and their relationships specified by the proposition. It is also sometimes possible to form a proposition with a concept that one possesses only partially and knows only some of its classificatory criteria. A person who has never seen a wombat and cannot recognize one, and merely knows that they are a kind of mammal living in Australia, can still believe that he or she has not seen a wombat in a Melbourne park, because the only animals that he or she saw there were birds. One should also be careful not to confuse propositions whose conditions of satisfaction are satisfied by the same event or situation: "John sold a house to Mary" and "Mary bought a house from John" do not express the same proposition: in the first John, and in the second Mary, had to perform a number of actions for the sentence to become true, although one and the same event (a house changed its owner) satisfies the conditions of both propositions. The proposition that the person who classifies as "Mary" also classifies as "someone who bought the house from John" is not the same as the proposition that the person who classifies as "John" also classifies as "the person who sold the house to Mary." Consider, similarly, Alfred Jules Ayer's claim that propositions about the past "are rules for the prediction of those 'historical' experiences which are commonly said to verify them."[7] G. C. Field responded that propositions about the past are "what they profess to be, namely, propositions about the past."[8] The point is valid, since the conditions of satisfaction of a proposition are its own conditions of satisfaction, and cannot be equated with the conditions of satisfaction of propositions formulated in the process of verifying it.

In his *Narration and Knowledge* Arthur Danto imagined an "Ideal Chronicler"—a device that describes every event at the moment it happens using the descriptions that are available at that moment. Such a device, Danto points out, could not use "narrative sentences"—that is, sentences that describe one event by referring to events in different times. Examples of such sentences are "Aristarchus's theories anticipated Copernican astronomy" or "The Thirty Years War started in 1618" (insofar we take into account that the Thirty Years War got its name because of its duration). In other words, such sentences express propositions that consist of concepts whose classificatory criteria are satisfied by events in different times. The first of these sentences says that what satisfies the classificatory criteria of "Aristarchus's theories" also satisfies the classificatory criteria of "something that anticipated Copernican astronomy." The second says that the event that satisfies the classificatory criteria of "the Thirty Years War" also satisfies the classificatory criteria of "something that started in 1618."[9] Danto's analysis of narrative sentences is thus unproblematic, but one should be careful about his further claims that events could not have been seen, or witnessed, under descriptions that were not available at the time. As discussed in the Appendix, his assumptions about visual perception and "witnessing under description" rely on 1950s "New Look" psychology of perception that has been abandoned by psychologists a long time ago. One should also be careful about Danto's formulations that introduce causal relationships in narrative sentences. He thus states that Aristarchus's anticipation of Copernicus's discovery "may in no sense have caused Copernicus to discover the heliocentric theory, but in a very definite sense it caused Copernicus to *re-discover* the heliocentric theory."[10] Similarly to Latour's statement about Pasteur, Pouchet and Napoleon III discussed above, this statement can only be metaphorical. Had Aristarchus's formulation of the heliocentric system really had any causal impact on what Copernicus did (for instance, if Copernicus knew about Aristarchus theory) then Copernicus would not have discovered a new theory but merely endorsed an existing one. Aristarchus's heliocentric theory had no such impact on Copernicus; rather, it produces a causal impact on modern historians of science and makes *them* classify Copernicus's formulation of geocentric systems as rediscovery.

CONCEPTS, PROPOSITIONS AND WORDS

It is not uncommon to confuse concepts and propositions with the words that express them. A good example is an old argument against the classical theory of concepts, originally formulated by Ludwig Wittgenstein and later advocated by Jerry Fodor.[11] The argument consists in pointing out in most cases one cannot actually state the definition of the concept expressed by a word. It is then inferred that the classificatory criteria of the concept expressed by the word cannot be specified. For instance, in the case of the verb "to paint" one cannot say that it simply means "to cover with paint"—if a paint factory explodes and covers people present nearby with paint, this would not count as "painting."[12] When Michelangelo dropped his brush into the paint, we do not say that he was painting the brush itself. The argument concludes from this that classificatory criteria do not govern the concepts expressed by these words. The implications of this argument are very inconvenient for a historian: if concepts expressed by words did not have specifiable classificatory criteria, then in the case of the sentence "Caesar ordered his troops to cross the Rubicon" we would not be able to say what action Caesar's troops had to perform in order to obey his order.

Rather than defeating the classical theory of concepts, the argument shows that it is typically impossible to state a single rule that covers the great variety of concepts that individual words come to express through the history of a language. Words typically express more than one concept. Most entries in any decent dictionary list more than one meaning for each given word. It is also common that there are many distinctions in the use of words that dictionaries do not cover. The verb "to paint" thus came to express the action of covering with paint in some situations, but not in others. The expectation that it should be possible to state *the* definition of *the concept* expressed by a word assumes that words do not change their meanings relative to the context of their use.[13] It is reasonable to expect that the rules for the context-dependent use of words that natural languages develop are going to be very complex and elaborate. Words normally express great variety of concepts and they do so in context dependent ways. However, this has no consequences for the understanding of concepts as sets of classificatory criteria that words express. The very example about the verb "to paint"—the difference between covering a wall with paint and a person being covered with paint from a paint factory that has exploded—could not be made if one did not differentiate between the two concepts of these two events. Wittgenstein's and Fodor's argument merely illustrates the deep rift that exists between language and thinking.

Words or their combinations may be taken to express a variety of concepts and can be understood in different ways. However, this does not apply to concepts or propositions, since they are precisely the meanings of words. If their classificatory criteria or conditions of satisfaction were understood differently, it would be another concept or proposition that is understood. The study of different concepts that words came to express through history is an important topic of historical research and can significantly contribute to our understanding of different eras.[14] Since concepts are the meanings of words and phrases, it makes no sense to talk about the "meaning of concepts." Usually, this phrase results from the confusion of words and concepts. It is sometimes stated that concepts changed through history, but this is merely a sloppy use of language. When they change, concepts become new concepts. What actually changes through history are people's beliefs, and in order to change beliefs people often need to acquire new concepts. Sometimes, new concepts are created from old ones. A new wider concept can be created by omitting some classificatory criteria from the list of classificatory criteria of an older one, and sometimes the old word is retained to express it. The word "text" thus came to be used in relation to non-verbal material, such as films or images.[15] The list of the classificatory criteria of the original concept expressed using the word "text" has been reduced by omitting some of them (e.g., "consisting of letters") and by retaining those that are satisfied by films and images (e.g., "ability to convey meanings"). In mathematics, the word "space" similarly came to express non-Euclidean or vector spaces.

In his or her work, a historian cannot rely on concepts that he or she does not possess.[16] If concepts were indeed able to change through time, one could not know what they were like once, and could not even know that they have changed. In other words, if concepts changed without becoming new concepts, we would have nothing to compare their new-acquired forms with and we could not know about it. We would also not be able to say that people's beliefs changed, because we could not grasp their older beliefs in order to compare them with new ones. In order to grasp how beliefs changed, one needs to assume that the concepts on which these beliefs rely do not change.[17] As the founder of *Begriffsgeschichte*, Reinhart Koselleck, pointed out, a word remains itself even when it changes its meaning because it is a physical entity.[18] A concept, however, becomes another concept if its content is changed. *Begriffsgeschichte*, the history of concepts, studies the way meanings changed through history—in other words, how words came to express different concepts.[19] Koselleck's example is Aristotle's phrase ἡ κοινωνία ἡ πολιτική ("political community"): the concept that Aristotle expressed cannot change nor have history, but its reception does have a history.[20] Another good example is the changes of the conceptualization of acidity through the history of chemistry.[21] For early atomists acidity resulted from the shape of atoms, the proponents of the phlogiston theory thought that acids were simple substances, Lavoisier thought that acids contained oxygen, in the nineteenth century it was thought that acidity resulted from the presence of hydrogen, in the twentieth century acids were identified as substances that donate protons or can accept an electron pair. These changes in conceptualization pertained to a set of substances with the same observable properties, and conceptualizations came about as a result of the effort to explain these properties. Beliefs about acids thus changed, but concepts such as "possess sharply formed atoms," "simple substance," "contain oxygen," "donate protons or can accept an electron pair" have remained the same; had they changed, we would actually not be able to say that beliefs about acids changed.[22]

It may also happen that words continue to express the same concepts, while the items that satisfy the classificatory criteria of the concepts may change. One famous example pertains to the cause of (or the pretext for) the second Punic war. Polybius describes that the original treaty between Rome and Carthage stipulated that none of the sides would attack other sides' allies.[23] Romans made alliance with the Iberian city of Saguntum after the treaty was made. When Hannibal attacked the city, the dilemma was whether the treaty was violated as Romans claimed, or not, according to Carthaginians. What happened was that the concept expressed with the term "Roman ally" remained unchanged, but the set of polities that satisfied the classificatory criteria of the concept changed. The treaty said nothing about such situations and both sides interpreted it as it suited them. The situation illustrates the important difference between historical and legal hermeneutics. A lawyer or a diplomat may need a standard or rules in order to establish *the correct* interpretation of a text—hence the efforts to identify the meaning of a text, for instance, with the author's meaning, establish it on the basis of the standard meaning of words in the era when the document was written and so on. For the historian, however, it is often relevant to establish how a specific person or public understood or misunderstood a document. As we shall later, the author's meaning is merely one possible meaning; the meaning of a document according to the standard use of the words of the era is merely the understanding a potential reader of the era would have. Alternative interpretations, that may have often motivated the actions of historical figures, may need to be taken into account in order to understand their actions.

CONCEPTS AND PROPOSITIONS AS MENTAL REPRESENTATIONS

The account of concepts and propositions presented here assumes that they are mental representations that result from human psychology and the biological functioning of the human brain. It aligns closely with John Searle's theory of human intentionality.[24] A core assumption of materialism, as described in the Introduction, is that mental is ultimately biological. Thus conceived, thought-contents and not abstract, immaterial entities that exist independently of human minds—and our topic here is to see what it means for historical research if we assume that this is the case. A book on the philosophy of history is not a place to discuss in general terms whether it may be necessary to assume that concepts and propositions (can) exist outside or independently of human minds.[25] Nevertheless, it is useful to consider some established arguments that have been made in favor of such ontological expansion in order to see how they can be responded to and what these responses entail. Arguments about externalism that will be discussed in the next chapter belong to this dilemma as well—but for now, let us consider more elementary ones listed by Gottlob Frege early in the twentieth century.[26]

Frege's view was that the identification of thought-contents (*Gedanke*) with mental representations (*Vorstellungen*) is insufficient in order to explain human thinking.[27] If different individuals are to recognize as true the thought that is expressed when one states Pythagoras's Theorem, he argued, then this thought cannot belong to the contents of their consciousness; they cannot be its bearers, although they can recognize it as true. Otherwise, if it were not the same thought that different people regard as the content of Pythagoras's

Theorem, then one could not say that there is a single Pythagoras's Theorem, but every person would have his or her own Pythagoras's Theorem, different from other people's Pythagoras's theorems. The qualification "true" or "false" about Pythagoras's Theorem would then apply only in the realm of an individual's consciousness, and it would be unclear whether something similar existed in the minds of other individuals. In Frege's view, if it is assumed that every thought requires a bearer, and belongs to this bearer's consciousness, then knowledge that is shared by many individuals will be impossible. Rather, in that case, every person will have his or her science and it will be impossible to establish what people agree or disagree about. From these arguments Frege inferred that in addition to the physical world and the realm of human mental representations (which he regarded as two separate realms), it is necessary to postulate a third realm to which thought-contents belong. This expansion of ontology is then meant to enable, for instance, that Pythagoras's Theorem is eternally true, and true independently of whether anyone holds it true or not. It exists on its own, it does not require a bearer, and it docs not become true only after it has been discovered.

It can be, however, responded that there simply can be no thoughts (or thought-contents) without bearers, that is, beings to whose mental life they belong. Thought-contents (concepts and propositions) are identified by their classificatory criteria or conditions of satisfaction, and we can say that different individuals can have thoughts with the same thought-content insofar as their thoughts have identical classificatory criteria (in the case of concepts) or conditions of satisfaction (in the case of propositions). One and the same thought-content can be present in different minds the way redness can be distributed in different red objects; there is no need to believe that redness exists independently of individual red objects nor, similarly, to postulate thought-contents that exist independently of the minds in which they are instantiated. As Searle pointed out, if two persons share the same thought, the sense in which they have an abstract entity in common "is the utterly trivial sense in which, if I go for a walk . . . and you go for the exactly same walk, we share an abstract entity, the same walk, in common."[28] It is consequently unproblematic that different people whose minds contain the same proposition—that is, share thought-contents that stipulate the same conditions of satisfaction—can discuss whether these conditions are satisfied or not. In the case of Pythagoras's Theorem, various individuals may entertain the proposition whose conditions of satisfaction state that an item that can be classified as a right-angled triangle is always also classifiable as a triangle such that the square of its longest side equals the sum of the squares of its two other sides. This thought-content could be instantiated in a person's mind, and that person could even believe that it is false although it is true. It could also be true even if all individuals in whose minds it is instantiated thought it was false. For this to be the case, it is not necessary that it exist outside their minds.

Different individuals can thus have thoughts with the same content and believe that the content is true or false, but it is not necessary to assume that this content exists outside their minds. Finally, a thought-content that is only instantiated in the minds of individuals (such as the Pythagoras's Theorem) can also be timelessly true. Nothing prevents it to be true about every item that satisfied the description of a right-angled triangle even before the Theorem was first discovered. A thought about an object can be true without being contemporaneous with the object. The only thing that matters is whether these right-angled triangles satisfy the proposition's conditions of satisfaction.

These responses to Frege now announce an important theme of this book. It will be necessary to explain the way understanding, interpretation, translation and similar procedures, common in historical research, function once extra-mental thought-contents are precluded. Since concepts and propositions are the meanings of words and sentences, then, insofar as they are contents of mental states and do not have separate, immaterial and abstract existence, it follows that there can be no meanings of texts, documents, historical works and so on that would exist independently of someone's mental states. There can be no semantics independently of the mental processes that enable it. From the materialist point of view, meanings cannot inhabit, inhere, reside or be present in linguistic artifacts as such; they are psychological, ultimately neurological, phenomena inseparable from the mental states that enable them and can be only communicated using various linguistic artifacts, written or spoken. The rejection of abstract, immaterial meanings that is necessarily one of the core assumptions of the materialist approach to historical research has wide-reaching implications. In the forthcoming chapters we shall repeatedly encounter arguments in favor of the view that meanings of linguistic artifacts that historians have to work with require ontological expansion beyond the material world and it will be necessary to review the responses that can be given to such arguments.

Although concepts and propositions are psychological in the sense that they are the products of the human brain, attempts at identifying them with specific processes in the human brain are likely to be futile, since it may happen that quite different processes in different brains produce identical concepts. The mental nature of concepts also means that the possession of a concept should not be identified with the ability for sorting behavior. Materialism as discussed here should not be confused with behaviorism. Behaviorist psychologists were inclined to argue that sorting behaviors are decisive in order to establish concept possession.[29] However, if two persons are given the same sets of drawings of geometrical figures and one of them told to separate the drawings of triangles from the pile, and the other person the drawings of trilaterals, the results of their work, their sorting behavior, will be the same, but they will have operated with different concepts.

FACTS AND REFERENCE

The contents of mental states stand in complex relationships with the words used to express them. An item belongs to the extension of a concept if it satisfies the classificatory criteria of that concept. Accordingly, when a word expresses the given concept, we can say that the item falls under the extension of that word. One and the same concept (or proposition) can be expressed using different words in different languages or even in one and the same language—thus German *Tisch* and Italian *tavola* express the same concept as the English word "table." A word or a phrase can express more than one concept: a "hot soup" can be a soup that is spicy or a soup that is too warm. Through this book I will use the term "meaning" for the concepts and propositions that words, phrases or sentences express. I will use the word "sentence" for the combination of words that expresses at least one proposition. Sentences often express more than one proposition. Also, there exists a substantial literature about the propositions that sentences may imply—words such as "but," "however," "although," "anyway" and similar often suggest that the author implies more than just the propositions that the sentence explicitly states.[30]

In the case of concepts, reference is the relationship between concepts (words or phrases that express them) and the items that satisfy their classificatory criteria.[31] One should not attribute a separate ontology to such relationship; rather, if an object satisfies the classificatory criteria of a concept, we say that the concept refers to it. I will use the term *relatum* for the specific objects that are referred to and "extension" for the set of all relata of a concept or a proposition (words, phrases or sentences that express it).[32]

One can define the relata of propositions (and the sentences that express them) in a number of different ways. (One has to be particularly careful with the way relata are understood, since anti-realist authors, such as those discussed in Chapter Nine, sometimes say that certain types of propositions or their combinations do not refer.) The view that the relatum of a proposition is its truth value—its being true or false—goes back to Frege, who simply introduced it by definition.[33] This understanding is inconvenient, since it suggests that all true propositions or sentences have the same relatum (truth) and the same is the case with all false propositions or sentences (their relatum is falsity). In the writings of contemporary philosophers of history it is commonly assumed that propositions (and the sentences that the express them) refer to the events or situations that make them true. As Goldstein put it, a statement about Caesar crossing the Rubicon refers to a specific action of Caesar.[34] Arthur Danto similarly defined narrative sentences as sentences that "refer to at least two time-separated events."[35] The intuition that motivates this use of the word is reasonable. If concepts (and the words that express them) refer to those items that satisfy their conditions of satisfaction, then, by analogy, one should expect that the relata of propositions (and the sentences that express them) should be the events, situations, relations and so on that satisfy the truth conditions (conditions of satisfaction) of propositions. When reading the authors who make this assumption, one should bear their usage in mind. However, while their reasoning is convincing, it is not always unproblematic.

Since the conditions of satisfaction of false propositions are not satisfied, it would follow that such propositions do not refer. The proposition "Columbus arrived to the American continent" is true and on this account it refers to Columbus's arrival to the American Continent. The proposition "Columbus failed to reach the American Continent" is false and it does not refer. The same applies to the false proposition "Columbus reached China"—it also has no relatum. This is arguably unproblematic since it is analogous to case of concepts whose classificatory criteria are not satisfied. Problems, however, arise with the true propositions that assert the non-existence of certain types of relata. For instance, the proposition "Columbus did not reach China" is true but it is hard to say what physical event it might refer to. It is equally difficult to say what might be the relatum of the true proposition "It is false that Columbus reached China." True propositions that deny the presence of properties ("My table has no white spots") are another difficulty. The same problem arises with the true propositions that assert the non-existence of various imaginary items such as "Werewolves do not exist." Complications also arise with the reference of hypothetical sentences, such as "Had Napoleon not invaded Russia, he could have dominated Europe for the rest of his life."

Speaking in general, there are events that happened and make some propositions true and these propositions can be said to refer to them. But events that did not happen sometimes do the same, and it is not clear how one can refer to them. One possible response would be to accept that many true sentences do not refer although, since they are true, their conditions of satisfaction are satisfied. Another possible response is to shun all talk about the reference of sentences and propositions altogether. Arguably, this approach has merits. The fact that concepts (or the words that express them) refer does not mean that this needs to be the case with propositions (or the sentences that express them).

In what follows, I will assume that propositions (the sentences that express them) refer to the properties of the world that make them true. The world has the properties of including or not including certain items (events, phenomena and so on). A true proposition that states that a historical figure performed a certain action states that our world has the property that in it the historical figure performed this action. This property is then the relatum of the proposition. True sentences that state that certain types of objects do not exist or that some events did not happen state that the world has the property of not including certain things or events and such sentences refer to these properties. In the case of hypothetical propositions, they state that our world has the property (they refer to the property) that some events in our world would have happened differently had some other event not happened or happened differently. Finally, false propositions (the sentences that express them) obviously do not refer.

The word "fact" is commonly used in two ways: a "fact" is sometimes a situation and sometimes a true description of a situation.[36] As mentioned, some philosophers of history assume that propositions or sentences refer to something that happened in the past and these events may be called "facts." Alternatively, it may be said that facts are true propositions that refer to past events. This inconsistency of everyday language use can also be taken to imply substantial ontological expansion beyond the material world. It may suggest the view according to which mental propositions (and the sentences that express them) refer to eternal, immaterial, abstract true propositions ("facts") that, on their own, then refer to the physical world. This is precisely the kind of ontological expansion that the materialist perspective that this book describes has to reject. I will assume here that facts are properties of the world. Consequently, it makes no sense to say that a fact refers to or pertains to something. Propositions (sentences that express them) refer to facts, but facts themselves do not have relata.

The discussion of reference presented here leaves aside the problem of the reference of mathematical concepts and propositions. There exists a long tradition that assumes that they refer to abstract and immaterial entities and there also exists the view that they do not. This is a specialist debate that cannot be addressed here. It is also not clear that, in the case mathematical concepts and propositions actually do refer to immaterial or abstract entities, this needs to affect, for instance, the work of a historian of mathematics. Insofar as a historian of mathematics is describing the work of and discoveries made by mathematicians, he or she is really describing the contents of their mental states and it is quite possible that such accounts can avoid reference to entities that do not have physical descriptions.

CONCEPTS AND THEORIES

In the final decades of the twentieth century, an alternative theory of concepts—the so-called "Theory"-theory—exercised significant impact on the humanities. The "Theory"-theory directly opposes the classical theory on which I have relied here and provides grounding for an anti-realist perspective not unlike the one discussed in Chapter One. The idea is that concepts are identified by their relations with other concepts and in relation to their positions within theories in which they participate. The concept of an electron, in this case, is relative to the theory, and two persons who subscribe to different theories of electrons necessarily have different concepts of electrons as well. One possible implication can be that concepts cease to refer to material items as well—since they are defined merely in relation to other concepts, it can be argued that it is not clear how they can establish relationship with material or historical reality. Further on, the experience and realities of individuals (e.g., scientists) who rely on different conceptual systems, paradigms or theories may be parceled into units so radically different that there could be no communication between them. Their views are said to be incommensurable.

In spite of its popularity in the final decades of the twentieth century, there have been too few clear and explicit attempts to define the "Theory"-theory of concepts, especially in relation to the ways the term "concept" and "incommensurability" need to be understood.[37] In historiography, Thomas Kuhn's theory of the paradigmatic shifts that occur in scientific revolutions has often been interpreted as a "Theory"-theory based position, though his statements are notoriously lacking an explicit commitment to this view.[38] According to this interpretation of Kuhn's views, "incommensurability" is to be understood as a radical incapacity of scientists who work within different paradigms to communicate and compare their beliefs. Radically different paradigms that organize their realities rely on concepts that make translations of their statements impossible. It is, however, not at all clear that such a radical position was really articulated by Kuhn, whose statements about incommensurability or that "when paradigms change, the world changes with them," were regularly qualified and made to sound like metaphors.[39] Unlike Goldstein who explicitly stated that "before the history of biology reached a certain point, there weren't any bacilli at all," Kuhn was careful to make his anti-realist statements sound metaphorical.[40] Historians often stretch their terms in order to emphasize the point they want to make, while it is simply historically not true that older scientific theories become incomprehensible to the scientists who worked after a scientific revolution. They become obsolete precisely because one understands them and knows the reasons why they are wrong. Nevertheless, as discussed in the Appendix, Kuhn did rely on an understanding of human perception that has direct anti-realist implications. The popularity of anti-realist interpretations of Kuhn's book could also be related to the fact that its publication happened to coincide with the rise of anti-realism in the 1960s. Ernst Gombrich similarly wrote in his 1960 book *Art and Illusion* that "there is no reality without interpretation" and then spent decades fighting against the anti-realist appropriations of his book.[41]

Radical incommensurability presents problems for historians. If two conceptual frameworks are indeed mutually incommensurable, one needs to explain the fact that they are nevertheless commensurable with the historian's own, and in a way that enables the historian to report on and compare them.[42]

Otherwise, if the historian cannot understand and compare them, then he or she cannot know that they are incommensurable. It is also not easy to deny incommensurability, because it is certainly present in some sense when paradigms are different: one does not expect Copernicus's astronomical system to be commensurable with Ptolemy's in the sense that it provides an account of epicycles or that Einstein's theory of relativity provides an alternative account of ether. But then, since they do not, in what sense can we expect concepts from radically different theories to be commensurable, or how is a historian going to report about the difference between two theories?

These problems do not necessarily relate to the historian's position in the debate about anti-realism. A realist historian may endorse the view that different theories indeed slice reality differently and according to different conceptual systems. Even then, if conceptual systems parcel out and organize our reality, concepts that participate in them still define the classificatory criteria that some elements of this reality must satisfy. Ptolemaic astronomy assumes that the concept of a planet as a body that moves according to the theory of epicycles is satisfied by some heavenly bodies. In other words, it assumes that there are planets that actually move the way the theory of epicycles describes it. Problems arise when this does not happen—when a theory assumes that the satisfaction conditions of certain concepts will be satisfied by some elements of reality and they are not. A theory is defeated when we cannot slice reality the way it says we should be able to. It will be therefore pointed out that one cannot say that our experience of reality is always already predetermined by the beliefs and theories with which we approach reality—because that is precisely not what happens. There are numerous examples in the history of science. Consider the eighteenth-century testing of the Newtonian view that the rotation of the earth would cause a protrusion along equator and a constriction at the poles.[43] The alternative view in the eighteenth century was the Cassini-emended Cartesian view that postulated the oblong form of the earth. The systematic measurements made by the expeditions to Lapland and Peru organized by the French *Académie des Sciences* eventually confirmed the Newtonian hypothesis. However, even a realist position that endorses the "Theory"-theory still needs to explain how communication between individuals who subscribe to incommensurable conceptual frameworks is possible. The dilemma between realism and anti-realism is a different one from the problem of incommensurability.

It should also be mentioned that this argument against the anti-realist implications of the "Theory"-theory cannot be rejected by invoking Quine's underdetermination thesis.[44] In his "Two Dogmas of Empiricism," Quine argued that scientific systems are underdetermined by their boundary conditions (empirical facts).[45] Regardless of recalcitrant experiences, in his view "[a]ny statement can be held true come what may, if we make drastic enough adjustments elsewhere in the system."[46] This is the thesis that negative instances cannot disprove a theory because a theory can be always saved with sufficient internal adjustments.[47] Quine's view was that "Any statement can be held true come what may, if we make drastic enough adjustments elsewhere in the system."[48] (Critics such as Larry Laudan have pointed out that this formulation comes very close to the claim that "it is as reasonable to believe in fairies at the bottom of my garden as not."[49]) The idea is that no individual proposition can be verified by means of experience; the confirmation of a proposition is always holistic and our beliefs face the tribunal of sense experience as a whole. Quine's position enjoyed huge popularity for decades and it may seem to be an important argument in favor of the "Theory"-theory. It is, however, important to notice that his thesis is not that all conceptual systems are equivalent in relation to experience—rather, he says that they can always be adapted to it. He precisely admits that theories need internal adaptation when faced with recalcitrant experiences and claims that this can always be done if they are treated in *in toto*. The position he describes in "Two Dogmas of Empiricism" does not entail that theories determine or construct experience. He is not denying that theories face recalcitrant experiences and he is certainly not saying that our experiences are constructed by our theories.[50]

INCOMMENSURABILITY

There are thus serious complications for historians who endorse the "Theory"-theory of concepts, in spite of its popularity in the final decades of the twentieth century. Problems are particularly likely to arise in the history of science, the history philosophy, and other fields of historical research that may seek to establish differences in conceptual contents that belong to individuals from different contexts. The fact that different theories will define one and the same item differently can cause concern only if one assumes that there can be only one concept of a physical or historical item within a given theory. If we look at the problem from the perspective of the classical theory of concepts and understand concepts as sets of classificatory criteria, the situation is far more straightforward. In the case of theoretical concepts defined differently by different theories (e.g., electron) the question will be whether two concepts that originate from different theories specify different lists of classificatory criteria.[51] If they do, then the question is whether these classificatory criteria are satisfied by the same and only the same segment of reality. If they are, then these are different concepts of one and the same item; if not, they are different concepts of different items. At the same time, it is quite possible that two concepts from different theories state the same classificatory criteria and are thus one and the same concept. Such concepts can then enable commensurability between theories.

The last point requires some elaboration. Consider how a historian can convey a different conceptual framework to his or her public—for instance, a modern historian who tries to explain the concept of epicycle to a modern public that believes planets go around the Sun. In order to formulate the explanation of an unknown concept, the historian will have to use a suitable combination of available concepts. According to Ptolemy, an epicycle is something that satisfies various sets of classificatory criteria (it can be identified using various descriptions). Many of these sets will rely on the Ptolemaic understanding that planets revolve around the earth. However, planets are clearly identifiable entities and their concepts participate both in heliocentric and Ptolemaic astronomy theories. There are a number of identifying descriptions of planets that both theories share (heavenly bodies that differ from others by the way they move across the sky, the way they shine, etc.).[52] There are thus a number of beliefs about planets that are shared by believers in the heliocentric and the geocentric systems. Starting from a clearly identified concept that both theories share, one will establish which beliefs about planets are different. The historian will explain that according to Ptolemy planets revolve around the earth, and then explain epicycles as segments on their paths. The explanation is possible because the crucial items, planets, that satisfy various sets of classificatory criteria in the heliocentric and the Ptolemaic system, still satisfy a number of sets of classificatory criteria that are valid in both systems and because other terms in the explanation (movement, sky) express concepts that are available in both worldviews.

Two points need to be made here. First, the account thus fundamentally depends on the possibility of making a conceptual link between these two theories. In the cases when no conceptual links can be made (i.e., when no part of reality is classified the same way or we do not know how they were classified) conceptual frameworks will indeed be "incommensurable" in the sense of being incommensurable in those segments where no links can be made. Consider the case of Inca builders. It is possible that they classified stones in accordance with what could be done using their stone-cutting technology. But since we know nothing about their stone-cutting technology, we cannot say how they classified stones. Additionally, if the question is whether it can happen that some people organize their experience in radically different conceptual frameworks so that the totality of these frameworks is incomprehensible to us, the answer is simple: should this be the case, then we would not know about it and no historian could report it.

Second, in the above example the historian's account assumes that his or her public can perceive and identify the stars the same way as Ptolemy did—in other words, that seeing can be theory-independent, that not all seeing is seeing-as. The account assumes that visual perception of stars is the rock-bottom of communication, to use Searle's phrase. The historian's explanation would be impossible if the members of the public did not see stars, could not identify them, did not operate with the concept of a star, and consequently did not know what the historian was talking about. At the same time, if perceptual experience is to underwrite the possibility of human communication, it has to be (on a certain level, at least) independent of the ways various individuals classify its contents. People classify things on the basis of their previous experiences and if all perception depended on classification, people might experience the world in such a diversity of ways that communication would indeed be impossible. A Ptolemaic astronomer would then *see* stars differently than an astronomer who assumes the validity of the heliocentric system. The possibility of theory-independent perception is thus crucial for the rejection of the "Theory"-theory of concepts. At the same time, the idea that the contents of perception are or can be detachable from the conceptualization of these contents was widely rejected for a number of decades during the second half of the twentieth century. This rejection was largely motivated by the "New Look" psychology of perception that was influential in the 1950s and the 1960s. Historically, the rise of the "Theory"-theory coincided with the influence of the view that "all seeing is seeing-as" and can be seen as a development of its implications outside the fields of the philosophy and psychology of perception. (See the Appendix.) However, in the case it is possible to perceive things and their properties independently of how one classifies them, then it will also be possible to classify them (and form concepts) merely according to the properties one perceives on them, independently of any other concepts one operates with. This would mean that it is possible to form concepts from (and more generally base them on) sense experience, independently of other concepts and conceptual systems (theories) one operates with. Such concepts would be identified in relation to sense experience and not based on the theories in which they participate. They would enable for the formulation of further concepts, systems of concepts and theories that are based on sense-experience. It would follow that not all concepts are therefore theory-relative and that conceptual systems and theories can be anchored in sense experience as their rock-bottom base. From this position one can reject the "Theory"-theory of concepts by rejecting its anti-foundationalist assumptions. At the same time, the view that all perceptual contents are always already predetermined by the way we conceptualize them, in the strong form that is necessary in order to support the "Theory"-theory, is nowadays generally rejected in the philosophy and the psychology of perception. Although the position was very influential in the mid-decades of the twentieth century, it is regarded as obsolete today, which makes the "Theory"-theory, and anti-foundationalism more generally, difficult to defend. The reasons for this and the relevant arguments from this debate are presented in the Appendix.

NOTES

1. Margolis and Laurence, "Concepts and Cognitive Science," 10, define the "classical theory" as the understanding of concepts as "structured mental representations that encode a set of necessary and sufficient conditions for their application." Similarly, Rey, "Concepts and Stereotypes," 280, calls the "classical theory" the view that a concept is "a summary representation of some set of things in terms of conditions that are singly necessary and jointly sufficient for membership in that set."
2. See Margolis and Laurence, "Concepts and Cognitive Science," 8–14.
3. Obviously, the term "concept" can be used differently. For instance, in experimental psychology there exists a body of research that seeks to identify concepts as prototypes. See Margolis and Laurence, "Concepts and Cognitive Science," Rey, "Concepts and Stereotypes," Rosch, "Principles," Smith and Medin, "The Exemplar View" and Osherson and Smith, "Adequacy."
4. Bruno Latour, "Partial Existence," 261, note 11.
5. For the explanation of satisfaction see Searle, *Intentionality*, 8–10, 22.
6. For an equivalent account see Braun, "Extension," 9. Braun gives as example "Barack Obama runs." The extension of "Barack Obama" is Barack Obama; the extension of "runs" is the set of things that run and the sentence is true if Barack Obama is a member of that set.
7. Ayer, *Language*, 102.
8. Field, *Problems*, 15.
9. "The Thirty Years War" is a name. According to metalinguistic descriptivism discussed Chapter Six, it means "the bearer of the name 'The Thirty Years War.'" This description and the name were not available in 1618.
10. Danto, *Narration and Knowledge*, 156.
11. Margolis and Laurence, "Concepts and Cognitive Science," 14–18. Rey, "Concepts and Steroetypes," 281.
12. Fodor, *Representations*, 257–316. Fodor, *Concepts*, 45.
13. This expectation is obvious from phrases such as "*the* meaning of a word." See for instance Putnam, "Semantics," 177. Fodor, Garrett, Walker and Parkes in "Against Definitions," 274, directly start from the assumption that "a definition gives the meaning of a word." Margolis and Laurence in "Concepts and Cognitive Science," 4, define their "lexical concepts" as those that correspond to lexical items in natural languages. Similarly, Rey, "Concepts and Stereotypes," 283, suggests that "the semantic structure of, for example, English, mirrors the structure of concepts."
14. There are numerous studies of this kind. Hon and Goldstein, *From Summetria to Symmetry*, analyzed how the meanings of the Greek term *symmetria* and its derivations changed through history. See Mitrović, "Giora Hon and Bernard R. Goldstein." Similarly, Gerring, "Ideology" provides a history of concepts expressed using the term "ideology."
15. Bal, *Concepts*, 26.
16. Partial possession is possible; see the earlier example about wombats in a Melbourne park.
17. This point is made by Peacocke, *Study of Concepts*, 3.
18. See for instance Koselleck, "Geschichte," 62–63, 67 and Koselleck, "Hinweise," 87–88. See also the analysis by Schultz, "Begriffsgeschichte," 65–67.
19. Koselleck, "Geschichte," 88.
20. Ibid., 88.
21. Thagard, *Conceptual Revolutions*, 37–38.
22. See Kuukkanen, "Conceptual Change," for an attempt to formulate an account of conceptual change that assumes that concepts actually change through history. According to this account, every concept has certain components, for instance, A, B and C. A dynamic understanding of concepts then assumes that one and the same concept evolves through history. In some periods a thing must have properties A, B and C in order to be subsumed under a given concept; in some other time D, E and F and in yet another epoch G, H and I. As Kuukkanen admits, such a dynamic theory allows concepts to change so much that one and the same concept may become unrecognizable and consequently it becomes difficult to say that we are

still dealing with one and the same concept. In other words, in order to recognize differences between new and old concepts, we must retain the original concept, which is a different concept from the new one.

23. Polybius, *Histories*, 3.29.2–7.

24. For Searle's own summaries of his position, see his articles "Intentionality 1" and "Intentionality and the Use of Language." In the discussion here, I replace Searle's term "intentional content" with "thought-content." In his *Intentionality* Searle mainly discusses propositions, and does not expand his discussion on concepts. This is, however, necessary for the present discussion. The great advantage of Searle's theory of intentionality is that it avoids the claim that intentional contents are directed to immaterial intentional objects—and consequently, it avoids problems with intentional contents that have no intentional objects as well as the need to explain the ontology of "directedness." For an alternative theory of intentionality, that also successfully avoids the need to expand ontology see Crane, *Objects of Thought*.

25. See Margolis and Laurence, "Ontology of Concepts" for a good survey of responses to standard arguments against the mentalist understanding of concepts.

26. Frege, "Gedanke."

27. Frege, "Gedanke," 68–69.

28. Searle, *Intentionality*, 198.

29. Fodor, "Concepts."

30. See the discussion of implicature in Chapter Nine. See also Horn, "Implicature," Bach, "Speech Acts," and Bach, "Top 10."

31. See for instance explanations of the term in Neander, "Naturalistic Theories," 374, Lycan, *Philosophy of Language*, 3, Robinson, "Reference," 189.

32. Analytic philosophers sometimes use the term "referent" for the purpose, but I will avoid it in this book. The readers who know Latin may be mislead by the derivation of this word from the Latin active participle and take it to refer to the person or the sign that refers and not the object referred to.

33. Frege, "Sinn und Bedeuting," 30. Frege used the same German term *Bedeuting* for both the relationship of reference and the object of reference. Since he introduced this use of the word by definition, he did not provide any arguments for his choice. Here is a standard explanation of this view from modern literature: "If we assume that they [declarative sentences] have extensions, and we also assume that the extension of every complex expression is completely determined by the extensions of the simple expressions in it, then we are naturally let to the conclusion that the extension of a declarative sentence is its *truth-value* (either *truth*, if the sentence is true, or *falsehood*, if the sentence is false)." Braun, "Extension," 9. Similarly, Gauker, "Semantics and Pragmatics," 19.

34. Goldstein, "History," 51.

35. Danto, *Narration and Knowledge*, 159.

36. See discussion in Kosso, "Philosophy," 11–15.

37. See for instance Achinstein, "On the Meaning," 497. However, Achinstein's discussion is limited to the ways terms are used in theories. Fodor, "Concepts," 113, observes that the key notions like "discontinuity" and "incommensurability" have never been properly explicated—"the buck is simply passed to philosophers." Margolis and Laurence, "Concepts and Cognitive Science," 50, note 67, similarly state "the 'Theory'-theory hasn't been subjected to as much critical scrutiny as previous theories." For a description of the problems related to the "Theory"-theory, see their account in Margolis and Laurence, "Concepts and Cognitive Science," 43–51.

38. For such understanding of Kuhn see for instance, Nersesian, *Faraday*, 17–29, Thagard, *Revolutions*, 4, 49, and Davidson, "Very Idea," 190. Fodor, *Concepts*, 113, also cites Kuhn as a proponent of the "Theory"-theory.

39. Kuhn, *Structure*. For the qualifications of the statements that "the world has changed" see: "the historian of science may be tempted to exclaim" (ibid., 111); "wish to say that" (ibid., 117); "will urge us to say that" (ibid., 118); "Is there any legitimate sense in which we can say that they pursued research in different worlds?" (ibid., 120); "though the world does not change with the change of a paradigm, the scientist afterwards works in a different world" (ibid., 121). However, no such qualification accompanies the statement that after Dalton's discoveries

"chemists came to live in a world where reactions behaved quite differently from the way they had before" (ibid., 134). For incommensurability see ibid., 112.

40. Goldstein, *The What and the Why*, 216. Claims of this kind are common among postmodernist authors. Following the same reasoning, global warming does not result from the emission of greenhouse gasses, but from the work of the scientists who measure it.

41. Gombrich, *Art and Illusion*, 363. A summary of the anti-realist reception of Gombrich is in Krieger, "Ambiguities." See also Gombrich's reaction in his "Representation and Misrepresentation." For a general survey of the debate see Mitrović, "A Defence of Light."

42. "Kuhn is brilliant at saying what things were like before the revolution using—what else?—our post-revolutionary idiom." Davidson, "On the Very Idea," 184. As mentioned in the note above, I do not think that there is enough textual evidence to attribute to Kuhn such radical views.

43. Todhunter, *Theories of Attraction*, vol. 1, 93–102. Todhunter's presentation is not quite clear; see the summary in Laudan, "Underdetermination," 287.

44. Quine, "Two Dogmas," 42–46.

45. Ibid., 44.

46. Ibid., 43.

47. See Laudan, "Underdetermination," for an analysis of the problems that arise from Quine's principle of underdetermination and also Bricmont and Sokal, "Defense."

48. Quine, "Two Dogmas," 43.

49. Laudan, "Underdetermination," 277.

50. Quine does consider the possibility of dismissing recalcitrant experience as hallucination—and from the point of view that he describes, this could count as an adaptation of theory too. But he is not saying that theory determines sense experience, let alone reality.

51. Obviously, all this happens from the perspective of the person (historian) that compares their views.

52. Additional caveats will be necessary—for example, that one is only counting planets that can be seen without a telescope.

Chapter Five

Language

Historians' works are always in a language and their research is largely based on the study of language-based materials. At the same time, in the philosophy of language there exist extensive debates about the ontology of linguistic phenomena (such as meaning or reference). Arguments for the view that the functioning of languages cannot be understood without postulating abstract and immaterial entities have been highly influential since the 1970s—and there is also a substantial corpus of arguments intended to disprove these views. The aim of this chapter is to analyze the implications of these debates for historical research. Obviously, the credibility of the materialist perspective on history would be seriously damaged if it were impossible to conceive of languages without expanding ontology beyond the material world. It is therefore important to see how arguments in favor of such views can be responded to. An additional point that also needs to be made is that the arguments stated in favor of such ontological expansion—those proposed by Hilary Putnam and Tyler Burge—rely on assumptions that are incompatible with standard approaches to historical research and the understanding of historical documents. Abandoning the materialist paradigm in matters of language easily ends up in anachronistic attributions of beliefs to historical figures.

ANTI-MENTALISM

In the previous chapter we have already seen some elements of the terminology involved in the discussion of linguistic phenomena. There are words and sentences and they are physical entities, such as lines on paper or vibrations of air. They are used to express concepts and propositions, which are the contents of mental states identified by their classificatory criteria (in the case of concepts) or conditions of satisfaction (in the case of propositions). Concepts and propositions are the meanings of the words and the sentences that express them. The items that satisfy the classificatory conditions of concepts are the relata of these concepts; the relata of propositions are the properties of the world that make them true. The relationship between concepts and propositions and their relata is called reference and this term is also used for the relationship between the words or sentences that express these concepts and propositions and their relata.

For a long period during the twentieth century it was a common view among philosophers of language that the materialist perspective on language must preclude the consideration of mental states and their contents. The idea that mental states are somehow not properly material was highly influential among analytic philosophers for a very long time.[1] The assumption resulted in attempts to describe and explain linguistic phenomena in ways that left aside the meanings of words and relied exclusively on reference as a relationship between words and their relata. This approach produces numerous difficulties. It is useful to survey briefly these well-known problems in order to clarify the reasons why the concept of reference has limited explanatory capacities in the understanding of how languages work. The point to be made is that in order to explain the use of language by historical figures and historians, it is necessary to rely on their mental, ultimately biological states.

From the materialist point of view, the problem with reference-based accounts of linguistic phenomena is precisely the ontology they have to rely on. According to the account based on meanings, meanings as contents of mental (i.e., biological) states underwrite reference—that is, we say that concepts or propositions refer to their relata when these relata satisfy the classificatory criteria or the conditions of satisfaction of these concepts or propositions. Words are said to refer insofar as they express such concepts or propositions. Problems start if we try to exclude meanings from the account—it becomes difficult to explain what reference is (its ontology) and what sustains this relationship between words and their relata. In other words: what does the word "reference" in that case refer to? Since the response cannot rely on mental states, it becomes necessary to expand ontology and assume that referential relationships are immaterial abstract entities.[2] The attempt to reduce ontology by omitting mental states thus ends up by expanding it in the direction of immaterial things.

At the same time, the perspective on languages that relies on reference without meanings has limited explanatory capacities when it comes to numerous phenomena of language use. One important problem pertains to words that "refer" to non-existent things, such as phlogiston or vampires. It is not clear that one can refer to non-existent things (hence scare quotes in the previous sentence). The same problems arise when one attempts to refer to nothing, vacuum and similar items. Further on, since neither phlogiston nor vampires exist, the words "phlogiston" or "vampire" refer to nothing and since they have the same relatum (nothing is nothing), we have to conclude that vampires are identical to phlogiston. The same applies to anything else that does not exist.

Complications also arise when it comes to the attribution of beliefs. Columbus may have thought that the island that we call Cuba is China, and people today may describe Cuba as "Castro's island," but it would be quite wrong to say that "Columbus thought that Castro's island is China." In other words, the fact that some words and phrases share the same relatum does not mean that they can be substituted for each other in sentences that describe attitudes of individuals—which should be the case if their reference governed their role in a language. Further on, there are problems with objects that have multiple names or can be identified in different ways. "The Morning Star" and "the Evening Star" refer to the same planet, Venus. If the role of words in a language were regulated by their reference, and if meanings played no role, then saying "the Morning star is the Evening Star" would be the same as saying "the Morning Star is the Morning Star," since "the Evening Star" has the same reference as "the Morning Star." But this is not quite the same, since someone may not know that the Morning Star and the Evening Star refer to the same planet. For such a person, "the Morning star is the Evening Star" conveys new knowledge, while "the Morning Star is the Morning Star" does not.

If we say, however, that the role of words in a language is regulated by what people mean, the thought-contents that they express when they use them, problems of this kind vanish. Columbus could not have had thoughts about Fidel Castro. Anyone who says that "Columbus thought that Castro's island is China" is expressing a false proposition that attributes to Columbus thoughts about Castro. The words that refer to non-existent entities such as "phlogiston" or "vampires" express concepts whose conditions of satisfaction are different. It is true, but irrelevant that in both cases they are not satisfied by any existing thing. Finally, the classificatory criteria that something must satisfy in order to be the Morning Star are different from those that something must satisfy in order to be the Evening Star. Saying that they are one and the same heavenly body, provides significant new information about their identity. While denying the role of mental states when explaining linguistic phenomena is bound to generate problems, the materialist perspective on language, insofar as it is assumed that mental phenomena are neurobiological, has no reason to adopt this approach.

Chapter 5

A MATERIALIST PERSPECTIVE ON LANGUAGE: *DE VERBIS* AND *DE SIGNIS* BELIEFS

The most obvious aspect of the materialist perspective on language with its exclusion of abstract, immaterial entities is the rejection of the view that the meanings of words and sentences could exist independently of the mental states of individuals. The result is the identification of meanings with the contents of individuals' mental states. One elementary problem is that this view may seem to end up in a position similar to that of Humpty Dumpty in Lewis Carrol's *Alice through the Looking Glass*: "'When *I* use a word,' Humpty Dumpty said in rather a scornful tone, 'it means just what I choose it to mean—neither more nor less.'"[3] Languages and their use, it will be pointed out, are social phenomena; meanings of words are not just a matter of the whim of the individuals who use them. Even if we postulate private languages, this will not get us very far when we have to explain how one can understand, interpret or translate historical documents, works of historians, or engage in language-based communication of any kind. The point is certainly well made. Languages are indeed social phenomena, although this does not necessarily imply that they have to be abstract, immaterial entities existing independently of individuals' mental states.

Speaking in general terms, a language is a social phenomenon because it enables communication within society, and this communication is always between individuals. Consider the referential use of sentences—a phenomenon that was described by Keith Donnellan and has been widely discussed among philosophers of language.[4] Donnellan imagines that during a court trial two persons observe and discuss the odd behavior of the person accused for murder. One of them says, because of the way the accused behaves: "The murderer is insane." The proposition expressed by the sentence may be false, since the accused may not be the murderer; but it can be taken to convey the true proposition that the accused is insane. (Historical texts are replete with conventional referring similar to Donnellan's example. For instance, many historians use the word "Hapsburgs" to talk about the dynasty that ruled Austria until 1918, although that dynasty actually became extinct in 1740.) Communication is enabled by the beliefs that the participants in communication share about the meaning of the sentence, not by some immaterial, abstract meanings that exists independently of the content of their mental states. Even if we accept that meanings (as social phenomena) may be abstract entities that exist on their own, independently of the mental states of individuals, this does not explain their use by individuals in communication. In order to use a combination of words in order to convey a certain meaning, the individual must believe that the combination of words will perform that job, while the person receiving communication must believe that the words are intended to convey that content. They must share the same beliefs about the capacity of the words used on the occasion to convey the meanings. If the speaker (author) does not believe that the words will convey the thought-content, he or she will not choose them in order to communicate. If the recipient does not have the appropriate belief about the meaning of the words the speaker used, or believes that they are intended to convey a different content, then communication fails. The view that communication is impossible without such beliefs and assumptions has a long history in the philosophy of language that goes at least back to John Locke.[5]

Communication requires that participants share the same beliefs about the capacities of specific signs or combinations of words to convey specific thought-contents. One should differentiate between such beliefs about words and beliefs about other signs. A *de verbis* belief is such a belief that pertains to words; a *de signis* belief is a belief that pertains to other kinds of signs, including the cases when a thought-content expressed using words functions as a sign of another thought-content. (This happens in the case of ironical statements or metaphors: the meaning of a sentence is itself a sign of another meaning. In order to grasp irony or a metaphor, one needs to form both *de verbis* and *de signis* beliefs about the words used to express it. Mao Tse-Dung's statement that a revolution is not a matter of inviting people to dinner has a literal meaning that can be understood on the basis of *de verbis* beliefs and also an additional metaphorical meaning that is conveyed by the literal meaning and understood on the basis of an additional *de signis* belief about this literal meaning.[6]) In Donnellan's example, a person who hears the sentence "the murderer is insane" may have the *de verbis* belief that the proposition it expresses may be false, and still have a *de signis* belief that the proposition conveyed by that proposition is true. Since words are also a kind of sign, one may count *de verbis* beliefs as a kind of *de signis* beliefs. In any case, without shared *de verbis* and *de signis* beliefs, no communication is possible. If an author does not believe that certain words can convey his or her thought-contents to recipients, he or she has no reason to use them for the purpose of communication; if a recipient does not believe that certain words can be used in order to convey a certain thought-content he or she will not understand them as conveying it.

De verbis and *de signis* beliefs are mental states and consequently assumed to be generated by human neurobiology. Throughout this book I will extensively rely on them in order to provide materialist accounts of various ways historical figures and historians use language. The aim is to show that the linguistic behavior of historical figures and historians can be accounted of without the expansion of ontology beyond the material world. (It should also be mentioned that *de verbis* and *de signis* beliefs can be understood as a version of *presuppositions* that are widely discussed in the philosophy of language and linguistics.[7])

An important point about *de verbis* and *de signis* beliefs is that they are as much beliefs about the participants in communication as they are beliefs about the words used. In order to successfully use a term in communication, the person using it must have the true belief that words and sentences will be understood by his or her recipients as he or she wants them to understand these words and sentences. At the same time, the recipients must have the true belief that such understanding was the intention of the person who used it. *De verbis* and *de signis* beliefs are thus not merely beliefs about the capacity of words to convey certain thought-contents, but rather about their capacity to convey them to specific recipients. They are also beliefs about the capacity of the intended recipients to grasp the meaning that the words or signs convey. On the recipient's side, they are also beliefs about the author (speaker) and his or her capacity to use certain words or signs in order to communicate specific thought-contents. For both the author (speaker) and the recipient, they are, ultimately, beliefs about communicative abilities of other individuals. Most times one takes this aspect—that these are beliefs about other individuals—for granted. One thus typically assumes that one can always use the local language of the country where one finds oneself. The assumption that a certain language is spoken in a certain area is an assumption about individuals who live there and it is reliable as long as one keeps coming across the locals who indeed speak the local language. However, communication falls apart when one runs into someone who does not know the local language. Also, even the fact that individuals speak the same language (and even the same dialect) does not guarantee perfect communication: individuals may have different beliefs about specific words or may use certain words in non-standard or unexpected ways. Early in his *Annales* Tacitus makes an apparently startling statement that after Brutus, Pompey, Marc Anthony and other Roman leaders perished in civil wars, only Caesar remained.[8] The statement is astonishing only until one grasps that he does not mean Julius Caesar, but Octavian—and that this implies that Tacitus could expect that his Roman readers will grasp whom he meant. They, we can infer, understood reference to Octavian as "Caesar"—and similarly a paragraph later, when he talks about "Nero" but it is clear that he is referring to Tiberius. In order to understand Tacitus properly, one must take care about his *de verbis* beliefs, and the *de verbis* beliefs he attributed to the readers he thought he was writing for. (Note also the dilemma that a translator needs to resolve: either one will translate "Caesar" with "Octavian" in order to avoid confusion and accurately convey what Tacitus meant, or one should translate "Caesar" with "Caesar" in order to convey to the readers both what Tacitus meant and his *de verbis* beliefs. The translator has to make that decision, and it should be made on the basis of the translator's own beliefs about the expectations, knowledge and beliefs of his or her readers.)

Anomalies in the ways individuals use languages can only be of marginal interest for linguists or philosophers of language, since they are typically interested in the functioning of languages in general. It is natural that their interests are directed towards a much wider, general, picture. But a historian's dilemmas often pertain to those situations that a linguist or a philosopher of language regards as uninteresting. Methodological dilemmas in historical research (such as the understanding, the interpretation or the translation of documents) often pertain to the complications that arise when the author used words in a non-standard way and communication threatens to break down. More generally, a historian who analyzes communication between historical figures is not going to get very far without reconstructing the *de verbis* and *de signis* beliefs on which the communication was based. Christopher Gauker, who should be credited for being one of rare analytic philosophers of language to discuss the problem of translation, proposed that translations of statements by two members of the same linguistic community should be made uniformly.[9] But this is precisely *not* how translations should be done. Consider, for instance, translations of philosophical works—a standard job for a historian of philosophy. Aristotle's written Greek, for instance, is simple and straightforward and his use of words, and as long as it conforms to the standard usage of the time unlikely to cause much problem. Immense amount of scholarship, however, has been spent on his *non-standard* use of words—that is, the technical terminology of his philosophy. Notoriously, these are the moments in which the standard tools of the analysis of meaning based on assumptions about language as a collective phenomenon fall apart. In such situations dictionaries cease to be helpful; one needs a tool such as Herman Bonitz's *Index aristotelicus*. What matters when such problems are encountered are the *de verbis* beliefs that motivated the use of certain words in the given context.

An analysis of the use languages based on *de verbis* and *de signis* beliefs thus clearly emphasizes the study of pragmatics of word use. The important assumption of the pragmatic perspective is that words or sentences cannot have meanings on the basis of their participation in an abstract system (such as language) and independently of the meanings that one attributes to them. A sentence that nobody ever pronounced, wrote or contemplated cannot mean anything since meanings are assumed to be the contents of mental states. In the philosophy of language, the study of the pragmatics is typically limited to communication between two persons, the speaker and the listener or the author and the recipient. For a historian this analysis is very elementary. Very often, in historical research, it is not enough to provide an account of communication between two historical figures; the *de verbis* and *de signis* beliefs of various other individuals reporting such communication (including other historians) have to be relied on. The moment one has to report, for instance, the content of a document to a public different from the public it was intended for, let alone when translation gets involved, everything becomes much more complex. A translator, we shall see in Chapter Eight, typically works with at least two sets of *de verbis* beliefs: beliefs about the author of the text he or she is translating and beliefs about the public the translation is intended for. Consider the case of a modern scholar translating some of Aquinas's commentaries on Aristotle. It will be necessary to include translations of the relevant sections from Aristotle—and not from original Aristotle but from the Latin version that Aquinas worked with, conveying his understanding of that translation. Also, Aquinas's own comments cannot be simply understood on the basis of standard scholastic Latin—philosophers often change the meanings of words and make them into technical terms in order to convey new concepts to their public. The translator has to reconstruct the *de verbis* beliefs that motivate the use of specific terms, and find a way to convey a text based on them to his or her own public, on the basis his or her *de verbis* beliefs about that public.

ONTOLOGICAL CONSIDERATIONS

The view that the assumptions historians need to make about languages are ultimately assumptions about (widespread) clusters of *de signis* and *de verbis* beliefs removes the need to expand ontology beyond the mental states of individuals in order to explain the role of languages in historiography. Insofar as beliefs are mental and consequently biological phenomena, language, on this account is ultimately a biological phenomenon as well.[10] This perspective may seem to contradict the view of languages as public, intersubjective or social phenomenon, insofar as being a public, intersubjective or social phenomenon is conceived as being something over and above individuals, their properties (mental states) and interactions. The response to this concern, made by Noam Chomsky among others, is that the biological understanding of the human capacities that enable the use of language does not preclude the social perspective; rather, it is hard to see how the social perspective could be endorsed without taking into account the actual biological properties of individual minds that enable it.[11]

Linguists and philosophers of language typically differentiate between semantics and pragmatics in the sense that semantics studies literal meanings of words and phrases, while pragmatics is the study of the use of language in order to communicate messages.[12] The question that concerns us here pertains to the ontological assumptions that sustain the study of semantics. One possible perspective, that is not ontologically controversial, is that semantic meanings are statistical generalizations about *de verbis* beliefs within a certain population (linguistic group). People are classified into their linguistic groups because they share large clusters of *de verbis* beliefs. Those *de verbis* beliefs that are sufficiently widely shared define the semantic meanings of words. A speaker of a language relies on and assumes this wide agreement about *de verbis* beliefs in order to engage in communication in his or her community (although they may also opt for non-standard use in some circumstances, as we have seen that Aristotle did). The standard meaning of words in that case is nothing more than their meaning that has been codified on the basis of widespread agreement about *de verbis* beliefs within the community. One could call this view a bottom-up perspective. The alternative, top-down perspective would be that members of a linguistic community have *de verbis* beliefs *because* they belong to their linguistic community. This means that the community is the primary explanatory entity; it typically requires the expansion of ontology beyond the material world and the assumption that a linguistic community (or language) is something over and above individuals, their mental states and interactions. It assumes that semantic meanings are abstract entities that somehow exist independently of what goes in individuals' minds. Jerrold Katz, for instance, argued that languages or linguistic structures are Platonic entities that exist on their own, independently of mental states of individuals—that they are abstract objects, on par with numbers or geometrical figures in the philosophy of mathematics.[13] Chomsky's response to Katz was that the Platonist view of mathematics is plausible since facts of arithmetic are independent of any facts about individual psychology and the way they are discovered is somewhat comparable to the discovery of facts about the physical world—which is not the case with languages.[14]

Speaking in more general terms, these dilemmas about the ontology of linguistic contexts are a specific case of dilemmas about the nature of historical-social items that was discussed in Chapter Two. We are here, however, interested in the implications of different views on the ontology of language for historical research. It may well be that languages or their elements indeed exist as Platonic Forms, independently of mental states of individuals. Maybe Chomsky is wrong, Katz is right and there are genuine linguistic phenomena that are not ultimately biological. The view is, after all, not unknown to historians. Among architectural historians there exists a tradition influenced by Martin Heidegger and initiated by Christian Norberg-Schulz that claims to analyze and study "the meanings of buildings" whereby these "meanings" are understood to pre-exist architectural works (and possibly humans in general) and are merely discovered by architects.[15] The question of whether languages (or the meanings of words) can be something more than the biological phenomena could have significant implications for history-writing. Later in this chapter we shall consider the two well-known arguments that deny the mentalist perspective on languages. For a historian or a philosopher of history it will be important to notice that they result in anachronistic attributions of beliefs to historical figures. But before proceeding, it is useful to remind here of the complications that arise in historical research from the view that meanings exist independently of the mental states of individuals.

Let us assume that there are indeed linguistic or philosophical reasons that require the introduction of linguistic structures as abstract, immaterial, phenomena over and above the mental states of individuals. Nevertheless, the relevant *de verbis* beliefs will have to be instantiated in individuals' minds in order to enable their communication. Even if meanings existed independently of individuals' minds, individuals could communicate only on the basis of their beliefs about the use of words. It is consequently not clear that a historian needs to postulate anything more beyond the contents of mental states in order to describe and explain their communication.

At the same time, the meanings and the thought-contents that people express using words are not merely in their minds waiting to be expressed. These thoughts influence and motivate their actions and historians often rely on the statements of historical figures in order to explain why they acted the way they did. A theory that takes the meanings of words and sentences to be abstract entities that exist separately from the minds of individuals needs to explain the relationship between, for instance, a person's statement that he or she intends to act in a certain way and the subsequent action. If a person says that he or she intends do something and why, and one takes the meaning of that statement to be an abstract entity separate from the mind of that person, then when the person does what he or she said he or she would do, we cannot take the statement as an expression of the motivation for the action. In order to motivate the person, it would have to have been a mental state. If one says that the historical figure thought the thought whose content was the abstract entity expressed by the sentence, one needs to explain the nature of this relationship between the abstract entity which is the content of the thought and the subsequent action. How can a thought-content that is a causally inert abstract entity, and not instantiated in the neuro-system of the individual, still make the neurons of that individual perform physical actions in accordance with that thought-content? Vice versa, it is not clear why one needs the abstract entity at all, if one can say that people have thoughts, that these thoughts have contents and that contents motivate their actions.

Consider Stalin's speech in the Central Committee of the Bolshevik party on 3 March 1937. In Soviet history 1937 is known as the year of the Great Purge. As Stalin's biographer put it, this speech concluded a nine-days session of the Central Committee during which, under Stalin's guidance, the country's top communists discussed and planned the logistics of their own liquidation.[16] In the speech Stalin pointed out that wrecking and activities of foreign spies, that hurt all Soviet institutions, have been enabled by the carelessness, indifference and naiveté of the Central Committee members present in the meeting. The demand that he then stated—that every Party official needed to find two young assistants and teach them in his job—

clearly implied, as the biographer observed "that Stalin planned to liquidate two-thirds of the Party apparatus, an assessment which events were to show to have been on the conservative side."[17] A historian may have good reasons to explain the horrors of the Great Purge by Stalin's beliefs that he expressed at the meeting—but this explanation can only be formulated if the meanings of his words were somehow present in his mind; if they were not, and if they were abstract immaterial contents that exist on their own in a way comparable to Platonic Forms, then his decisions to act had to be separated from the meanings of his words in a way that prevents this kind of explanation.

EXTERNALISM

Externalism about mental contents is the view that contents instantiated in the minds of individuals are not enough to determine the meanings of words and sentences they use and that consequently meanings of verbal acts have to be external to the minds of people who make them. The view became very influential as a result of two arguments in its favor formulated in the 1970s by Hilary Putnam and Tyler Burge.[18] Putnam's and Burge's attack was directed against the view that an individual's understanding of terms determines the meanings that the terms he or she is using; they strove to show that it is rather the wider social context that determines meanings.[19] Their arguments have generated a huge literature and it is important to describe here why they have to be rejected—otherwise materialism in general, and not only in relation to history would not be credible. It is also important to describe here the implications of these arguments for historical research as well as the methodological problems that externalism generates.

Putnam's aim was to show that the meanings of words must be independent of the mental states of the individuals who use these words. His Twin Earth argument pertains to an imaginary planet that replicates in the smallest details our Earth. Every person on Earth has an identical twin sharing the same thoughts on Twin Earth. The only difference is that water on Twin Earth is not H_2O but some complicated substance XYZ. This substance looks like and has the same properties as our water. It can be distinguished from our water only in a laboratory. Since Twinearthians speak the same languages as we do, they call XYZ "water." If our spaceship today visited Twin Earth it would report that "On Twin Earth the word 'water' means XYZ" while if a Twin-Earthian spaceship visited Earth, it would report: "On Earth the word 'water' means H_2O." The situation is unproblematic, since the inhabitants of the two planets call two different substances "water." However, in 1750, when the chemical structure of the substance called "water" was unknown on both planets, two identical speakers on the two planets would have had completely identical beliefs about "water." At the same time, Putnam claims, the extension of "water" at that time on Earth was H_2O as much as today and XYZ on Twin Earth. Consequently, he says, two identical twins on the two planets "understood the term "water" differently in 1750 *although they were in the same psychological state*." It follows that the extension of the term "water" "is *not* a function of the psychological state of the speaker by itself." And if extension is different, while the thought contents are identical, it follows that their mental state does not determine extension of a term—meanings cannot be in the head, Putnam concludes.

Burge's argument has similar implications as Putnam's. Burge formulated it as part of a wider collectivist project that aimed to show that social cooperation *determines* (not merely influences) what an individual thinks.[20] Burge imagines a patient who has a number of correct beliefs about arthritis, but also thinks that he has developed arthritis in the thigh. He reports this to the doctor who responds that this is impossible, since arthritis is specifically an inflammation of joints. The patient, says Burge, "relinquishes his view and goes on to ask what might be wrong with his thigh."[21] Burge then considers an imaginary situation in which the same patient, with the same pains, social and phenomenal experience lives in a community in which the word "arthritis" is taken to apply to various rheumatoid ailments, including both what we call arthritis and the one on the patient's thigh.[22] In this counterfactual situation the word "arthritis" does not mean the same as what we call *arthritis*.[23] Assume that no other word in the patient's vocabulary means "arthritis." Then, if we attribute to the counterfactual patient belief-contents using the word "arthritis," our attributions "would not constitute attributions of the same contents that we actually attribute. However we describe the patient's attitudes . . . it will not be with a term or phrase extensionally equivalent with 'arthritis.'"[24] Burge infers that the two patients' mental contents differ in accordance with the languages of their communities while their mental histories, internal qualitative experiences and physiological states remain the same. It may be interesting to compare Burge's account of the beliefs of the patient who suffers from arthritis with Latour's view that it is anachronistic to assume that Ramses II died of tuberculosis because Koch's bacillus was discovered only in 1882.[25] Since "discovered" for Latour means the same as "invented, or made up, or socially constructed" one can say that the bacillus was in the Pharaoh body all along only insofar as the bacillus was retrofitted by the modern scientists who examined the body.[26] For Burge, the existence of the disease in the patient is an independent fact, but beliefs about it are linguistically constructed; for Latour, the disease in the Pharaoh's body itself is a modern social construct.

Putnam's and Burge's arguments suggest the view that individuals have thoughts, these thoughts have contents but these contents do not fix the extension, that what these thoughts pertain to. This extension can be fixed only by taking into account the collective socio-linguistic body to which the speaker belongs. The arguments rely on the assumption that languages are social phenomena and that consequently the meanings of words are socially determined. This assumption is used in order to oppose the intuition that human minds are biological phenomena and that what people mean ultimately must result from the biology of their brains. In the Introduction of this book it was assumed that different mental states entail different brain states. Both Putnam and Burge argue the opposite. A person on Earth and his or her twin on twin Earth are identical molecule-for-molecule but they understood the term "water" differently, on Putnam's account. The suggestion is that they can differ mentally, while being identical at the molecular level. Consequently, one might be tempted to reject externalism by pointing out that it is biologically impossible for meanings to exist outside human brains—that "there is nowhere else for them to be," as Searle put it.[27] Nevertheless, dismissing externalism because of its incompatibility with the materialist worldview is not a straightforward matter. Jerry Fodor extensively elaborated this line of counter-argument.[28] His discussion pressed the problem that would be a major concern for a historian (as we have seen on the example about Stalin's speech): if externalism is true, and meanings exist independently of brain states that control the actions of individuals, then how can mental states such as beliefs or desires cause behavior? Insofar as the contents of individuals' beliefs and desires are external to individuals' minds and belong to the socio-linguistic context, it is hard to see how they can contribute to individuals' decisions to act. The argument is convincing from the point of view that assumes the validity of the materialist perspective on the human mind—but its weak side is that psychologists actually still know very little about the way mental states, such as beliefs and desires, are generated by the states of the brain. As Tim Crane pointed out in his discussion of externalism, the scientific explanation of the contents of human thoughts "is as yet waiting on its wings."[29] The proponents of externalism may thus respond that such explanation may still eventually rely on externalist terms. This was indeed the line of Burge's response to Fodor: it is merely a metaphysical conjecture, he said, that none of an individual's beliefs or desires could not have been different unless his or her brain states were different.[30] The question of whether materialism is the correct metaphysical view of the mind "depends on among other things *exactly* what the relations are between thoughts are the underlying physical material."[31]

Externalism about mental contents is thus not compatible with the materialist perspective on historical research that is discussed in this book. It is, however, useful to point out that it has significant and complex implications for historical research. At least since Descartes, it has been commonly assumed that our experience of the world (and consequently the beliefs we have about it) could be the same even if the world were (in fact) quite different. Traditional examples of such situations are hallucinations and dreams; since recently, computer-generated virtual reality has provided ample support for this kind of view. In theory, one can imagine that a brain in the vat, fed externally with information in a way that replaces senses, could believe to be in an imaginary world and have beliefs and desires about objects in that world that are the same as a brain in the real world. Burge and Putnam deny this. In particular, their view implies that although a brain-in-the-real-world and a brain-in-the-vat may share the same brain states, the thoughts they have and the meanings of their words will be different. Brain states, on their account, are not enough to determine the contents of thoughts. A copy of Stalin's brain kept in the vat could have the same brain states but different thoughts and no murderous intentions. The problem that Fodor pointed out is that, from the psychological point of view, it is these same brain states that cause physical action—in other words, it is because of these same brain states that Stalin performed specific physical actions such as signing execution orders. But if mental states are not translatable into brain states because two brains can be in the same brain state without being in the same mental state (such as beliefs), then it follows that Stalin's brain states cannot explain why he signed execution orders. For Burge, materialism is merely an assumption and not an established fact, and consequently the same applies to the view that socio-linguistic context cannot affect (or cause) physical actions of individuals (such as rising a hand or signing an execution order) independently of their brain states. In other words, if the meanings of Stalin's words had not been "in his head" or if the meanings that he had were not ultimately his brain states (for instance, if he could have had the same brain states while having different and less murderous thoughts) then either what he said in his speech cannot contribute to the explanation of his actions, or these external meanings could have caused him to act in some way that is independent of the material causation that the mind uses in order to make body act the way it wants it to act. In the latter case we have to assume that physical actions performed by individuals' bodies can be caused by the social environment in a way that is incompatible with the principle of causal closure. Burge actually related his views to the Hegelian tradition—and indeed, on his account the social environment becomes a force that can act via immaterial causation in a way that hardly differs from divine causation, providence, *Geist* or some other similar models of historical explanation.

EXTERNALISM AND *DE VERBIS* BELIEFS: A RESPONSE TO BURGE

If they are endorsed, Putnam's and Burge's arguments have wide reaching counterintuitive implications for the understanding and interpretation of historical texts and statements—and it is therefore important to see how they can be responded to. A good way to start is to consider the understanding of language on which Putnam and Burge relied in their arguments. Very early in the history of the debate their assumptions about what counts as a linguistic community were challenged. As Eddy Zemach put it, if Twin-Earthians speak English, then their view that "water" is XYZ is as valid as the Earthian belief that it is H_2O.[32] Water is then neither H_2O nor XYZ, but both (H_2O or XYZ)—and consequently the extension of "water" on Earth and Twin Earth is identical. Consider a similar situation with the English word "plunger." In most English dialects it names a device that consists of a stick and a rubber cup and is used to clear blocked pipes by means of suction. In New Zealand and Australia, however, this word also refers to a device used to make coffee—called *cafetière* or "French press" in some other English dialects. The response is then that Twin-Earthians talk about XYZ when they talk about "water" in their English dialect, the way New Zealanders talk about a device one makes coffee with when they talk about "plunger." In that case one cannot accept Putnam's claim that "water" had a different extension in Earth English and Twin-Earth English: the extension is the same and it includes both H_2O and XYZ. Consider what happens if a person who speaks Earth English arrives to Twin Earth and talks about "water." Is he or she talking about H_2O or XYZ? Some authors have suggested that because the visitor arrived from Earth, when he or she says "this is water" about a puddle of XYZ, this is false.[33] It is not clear why this should be the case. The situation depends on *de verbis* beliefs involved in making the statement. He or she may actually mean XYZ and use the word "water" because of his true *de verbis* belief that "water" is the right word to talk about XYZ to the locals. (A New Zealander who comes to a London shop and asks to buy a "plunger" "to make coffee with" will have some explaining to do. But if he or she relies on the *de verbis* belief that the right term to use when speaking with locals is *cafetière*, he or she may use that word in order to avoid misunderstandings.)

More generally, the introduction of *de verbis* beliefs into consideration changes the perspective on Putnam's and Burge's arguments. In Burge's example problems pertaining to the meaning of the word "arthritis" can be avoided if one reports both the patient's belief about his or her medical state and his or her *de verbis* belief about the word. The correct report is "the patient believes to have a medical state that he believes is called arthritis." We have seen that Burge compares two types of situations. In the first, when the patient is in a community in which arthritis is located in joints, this belief is false; in the second community, where "arthritis" means "any kind of rheumatoid ailment" it is true. What is true or false, however, are the patient's *de verbis* beliefs, not beliefs about the illness. The beliefs that the patient has about his or her illness, independently of his or *de verbis* beliefs coincide. Tim Crane made a response of this kind.[34] As he put it, "For beliefs to be expressed in words, they have to go via second order beliefs about which words are the right ones . . . sentences do not, as it were just 'squirt out' beliefs."[35] Let us assume that the term *tharthritis* pertains both to arthritis and whatever ailment the patient in the example has in his thigh. In the situation described in Burge's article, in both cases the patient actually thinks that he has *tharthritis*. In the context of our linguistic community, the patient also has the false belief that the word arthritis expresses the concept that we would express using the word *thartritis* while in the counterfactual community his or her belief about the term "arthritis" is true.

Burge's response to this line of argument illustrates the problems that arise when one attempts to describe how people use language while disregarding the assumptions that people make about the use of language. He actually admits that there are numerous situations in which we reinterpret or discount what people say when establishing what they think. (These would be obviously the situations when we recognize that what people say is based on false *de verbis* beliefs.) A non-native speaker may misuse a word; a person's deviance in the use of words may derive from speaking a regional dialect. In the latter case, regional standards are to be taken as relevant for attributing the content; reinterpretation is also necessary in the case of tongue slips and Spoonerisms, Burge admits.[36] If a person thinks that "orangutan" is the name of a fruit drink, one would be still reluctant, "and it would be unquestionably misleading" to take the person's words as revealing that he drinks orangutans for breakfast.[37] However, Burge then tries to differentiate between the cases in which reinterpretation is standard and those in which it is not. In his view, when a generally competent native speaker mistakenly uses a word in non-standard way, we should not try to re-interpret his or her statement in order to understand the belief that it was meant to express—rather, we should attribute to him or her the belief indicated by the statement, even though this statement may be based on a genuine ignorance about the proper use of a certain word. Burge actually insists that "It does not follow from the assumption that the subject thought that a word means something that it does not (or misapplies the word, or is disposed to misexplain its meaning) that the word cannot be used in literally describing his mental contents."[38] The response here has to be that this is simply not how communication works. People think and then they express their thoughts; if they choose the wrong word their audience will misunderstand what they mean. It is certainly a duty of participants in communication to choose the words that will not be misunderstood, but people can do this only on the basis of their *de verbis* beliefs. It may be their responsibility to have true *de verbis* beliefs, but they can act only on the basis of the *de verbis* beliefs they have. The content of their thoughts is such as it is; if we attribute them the content that we infer from what they say then it may not be our fault that we do misunderstand them, but we will still misunderstand them. The thought-contents that we attribute to people on the basis of their words will be false and will not be able to explain their actions—a problem that, as we have seen, can be a major concern for a historian. The second of the two problems, pertaining to the intended non-standard use of words (as we have seen in the case of Aristotle) also applies: on Burge's approach, that assumes that meanings of words are those shared by the community, when reading Aristotle in Greek one would have to impose the standard meanings of words on the text even when one can obviously see that Aristotle intentionally changed the meaning of words and used them as technical terms.

EXTERNALISM AND *DE VERBIS* BELIEFS: A RESPONSE TO PUTNAM

When Putnam's Twin Earth argument is considered in the context of historical research it generates a different kind of problem. The argument fundamentally relies on the assumption that English language (both on Earth and on Twin Earth) has not changed for the past two hundred years. Because they belong to the same linguistic community, Putnam assumes, Earthian English speakers' statements about "water" from 1750 and 1950 equally refer to H_2O, even if the former are not aware of that (meanings are not in the head). The same way, statements of Twin Earthian English speakers about "water" from 1750 and 1950 refer to XYZ. Without this assumption the argument does not work. If it is recognized that in 1750 "water" for both Earthian and Twin-Earthian English speakers referred to transparent and odorless fluid substance that seas and lakes are made of, then the word had the same meaning and the same extension for them (approximately H_2O or XYZ or anything else sufficiently similar). The meanings that they had in their heads then determined the extension of the word "water" as they used it.

In other words, the core problem of Putnam's argument is anachronism—the assumption that English language has not changed for two centuries and that English speakers two centuries apart constitute the same linguistic community. In fact, the two linguistic communities are constituted by very similar clusters of *de verbis* beliefs, but nevertheless, many words have in the meantime come to express different concepts and their extension has changed. For instance, in the meantime English speakers on Earth have acquired the *de verbis* belief that for something to be called "water" it has to be H_2O which they did not have two hundred years ago. Twin Earth English speakers have acquired the corresponding belief about XYZ. In the 1750s Earthians and Twin-Earthians did not know the chemical structure of water and could not differentiate between two substances that are abundant on their planets. They would have conceptualized (classified) H_2O and XYZ the same way and the mental states that constitute their conceptualizations would have been identical in identical Earth/Twin Earth twins. Both twins would have used the word "water" to express the concept and to refer to the respective substances. Anything that satisfied the classificatory criteria of the concept would have counted as "water" (H_2O or XYZ, as Zemach stated). But subsequent scientific developments have changed the meaning and the extension of the term "water" which is nowadays used to express the concept that includes, in its classificatory criteria "being H_2O" on Earth and "being XYZ" on Twin Earth. In other words, in the meantime the two dialects diverged.

Putnam's argument is thus a fine example of differences in intuitions between historians and analytic philosophers. The assumption that the meanings and the reference of words have not changed through history is going to be highly counterintuitive for a historian: it can be made only if one rejects the established results of historical linguistics as well as Koselleck-style *Begriffsgeschichte*. It should be mentioned that the dilemma here does not pertain to reference realism, understood as the view that entities such as (that what we call) gold, water, gravity and so on have remained the same through history. This should be beyond doubt. However, through history things have been classified differently over time, some classificatory criteria were omitted from and others added to the concepts that words expressed and the same words came to express new concepts. As a result, the pool of substances that satisfy the classificatory criteria of these new concepts also changed, as well as the relata of the terms that express them. This account is precisely what Putnam cannot accept, because in that case the mental states of twins on Earth and Twin Earth in 1750 would have been the same as a result of their identical brain states, and they would have understood the term "water" the same way, unlike modern twins. Putnam actually insisted that "the meaning of the word 'water' [i.e., our modern meaning] existed even *before* chemistry was developed on either Earth or on Twin Earth (say, in 1750); it is just that in 1750 neither community knew the chemical nature of the substance each called 'water.'"[39] Similar statements were made by a number of analytic philosophers who wrote about the Twin Earth argument. D. H. Mellor agreed that "'water' had tenselessly the same extension in 1750 and 1950."[40] He also denied that at either time the extension was different on Earth and on Twin Earth. Kim Sterelny similarly stated that "there is not reason to think" that it could have happened that the reference of "water" changed from 1750 to 1950 as a result of the discovery of the chemical structure of water.[41] Stephen Schwartz put the same thought into much stronger words—in his view: "Nobody who is not in the grip of a theory would not imagine that the word "gold" changed its meaning when chemists discovered the atomic structure of gold."[42] But, it may be pointed out that the "theory" Schwartz is talking about is the well-established discipline of historical semantics. The historian Arthur Marwick stated the opposite view in equally strong words:

> ... in all uses of language we encounter changes and shifts of meaning. Only the stupid and the bigoted insist that each word must have one meaning and one meaning only, that is the meaning defined by them. What we have to do in a serious study is to understand how words shift in meaning, and always be clear which particular meaning is being used at which particular time. [43]

Admittedly, historians' methodologies may differ, but few will deny that it is simply bad methodology to assume that statements made by speakers of English in the past should be always taken to mean or to refer to what they mean or refer to in modern English. This would imply that when Newton wrote about gravitation, a historian of science is to understand his statements according to the modern, post-Einstein meaning of the term. Aviezer Tucker similarly warned against the danger that arises when historians are not aware

> that words can have different meanings in different contexts and therefore assumed that other historians were using words in the same way as they were, and therefore were offering explanations that appeared implausible to them. [44]

The next chapter will further analyze the problems that arise when Putnam's position is applied to translation and the understanding of historical texts.

NOTES

1. See the historical account in Searle, *Rediscovery*, 1–26.
2. See Neander, "Naturalistic Theories" and S. C. Wheeler, "Indeterminacy," 91–92.
3. Carroll, *Through the Looking Glass*, 81.
4. Donnellan, "Reference."
5. Locke, *An Essay*, 324. See similarly Davidson, "Structure and Content," 311: "What matters to successful linguistic communication is the intention of the speaker to be interpreted in a certain way, on the one hand, and the actual interpretation of speaker's words along the intended lines through the interpreter's recognition of speaker's intentions, on the other." See also Fodor, *Language of Thought*, 103–109. We shall also see later in this chapter that Tim Crane relied on these assumptions in his refutation of Tyler Burge's argument about externalism.
6. Stern, "Figurative Language," 170.
7. For a summary of these works see Dekker, "Presupposition." See also Karttunen, "Presuppositions of Compound Sentences," Karttunen, "Presuppositions: What Went Wrong," Stalnaker, "Presuppositions," and Stalnaker, *Context and Content*, 47–62. Presuppositions are the propositions that an author takes for granted, assumes that the audience does the same, and that need to be taken for granted in order to make sense of a linguistic act. (It has been debated how this "taking for granted" is to be understood and whether it is to be understood as a belief.) Although presuppositions discussed in literature typically do not pertain to the beliefs about the words that are used in communication, we shall see later that this view has its advantages. (See Gray, "Name Bearing.") Also, the existing literature concentrates on the presuppositions that are shared by the author and the audience; later in this book we shall have to consider more complex situations that arise, for instance, when a historian or a translator needs to grasp that communication and convey it to his or her audience.
8. Tacitus, *Annales*, 1.2.
9. Gauker, *Thinking*, 289.
10. For the ontology of language see McDonald, "Linguistics" and Pateman, *Language and Mind*, 41–80, esp. 54–56 for the nominalist perspective. Pateman describes this position as the view that languages are names—presumably, in the sense that they are joint names for certain types of mental states, such as *de verbis* beliefs. He describes the view as "uncontroversial in the extreme." Ibid., 54. "It is also a view which attracts linguists whose focus of interest is the individual idiolect, or mentally represented grammars, and all linguists in so far as they see that no two speakers are ever linguistic twins: there are always differences in their idiolects or mentally represented grammars." Ibid., 54. The view is compatible with Chomsky's description of "I-language" as "some element of the mind of the person who knows the language, acquired by the learner, and used by the speaker-hearer." Chomsky, *Knowledge of Language*, 22.
11. Chomsky, *Knowledge of Language*, 18.
12. This is a standard formulation, see for instance Davis, "Foundational Issues," 19.
13. See Katz, *Language*. This would be the position, for instance, that English language is an abstract object, whereby speakers who use it have partial and imperfect knowledge of it. For Chomsky, on the contrary, that what is individuated as a language (e.g., English or Latin) is not linguistically definable, but merely a sociopolitical fact. See the discussion in Pateman, *Language and Mind*, 49–54.
14. Chomsky, *Knowledge of Language*, 33.
15. Norberg-Schulz, *Mellom jord og himmel*, 110.
16. Ulam, *Stalin*, 429–430.
17. Ibid., 430.
18. Putnam, "Meaning and Reference." Putnam, "The Meaning of 'Meaning.'" Burge, "Individualism and the Mental."
19. See Putnam, "Introduction." Putnam says that his article was directed against the traditional view that an individual can, in principle, grasp any concept whatsoever, and that "the individual's grasp of his or her concepts totally determines the extension of all individual's terms." He wanted to argue that "knowledge of meanings is not something that is possible for a thinker in isolation."

20. Burge, "Individualism and the Mental."
21. Ibid., 77.
22. Ibid., 78.
23. Ibid., 79.
24. Ibid., 79.
25. Latour, "Partial Existence," 248.
26. Ibid, 248, 266.
27. Searle, *Intentionality*, 200.
28. For Fodor's wider position see his "Methodological Solipsism." For his contributions to the debate see Fodor, *Psychosemantics*, 27–54 and Fodor, "A Modal Argument." For the subsequent development of these arguments see Dretske, "Burge."
29. Crane, "All the Difference."
30. Burge, "Individualism and Psychology," 17.
31. Burge, "Epiphenomenalism," 402.
32. Zemach, "Putnam's Theory."
33. Fodor, *Psychosemantics*, 36.
34. Crane, "All the Difference."
35. Ibid., 18.
36. Ibid., 90.
37. Ibid., 91.
38. Ibid., 101.
39. Putnam, "Introduction," xvi.
40. Mellor, "Natural Kinds," 71.
41. Sterelny, "Natural-Kind Terms," 100.
42. Schwartz, "General Terms," 278.
43. Marwick, *The Nature of History*, 276.
44. Tucker, "Historical Counterfactuals," 9.

Chapter Six

Essentialism

The understanding of concepts as clusters of classificatory criteria implies that one and the same item can be classified in different ways and subsumed under different concepts. Similarly, different descriptions can identify an object with equal precision and in such situations we have no grounds to say that some description is more important than others, that it states the essence of the object, its nature, that what the object really is. Various items have various properties and people can classify and identify them sometimes with equal precision according to various classificatory criteria, depending on the situation, practical needs or what one knows about them. Historically, materialism has been associated with anti-essentialist positions and the rejection of Aristotelian essentialism during the scientific revolution of the seventeenth century was one of the crucial steps in the formulation of the modern materialist worldview. It is, in fact, hard to imagine how materialism could be squared with essentialism, since if all properties of things result from particles in the fields of force, then one description of these particles should be as good as any other as long as they are all equally precise and accurate. Nevertheless, since the 1970s essentialism has been widely endorsed by many analytic philosophers as a result of the influence of Saul Kripke's work. The arguments in favor or against essentialism formulated in analytic philosophy have important implications for the methodology of historical research, since essentialism is notorious as a breeding ground for anachronistic attributions of beliefs to historical figures. An approach to historical research that is careful about avoiding anachronism will thus seek to avoid essentialism, and may thus seem necessarily aligned with materialism. Finally, the need to avoid reference understood as an immaterial, abstract relationship results in problems when it comes to the use of names (including, for instance, the names of historical figures and localities) and the final section of the chapter presents a treatment based on *de verbis* beliefs.

ESSENTIALISM

Essentialism is the view that among many different, equally precise, descriptions of an item one states its real, true, essential nature and that the definition of the item should state this nature. (A definition is understood as a verbal specification of the concept's classificatory criteria.[1]) The opposite view, anti-essentialism, assumes that since one and the same item can be identified with equal precision on the basis of different sets of its properties, there is no reason to give priority to any of these sets. In other words, there are no grounds to regard any of these sets as "essential," and no description (definition) should be privileged over others. Consequently one cannot talk about the concept or the definition of something but only about a concept or a definition. Gold, for instance, can be identified with equal precision as "the chemical element with atomic number 79" or "the only metal that melts at 1063°C" or "The metal that Francisco Pizarro desired the most." All these descriptions identify gold with equal precision, but the proponents of essentialism will claim that one of them (typically, the first one) expresses the real nature of gold. Their opponents' view will be that it is impossible to state criteria that would justify the preference for one among numerous possible equally precise definitions. While the first definition of gold relies on physical facts about gold that have been more recently discovered by science, it does not necessarily get us very far when it comes to specific historical explanations: when explaining why the Inca king Atahualpa despoiled Inca temples of gold we have to rely on the third description.

Essentialism has a long history. Famously, Aristotle and his followers believed that each thing has its own proper nature, essence, the that-what-it-is-to-be-that-thing and that to have the concept of a thing is to know what it is, to know its nature. This means that there can only be one *proper* concept of each thing pertaining to its real nature, that what that thing is, and that there can be only one definition expressing it (though they may be in different languages). The descriptions "animal endowed with reason" or "animal able to laugh" or "featherless biped" differentiate human beings equally well from all other species, but, the argument goes, only the first states the human essence. As mentioned, the rejection of Aristotelian essentialism was one of crucial steps in the formulation of modern scientific worldview. This entailed the understanding that natural phenomena result from interactions between minuscule particles (such as atoms) and not from some superior force (such as essence) that imposes properties on lumps of property-free matter. Modern science does not rely on essences in its explanations of the world; it seeks to explain the properties of things as consisting of atoms and molecules. According to Aristotle, the essence of a dog ensures that a puppy does not grow into a cat, but this top-down explanation is not a credible scientific explanation today—rather, it is understood that it is the biochemical processes that derive from the puppy's DNA that make it grow into a dog. While a dog's DNA may be decisive when it comes to the dog's properties, it seems hard to say that the knowledge of the DNA of a dog is necessary in order to have the concept of a dog—most people arguably have the concept of a dog without knowing its DNA.[2] All this is likely to predispose a materialist historian or a philosopher of history to reject essentialism.

Essentialist perspectives become even less credible when one considers their implications for historical research. The central problem for any attempt to introduce essences into theoretical discussions is to find a way to determine which descriptions of objects and phenomena should count as essential. Even if one relies on the Aristotelian (or a similar) worldview, in the case of history-writing it remains unclear how to decide what might be the essence of the Thirty Years War or the Council of Trent. Without metaphysics that can explain why some identifying descriptions are more essential than others, the introduction of essentialism in historical research easily ends up in arbitrary claims. Here are some examples.[3] Alexandre Koyré noted that Galileo's mathematical description of the free fall of bodies relied on and mathematically articulated the concept of inertial mass.[4] It is, however, commonly assumed that inertial mass was conceptualized[5] much later. Galileo certainly knew nothing about the ways inertial mass would be conceived of by Newton or Einstein. Can we then say that he conceptualized inertial mass merely because his equations clearly identified this property of physical objects? Should we not say that such attribution is inappropriate because theoretical concepts are articulated in relation to other concepts within a theory and Galileo could not have had access to the knowledge that is necessary to formulate modern theories of inertial mass.[6] Here is another similar dilemma. Carl Wilhelm Scheele in 1772 and Joseph Pristley in 1774 separated oxygen through a chemical process; Pristley regarded it as common air. It was only Lavoisier in 1777 who conceptualized the gas as one of the constituents of the atmosphere. Now, the question is, who discovered oxygen—Scheele, Pristley or Lavoisier? Similarly, between 1690 and 1781 numerous European astronomers observed Uranus and thought that it was a star. In 1781, Herschel, who was using a stronger telescope, observed its disk, and some months later he established that its orbit was that of a planet. Again, the question is, who discovered Uranus—the early astronomers who individuated it as a heavenly body or Herschel who first classified it as a planet? If we say that it was Herschel, do we have to say that pre-Copernican astronomers did not have the concepts of the planets Venus, Mars or Jupiter because they inaccurately conceived of them as bodies that revolve around the Earth and not around the Sun?

The *non-essentialist* response to these dilemmas is straightforward. This view, we have seen, assumes that one can have only a concept but not the concept of something, and that consequently no historical figure ever had the concept of inertial mass or any other thing or phenomenon. It follows that Galileo had a concept of inertial mass insofar as he found one way to identify and clearly single out this property of material objects. Of course, he did not have the Newtonian or Einsteinian concepts of inertial mass and could not have known different ways to identify and define the same property discovered by physicists in later centuries. Similarly, seventeenth-century astronomers identified the heavenly body which we call Uranus but thought it was a star; they singled it out as a heavenly body with a certain position in the sky and then formed false beliefs about it. Herschel formulated a different identifying description (a new concept) of the same heavenly body. A similar reasoning applies to the discovery of oxygen. The *essentialist* position, however, will be that there are singular descriptions of inertial mass, Uranus or oxygen that state their real natures and that the honor of discovery belongs to the scientist who first comprehended the item under that specific (essential) description. In history-writing, this is going to lead to problems, because it makes no sense to attribute the knowledge of modern scientific definitions to historical figures who lived in the past and yet were able to identify these items. Euclid certainly knew what a circle was, even if he did not have access to modern mathematical ways of defining it. Essentialism thus easily results in anachronism. The non-essentialist response to the essentialist view on scientific discoveries is thus going to be that it is one thing to discover a gas, a heavenly body or a property of physical bodies and something quite different to discover a new way to identify it—to discover that the gas is one of the constituents of the atmosphere, that the heavenly body is a planet or to understand inertial mass according to Newtonian or Einsteinian physics. It is fair to say that in such cases we are dealing with discoveries of new identifying descriptions of items that one already knows how to identify.

This non-essentialist perspective can be challenged by the claim that the essences of natural substances and phenomena are what modern science says they are—for instance, that a description of a dog's DNA states its essence or that by describing the atomic structure of a chemical element one states its essential description. Since the publication of Saul Kripke's *Naming and Necessity* in 1972 a particular brand of essentialism that follows this line of reasoning has been very influential among analytic philosophers. Kripke's book largely concentrated on the problem of naming and identification across so-called possible worlds—imaginary situations in which the world could have been different from the world as we know it. The idea is that the essential properties of an item are those that are necessary, in the sense that we cannot imagine that item without such a property. In other words, some properties of objects are necessary, and some are not; it is impossible to imagine a world in which things would not have their necessary properties. *Grosso modo*, Kripke's test for what is necessary (or not) is based on what can be imagined and what cannot be imagined.[7] It is possible, for instance, that there could exist a world in which Richard Nixon did not win elections and failed to become the president of the United States, so having been an American president is not a necessary property of Nixon. But, according to Kripke, it is impossible that there could be a world in which gold would not have atomic number 79, simply because gold *is* the metal that has atomic number 79. Gold could be identified with equal precision as "the metal that Pizarro desired the most," but this cannot be its essence since one can imagine a world in which Pizarro did not care about gold. Essences thus understood are not quite the same as those of the Aristotelian tradition. The latter were singular for each natural kind, while natural kinds as understood by modern sciences can have more than one necessary identifying description: gold is not only the element with atomic number 79, but also the heaviest monoisotopic element, the only metal that melts at 1063°C, the only metal whose specific weight is 19.32 times greater than the specific weight of water, and so on. In other words, gold has numerous necessary identifications that differentiate it from all other chemical elements.

Because of the discussion that follows, it is important to point out that the *names* of individuals or natural kinds (such as chemical elements or biological species) are not among their necessary characteristics. One can easily imagine that in another possible world a different language would be spoken and the word "gold" would be used to refer to mud, while "Aristotle" may be the name of Emperor Augustus. But, at the same time, as Kripke pointed out, such names are *rigid designators* in the sense that they refer *from our perspective* to the same individuals or natural kinds wherever (in whichever world) these individuals or natural kinds exist.[8] When describing a specific possible world, we do it in *our* language. If we imagine that a different language is spoken there, and that "gold" refers to mud in that world, we will still use the word "gold" to talk about the chemical element with atomic number 79. We normally present a description of a possible world in the language we speak; we do not switch to the language spoken in that world (unless we are communicating with locals and talking their language). As Kripke pointed out, when describing a possible world or a counterfactual situation in which people (including ourselves) speak differently, we are still describing that world in our language: we still use our words with their meanings and references that they have in our language.[9]

Chapter 6
ESSENTIALISM AND ANACHRONISM

Essentialism in the form that Kripke presents it is unlikely to be controversial for a historian. Nevertheless, one needs to be careful because in some formulations it can easily lead into anachronistic perspectives. Putnam's analysis of Archimedes's use of the Greek word for gold, χρυσός, shows what happens when essentialism is combined with the belief that words are translated between languages straightforwardly and one-for-one. In most cases, what Greeks called χρυσός is what we would call "gold." Nevertheless, the techniques that ancient Greeks used to identify gold were not technologically as advanced as ours and it may have happened that some items that passed Archimedes's test for χρυσός would not count as "gold" for us today. In Putnam's view:

> when Archimedes asserted that something was gold (χρυσός) he was not just saying that it had the superficial characteristics of gold . . . ; he was saying that it had the same general *hidden structure* (the same "essence" so to speak) as any normal piece of local gold.[10]

This "essence" Putnam says, can only be our modern understanding of gold.[11] In the case of a piece of metal that does not pass our modern tests for gold, Archimedes would have said that it was χρυσός, but he would have been wrong. Putnam claims that:

> If, now, we had gone on to inform Archimedes that gold had such and such a molecular structure . . . and that X behaved differently because it had a different molecular structure, is there any doubt that he would have agreed with us that X isn't gold?[12]

But the response is that this may be so, if he spoke modern English with Archimedes and Archimedes was learning how to use the word "gold." If they talked in Greek, Archimedes could point out that χρυσός is a shiny yellow material that has certain specific weight, while according to this latest theory they are explaining to him, in most cases it has a certain molecular structure. Presumably, the reason why Putnam thinks that χρυσός is "gold" is that dictionaries say so. This suggests the view that Greek words did not have their meanings because ancient Greeks used them the way they used them, whereby our modern dictionaries strive to convey that usage the best they can. Rather, Greek words had their meanings and reference in ancient times because our modern Greek-English dictionaries happen to define that meaning and reference in a certain way. As a result, the meanings of Greek words are independent of any thoughts or beliefs ancient Greeks might have had. (This clearly aligns with Putnam's view that meanings are not "in the head," as discussed in the previous chapter.) Consider the English sentence "this is gold," which is the standard translation of the Greek sentence "οὗτος ἐστί χρυσός." As mentioned, Archimedes might have said this about a piece of metal that satisfied his tests for χρυσός while the same metal would not be gold by our modern standards. Putnam would say that the Greek sentence is false, because its English translation is false. But the response is going to be that this claim is based on a simplistic understanding of the way translation between languages works. In fact, it hardly ever happens that words in different languages can be always translated one-for-one. The fact that the English word "gold" translates into Greek as "χρυσός" in most cases, does not mean that it always does. A German may say that a soup he or she is eating is *scharf* and if we translate German "scharf" as "sharp" his or her statement will be either meaningless or false. But the statement may be perfectly true—if we consider that German "scharf" can also mean the same as English "spicy." In the case of ancient Greek "χρυσός" and modern English "gold" it is normal that there will be some discrepancies in what they refer to and a good translator will indicate such situations (e.g., in a footnote) when they occur.

Here is another way to look at the same problem. Imagine that Archimedes's tests for gold did not enable him to differentiate between the substance that is called "gold" in modern English and an alloy, call it PQR. In that case he would have used χρυσός both for gold and PQR. Putnam says that when he used χρυσός to refer to PQR his statements were false because "χρυσός" means "gold" in English. But there could exist another modern language in which the same word (e.g., RST) is used both for gold and PQR. Scientists who work in that language would differentiate between gold and PQR but use the word "RST" for both. (Something similar happens with the word "jade" in English, which is actually used to refer to two different minerals.) In that case one and the same Greek sentence that Archimedes used when he classified a piece of PQR as χρυσός would be false (because "χρυσός" translates into English as "gold") and true (because "χρυσός" translates into this other language as "RST")—which certainly cannot be the case.

Collingwood in his *Autobiography* describes a similar situation.[13] He imagines a discussion with a man who insists on translating Greek τριήρης ("trireme") as "steamship." If it is pointed out that descriptions of τριήρης by Greek authors do not fit very well a description of a steamship, the person responds: "That is just what I say. These Greek philosophers . . . were terribly muddle-headed, and their theory of steamers is all wrong." However, in Collingwood's example, if one tried to explain that τριήρης means something else and not "steamship" one could still say "trireme." But in the case of χρυσός the closest word we have is "gold." For something to be "gold" in modern English, it must have atomic number 79—but this does not mean that χρυσός necessarily had atomic number 79. When we read in a book about the Bronze Age in the Middle East that historians in the past thought that the

Assyrian word *annukum* meant "lead" while "it now it seems certain that the metal in question was tin," this certainly does not refer to lead and tin defined according to their atomic number.[14] *Annukum* could have been lead or tin only as identified within technological means available at the time. Historian's work will precisely consist, as Collingwood described for τριήρης, in careful sifting and interpretation of evidence in order to establish what substances Greeks would have classified as χρυσός. When did they, for instance, start testing specific weight in order to establish whether a substance is χρυσός? In Homer's time this kind of testing was probably not in use, which further suggests the difference between the substances that Archimedes and Homer-era Greeks would classify as χρυσός.

Putnam's description of Archimedes's beliefs strikes one as an extreme opposite of Latour's view (described earlier) that it is anachronistic to say that Ramses II died of tuberculosis. Latour expands historicity on physical facts that could not have been affected by what people knew or believed at the time; he assumes that facts such as the presence of Koch's bacillus are socially constructed. In Putnam's view, however, even beliefs of historical figures should not be analyzed in relation to their historical context—rather, on the basis of the words they used, they should be attributed beliefs according to the modern meanings of these words. It should be mentioned that Kripke (who discussed situations similar to the example about Archimedes before Putnam) presented a different account.[15] He noted that a substance often originally receives its name in a "baptism" that pertains to a sample of material. The name given to it may pertain to almost all of the given sample—"almost all" because, for instance, in the case of gold, some fools' gold may also be present. From that point on, various situations may happen: if the original sample has a small number of deviant items, they will be rejected as not really gold. On the other hand, if the supposition that there is one uniform substance or kind in the initial sample proves more radically in error, one might declare that there are two kinds of gold, or one may drop the term "gold." The reference and the meaning of the word "gold" will thus change with time. Consequently, when we deal with documents from the time before it changed, we have to take into account that the word is used differently.

CONCEPTUAL CONJUNCTIONS AND DISJUNCTIONS

One and the same item can satisfy numerous identifying descriptions and be subsumable under different concepts. If two or more concepts are satisfied by the same and only the same item(s) then we say that they are co-extensional: for instance, Venus, the Evening Star, the Morning Star and so on. When such co-extensional concepts are connected with "and" the result is a *conjunction* of concepts. (Venus *and* Morning Star *and* Evening Star *and* . . .).

One can call such concepts pleonastic concepts. Such conjunction is still a concept and its extension is the same as that of each participating concept. Vice versa, a *disjunction* of concepts is created if co-extensional concepts are connected using "or." (Venus *or* Morning Star *or* Evening Star *or* . . .). In this case too, the extension of such a concept is going to be identical with the extension of any of its participating parts.

Conjunctions of concepts are sometimes used in order to introduce essentialist assumptions in historiography by arguing that no single identifying description, but only a number of them taken together, that is, a conjunction of specific identifying descriptions, is the concept of an item. For instance, it may be argued that the way seventeenth-century astronomers identified Uranus is not enough in order to have the concept of Uranus and that it is *also* necessary to know that it is a planet and so on. Or, it may be argued that the way Galileo identified inertial mass is not enough in order to say that he operated with the concept of inertial mass, but that he also needed to have Newton's or even Einstein's understanding of this property of objects in order to be attributed the possession of the concept. The word "also" in such demands implies that the possession of a concept is the possession of more than one identifying description. This perspective on concepts brings back the standard problem with essentialism: it remains unclear which identifying descriptions are to be included in the conjunction and why. This decision is going to be arbitrary and different historians are going to adopt different conjunctions as the concepts of a specific thing. The availability of such conjunctions changes over time, which can generate anachronistic arguments. For instance, a historian who insists that "the" concept of Aristotle must include classifications such as "the tutor of Alexander the Great" and "the most famous disciple of Plato" is at the same time arguing that before Aristotle left for Athens to study under Plato, his mother did not have "the" concept of Aristotle.

One normally expects concepts to participate in propositions and inferences that are made from them. Conceptual conjunctions are poor at performing that role, and cannot replace simple concepts. Assume, for instance, that concepts are indeed conjunctions of identifying descriptions. In that case, for instance, in order to have the concept of Venus, one has to have the concept of a heavenly body that revolves around the Sun on the second closest orbit and that it is also the Evening Star and that it is also the Morning Star and so on. None of these specific identifying descriptions, the argument would be, can be said to express the concept Venus, but only all of them together. But the problem is that we do not use pleonastic clusters of identifying descriptions in order to make inferences—rather, we use the specific identifying descriptions that are suitable to make a specific inference. When we want to infer that Venus is closer to the Sun than Mars, because it is on the second while Mars is on the fourth orbit from the Sun, the fact that Venus is the

Evening Star plays no role in our reasoning. Consider what it means to say that only a pleonastic concept of inertial mass (that includes Newton's and Einstein's articulations) should properly count as *the* concept of inertial mass. Insofar as Galileo's equations identify inertial mass as a property of physical bodies in a way that enables the calculation of the time bodies need to fall, we have to say that the possession of *the* concept of inertial mass (which in that case Galileo did not have) is not necessary in order to calculate the time that bodies need to fall.

It may be suggested that the same word is used to express a number of different concepts, all of which are identifying descriptions of the same and only the same items. Words or phrases, from this point of view, often express disjunctions of co-extensional identifying descriptions in a way that makes them similar to abbreviations of such disjunctions. In order to avoid anachronism, when a historical figure uses a certain word or phrase, the cluster of concepts the word is taken to express may be assumed to contain only those concepts that were available to that historical figure in a given moment. When reading Ptolemy, we can assume that the word "Venus" expresses the concepts of "Evening Star" and "Morning Star," but not the concept "the planet that revolves around the Sun on the second closest path." Similarly, Copernicus's understanding of planets implied that their orbits around the Sun are circular and not elliptical, as we have known since Kepler. Does it mean that his concept of a planet was different from ours? We have already seen the response that there is no such a thing as the concept of a planet; there are various concepts which we express using the word "planet." Copernicus used that term to express a disjunction of concepts somewhat different from ours, and when it comes to Ptolemy his disjunction differs even more. Or, consider an imaginary debate between a medieval schoolman and a rabbi. They were certain to agree, and a historian may write that they agreed, about the sentence "God exists" but not about the sentence "Jesus is God." One way to explain their agreement in the case of the first sentence is that they both used the word "God" to express a number of identical concepts; a more complete account should certainly add that they disagreed about some descriptions of God. But if we assume that each of them used the term "God" to express the conjunction of all the concepts of God known to him (a pleonastic concept), then one could not say that they agreed about God's existence. It may thus seem unclear whether we can say that they agreed or not, although they both assented to the sentence "God exists."

THOUGHT-CONTENTS AND LANGUAGE

This example about (dis)agreements between a medieval rabbi and a schoolman indicates a wider range of problems. Such (dis)agreements are common in the case of many words. An architectural historian and a historian of literature will agree that "Renaissance happened," but the former may claim that it started with Brunelleschi's departure for Rome in 1401, the latter may insist that it started with Petrarch's ascent of Mt Ventoux in 1336. Do they actually agree about the Renaissance, considering that they possibly mean different things by what they say? Dilemmas of this kind are variations of problems well known in the philosophy of language. Once again, it is important to show here that they can be resolved without relying on reference conceived of as a non-mental, immaterial or abstract relationship between words and what they refer to.

The view that words and phrases express the concepts that the speaker has in mind is a variation of the descriptivist theory of proper names that was developed early in the twentieth century by Bertrand Russell and further refined by John Searle in the 1950s. Russell conceived of names as equivalent to or abbreviations of descriptions—for instance, "Aristotle" may stand for "Plato's most famous student" or "the author of *Metaphysics*."[16] However, different people associate different descriptions with one and the same name, and if a name merely abbreviates a single description that a person has in mind, then we will never be sure whether people agree or disagree about when they talk about Aristotle. (This will also apply to the above example about the medieval rabbi and schoolman.) Searle's solution was to argue that names do not stand for individual descriptions that a person who uses the name has in mind, but clusters of such descriptions.[17] A name then refers to any object that satisfies a sufficient but vague and unspecified number of descriptions that are associated with it. In literature, the descriptive theory of names is usually discussed in relation to names of persons—but boundaries are not clear and it is reasonable to think that it applies to words such as "God," "April" or "autumn."[18] One may also be tempted to generalize the descriptivist theory, assume that words and phrases express disjunctions (or Searle-style clusters) of concepts, whereby concepts are the sets of classificatory criteria that identify the objects that words refer to.

An alternative view of names was proposed by Kripke in the late 1970s. Kripke pointed out that when people use names they sometimes know very little or almost nothing about the individuals to whom the name refers. One can therefore not expect that they have a ready description of a person when they use his or her name. Sometimes, everything we know about a person may be wrong—for instance, it may be the case that Moses did not do the things that the Bible attributes to him. In that case no identifying description of Moses that the Bible provides us with would be true, but this would not mean that Moses did not exist—he could have existed, under that name and could have done other things in his life that we do not know about. We would still be able to identify him by his name. Finally, if names stand for, mean or abbreviate descriptions, then they should be replaceable by these descriptions in every context. But this is not the case, especially when we talk about the way events might have happened. Assume that we take that "Richard Nixon" means, stands for or abbreviates "the 37th President of the USA." Counterfactually, one can imagine that (e.g., in another possible world) he might have lost elections and that he never became a president. In other words, the sentence:

> It may have happened that Richard Nixon was not the 37th President of the USA.

is true. But if "Richard Nixon" stands for "the 37th President of the USA" then we should be able to replace this latter phrase with his name. However, we then get the false sentence:

> It may have happened that Richard Nixon was not Richard Nixon.

Kripke argued instead that things and people are given names in an original baptism and this name spreads through a chain of communication between the individuals who use the word. A person at the end of the chain may use the name even though he or she does not remember from whom he or she first heard it. He or she may know something or very little about the bearer of the name, and often not enough in order to identify him or her. Kripke's theory of names has had wide acceptance since the 1970s. It strives to replace an explanation of how names are used that is based on the speaker's thought-contents (meanings, descriptions that the speaker has in mind) with the one that relies on the reference of a name. As a result, it has to face the problems typical for reference-based theories. For instance, it cannot account of reference to non-existent entities. While Kripke's arguments against the descriptivist theory are convincing, it is not clear that reference that speakers borrow from each other on his account can be understood in materialistic terms. Since reference in that case is to be conceived of as independent of the descriptions available to individual speakers (and consequently their mental states), it seems necessary to conceive of it as some kind of abstract and immaterial relationship, existing on its own, independently of the mental states of speakers. The implication would be that when historians use names of historical figures, they cannot do it within the materialist paradigm.

There is, however, a third approach, closely aligned with the discussion of *de verbis* beliefs in Chapter Five. In recent decades philosophers of language have increasingly paid attention to a position called "metalinguistic descriptivism" that successfully avoids the problems of both descriptivism and Kripke's approach. The position is also relevant for us here because (like other descriptivist positions) it explains the use of names by relying on the mental states of language users and avoids the need to postulate reference as an abstract, immaterial relationship. Metalinguistic descriptivism is the view that the meaning of a name X is "the object (person) called X" or "the bearer of X."[19] The view implies that being named X is a property of objects like any other and can be used in descriptions that identify items that bear that name.[20] Simply, items can be classified and identified according to various properties they have, and being called a certain name is one of such properties as well. Imaginary non-existent things are then assumed to be that what is named by words such as "Pegasus," "gryphon" and so on. We can easily say that such an item does not exist and still not confuse it with other non-existent things that are identified on the basis of their own names. The approach is applicable not only to names. Saying that items called "vampires" do not exist is a different thing to say from saying that the item called "phlogiston" does not exist. Metalinguistic descriptivism is also resistant to Kripke's arguments against descriptivism. Since Moses's name means "the person called Moses," this description would be enough to identify him even if everything else the Bible reports about him were false. Similarly, metalinguistic descriptivism can overcome problems that result from Kripke's modal argument (see the footnote).[21]

Metalinguistic approaches were originally rejected by both Kripke and Searle, on the basis of the argument that they do not really fix the relata of names.[22] Both Kripke and Searle argued that saying that Socrates was the person called "Socrates" does not get us very far if we want to determine the identity of the person. The response to this view is that it is the context and the use that resolve this problem. Consider a conversation in a bar: a person sits with a group of friends who are talking about someone called Phil of whom this person has never heard before. After some time, the person gets interested in conversation and asks: "And what did Phil do then?" There should be no doubt that he or she has successfully referred to Phil—though he or she may know very little about Phil and certainly not enough to identify him. What enables that this act of reference is successful is not this person's interaction with his friends as the sources from whom he learnt to use the name, for he or she could have learnt the name from other people. Rather, it is *their* capacity to perform the role as listeners. Phil is uniquely identified on the basis of his listeners' *de verbis* beliefs. In fact, one can use names without ever having learnt them from anybody: if I know how streets in Philadelphia are numbered, I can talk and successfully communicate about the "Tenth Street" even though I have never heard someone talk about it. Speakers (and authors) have to adjust the words (including names) they use to their public and they do this on the basis of their *de verbis* beliefs about their public.[23]

The metalinguistic approach is thus a way to think about the use of names in terms of *de verbis* beliefs. It avoids the need to expand ontology beyond the material world—whereas such an expansion would be necessary in the case of a reference-based account of names. When a person uses a name N (or another term) in communication and means "the bearer of N" he or she also relies on *de verbis* beliefs of his or her listeners. This is not the Humpty-Dumpty view that the word used by a speaker merely means what the speaker decides to; insofar as the user wants to communicate, the use of words must be regulated by the speaker's *de verbis* beliefs about the capacity of listeners to identify the bearer of "N." If the bearer is going to be identified, the beliefs must be true as well. In the above example, the medieval schoolman and the rabbi belong to different religious communities but to the same linguistic community. When one of them pronounces "God exists" he uses the term "God" to express a proposition about the bearer of the word "God." He makes the pronouncement on the basis of his belief that his conversation partner belongs to the same linguistic community and will identify the same bearer. Insofar as they agree, they agree about the proposition that "that-what-is-called-'God'" exists, even though they know that they disagree about the bearer of "God" in many other ways. Nevertheless, the proposition that they agree about—that God exists—is quite different from other propositions that they may also agree or disagree about: that God is creator of the Universe, that Jesus is God or others. One can agree about a single proposition without agreeing about the totality of the worldview. The factual existence of God, at the same time, is irrelevant for their agreement. What matters is that they assume that they agree about the bearer of "God."

NOTES

1. Similarly, Smith and Klein, "Concept Systems," define a definition as a " representation of a concept (as agreed meaning of a term) by a descriptive statement or a formal expression which serves to differentiate it from related concepts."

2. However, see the opposite view, advocated by Putnam and described later in this chapter. Barber, "Pleonasticity," 79, defended his theory of concept attribution from the criticism that it does not provide an account of concept mastery, by asking what concept mastery was: when it comes to the concept of a butterfly, does it include the knowledge of a butterfly's DNA structure, its evolutionary history and so on? If this were the case, then most people would not have the concept of a butterfly. His critic, Stainton, "Deflation," 71, admitted that he did not know what the mastery of a concept could be.

3. The widespread expectations to establish that a historical figure possessed the concept of something illustrate widespread and strong essentialist commitments among many historians. Gerring, "What Makes," 363, observes that saying that human beings are featherless bipeds successfully picks out humans from other species. However, he says, such a definition is not "sufficient" and that "essentialising approach to definition" is "often justified." Similarly, Davis, "Concept Individuation," 167, differentiates between the understanding of a triangle as a polygon with three sides from the understanding of a polygon whose internal angles add up to 180°. In his view, "a polygon is a triangle in virtue of the number of sides and angles it has"—in order words, he assumes that there are specific properties that make a triangle that what it is, although some other properties identify it with equal accuracy. Neither Gerring not Davis explain how to establish what these essences are and how we know that a concept is really *the* concept of something. When Gerring talks about the concept of a thing and expects definitions to be "sufficient" in a way that is more than a mere ability to identify things accurately, he does not tell us where to find a metaphysics and epistemology that will credibly perform the job—or, at the level of the pragmatics of history-writing, where to find a description of the world that will provide us with the real essences of every item historians may need to write about.

4. Koyré, "Galileo's Treatise," 61–62.

5. The term "conceptualized" is used here in order to avoid the dilemma between the use of "a concept" and "the concept" and thus prejudice the position in essentialism versus non-essentialism debate.

6. See discussion in Prudovsky, "Can We Ascribe."

7. "But if it [a statement] is true, might it have been otherwise? Is it possible that, in this respect, the world might have been different from the way it is? If the answer is 'no,' then this fact about the world is a necessary one. If the answer is 'yes,' then this fact about the world is a contingent one. This . . . has nothing to do with anyone's knowledge of anything." Kripke, *Naming*, 36. Later through the book one's capacity to imagine is said to decide what counts as necessary. For instance: "If we can't imagine a possible world in which Nixon doesn't have a certain property, then it's a necessary condition of someone being Nixon." Ibid., 46.

8. Kripke, *Naming*, 46. See similarly ibid., 126–7.

9. Kripke, *Naming*, 77.

10. Putnam, "The Meaning of Meaning," 20–25.

11. "But who's to say that he [Archimedes] would have been wrong? The obvious answer is: *we are* (using the best theory available today)." Ibid., 20.

12. Ibid., 22.

13. Collingwood, *Autobiography*, 64.

14. Bryce, *Hittites*, 27.

15. Kripke, *Naming*, 136.

16. Russell, "On Denoting." Russell, "Descriptions."

17. Searle, "Proper Names."

18. The examples are from Kripke, *Naming*, 26 and Fara, "Literal Uses," 277.

19. The view has a long history and it was even discussed by Russell. The early attempts to develop metalinguistic descriptivism go back to the 1970s, see Loar, "Semantics" and "Names and Descriptions." (The latter article is a response to Devitt, "Brian Loar"). Since the 1980s the view has been defended by Kent Bach, see Bach "What's in a Name," and Bach, "Giorgione."

For more recent treatment of the idea see Katz, "Names without Bearers," Geurts, "Good News," and Fara, "Literal Uses."

20. Note that this is view does not imply regress. Burgess, "Metalinguistic Descriptivism," 445, argued that it does, insofar as "the bearer of 'Galileo'" stands for "Galileo":

(G0) Galileo came to the party.
(G1) The bearer of "Galileo" came to the party.
(G2) The bearer of the bearer of "Galileo" came to the party.
(G3) The bearer of the bearer of the bearer of "Galileo" came to the party.

In fact, this replacement is not legitimate, "Galileo" in "the bearer of 'Galileo'" is under quotation marks and refers to the word "Galileo" and not Galileo himself.

21. It may seem that the modal argument defeats metalinguistic descriptivism. If one takes "Richard Nixon" to mean "the person called 'Richard Nixon,'" then the equivalent of the above example about the 37th President of the USA may seem to be:

Richard Nixon may not have been the person called "Richard Nixon."

This sentence is true, since he could have been baptized differently. When we then replace "the person called 'Richard Nixon'" with "Richard Nixon" we get:

Richard Nixon might not have been Richard Nixon.

This latter sentence is obviously false, which would suggest that metalinguistic descriptivism cannot resolve problems with the modal argument (since a legitimate replacement of words in makes a true sentence false). This argument is, however, not valid. As Kripke pointed out, names are rigid and to be applied the way we apply them: people or things may have had different names in the past, but when we identify them by their names we do so on the basis of the names we use. The appropriate starting sentence in the argument is thus not:

Richard Nixon might not have been the person called "Richard Nixon."

but:

Richard Nixon might not be the person we call "Richard Nixon."

Which is false, since Richard Nixon, according to Kripke, is the person we call "Richard Nixon." Then, after replacement, this false sentence gives another false sentence:

The person we call "Richard Nixon" might not be the person we call "Richard Nixon."

And the problem with Kripke's modal argument does not arise. For a detailed discussion of the modal argument in relation to metalinguistic descriptivism see Bach, "What's in a Name," 374, Loar, "Semantics," 373; Bach, "Giorgione," 84; Katz, "Names Without Bearers," 14; Bach, *Thought and Reference*, 150.

22. Kripke, *Naming*, 70. Searle, *Intentionality*, 242.

23. A similar point was originally made by Loar, "Semantics," 353 and 371 and Loar, "Names," 88. The importance of presuppositions was analyzed into detail by Gray, "Name Bearing."

Chapter Seven

Contexts and Rationality

In Chapters Two and Three we have seen the implications of materialism for the understanding of historical-social entities, forces and phenomena and the way they can be taken to affect explanations of actions of historical figures. Chapters Four, Five and Six presented the materialist perspective on the mental states of historical figures and the use of language. It is now possible to address the relationship between these two topics and analyze the impact that historical and social contexts can exercise on the contents of the mental states, and more generally on the intellectual lives of historical figures and historians themselves. The view that historical, social and cultural contexts determine or delimit (and not merely affect) the mental and intellectual capacities of historical figures, their beliefs and creativity, has a long history. The chapter discusses three problems that pertain to the role of contextualization in historical explanations and research.

First, there is the understanding that some ideas, views, beliefs and so on could not have been formulated by individuals from certain contexts because the concepts that are necessary in order to form those ideas, views or beliefs were inconceivable for them. Such claims about inconceivability can be formulated in two ways. One can point out that a concept could have been inconceivable to individuals from a certain context because in that context they could not acquired, through interactions with other individuals, the knowledge that is necessary in order to form it. Alternatively, one may simply assume that the context *qua* context had the causal power to delimit their intellectual capacities and prevent them from conceiving of certain concepts, independently of their interactions with other individuals in the same context. This latter model has been often proposed by cultural historians for the past hundred years. It attributes to historical-social contexts causal powers over the intellectual capacities of individuals that are different (or exceed) the causal impact that can be exercised through interactions with other individuals. It thus relies on variations of ontological holism that was discussed in Chapter Two. If historical claims based on the assumption that a historical-social context can have causal power over mental states of individuals independently of interactions between individuals (i.e., immaterially) can be sustained, this would suggest the necessity to expand ontology beyond the materialist perspective and its individualist implications described in Chapter Two. It is therefore important to see how such claims can be answered.

Second, there is the view, also very influential in the second half of the twentieth century, that linguistic contexts, the languages that people use in order to communicate, delimit the pool of the thoughts they can have. This is the view that all thinking is verbal and always in a language and that consequently, the capacity to have a thought does not differ from the capacity to express it in words that are available within a linguistic context. Since individuals learn languages through interactions with other individuals, there is no need to assume that this view requires the expansion of ontology beyond the individualist understanding of contexts described in Chapter Two. However, it does generate serious complications in historical research, especially when it comes to the reporting of the beliefs of historical figures who expressed them in languages different from the one in which the historian is writing. The analysis of this problem presented here prepares the discussion of understanding, interpretation and translation in Chapter Eight.

The third problem that needs to be discussed pertains to the reflexive argument. Historians are historical figures too, and if historical-social contexts determine and delimit the mental states of historical figures, they must do so with historians' mental states as well. In that case it is not clear how historians can get outside their contexts in order to understand the statements made by historical figures who inhabited contexts different than their own. Here too, the discussion relies on the consideration of the causal capacities of historical-social contexts discussed in Chapter Two. The discussion of the problem enables the analysis of the shared rationality that needs to be postulated in order to enable the assumption that historians can understand documents from contexts different than their own.

INCONCEIVABILITY

Claims about the inconceivability of certain mental contents to members of specific groups have a long history in cultural and intellectual historiography. Spengler, for instance, was the great master of this kind of argument; in his *Decline of the West* we read that the ancient Greeks and Romans were incapable of writing history beyond discussing contemporary events (he forgets about Herodotus or Livy); that a "real Russian" finds Darwin's theory incomprehensible, that a "real Arab" cannot understand the Copernican system or that the Greeks had no sense for ceremony in public life.[1] His claim that ancient Greeks could not conceive of infinity was widely repeated in the 1920s and the 1930s.[2] Another good example of a widely circulated Weimar-era thesis about inconceivability is Erwin Panofsky's erroneous claim that before the early Renaissance people could not conceive of space as a homogenous and isotropic medium.[3] Until he left Germany in 1933, Panofsky often relied on arguments about inconceivability in his writing.[4] In his 1920 article "The Concept of *Kunstwollen*" he argued that Polygnotus did not paint a naturalistic landscape because, as a result of the "necessity that predetermined his will," he could only have wanted to paint an unnaturalistic landscape.[5] The idea of the argument is that membership of a group constrains an artist, a scientist or a philosopher from creating a work that would have certain properties that are (allegedly) inconceivable within his or her historical-social context, ethnicity, class and so on. (Such claims often reflect the ideological prejudices of the historian.) The same assumption that necessity precludes the availability of certain ideas in certain eras one can find in Foucault. His theory of *épistémè* is precisely intended to enable such claims—for instance that ". . . knowledge of nature, and reflection or practices concerning money, were controlled during the Renaissance by one and the same configuration of the *episteme*."[6] Similarly, when he says that Plato replaced the ritualized act of enunciation of earlier Greek poets by introducing the division between truth and falsity, he is *de facto* claiming that the distinction between truth and falsity was inconceivable before Plato (otherwise one could not talk about Plato's "introduction" of the distinction).[7] Burge's arthritis example, discussed earlier, also implies a claim about inconceivability. The argument depends on the assumption that in the counterfactual community (where the term "arthritis" refers to rheumatic ailments in bones, and not only in joints) the patient could not have operated with our concept of arthritis. The implicit idea is that the available linguistic practice delimits individuals' conceptual frameworks and makes ideas that step out of the linguistic practice inconceivable. It is, however, not clear why this should be the case. It may be responded that the counterfactual patient could have remembered that his father's arthritis was limited to joints, noticed that this happens to many other people and formed the concept of arthritis-in-joints, equivalent to ours. Burge's argument can be made only if one assumes that the linguistic context has the causal capacity to delimit the cognitive abilities of individuals who belong to the context and makes certain ideas inconceivable to them. A collateral problem is that if the concepts available to individuals were limited only to those that could have been acquired through common linguistic practice within a certain community, then it would be hard to see how new discoveries in science or technology could ever be made; after all, things typically do not have names before they are discovered.

Claims that members of certain groups could not conceive of certain ideas easily remind of ethnic prejudices. But there is also a reasonable sense in which, for instance, Archimedes could not have conceived of quantum physics because in the context in which he lived and worked he could not have acquired the necessary knowledge or performed even the elementary experiments. There are thus situations when assumptions about the inconceivability of certain ideas, beliefs, concepts and similar in various historical, social, cultural, linguistic and so on contexts, can be useful in historical research: insofar as they are true, they enable the historian to preclude the possibility of certain explanatory approaches and chose others. Also, the term "inconceivability" can be used to justify claims that pertain to the acting of historical figures in general and not only intellectual creativity—one may thus argue that in a given situation, because of his or her membership of a specific group, a historical figure could not conceive of acting differently than he or she did.

Consider an example presented by Arthur Danto. Historians of literature sometimes state that Petrarch initiated the Renaissance when he climbed Mt. Ventoux. Petrarch's brother was with him and witnessed the ascent. Had someone asked the brother at the time whether he was aware that Petrarch was initiating the Renaissance, he would not have understood the question. Does this mean that the Renaissance was *inconceivable* to Petrarch's brother? Would he have been able to conceive of the Renaissance if the term had been explained to him as a series of future events such as numerous discoveries of ancient manuscripts, a discovery of a machine to multiply books, immense progress in the visual arts and so on, which would all lead to a profound change in European culture within the next two centuries? If we accept that Petrarch's brother could have understood this description and consequently conceived of such events, then the concept was inconceivable to him only in the sense that he lacked the necessary knowledge; had that knowledge been made available, he would have been perfectly able to conceive of the Renaissance. The alternative understanding of inconceivability would be that no amount of new information would help Petrarch's brother step out intellectually from the context he belonged to. From this point of view, membership of a group (historical or social context, era, culture, ethnicity or similar) constitutionally delimits the pool of thoughts an individual can have. Simply, some ideas are unavailable to individuals from certain groups; the group has causal powers over the cognitive capacities of individuals. In this case, the group is understood holistically, and it is assumed that individuals' cognitive capacities can be causally affected by the group *qua* group in a way that is additional to and different from the way they are affected by all their specific interactions with other individuals. One should thus differentiate between *strong* and *weak* inconceivability. *Strong inconceivability* is the assumption that individuals' capacities to form concepts and acquire beliefs are determined by the collectives they belong to, and that individuals' membership in collectives constitutes them as incapable of having beliefs inconceivable in their context. Vice versa, *weak inconceivability* is the claim that certain concepts, knowledge and information are not known to individuals who belong to certain collectives; they could be learnt, but, typically, the necessary information cannot be acquired in the given context. If we talk about inconceivability in the weak sense, then Archimedes was not able to conceive of nuclear physics because the available technology prevented ancient Greeks from making the necessary experiments; since the necessary concepts were not available to any of his individual contemporaries, he could not have acquired them. But if we say that Archimedes, because he was an ancient Greek, was constitutionally incapable to form thoughts or acquire beliefs about nuclear physics, this is a claim about strong inconceivability. In this case the collective, taken holistically, has causal powers over the cognitive capacities of participating individuals.

The dilemma between strong and weak inconceivability is a variation of the dilemma between individualist and holist understanding of historical-social items discussed in Chapter Two. Weak inconceivability is compatible with the individualist position on historical, social and cultural contexts: it assumes that the incapacity to form specific beliefs (or acquire knowledge) results from the lack of the necessary interactions with other individuals (or the physical environment). Contexts, according to this view, do not have causal or explanatory powers beyond the causation generated by actions and interactions of individuals. Strong inconceivability, however, implies the holist position that the community, the context or the group to which the individual belongs has additional causal capacities over and above the causal capacities exercised by the participating individuals and their interactions. The context or the group is assumed to cause mental incapacities in a historical figure independently of how and whether he or she interacts with other individuals (or the physical environment). Claims about strong inconceivability attribute causal capacities to social contexts independently of the individuals that make them up, interactions between individuals or the relevant physical environment.

DILEMMA BETWEEN WEAK AND STRONG INCONCEIVABILITY

The dilemma between weak and strong inconceivability has potentially significant consequences. In the case one could show that genuine cases of strong inconceivability indeed exist, this would be a clear case of holist historical-social causation. It would mean that historical-social items could produce causal impact on historical individuals independently of these individuals' interactions with other individuals and the physical environment. This would obviously ultimately present a serious challenge to the materialist perspective on history in general. It would mean that for the explanation of some historical events or some properties of historical artifacts it is necessary to postulate causally active, immaterial, abstract, or maybe even spiritual historical-social forces. An additional complication derives from the fact that whenever we can establish that certain mental contents were inconceivable to individuals in the weak sense, it is also possible to claim that these individuals were actually constitutionally incapacitated to form them. Archimedes may not have had the opportunity to acquire knowledge that would enable him to form beliefs about nuclear physics, but it is also possible to make a stronger claim that he was constitutionally incapacitated to do so. Nevertheless, historical facts that can be explained equally well by both kinds of inconceivability do not strengthen the holist's case because it can be responded that in such situations it is not clear why we need holist explanations. (It is enough to say that no single contemporary of Archimedes had the information and knowledge necessary to conceive of nuclear physics. We do not need to claim, and it is unclear how we could prove it, that it would have been impossible for any of them to conceive of nuclear physics had the necessary information and knowledge been made available.)

The outcome of the debate between the individualist and the holist perspective (and the possibility of refuting the materialist philosophy of history), hinges on the existence of cases that cannot be explained by relying on weak inconceivability, but could be explained by strong inconceivability. For the holist program to be convincing, it must be able to provide explanations that are beyond the reach of individualist methodology. A good example could be, for instance, Archimedes's (in)ability to conceive of Galilean physics: the necessary mathematical and physical knowledge was available, but nevertheless, unlike Galileo, Archimedes and ancient Greeks in general seem to have never come to the idea of the systematic quantification of physical phenomena the way Galileo did. It is impossible to say that such quantification was weakly inconceivable in Archimedes's time, since the necessary conceptual framework was available to his contemporaries as much as to Galileo's. In this case it may be indeed possible for the holist to press his or her case by arguing, for instance, that the idea of the quantification of physical phenomena was strongly inconceivable to ancient Greeks—and the result would be a potentially strong challenge to the materialist perspective on history in general.

Let us therefore analyze what happens in situations when a historian has to explain the presence (or absence) of a certain property (P) on an artifact (a scientific or a philosophical theory, an artwork and so on) made by a certain author whereby:

(a) That property (P) is also present (or missing) on all artifacts made by the authors who belong to the same collective as the author and
(b) There is no reason to assume that the absence of such a property (P) (in the case it is present) or its presence (in the case it is missing) was weakly inconceivable to the author of the artifact.

There are numerous examples of such situations in history, such as artworks of the same style from the same period, the absence of Galileo-style quantification of physical phenomena in Hellenistic authors, the fact that ancient Greeks and Romans did not discover the printing press or the fact that pre-Columbian civilizations did not use the wheel. In all these cases, the knowledge necessary to make a given discovery was present in the given historical, cultural or social context, but the discovery was not made. The individualist (materialist) will explain the systematic presence (or absence) of specific artifacts or their properties by the individual decisions of the authors of these artifacts, who may have been influenced by other individuals belonging to the same collective. For instance, the fact that an artist's work conforms to the stylistic practices of its time will be explained by the influence of the author's contemporaries, the education the artist received and so on. The individualist will deny that it was strongly inconceivable for an author belonging to a given group to make an artifact with(out) the given property. According to this point of view, discoveries such as the printing press or the wheel happen or do not happen; interactions in the social environment may enable, stimulate or prevent them but if some individual does not come up with the idea, they will not happen. The holist, however, will claim that the systematic presence or absence of artifacts with or without a specific property among the artifacts made by members of a certain group results from the fact that such artifacts were strongly inconceivable for their authors, and that this inconceivability is caused by the authors' membership of specific groups. The holist's explanation will be that:

> An artifact of the given kind with (without) the property P was strongly inconceivable to the author because the author was a member of the given group.

Which implies:

> There could not exist a person who was a member of the given group and believed that an artifact such as the one under consideration should not have (or: that it should have, in the case such property is systematically absent) the property P.

The response to this claim that saves the individualist position is that no amount of historical research can prove that this claim is true. One can only state examples that support it: for instance, that artifacts of a specific type, produced by a series of authors who all belong to the same group, have the property P. This fact is not sufficient to justify the claim that these authors could not conceive of an artifact, such as the one under consideration, without the property P—and then further, that *because* a given author belonged to the same explanatory collective, therefore his or her works necessarily had the property (P) (i.e., that he or she could not conceive of a work such as A without P). Such claims can be made only as generalizations on the basis of a limited number of instances. However great the number of available instances, this does not prove that there *could* not have existed an author who conceived of an artifact without P. A generalization that makes such a claim is the fallacy of false generalization: one cannot explain the fact that a certain cat lives in London by listing numerous examples of cats that live in London and then inferring that it is *impossible* for a cat *not to* live in London. Consider, as an example of such false reasoning, Foucault's attempt to show that resemblance played a crucial constructive role in Renaissance culture.[8] The claim is a generalization based on a thin list of examples: he considers a total of only fifteen Renaissance authors and from a very limited field, since most of these authors wrote about topics such as magic, alchemy or astrology. The Aristotelian tradition that dominated Renaissance academic life is missing, while a historian of some other field of Renaissance studies is likely to be puzzled how to relate Foucault's claims about resemblance to materials in his or her field.[9] However, the real problem is that even if one could show that resemblance, as Foucault describes it, really dominated Renaissance intellectual life and was omnipresent in the writings of the era, and made non-resemblance-based views inconceivable, this would still not justify the claim that there *could not* have existed an author who conceived of the world in a way that did not depend on resemblance.

The problem with claims about strong inconceivability is that the number of historical examples is always limited, and insufficient for universal claims, of the kind that can be made in natural sciences on the basis of experiments that are infinitely repeatable. (This is a variation of the problem with the formulation of causal laws in disciplines such as history, astronomy or geology that was mentioned in the Introduction. In disciplines in which it is impossible to make experiments in order to confirm regularities which one observes, it can easily happen that one observes an accidental regularity of a certain phenomenon that occurs in a limited number of available instances.) At the same time, it is often hard to say why counterexamples to holist historical claims in favor of strong inconceivability should be impossible. Imagine, for instance, the claim that before Copernicus the heliocentric system was strongly inconceivable. Even if one could establish, by surveying all the material available, that no European astronomer known to us conceived of the heliocentric system in the century before Copernicus, this still does not prove that some unknown astronomer did not carry out equivalent observations and did not reach the same conclusions as Copernicus a hundred years earlier, but that his manuscript was destroyed in the intervening centuries. Similarly, it is impossible to prove that there *could not* have existed a young astronomer in the late 1300s who *would have* carried out the same observations as Copernicus and reached the same conclusions, *had he not* prematurely died of plague; strong inconceivability is precisely the claim that this could not have happened. In other words, the problem with the application of holist methodology to assert strong inconceivability is that no amount of evidence can warrant the move from "is not known to have been conceived" to "could not have been conceived"—except trivially, if we talk about weak inconceivability. In historiography, the problem will manifest itself as the tendency to base the historical explanation on an incomplete survey and disregard counter-examples. Subsequently, this approach generates endless debates about relative merits of explanatory collectives such as culture, class, ethnicity and so on. Because they are based on unjustified generalizations, such explanations often merely reflect the ideological bias of the individual historian.

NOVEL PROPERTIES

As Foucault repeatedly admitted, scientific discoveries, inventions and other situations in which an author produces an artifact with novel properties (properties that are not present on any artifact previously produced by the members of the same group) present an irresolvable problem for holist approaches to intellectual history.[10]

The problem with the holist perspective is that insofar as one wants to provide holist explanations of the creative actions of individuals, one needs to formulate its explanations in terms of collectives. We must be able to say that an author was a member of a collective of authors (or potential authors) who produced (or would have produced) an artifact with identical properties (including the absence of those properties which were inconceivable). If a given artifact made by the author has the property P, then, according to the holist, this fact has to be explained by the author's membership in a certain collective. But even if we could establish the beliefs, thoughts or ideas an individual possessed because he or she was a member of a certain collective, this could be done only when it came to the beliefs, thoughts and ideas that were shared by other members of that same collective. Explanations of this kind cannot be applied to those ideas, thoughts and beliefs which were formulated for the first time by specific individuals, simply because no generalization can be made from a set of non-existent instances. It is also going to be of little help to refer, for example, in the case of novel scientific theories, to the existence of irresolvable problems in an existing and widely accepted theoretical paradigm—because many members of the scientific community would be aware of such difficulties, but their solution (and the introduction of a novel paradigm) would still have to be individualized to one person (or a group of individuals). Before Brunelleschi, many *trecento* painters had worked on resolving the problem of the distance point. But this does not explain his geometrical solution of the problem (other solutions could have been formulated as well) nor does it explain how he actually made the discovery, or why others before him failed.

The individualist position, however, is better at providing a *quomodo* explanation. Imagine, for the sake of the argument, that in some Florentine attic an art historian finds the complete documentation about the discovery of the geometrical construction of perspective, as Brunelleschi himself assembled it before his death. This would include Brunelleschi's diaries with his early observations about the representation of space in *trecento* Tuscan paintings, attempts to formulate and resolve the problem of the distance point, his famous (and now lost) experimental paintings, even, possibly, a manuscript of a previously unknown Italian *trecento* translation of Euclid, annotated by Brunelleschi himself; dairy entries could even describe how he obtained the books he needed from his friends. The documentation would constitute a *quomodo* explanation and it would allow us to trace, day by the day, how the discovery of perspective evolved and an individualist explanation of the contribution that the social context made to the discovery. As discussed in Chapter Three, we cannot know what happened in his mind and brain when the discovery was made, but we can specify and individuate the way social influences, in the form of interactions with other individuals, contributed to the discovery of perspective. It hard to see how a historian can expect to achieve more.

IS ALL THINKING VERBAL?

The second problem that needs to be addressed in this chapter pertains to the relationship between the contents of mental states of historical figures and the linguistic contexts, the languages these individuals used. For the past two centuries a number of philosophical traditions have emphasized the idea that all thinking is verbal and language-based. This would be the view that an ordinary language such as French or Russian is a vehicle of thought and not merely a vehicle of communication, and that there can be no thoughts independent of their articulation in a language. Such views amount to the claim that the linguistic context delimited the pool of thoughts a historical figure could have had and that he or she would not have conceived of ideas for which his or her language had no words. In European continental philosophy the idea goes back at least to early German Romanticism and Johann Gottfried Herder.[11] Early in the twentieth century this view was promoted by Ferdinand de Saussure.[12] According to Saussure, the relationship between concepts and the words that express them is comparable to the one between two sides of the same paper, whereby one cannot cut one side without cutting the other.[13] Slavic languages, he pointed out, differentiate between the finished and unfinished aspect of verbs; these categories are difficult to understand for French native speakers since they are non-existent in French.[14] The view that all thinking was verbal came to be immensely influential in analytic philosophy during the "linguistic turn" and it was promoted by a number of prominent analytic philosophers, such as Quine, Dummett, and Gilbert Harman.[15] Dummett even identified analytic philosophy with the rejection of the view that there can be nonverbal thoughts.[16] Donald Davidson attempted to argue that neither language nor thought have conceptual priority over each other, but ultimately the way he phrased his arguments can be taken to suggest that he assumed the priority of language.[17] As the opponents of the priority of language, one should mention Paul Grice, Jerry Fodor, Jerrold Katz, and John Searle. Fodor's important observation was that the sentences that we encounter in our conscious thinking often suffer from ambiguities—for example, the sentence "Visiting philosophers can be unpleasant" can be taken to express two different thoughts—whereas, he points out, "thought needs to be ambiguity free."[18]

For the past two centuries various arguments that belong to the realm of armchair psychology have been introduced in order to argue in favor or against the view that all thinking is verbal. Some authors are inclined to assume that they think in words on the basis of introspection.[19] Others claim, also on the basis of introspection, that their thinking is pre-verbal. Those who believe that thinking precedes its verbal articulation may base their opinion on experiences such as occasional difficulties in finding the suitable word to express a certain thought or recognizing a person without being able to remember the person's name. Some of these arguments can be answered by saying that the process of finding a suitable word *is* the process of formulating a thought. Similarly, it may be argued that animals or prelinguistic infants are able to think and have beliefs.[20] But it is possible to answer this argument by saying that thinking in a language is indeed particular to grown-up humans. It may also be argued that human beings are able to differentiate among numerous properties of objects (such as nuances of colors) without being able to name them. This argument can be answered by saying that such differentiation really occurs as part of perception and does not count as thinking. Visual imagination, including the capacity to "rotate" objects in imagination and imagine them from different sides, for instance, may be stated as a particularly prominent example of a nonverbal mental process: it may be argued that its operation is necessary for solving complex, three-dimensional, geometrical problems and that it should therefore count as thinking. Some philosophers, such as Quine, however, have denied that there is such a thing as visual imagination.[21] Dummett, another strong proponent of the view that all thinking is verbal, answered this dilemma about visual imagination by saying that it does not count as thinking.[22] This response is open to the criticism that it first excludes nonverbal mental processes from the definition of thinking and then claims that all thinking is verbal. Various arguments of this kind can be proposed in one direction or another. The development of cognitive science and the problems that the view that all thinking is a linguistic affair generates in the philosophy of language have ultimately led to the general rejection of this view in recent decades. Today, authors such as Peter Carruthers or Christopher Gauker who insist that thoughts are language-based are careful not to formulate their claims as universal claims about all thinking.[23]

PROBLEMS WITH TRANSLATION

The idea that all thinking is verbal is not necessarily opposed to the materialist worldview. It does not necessarily imply ontological expansion beyond the material world or the belief that languages are abstract, immaterial entities that exist independently of the mental states of individuals and the biology of their brains. It is, however, opposed to the account of language and communication based on *de verbis* and *de signis* beliefs, that assumed separation between thoughts and languages used to express them. The important difficulty with the view that all thinking is verbal, however, that needs to be pointed out here is that it makes translation between languages impossible. Because it has been influential both among analytic and continental philosophers, the view has been also often endorsed by historians and philosophers of history. However, the problems that result from this view when it comes to explaining translation between languages mean that a historian who endorses it will never be able to report beliefs of historical figures who expressed them in a language different from the one the historian is using.

The immediate implication of the view that all thinking is verbal is the understanding that when historians report beliefs of historical figures, they report *the sentences* and not the language-independent propositions that these individuals believed to be true or false. More generally, the view also assumes that only properly formed sentences of ordinary languages (but not thought-contents, conceived of as independent of any language) can be said to be true or false. Among English-speaking philosophers of history, Arthur Danto promoted this kind of view, while the opposite position was endorsed Quentin Skinner and Mark Bevir.[24]

For a historian, and anyone working with language-based artifacts, the view that all thinking is verbal introduces significant problems in various situations that arise in relation to homonyms and translation between languages. (Translation in general will be discussed in the next chapter; this section merely describes the problems that arise from the view that all thinking is language-based.) Different languages normally have different homonyms, there is no one-to-one fit between words in different languages. Translations become a serious problem if one assumes that there are no non-verbal thoughts that would make it possible to differentiate between words on the basis of their non-verbal meanings. The human capacity to recognize homonyms presents significant difficulties for a position that delimits human reasoning capacities in accordance to the classificatory whims of natural languages. If Saussure is right, and the relationship between thoughts and words is indeed comparable to the one between two sides of the same piece of paper, whereby one cannot cut one side of paper without cutting the other, then an English speaker would never be able to differentiate between a soup that is "hot" in the sense of "very warm" and another that is "hot" in the sense of "spicy." The claim implies that insofar as a language possesses a homonym, its users simply cannot grasp the difference between the concepts it expresses. (The fact that, at the same time, there can exist alternative ways to express these concepts in English then becomes unexplainable.[25]) Similarly, if Saussure is right about the way languages form human thinking, then it should be impossible, and not merely difficult, for French speakers to grasp the difference between completion aspects of Slavic verbs. If French speakers' thinking were fully formed and delimited by the structures available in French language, it should be impossible for them to grasp differences in meanings that exist in other languages but do not exist in French.

Further problems arise when one has to translate English sentences that contain words such as "hot" into languages that do not have equivalent homonyms. Since, according to the argument, English speakers cannot differentiate between the two meanings, it follows that for them it is also impossible to decide how to translate the word. One may argue that the correct translation is to be established on the basis of the systematic contribution of homonyms to the truth conditions of the sentence in which they are used. For instance, the truth-conditions of the sentence "this soup is hot" may be satisfied if the soup is spicy or if it is very warm. It may be said that in such cases the contribution that the word makes to the truth of the sentence should decide on the correct translation would employ German "scharf" or "heiß." (This would be in line with the view that the role of words in a sentence is defined by their systematic contribution to the truth conditions of the sentence.) However, this translation imputes to the English speaker a distinction that he or she, according to Saussure, cannot make. If the sentence "this soup is hot" does not express two language-independent propositions, then the systematic contribution of the word "hot" can only be that it makes the sentence both true and false at the same time. One cannot say that the sentence can be understood in two different ways, because according to this view there are no extralinguistic thoughts (meanings) that would differ in truth-value; simply there is only a sentence that is both true and false at the same time.

As a result of all this, homonyms substantially exacerbate problems with translations. When establishing the English translation of a sentence written, for example, by Aquinas, one is likely to encounter situations in which there is more than one equivalent sentence in English. Sometimes these English equivalents may even be contradictory. In such a situation a historian of philosophy may think that Aquinas did not express clearly the *proposition* he intended to express. One need not assume that Aquinas had contradictory beliefs—it is often more likely that Aquinas did not clearly state which (one of a number of) propositions that his sentence expresses he believed to be true. It may still be assumed—and in most cases it will be reasonable to assume—that Aquinas believed only one of them to be true. Arguably, this is also the way historians of philosophy would react in this situation; one does not assume that great thinkers subscribed to contradictory beliefs whenever their statements can be translated with contradictory English sentences. Rather, one tries to establish what Aquinas meant—which of these propositions he wanted to express—through further textual analysis. This highly plausible interpretative assumption is, however, not available to a historian who assumes that all thinking is verbal. If one assumes that all thinking is verbal, then there are no extra-linguistic propositions that are merely expressed using sentences. If Aquinas believed that a Latin sentence that has three mutually contradictory English equivalents was true, then he had contradictory beliefs—and it is pointless to ask which of the three sentences articulates his real belief.

Moreover, some English sentences may translate more than one Latin sentence written by, say, Aquinas. If one assumes that all thinking is verbal, it will follow that the Latin sentences that a single English sentence translates are either all true or all false in Aquinas's view. Imagine, for instance, that a certain English sentence "E" translates five Latin sentences. Aquinas may, however, have understood the first, second, and fourth sentences and believed them to be true, but did not understand the third and fifth, and consequently, did not believe them to be true. Simply, the third and the fifth sentences may have contained words or phrases unknown to him—which may also happen to any speaker of any language. Since E is the English translation of all five Latin sentences, and since according to the view that all thinking is verbal beliefs are always beliefs that certain sentences (and not propositions) are true or false, we have to say that Aquinas believed that E was true and that he did not believe that E was true. This kind of situation cannot arise if we assume that sentences express mental propositions, since in that case it is the proposition an individual believed to be true that is reported, even though the sentence that reports it may have multiple meanings and it may be necessary to clarify which proposition the person actually believed to be true.

REFLEXIVE ARGUMENT

Aquinas's famous dictum that *Quicquid recipitur, ad modum recipientis recipitur*—whatever is received, can be received only in accordance with the capacity of the recipient—indicates a major dilemma present in every attempt at historical understanding and interpretation. On the one hand, one needs to understand historical figures in relation to their historical context[26], which is presumably different from the historian's own in its conceptual frameworks, fundamental beliefs or reasoning principles. (Why would a historian worry about contextualization if other contexts were not genuinely different?) On the other hand, the content cannot be intelligible to the historian if the conceptual frameworks, fundamental beliefs or reasoning principles are so different from the historian's own that he or she cannot understand them. (How could a historian grasp ideas based on conceptual frameworks that he or she does not share?) But then, how can one claim to be dealing with a *different* conceptual framework or a context, if one shares it or participates in it? The dilemma suggests that it is either pointless to contextualize, or that it is impossible to understand anything outside one's own context. Problems related to contextualization permeate not only the understanding of historical documents and artifacts but also historical works themselves and the meanings that can be attributed to them; readers of historical works necessarily approach historical works from their own perspectives as well.

The corresponding dilemma between the claim that the reasoning capacities of historical figures are relative to their historical, social, linguistic and so on contexts and the need to postulate their trans-historical rationality that would explain how one can (claim to) understand their beliefs, actions and statements, was a major problem for hermeneutic and historicist traditions. The problem is actually resolvable from the point of view of the materialist and the individualist approach—which suggests significant advantages of these latter perspectives. Here are some traditional formulations of the problem.

In his *Der Aufbau der geschichtlichen Welt* Wilhelm Dilthey famously argued that the individual is to be understood within the context of his community.[27] Every action or thought has its meaning through its relationship to the totality of the epoch or time, he says.[28] He further infers that since the context determines the individual, all that can be studied in history are contextualization's of individuals.[29] Problems with this view start, however, when one has to account of the historian's own cognitive capacities. If the historian's own social context determines his or her worldview, then how can the historian understand the worldviews of the past? To resolve this problem Dilthey unexpectedly introduced the claim that when understanding historical documents, one relies on that which is immutable in time and has universal human validity.[30] In other words, it turns out that some aspects of human experience are still independent of their historical contexts and they constitute the only possible object of a historian's study. Contextualization, it seems to follow, is both impossible and unnecessary.

Ernst Troeltsch in his *Der Historismus und seine Probleme* resolved the same dilemma by introducing claims about occult forces. It is only in the context of a greater totality, such as a family, class or nation that human individuals can be understood, he says.[31] These totalities are marked by their own, shared, spirit (*Gemeingeist*), constituted by a consciousness that is external to participating individuals.[32] It is metaphysics, Troeltsch says, that explains how a historian can comprehend individuals from other groups in which he or she does not participate.[33] The historian's understanding is enabled by the same Total Consciousness (*Allbewußtsein*) that, he claims, also explains the works of poets and occultist phenomena.[34] On his account, it is thus an extra-human spiritual force that enables historians' trans-contextual understanding.

Hans Georg Gadamer in his *Wahrheit und Methode* endeavored to overcome these problems by arguing that texts belonging to one context (horizon) are understood from the perspective of another horizon through "the fusion of horizons."[35] He also emphasized the historicity of the historian by criticizing the historicist assumption that one can simply project oneself into another historical horizon.[36] The understanding of the past must be based on the fusion of the horizons of the historian and the historical figures he or she is writing about.[37] But the notorious problem when reading Gadamer is that the meaning of the phrase "fusion of horizons" remains unclear; Gadamer neither explains how such "fusion" works nor does he provide examples of successful or unsuccessful "fusion."[38] E. D. Hirsch pointed out that the "fusion of horizons" rather exemplifies the problem than solves it; it remains unclear how an interpreter can fuse his or her own horizon with that of the text without appropriating in some form the latter and abandoning one's own.[39] In his view, "this intermediate perspective can no longer possess the meaning it pretends to carry."[40]

Modern historians have been often equally unsuccessful in proposing a solution to the problem. Martin Jay thus states: "surely, there is no self-evident transcendental version of rationality that can be applied historically and across cultures under all circumstances."[41] The statement seems plausible as long as one does not ask how historians can grasp, interpret or report the content of the statements made in the contexts marked by a radically different rationality. A different rationality could be the one, for instance, in which the thought contents of historical figures, or the contents conveyed in historical documents, do not consist of concepts and propositions or in which the principle of non-contradiction does not apply. The answer is that contents based on a different rationality simply cannot be understood—and if one cannot grasp, interpret or report (probably not even register) the thought-contents that were motivated by a radically different rationality, then it is also unclear how one can even know that such alternative rationality was operational in some historical contexts at all. Similarly, Joseph Fermia in his critique of Quentin Skinner described the historicist position as marked by the view that "[a]ll ideas and values are products of a given historical epoch, of a specific civilization, or even of definite national collectivity."[42] But then, when he takes as an example of the historicist approach Dilthey's view "that historical understanding must be firmly based in a reconstruction of the subjective experience of historical actors," one has to wonder how a historicist historian could ever believe to have achieved such a feat.[43] If a historian's own ideas are products of his or her context, then how can he or she understand ideas from a different context (if that context is really different)? Additionally, if a historian believes that all ideas are products of one's own context, then he or she must believe that this applies to his or her ideas about "subjective experiences of historical actors" which are then not "reconstructions of the subjective experience of historical actors" but can only be "products of a given historical epoch, of a . . . civilization, or . . . national collectivity." Like Dilthey, Fermia makes the effort to resolve the dilemma by curbing the implications of historicism and scaling down the claim that "there is . . . no universal human nature."[44] He therefore postulates (and attributes to Gramsci, whose views he generally endorses) the "permanent substratum of human needs and concerns."[45] As he puts it:

> Men have physical needs and sexual impulses, suffer from fear, are capable of using symbols, must work together in groups to satisfy mutual needs . . . [they] at all times become aware of needing such things as food, shelter, security, language, sexual satisfaction, and human companionship.[46]

Fermia stops short of attributing shared cognitive structures to humans, but it is hard to see how they could share the awareness that he describes without sharing the cognitive capacities that enable it.

Spengler, one should observe, was much more straightforward when it comes to responding to the reflexive argument. His historiographical schedule implied that ideas people have reflect their position within a standard scheme of development repeated by various cultures. He was prepared to admit that this applied to his writing as well. As he put it, "a thinker has no choice."[47] What a historian writes, from this point of view, is not true because of its correspondence to the past, but its correspondence to "the picture of the world that was born with him."[48] Spengler's position here is that the intellectual capacities of historical figures were determined, and not merely delimited, by the context. The point is not merely that certain views are inconceivable to individuals from certain cultures (this is anyhow the case for Spengler), but that what individuals, including historians think and write is dictated by their context. What one believes to have understood from documents that originate from other contexts is merely what one is compelled to understand on the basis of one's membership in one's own collective.

SHARED RATIONALITY

Individuals from different contexts must share at least some aspects of rationality if they are going to communicate at all—and if they do not communicate, they will not even know that, and in what ways, these other contexts are different. A historian cannot even know that there are cultures with whose members he or she shares no rationality at all, because if they existed no statement made by their members could be understood, nor could one know anything about these cultures. The understanding of a document will certainly fail if the recipient does not have the capacity to grasp the concepts, combinations of concepts, propositions or inferences that constitute the content of the document.

Consider what would be necessary in order to understand a Renaissance painter's recipe for the preparation of a paint.

First, it must be possible, *in principle*, to grasp the conceptual framework of the content of the document. The content may contain concepts that are unknown to us—for instance, it may rely on a classification of stones that is very different from anything known to us today. Insofar as we assume that we would grasp these concepts if we were provided with the necessary information, we are still assuming that we possess the same necessary rationality to understand the document. For instance, if the additional study of various contemporary sources may enable us to grasp the content, then our conceptual framework is not incommensurable with that of the content. (This is an equivalent of the example, discussed earlier, of a historian of science who explains the concept of epicycles to a modern public.) However, if we assume that we are constitutionally (or cognitively) incapacitated to form the necessary concepts, then no effort will enable us to understand the segments of the text that rely on such concepts. Explaining such concepts would be comparable to trying to explain what red color is like to a color-blind person.

Second, if we are to understand the content of a document, it must consist of propositions made using the conceptual relationships that we can grasp. As discussed earlier, propositions establish relationships between concepts that, for instance, state that what satisfies classificatory criteria of one concept satisfies the criteria of another concept in all instances, or in no instances, or in some instances. But if the content of the document relied on some unknown relationship between concepts when combining them into propositions, we would not be able to grasp that content.

Third, the way new propositions are derived from given ones must be based on logical operations that we know how to perform. This requirement also applies to the inferences that are implicitly present between (can be made from) the various segments of the text. It includes the capacity to grasp contradictions in the content. The fact that we need to be able to recognize contradictions in the content of a document precludes the possibility that the principle of non-contradiction could be presupposed in order to understand the meaning of what someone says or does. At the same time, in the case of an author who systematically violated the principle of non-contradiction, and asserted both A and non-A, one will simply not know what that author is asserting—one will fail to grasp the content and will recognize that failure in the form of the impossibility of communication.

Fourth, while these requirements define the first level of coherence, they also need to apply at the level of *de verbis* and *de signis* beliefs: one needs to be able to think logically about the elements of the document such as words or signs in order to understand them. This implies the ability to think conceptually and form propositions about the elements of the document, such as signs, words or sentences in order to form the necessary *de verbis* and *de signis* beliefs. If the use of language is inaccessible to our reasoning (for instance, if we cannot recognize consistency in the use of terms) we will not understand the document even if its content has appropriate logical structure. The logical structure of the document is not reducible to the logical structure of its content, but also includes the logical structure of a coherent system of *de verbis* and *de signis* beliefs and the capacity to form it.

Consider a seventeenth-century refutation of Galileo cited by Charles Taylor:

> There are seven windows given to animals in the domicile of head, through which the air is admitted to the tabernacle of the body, to enlighten, to warm and to nourish it. What are these part of the microcosmos: Two nostrils, two eyes, two ears and a mouth. So in the heavens, as in a macrocosmos, there are two favorable stars, two unpropitious, two luminaries, and Mercury undecided and indifferent. From this and from many other similarities in nature, such as the seven metals, etc., which it were tedious to enumerate, we gather that the number of planets is necessarily seven.[49]

Taylor observes that "[t]he argument seems ludicrous to us today"—but one should note that this is because of its premises, not because of the logical procedure on which the argument relies.[50] The logical procedure is an ordinary syllogism:

> All objects of certain of importance in macro- and microcosm are seven.
> Planets are objects of such importance in macrocosm.
> Ergo, there are seven planets.

What makes the argument ludicrous to us today is the analogy that was used to generate the major premise. We do not regard analogy as a valid ground for generalization. The argument would be incomprehensible, rather than ludicrous, if we were not able to grasp its logical structure. It would also be incomprehensible if we did not share with the author the capacity to classify (conceptualize) objects as metals or planets or if the author combined concepts into propositions using some conceptual relationships that we cannot grasp (for instance, did not rely on the principle of non-contradiction).

Standard philological practices in the analysis of documents have been built around the assumption of shared rationality. Consider, for instance, the procedures developed in order to deal with errors created in transmission in various manuscript traditions. A good example is the efforts of scholars to reconstruct numbers in the original text of Vitruvius's *De architectura*. The medieval manuscript tradition introduced numerous errors when it comes to numbers, originally written in Roman numerals in the treatise. Since the Renaissance, efforts to reconstruct Vitruvius's original numbers often relied on the arithmetic analysis of what number would be correct in the context of Vitruvius's text. Such an analysis would make no sense without the assumption that the text must make sense arithmetically and that Vitruvius operated with the same arithmetic as we do.

Historians who work in some fields (history of music or architecture, for instance) often interpret various non-linguistic artifacts (musical scores, architectural drawings) whose interpretation may require necessary assumptions about shared reasoning capacities that go beyond shared rationality described here. The interpretation of architectural drawings, for instance, requires that the author and the interpreter share the understanding of the properties of three-dimensional space. Erwin Panofsky's thesis, mentioned earlier, that the newly acquired understanding of space as homogenous enabled the discovery of perspective at the beginning of *quattrocento* fails to convince, among other reasons, because it implies that before the 1400s people could not grasp that a distance (for instance, the length of a wall) is the same regardless from what end it is measured.[51] If Panofsky were right, we could not understand any architectural drawings that were made before the early 1400s.

It can be asked whether shared rationality, as described here, is sufficient for the understanding of a document. Certainly, there are other requirements that need to be satisfied for the communication to be possible. To use Kant's phrase, there are requirements that are based on the necessary conditions of every possible experience. Consider, for instance, Collingwood's criticism that when Kant talks about the possibility of experience, "he means by experience the kind of experience enjoyed by men of his own age and civilization. He was, of course, not aware of this."[52] It is, however, hard to see how Collingwood could know that there are types of experience different from those Kant described. The necessary conditions of every possible experience that Kant catalogued in the first half of the *Critique of Pure Reason* state, for instance, that all physical things are experienced in space, that no object can have contradictory predicates, that all experience happens in one time, that the existence of every object assumes the existence of something before it.[53] Imagine that there are indeed people in whose culture physical objects are experienced outside space, in whose experience the principle of non-contradiction does not apply, who experience events in more than one time order (so that in their experience there are events that are neither before, nor after, nor contemporaneous with each other) and who can experience physical things before which nothing happened. It is fair to ask how Collingwood could understand the statements made by these people, and know that they have thoughts at all, considering that he also claims that in order to understand the thought of a historical figure, the historian needs to re-enact that thought in his own mind.[54] More generally, the problem does not pertain merely to the re-enactment-based understanding of people from radically different cultural contents, as Collingwood describes. If a document were created by a mind that lives in a world in which physical objects, such as the document, are not in space-time, we would not be able to identify, let alone engage with such a document, since we can only engage with documents in space-time. Similarly, if a document had been created by a mind in whose experience of the world events happen in more than one temporal order (so that there are events that neither before, nor after, nor contemporaneous with each of other) its stricture, insofar as it does not reflect a single order of thoughts, could hardly be comprehensible. Maybe there are some people in whose culture things can have contradictory properties—but we could not understand what their descriptions of such objects state, because such descriptions would be self-contradictory. Claims about radical cultural diversity of human experience are merely superficial relativism if one cannot explain what such radically different experience may be like and how one can know and communicate about it.

It should also be mentioned that understanding the content of a document does not mean believing that the content is true. A modern historian of science who reads a treatise based on Ptolemaic astronomy will grasp the conditions that need to be satisfied if propositions about epicycles are going to be true, but need not believe that they will ever be true. What is necessary is *the capacity* to form certain thought-contents that correspond to the content of the document. Further on, in order to understand Ptolemy's *Almagest* one needs to be able to read Greek, and in order to understand his theory of epicycles one needs to know about the retrograde movements of planets. Learning to read Greek means acquiring the necessary *de verbis* beliefs. However, not having these skills and knowledge at a given moment does not *constitutionally* prevent one from understanding the text: such skills and knowledge can be acquired. What one needs to have is the capacity to acquire the necessary skills and beliefs.

CONTEXTUALIZATION

The dilemma about the impact of contexts on the reasoning capacities of the historian arises only if we endorse, together with the German theorists mentioned earlier, the holist understanding of historical, social, linguistic, cultural or ethnic contexts, and attribute them causal capacities to determine the cognitive powers of individuals. Since historians live in history too, they then have to be subject to such powers as well, and the reflexive argument becomes impossible to avoid. The individualist perspective avoids these difficulties because it denies that contexts are to be understood holistically and that they can have such causal powers over the cognitive capacities and beliefs of individuals. Contextualization, from the individualist point of view, consists in the consideration of the relevant interactions between individuals—it avoids the conception of contexts as holist structures over and above individuals and their interactions.

Once the holist perspective about contexts is adopted, the problem with the cognitive incapacity of the historian to understand documents or texts from other contexts becomes unavoidable. In that case, it is assumed that every individual's cognitive capacities are determined (delimited) by the holistically conceived context the individual belongs to, whereby an individual can acquire only the contents of mental states that are possible within the given context. Since this applies to historians too, and since humans belonging to different contexts have different cognitive capacities, it follows that a historian can only understand the contents that can be understood within his or her context. If a text or document belongs to another context, they can be understood only insofar as, and in those respects in which, the historian's context enables the cognition of the same contents as the documents—in other words, insofar as the context of the text or the document does not differ from the historian's own. (This was indeed Dilthey's conclusion, as we have seen.) In other words, historical contextualization is either impossible or serves no purpose.

An additional problem for the holist perspective is that it precludes the possibility of contextualization in a finite number of steps; if the holist perspective is right, contextualization could never be completed. (This argument would be particularly relevant if someone, for instance, assumed that a historian has a privileged position, exempted from history, that enables him or her to grasp the contents of documents or the mental states of historical figures in their holistically understood context, while remaining unaffected by his or her own context.) The problem is that from the holist point of view, knowledge about a finite set of the author's (or other individuals') documented interactions with contemporaries, sources, materials and so on can never be enough to grasp what needs to be known about the context, in order to understand a document. If they are holistically understood, contexts and consequently their contributions to the meaning of a text cannot be analyzed into individuals (including their mental states) and their interactions. The holist position is precisely the view that they causal capacities of contexts are different from those of the sets of participating individuals and their interactions. It becomes a problem to explain the possibility of historical contextualization, since a historian never encounters contexts as such ("the Renaissance" or "Antiquity") but only individual documents produced by individuals from these contexts. Contexts, from this point of view, are more than, or not the same as, sets of individuals and their interactions—and, as a result, it becomes unclear how a historian can grasp it, in order to understand a document that needs to be contextualized. Troeltsch, we have seen, avoided this problem by explaining the historian's cognition as comparable to interaction with occultist phenomena. Before Troeltsch, an attempt to resolve this same problem without relying on spiritualist phenomena was made by Karl Lamprecht. In his efforts to formulate a holist *Kulturgeschichte* he argued that generalization based on the impression the historian gets from sources is a legitimate equivalent of statistical induction, even though it uses no numerical descriptions; in his view, this impression was sufficient to understand the context.[55] It is, however, far from clear that this is indeed so, and his critics were quick to point out that such non-numerical statistics would amount to free-for-all scholarship.[56]

This same problem does not arise if contexts are understood individualistically, since in that case the context is a finite set of individuals (including their mental states) and interactions; it may be very big, but in order to understand or interpret a document one merely needs to know about a limited number of relevant interactions. Contextualization on this understanding may encounter *limited* regress: the understanding of a term in one text may require the ability to interpret another text and this may require the interpretation of a yet another text. Interpretation and understanding are possible if a finite number of such steps is possible, otherwise the document will be (partly) incomprehensible. It is fair to observe that if one assumes that contextualization necessarily deals with something that cannot be analyzed as the sums of documentable interactions between individuals (including historians), then some superior form of intellection, such as Troeltsch's occult phenomena, will be indeed necessary in order to explain the possibility of contextualization. For instance, Friedrich Ast in his 1808 *Grundlinien* claimed that the totality of Antiquity is a *Geist* from which all internal and external life derived; historical understanding consists in deducing everything, including the most individual aspects of Antiquity, from this higher unity.[57] The force that enables the cognition of this context from individual instances is also *Geist*: our understanding of Antiquity, says Ast, is possible because our *Geist* and the *Geist* of Antiquity are originally one *Geist*.[58]

INDIVIDUALIST UNDERSTANDING OF CONTEXTS

Difficulties with the historian's capacity to understand statements in their historical context described here are immaterial if contextualization is approached from the materialist point of view and its individualist implications taken into account. A historical context in this case is individuals and their interactions. Mark Bevir, in his book *The Logic of the History of Ideas* has provided a detailed individualist analysis of the way intellectual environments and contexts (which he calls "traditions") affect individuals.[59] As mentioned both in the Introduction and in Chapter Two, Bevir does not subscribe to the materialist worldview and his starting assumptions are antifoundationalist. However, the "procedural individualism" that he endorses precludes ontological expansions in a way that is equivalent to the materialist perspective. The idea is that meaning of a document is always the content of a mental state of the author or readers, and that such contents do not have an independent, non-mental existence. "Traditions" from this individualist point of view cannot be holist social structures, hypostatized entities, or have Platonic or occult existence, independent of the mental states of and interactions between specific individuals.[60] A historian, Bevir points out, can decide which individuals belong in a tradition only by tracing the temporal connections that bind a web of belief back to its predecessors.[61] The fact that various individuals share the same set of beliefs or experiences is not enough in order to establish that they belong to the same intellectual community or tradition—actual interaction is necessary as well.[62]

The transmission of ideas and knowledge is thus the defining aspect of contexts, traditions and intellectual environments. The standard model of interaction that defines them is an equivalent of teacher-pupil interaction, Bevir points out. He further introduces the concept of individual agency, which implies that traditions do not determine, but merely serve as the starting points of the beliefs of participating individuals.[63] Individuals thus can learn through a tradition, but they do not necessarily remain faithful to the views they receive. Traditions explain why people set out with the initial webs of belief they do, but they do not explain why they go on to change these initial webs in the ways they do.[64] As he puts it:

> Pupils learn what they do from individual teachers, not a social tradition: they listen to lectures by individuals, not society; they discuss affairs with individuals, not society; they read books written by individuals, not society, they watch television programs made by individuals, not society; and they reflect on beliefs held by individuals, not society. Intellectual traditions exist only as the sum of the beliefs of their individual exponents in their relations with one another.[65]

"Teacher-pupil relationship" (as this phrase is used here) obviously needs to be understood as the generic name for the situation when one individual learns from another. Historical, social, cultural, linguistic and so on contexts consist of such interactions through which individuals learn certain communication tools (e.g., words) and contextualization consequently seeks to reconstruct the meanings that these tools were employed to convey. The assumption is that through interactions within the context individuals learn the more-or-less standardized use of words. Contextualization then provides information about these interactions that is necessary in order to reconstruct the specific *de verbis* or *de signis* beliefs that an author or other individuals relied on. The understanding of a text from a different context can only happen if the necessary rationality is indeed shared and if enough is known about the *de verbis* and *de signis* beliefs on which communication in the given context relied. Problems with reflexivity do not arise, and since contexts are not something over and above individuals, and their interactions, the understanding of documents from different contexts is achievable within a finite number of steps.

It is interesting to see that it is these, individualist assumptions about contexts that the proponents of the hermeneutic tradition relied on in their explanations of the hermeneutic circle (i.e., the procedure whereby a document is to be understood or an event explained in its relevant context, while the necessary knowledge of the context derives from the understanding of other documents).[66] The views of the proponents of the hermeneutic tradition were traditionally aligned with the holist understanding of human collectives.[67] However, we have seen that if the context is understood holistically, then no finite amount of specific knowledge about elements of the context will be enough to understand a document that derives from that context—and since the original context must remain unknown, it will be impossible to understand the document. Understanding in this case can be possible only if one claims the support of a supra-human spiritual force such as *Geist*—and without it, holist contextualization is a dead-end street. Vice versa, if the context is understood individualistically (i.e., if the meaning of the document is the individual author's thought-content, the thought-contents of other readers or similar), the understanding of a document will depend on information about the specific aspects of the context (how individual authors used specific words, for instance) that can enable such understanding. In this case, the procedure will have the form of a series of attempts to grasp the content of the document (or its part) as consistent with such information. It will be an iterative procedure that formulates a series of interpretative hypotheses and tries to confirm them, but it will not have a circular form. Both Dilthey and Gadamer endorsed this latter approach and dropped their holistic assumptions about the nature of interpretative contexts when they had to explain the functioning of the hermeneutic circle. Dilthey's holist commitments have been described in the beginning of this chapter; in his view, historical analysis strives to find how specific purposes and views conform to something that he calls "the totality that rules the epoch."[68] However, when he comes to discuss the impact of historical contexts on individual authors, he does not say that one should explore the totality of a context but specific relevant causes. The examination of the context that produced certain effects (*Wirkungszusammenhang*) starts from one single effect and seeks to establish the limited set of causes that are relevant for that effect, he says. When one tries to find the causes for changes in German literature of a certain era, one looks for the specific groups of causes and evaluates their significance.[69] Although he insisted that thoughts and actions receive their meanings through their relationships with the totality of the epoch or time, when it comes to actual understanding and interpretation, it is nevertheless not the totality of the context, but specific causes that constitute historical explanations. Gadamer similarly avoids problems with the circularity of the hermeneutic circle by explaining it in individualistic terms. Following Schleiermacher, his model for the understanding of a text in the context of the works of an author, literary genre or the intellectual life of the author is that of a part of the text to the whole.[70] Interpretation of a text starts from an expectation about the context that needs to be confirmed, he says, and if this does not work, then we approach the text with a new expectation, until we achieve the unity of meaning.[71] This procedure works because there is nothing circular about it (even though Gadamer insists on calling it the "hermeneutic circle"): it consists in making iterative interpretative attempts until one comes up with an interpretative hypothesis that is satisfied by the context—a procedure that is actually not unlike the hypothetico-deductive method.[72] The context in this case is a set of specific situations (interactions) that can prove or disprove the individual interpretation; it is not the totality of such situations holistically understood.

NOTES

1. Spengler, *Untergang*, 11, 31, 79.
2. Ibid., 110, 192. About the wide influence of this view (that may have not originated only from Spengler) see the discussion in Mondolfo, *L'infinito*, 3.
3. Panofsky, "Die Perspektive." Because of the curvature of the retina, Panofsky claimed, the geometrical construction of perspective, (which provides an image on a plane) does not correspond to what is actually perceived. As subsequently pointed out by Pirenne, *Optics*, 148–149, we never see the retinal image but the object outside the eye; the geometrical construction of perspective merely depicts the intersection of the picture plane and the rays that connect the object with the eye. Panofsky's argument substantially depended on an inaccurate interpretation of the technical terminology of Euclid's *Optica* as well as Aristotle's discussion of space in the *Physics*. (For his misunderstanding Euclid's terminology, see Brownson, "Euclid's *Optics*." For the misinterpretation of the section about space in Aristotle's *Physics*, see Mitrović, "Alberti and Homogeneity.")
4. See Mitrović, "Humanist Art History" for the evolution of Panofsky's views on inconceivability.
5. "... weil er—kraft einer sein psychologisches Wollen vorherbestimmenden Notwendigkeit—nichts anders als eine unnaturalistische Landschaft *wollen konnte*." Panofsky, "Der Begriff," 1023.
6. Foucault, *Les mots*, 183: "... on voit qu'une seule et même configuration de l'*épistémè* a contrôlé...." One should note the deterministic implications of the "to control." He leaves the mechanism that enables this controlling power of *l'épistémè* unexplained. There exist significant similarities between Spengler and Foucault in the way they justify their claims about the limits of intellectual capacities available in certain eras. They both base their claims on analogies between different aspects of life in a given context. When Foucault in the Foreword to the English edition of *Les mots et les choses* compares biological knowledge of an era with what might have been said at the time about linguistic signs, the exchange of goods and all of them with the philosophical discourse of the period, his use of analogy is equivalent to Spengler's claim that that there exists a deep similarity between perspective, book-printing, credit system, point-counter-point, or similarly between a naked statue, polis, Greek gold coin. (Foucault, *The Order*, X. Spengler, *Untergang*, 66.) The claims of both historians are highly vulnerable to and known to be weak against counter-examples; also, they both refrain from describing the historical forces that actually cause the regularities that they describe.
7. Foucault, *Archaeology and Discourse*, 218.
8. Foucault, *Les mots*, 32.
9. Consider Renaissance architectural writings: it is hard to think of examples that would even vaguely justify Foucault's claims about resemblance, and it is even hard to imagine how interest in resemblances might have manifested itself in the writings of Leon Battista Alberti, Sebastiano Serlio, Daniele Barbaro or Andrea Palladio.
10. Foucault, *Les mots*, 229; 264. Foucault, Foreword to the English edition of *The Order*, xii.
11. Herder, *Abhandlung*, 85–86. For a general history of the view that all thinking is verbal, see Losonsky, *Linguistic Turns*.
12. Sassure, *Course*.
13. Saussure, *Course*, 113.
14. Saussure, *Course*, 117.
15. Harman, "Thought and Communication" and "Language Learning." Both essays are inconclusive. Harman, "Thought and Communication," 167, starts with the observation that the "view that language is used primarily in thought, need not imply that all or even most thinking or theorizing is in some natural language," though this is precisely what Harman subsequently attempts to argue. Harman, "Language Learning," 191 concludes with the observation that it is impossible to say whether the idea that we first think and then translate these thoughts in a language is better than the view that all thinking is in a natural language. Quine's view was that only material, physical token-sentences could be properly regarded as truth-bearers, so he was consequently obliged to argue that only such sentences can be believed to be true or false—in

other words, that there can be no non-verbal thought-contents that can be true or false. In Quine, "Meaning in Linguistics," 61, he stated that "there is in principle no separating language from the rest of the world. . . . It is not clear even in principle that it makes sense to think of words and syntax as varying from language to language while the content stays fixed." For Dummett, see, for instance, his essay "Language and Communication," as well as the essay "What Do I Know."

16. "The whole analytical school of philosophy is founded on the rejection of this conception, first clearly repudiated by Frege." Dummett, "What Do I Know," 97. See also a similar formulation in his "Language and Communication," 171.

17. Davidson, "Thought and Talk," says that he wants to defend the no-priority view, and he is indeed commonly cited as arguing that position. (See for instance Davis, "Foundational Issues," 30.) But throughout the article Davidson argues that it is impossible to have thoughts without being a interpreter of the speech of another (ibid., 160), and insists that it is sentences (and not thoughts) that are believed to be true (ibid., 161). The article was indeed interpreted by Searle as asserting the primacy of language over thought; see Searle, "Animal Minds."

18. Fodor, "Mentalese."

19. This is the view of Carruthers, *Language.*

20. For a summary and discussion of research on this topic, see Bermúdez, *Thinking without Words.*

21. "The Parthenon is visible; the Parthenon-idea is invisible. We cannot imagine two things more unlike, and less liable to confusion, than the Parthenon and the Parthenon idea." Quine, "On What," 2. The formulation leaves no space for the assumption that the idea of the Parthenon could be an imagined visual representation of the building.

22. Dummett, "Language and Communication," 170. More precisely, Dummett argued that a thought is capable of being true or false; a visual image, imagined or given in sensation, is true or false only in relation to external reality, whereas that which renders an image an image of an object is the concomitant thought to the effect that it represents that object. However, it is far from clear that all thoughts have to be true or false.

23. Carruthers, *Language,* 1 and 6. Gauker, *Thinking,* 1, 25.

24. Danto, *Narration and Knowledge.* Skinner, "Language." Bevir, *Logic.* Gad Prudovsky's criticism of Skinner's position as "licensing an absolute priority of talk over thought" is not justified. (Prudovsky, "Can We Ascribe," 28.) For instance, Skinner, "Meaning and Understanding," 51 makes a clear distinction between the concept and word, thought-content and its articulation: "When they spoke of 'egoism,' what they meant was something much more like what we should mean by solipsism." He also points out that "the words denoting the idea may be used, . . . with varying and quite incompatible intentions." Ibid., 55.

25. It does not help to point out that English speakers may be able to differentiate between the two meanings of "hot" in accordance to the descriptions "very warm" and "spicy" because Saussure's analogy with a piece of paper precisely implies that in the mind of an English speaker there can be only one concept that would correspond to the term "hot."

26. "Context" is here understood as the historical, social, cultural, linguistic and so on context. It does not pertain to the text itself, though the word is sometimes used that other way as well—for instance, when we say that the meaning of a word has to be established in relation to other words and sentences of a text.

27. Dilthey, *Aufbau,* 186.

28. Ibid., 189 and 218.

29. Ibid., 228.

30. "Die Bedingung für diese Interpretation der historischen Reste ist, daß das, was wir in sie hineintragen, den Charakter der Beständigkeit in der Zeit und der allgemein-menschlichen Geltung hat." Ibid., 196.

31. Troeltsch, *Historismus,* 33.

32. Ibid., 46.

33. Ibid., 71.

34. Ibid., 684.

35. Gadamer, *Wahrheit und Methode,* 401.

36. Ibid., 302, 304.

37. Ibid., 311.
38. Gadamer emphasizes that a historian cannot leave by side one's own conceptual framework when thinking historically. Ibid., 400. But he does not explain how one can understand these concepts of the past, or the nature of *Horizontverschmelzung*.
39. Hirsch, *Validity*, 254.
40. Hirsch, *Aims*, 49.
41. Jay, "Explanation."
42. Fermia, "Historicist Critique," 158.
43. Ibid., 159.
44. Ibid., 158.
45. Ibid., 165.
46. Ibid., 164.
47. Spengler, *Untergang*, vii.
48. Ibid., vii.
49. The example is from Taylor, "Rationality," 94.
50. Ibid., 95.
51. Mitrović, "Alberti and Homogeneity."
52. Collingwood, *Idea*, 224.
53. Kant, *Kritik der reinen Vernunft*, A26, A151, A177–179, B233–234.
54. Collingwood, *Idea*, 39, 215, 228.
55. Lamprecht, "Kulturgeschichte," 259.
56. Below, "Methode," 250. More importantly statistics (with numbers or not) can only pertain to what we already know. It cannot help with the interpretation of documents, since the fact that a certain term was used with a specific meaning 70 percent of times by the authors of a certain era is of little use if this meaning makes no sense in the document under consideration.
57. Ast, *Grundlinien*, 175.
58. Ibid., 164.
59. Bevir, *Logic*, 200–220.
60. Ibid., 203, 209.
61. Ibid., 209.
62. Ibid., 209.
63. Ibid., 203.
64. Ibid., 213.
65. Ibid., 203.
66. One also encounters the formulation that the individual (author or document) is to be understood in its context, while the understanding of the context derives from the interpretation of that very same individual. See for instance Schleiermacher, *Hermeneutik*, 95, and Droysen, *Historik*, 28 and 398. It would be an uncharitable interpretation if one attributed to these authors the view that contextualization does not require the consideration of other individuals belonging to the same context. Rather, these authors seem to be suggesting that the understanding of the individual that one derives from contextualization further enhances our understanding of the context and enables the fine-tuning of the original understanding.
67. See Mitrović, *Rage and Denials*.
68. Dilthey, *Aufbau*, 189.
69. Ibid., 192.
70. Gadamer, *Wahrheit und Methode*, 296–297.
71. Ibid., 296.
72. See Føllesdal, "Hermeneutics."

Chapter Eight

Understanding, Interpretation and Translation

Problems pertaining to the understanding and the interpretation of historical documents (and texts in general) are among the core methodological problems of historical research. This chapter is intended to elucidate these problems by providing an account that avoids the expansion of ontology beyond the material world and especially the need to rely on abstract meanings, rather than the mental states of individuals. In line with the discussion in Chapter Five, it also seeks to show that it is impossible to provide an account of understanding and interpretation that would avoid mental states. The result is an intentionalist account that relies on Mark Bevir's approach to interpretation.

An account of meaning and interpretation in historical research would be incomplete if it failed to include a discussion of its implications for translation between languages. Problems related to translation play the central role in every attempt to report the contents of the mental states of historical figures who expressed them in a language different from the one in which the historian is writing. The chapter presents an approach translation based on *de verbis* and *de signis* beliefs. The purpose of this chapter is to illustrate, in general terms, how such an account of translation can respond to questions and dilemmas that are likely to arise in historical research.

UNDERSTANDING AND INTERPRETATION

A historian's job largely consists of understanding and interpreting historical documents and other texts, including works of other historians. The two procedures—as I use these terms here—are not identical. In order to *under-*

stand a document one needs to form the thought-contents that have the same and only the same satisfaction conditions as the content conveyed (or believed to be conveyed) by the document.[1] This content may consist, for instance, of a certain number of concepts, propositions or inferences. Insofar as one does not understand the document as conveying (some of) these concepts, propositions or inferences, one will also fail to (fully) understand the content of the document. A person who attributes to the content of the document concepts, propositions or inferences that this content does not contain misunderstands the document. *Interpretation*, however, establishes the implications of the content of the document. It infers those propositions that can be inferred when one's own beliefs and knowledge (including one's beliefs and knowledge about the beliefs and knowledge of the author of the document and other people who read it) are combined with the content of the document. Understanding provides us with the concepts, the propositions and the inferences that have the same satisfaction conditions as those conveyed by the document. In interpretation, however, one combines them with propositions that fall outside the content of the document in order to make further inferences. (The meaning of the terms "content" and "to convey" will be defined into greater detail later in this chapter.)

This distinction between understanding and interpretation requires a number of clarifications. A simple example of understanding would be the case of a historian reading a document without knowing anything about the author or other people who read it before. The historian will recognize the language of the document and (attempt to) understand it on the basis of the *de verbis* and *de signis* beliefs that (he or she believes) are standard for the users of that language. Let me call such situations *zero external information understanding*. If I come across a piece of text in Latin, I may not know whether it was written by an ancient Roman, or by a nineteenth-century Russian aristocrat who trained himself to write classical Latin. All I may know about the author may be that he or she wrote the piece of text in question. Zero external author information understanding is possible because the author used certain communication conventions that the reader attributes as standard to the users of a specific language.[2] However, such readings will provide the meanings that the author intended to convey (or the meanings that other readers took it to convey) only insofar as the *de verbis* and *de signis* beliefs of the author or readers coincided with the standard ones as well. In the case they did not, the document will not be merely understood differently than the author intended. It may easily happen that one misses the inferences and logical connections between the propositions that the document conveys. Exclusive reliance on the *de verbis* and *de signis* beliefs that were standard within a linguistic community may easily produce results that are incomprehensible, contradictory, make little sense or can be unsatisfactory in some other way. It may also fail to provide accurate information about the motivation of a historical figure to act in a certain way, in the case he or she stated the motivation using words in a way that was not standard. Also, an author, a philosopher or a scientist, may introduce new technical terms that are not standard in a given language. Instead of a dictionary, the historian who studies such works may have to rely on a computer search or a concordance in order to survey systematically the use of individual terms and establish their meanings within the document. It may also happen that further information about the author—for instance, how the same author used the given term in other writings—needs to be taken into account. In many such cases, additional information about the author, his or her context, readers and so on may be necessary, and one can obtain such information only from interpretation. Alternatively, additional information about other readers may be necessary because one is interested to establish their understanding of the text. Historians of philosophy thus often strive to establish how Aquinas or Averroes understood Aristotle, independently of what Aristotle actually meant. The fact that understanding often depends on interpretation does not necessarily blur the distinction between the two. Interpretation often serves to infer the *de verbis* and *de signis* beliefs that are necessary for understanding, but once they are established, understanding is the procedure that derives contents purely on the basis of *de verbis* and *de signis* beliefs (including those established by interpretation). Interpretation relies on propositions not conveyed by the text as well.

There exists a long-standing debate about the question of whether the author's thought-contents constitute the meaning of the document. On the one hand it has been argued that meanings "reside" in texts independently of individual human subjects and that we can understand texts independently of (what we know about) their authors. The meanings of terms such as "reside," "inhere," "inhabit" and similar in such formulations are unclear. Similar views are also defended by pointing out that understanding can be derived by relying purely on specific social conventions, such as language; what one knows about the author as a human individual makes no contribution to understanding. On the other hand, their opponents point out that once the author's role has been suppressed, it is hard to see how some types of content, such as irony or understatement, can be grasped.[3] Many historians are also likely to argue that standard interpretative practices in historical scholarship are precisely built on the assumption that the meaning of a document is the thought-contents that the author expressed in it—and that consequently that the author's meaning determines the meaning of the document.[4] The view that the author's intention is *the* meaning of the text is sometimes dismissed traditional, or, vice versa, as Foucault claimed, as a view that has come about only in modern times.[5] However, it is hard to agree with Foucault since counterexamples are numerous. When medieval philosophers read and commented on Aristotle, they believed to read and comment on what the Philosopher had said.

Problems related to ontology loom large in the background of this debate. If meanings are the contents of the mental states of human individuals (the author, other readers) then their ontology is reasonably unproblematic. However, if this is denied, saying merely that they "reside" or "inhere" in the document is hardly a satisfactory clarification of their ontology. A document is a physical thing, typically a piece of paper with some ink marks. If meanings are not conceived as the contents of mental states associated with it in some way, then they have to be postulated as independently existent. Since it is hard to see how they can have material existence, it seems necessary to expand ontology beyond the material world and postulate them as immaterial or abstract entities. Even then, it is hard to say how readers can know about them if they are not somehow actualized in readers' mental states—and if they are, then it is not clear that we need to expand ontology beyond the mental states of readers.

An argument in favor of the view that the author's meaning is the meaning of the document that is often stated pertains to the source of the coherence of the document.[6] Insofar as a document is intelligible, it must have been organized with the intention to be intelligible. As Jorge Gracia put it, "It does not make any more sense to hold that texts can exist without causes than that there is rain without something that produces it."[7] The alternative would be to assume that some non-human agent gave to the text its intelligible form, or that it has come about as intelligible from nothing. This argument cannot be opposed by saying that the author may have provided the text with its coherence, but that once the text is coherent, the meaning resides in this coherence and not in the intentional states of the author. The response will be that the author had to organize the document to convey its specific content and to achieve this, the content needed to reside originally in his or her mind. The argument, however, has limited validity for a theorist who rejects the materialist perspective. The human author may be conceived of as a tool that acts according to the will of a super-human force (for instance, culture, or the spirit of the time). Historically, it has been often argued that various non-human or collective entities (understood as irreducible to the sets of individual humans) or spiritual forces are the sources of the content, its coherence and the coherence of the document that conveys it. Barthes, we have seen in the Introduction, replaced the author with *language*, conceived as an abstract force that "speaks" while individual authors are mere "scriptors."[8]

MARK BEVIR'S WEAK INTENTIONALISM

For our discussion here, Mark Bevir's analysis of the dilemma, in his *The Logic of the History of Ideas*, is particularly valuable. We have already seen that Bevir's reliance on the principle of procedural individualism aligns him with the materialist position, in spite of his proclaimed anti-foundationalism. Bevir uses the term "strong intentionalism" for the view that the meaning of a document is the meaning that the author wanted to convey, while "weak intentionalism" (that he endorses) is the wider conception that meanings are always meanings for particular individuals—authors, readers, authors re-reading their old texts and so on; these meanings are contents of mental states and can be conscious or unconscious. Methodological advantages of weak intentionalism are obvious: historians often have to consider not only the meaning the author wanted to convey with a text, but also how the text was understood by other individuals, at various times and in various contexts. Sometimes they also have to consider the unconscious meanings of the author or his or her readings. Bevir's principle of procedural individualism leads to the concept of (what he calls) *hermeneutic meaning*. This is the meaning an utterance has for particular individuals, regardless of whether they are authors or readers.[9] These hermeneutic meanings must relate to thoughts, he points out; if they did not, then people would be assigning meanings to utterances without having cognitive access to these meanings, which makes no sense.[10] He contrasts hermeneutic meanings of utterances to semantic meanings (understood as abstract and defined via truth conditions) and linguistic meanings (understood as conventional meanings within a certain group).[11] People may know the semantic meaning of a term, but still not understand the way it was used in a particular situation. Similarly, people may know the conventions that determine the linguistic meaning of a term but again fail to understand its use in a given context. Bevir argues that both semantic and linguistic meanings are reducible to hermeneutic meanings, understood as meanings that an utterance has for a particular individual. In the case of semantic meanings, utterances acquire meaning within conceptual frameworks, conceptual frameworks belong to individuals, and consequently, semantic meanings are generalizations based on hermeneutic ones.[12] Similarly, linguistic meanings are generalizations based on the statistical fact that a number of individuals take specific words to express specific concepts; they are thus also based on hermeneutic meanings.[13] It is, he further argues, hermeneutic meanings that historians are interested in. Let us call "structural meaning" any other kind of meaning, that is not defined as belonging to particular individuals. Such meanings are not of much use for historian, Bevir observes. Imagine that someone in the eighteenth century wrote an essay containing a section with the title "Hallelujah Lass." This term has been used since the nineteenth century to refer to female members of the

Salvation Army—and this contemporary, structural meaning of the term, is not the meaning that the historian would be interested in. The historian would be interested in the hermeneutic meaning of the term, the meaning that the term had for the author and his or her readers. It is valid to consider structural meanings, but they do not have historical existence, Bevir concludes. When we consider historical meanings, we are considering the meanings that the utterance had for individuals in a certain era, and this is always going to be the hermeneutic meaning.

One may thus imagine that a text has non-hermeneutic meanings ("structural meanings" as Bevir calls them), that do not belong to any specific person—for instance, by assuming that they have abstract immaterial existence or that they are mere generalizations based on the statistically established standard usage. From Bevir's point of view, this would obviously violate the principle of procedural individualism (that we have seen, aligns his theory of understanding and interpretation with the materialist perspective). For the materialist perspective that this book analyses, meanings as abstract entities are unacceptable in principle, while statistically established meanings are equivalent to what has been described as zero-author-information understanding.

It is possible to state two additional arguments in favor of Bevir's analysis, that further strengthen the argument that historians have little use for structural meanings. First, in the case of abstract meanings that have no grounding in mental states of individuals, it should be pointed out that from them one cannot infer anything about the motivation or actions of the author. If we want to understand the motivation or the acting of a person on the basis of that person's statements and explanations, one needs to consider the contents of the mental states of that person, and this means taking into account hermeneutic meanings. (This is equivalent to the anti-externalist argument about Stalin's mental states discussed in Chapter Five.)

Second, texts are not only combinations of words and sentences that convey concepts and propositions. They also convey logical reasoning such as arguments, syllogisms, or mathematical proofs. Very often, such reasoning is incomprehensible if we rely on the standard meanings of words. Dictionaries state that the standard meaning of the ancient Greek word χωρίον is "a particular space, a spot, country, a place in a book, a fortified post or town, a landed estate." However, Euclid in his *Elements* used this term with the meaning "geometrical figure" and if we try to read his geometrical proofs following the standard dictionary meaning, they are incomprehensible. The understanding of texts that express mathematical or logical reasoning is particularly vulnerable to departures from their author's meanings, since logical connection between propositions can easily get lost. Such texts are strongly tied to what Bevir calls "hermeneutic meanings." Arguably, this explains why historians who work in the history of mathematics or philosophy are less likely to endorse the rejection of intentionalism (weak or strong). It may be suggested that in such situations it is enough to postulate the specific, technical meaning of a term relative to a given text, and that it is not necessary to relate departures from the standard usage to the mental states of the author. A meaningless text may become meaningful if we systematically attribute a non-standard meaning to a word. However, this introduces the need to identify the source (or the cause) of the systematic departure from the standard usage. This cause can be only a human individual (unless one is prepared to expand ontology to include immaterial forces with reasoning capacities).

TRANSLATIONS: FOR WHOM?

Problems pertaining to meaning become particularly significant when it comes to documents in different languages and the methodological dilemmas that arise when a historian has to translate them. The need to deal with materials in various languages and to attribute thought-contents to historical figures who expressed them in different idioms introduces exceptionally wide range of genuine philosophical and methodological dilemmas into historical research. Unless they stay in the realm of monolingual research, historians simply cannot avoid dealing with translations. At the same time, it is a remarkable aspect of twentieth-century philosophy (both analytic and continental) that the great interest in language has produced remarkably few attempts to deal with the problem of translation between languages.[14] The rare statements about translation made by the most prominent analytic philosophers, such as those by Quine and Dummett (discussed below) tend to sound little credible to a scholar in the historical humanities who is used to working with materials in different languages. It is therefore important to see how an account based on *de verbis* and *de signis* beliefs can explain those aspects of translation that are relevant in historical research.

One may propose:

Principle of translation: Version 1
When reporting statements of individuals who expressed their beliefs in languages other than the one in which a historian is writing, the historian may (should) provide legitimate translations of these statements.

The critical phrases are "languages other than the one in which a historian is writing" and "legitimate translations." There is no clear criterion to decide what counts as one and the same language—which notoriously leads to endless debates about whether Dutch and Flemish, Serbian and Croatian, standard Italian and Sardinian are different languages or mere dialects of the same language. Vice versa, though one assumes that Chaucer wrote in English, we may need to translate his sentences in order to understand them.

Even when we deal with languages that are normally accepted to be different, some of them may be so similar that their speakers may understand each other and regard translation as unnecessary. Vice versa, even native speakers may need translations when sentences in their own contemporary language and their own dialect contain phrases that are incomprehensible to them. It is therefore much better to talk about idiolects, speech habits particular to individual persons. Idiolects are basically sets of *de verbis* beliefs of the individuals they belong to. Individuals who speak the same language can be assumed to share *grosso modo* the same sets of *de verbis* beliefs that enable their communication. It is in accordance to these beliefs that we classify them into linguistic communities. The boundary between linguistic communities is then often a result of historical, political and social factors, as Chomsky suggested. Since English language has evolved on an island this fact is not always obvious to English speakers. In continental Europe one can observe gradual geographical transition between dialects within Romance, Slavic and Germanic language groups. Very often vernacular dialects spoken in the vicinity of the border of another country whose language belongs to the same language group resemble more the language spoken across the border than the official language of the country to which that dialect belongs. Norwegian is a particularly good example: the language is not standardized and what counts as Norwegian is a great variety of dialects scattered along the western coast of Scandinavia.[15] Many speakers of Norwegian find it easier to understand Swedish than some Norwegian dialects. It is thus reasonable to say that clusters of *de verbis* beliefs that are shared by large groups of individuals are classified as languages as a result of social and political factors. This view is in line with the view that they are not abstract immaterial entities (the way we have seen Katz argued). One can thus reformulate the above principle into:

Principle of translation: Version 2
When reporting the statements of individuals whose sentences contain words or phrases incomprehensible to the public the historian is writing for, a historian may (should) provide legitimate translations of these sentences.

In other words, a translation is needed when recipients lack the *de verbis* beliefs that are necessary in order to understand a combination of words. We shall soon see various exceptions that may arise, but, in principle, the translator relies on the following *de verbis* beliefs:

1. That a certain content is conveyed in the original set of sentences.
2. That that same content can be expressed (can be conveyed to a different public) using a different set of sentences.

The content that is conveyed in a translation can be the "hermeneutic meaning" in Bevir's terminology, but it can be some version of imaginary "structural meaning," such as the "linguistic meaning." The translator may imagine "structural meanings" and decide to convey them in translation. Speaking in general terms, in the latter case the translator may seem to be able to rely on standard and established translation rules between the two languages, while in the former, his or her work will have to respond to the demand to establish the hermeneutic meaning first. In the process of translation, the translator will first, on the basis of his or her *de verbis* beliefs establish the content that the text conveyed (the hermeneutic meaning that the text had for the author or his or her readers or some form of its structural meaning). He or she will then, on the basis of his or her *de verbis* beliefs about his or her readers, produce a text that conveys this meaning to these readers.

A translation of a text needs to convey the same propositions, and this means that it needs to convey the same set of satisfaction conditions; if it does not, it is simply not accurate. A translation whose sentences can be true when those of the original are not, or vice versa, is simply not a translation of the original. Such a translation falsely states that the original contains propositions that it does not contain. In general, the requirement of legitimacy should state that:

> *Legitimacy*
> A translation of a text is legitimate if it conveys to the public it is intended for the same totality of propositions (has the same conditions of satisfaction) as the totality of propositions (conditions of satisfaction) expressed in the original text.[16]

The fact that the translation has to convey the same proposition(s) means that translating does not always work sentence-by-sentence, since it is not always the case that a single sentence expresses a single proposition. The good style in many European languages requires long sentences, typically expressing more than one proposition, while, for the last century at least, what is recognized as good English prose has been increasingly marked by short sentences. As a result, in the process of translation into English, a longer sentence from another language, expressing more than one proposition, may often have to be broken down into smaller sentences, each expressing singular propositions.

The legitimacy criterion is complicated by the fact that that there is no such a thing as *the* translation of a text; different translations need to be done for different kinds of public. A sentence of the original may be ambiguous and there may not exist a sentence in the language of translation that is ambiguous in the same way—and the translator will have to decide how to translate it on the basis of his or her beliefs about the public.[17] As described, the translator relies on his or her *de verbis* and *de signis* beliefs in receiving (establishing) the meaning of the original text and then on another set of *de verbis* or *de signis* in order to express them in a way that is appropriate, suitable, comprehensible and so on to his or her public. The sentences that the translator formulates result from his or her beliefs about the public and about the appropriateness of the words he or she uses in order to convey (he or she regards as) the original content to that public. Very often, the translation answers the questions that the translator expects his or her public would ask (want to know) about the original text. It often happens that a specialist who reads a translation of a text in his or her field may have questions that the translator (who may not be an expert) has not predicted and consequently the translation does not accurately cover.

The demand that the translation needs to convey the same propositions (and consequently concepts that make up these propositions) as those expressed in the original can lead to challenging situations when the original text is ambiguous or unclear. The demand that the translation must convey the same propositions as the original text and have the same conditions of satisfaction, means that in the optimal situation the translation will have the same, and only the same, ambiguities as the original—and given constraints present in different languages, this is often impossible to achieve.

A translation is normally required to replicate the criteria of satisfaction of the propositions and the classificatory criteria of the concepts expressed in the original. It does not merely refer to the same items that satisfy these criteria; it seeks to convey mental contents. It is not enough to merely state a translation in which phrases and sentences will have the same reference as the original. Typically, a translator will not achieve much if he or she attempts to rely on reference in translation, or try to render combinations of words with correferential equivalents in another language. This would be like translating "the Tsar who lost the battle of Narva" with the phrase equivalent to "the Tsar who won the battle of Poltava." The same applies to the translation of names. The correct translation of "Milano" is "Milan" and not "the second largest city in Italy." In translation, metalinguistic descriptivism about names implies that what is called "Milano" in Italian is that what is called "Milan" in English. In the case of cities, there may exist conventions about their names in certain eras. For instance, "Istanbul" is the name of Constantinople under Islamic rule the way "Leningrad" refers to Soviet-era St. Petersburg. The same applies also to the translation of phrases, such as German "der nahe Osten" (literally, "near East") with English as "Middle East"—the translation is a standard convention, chosen not only because the two phrases have the same reference but since geography makes them play equivalent roles in the cultural contexts in which these phrases are used.

The present discussion leaves aside the demand that the translation should replicate the stylistic aspects of the original. The existing literature about the theory of translation is largely marked by the fact that, traditionally, it has been the theorists of literature, rather than historians or philosophers, that have dedicated much attention to the problem of translation. Consequently, in "translation studies" the problem of translating and conveying the style, in addition to the accurate representation of the actual content plays a major role. The usual expectation in such situations is that the translation will not only be accurate but that it will produce on its recipient the same impression that the original would have done on the appropriate foreign-language reader.[18] The style that the translator chooses will also depend on the translator's *de verbis* beliefs about the public he or she is translating for and as well as his or her beliefs about the style of the original—i.e., either his or her beliefs about the author's *de verbis* beliefs that are relevant for the style, or the *de verbis* beliefs of the recipients that are relevant for the style. An important question is, whether the translator is concerned to convey the style in which the author wanted to write, or how his or her style was experienced by the work's recipients. These concerns, that are important in literary translation, however, are less important in scholarly translation and only sometimes in the translation of documents.

TRANSLATION: IS IT POSSIBLE TO CIRCUMVENT MEANINGS?

The core assumption of the account of translation presented above is that the translator needs to understand a text in order to translate it. It is the hermeneutic meaning (to use Bevir's term) that the text has for the translator that gets conveyed into another language. (As mentioned earlier, the translator may imagine "structural meanings," but they will be ultimately his or her hermeneutic meanings.) This assumption has been often denied. There exists a widespread view that translation can be performed without the understanding of the text and that it can be explained purely by manipulating words according to grammatical rules. The view is particularly supported by the belief in the possibility of computer translation. Michael Dummett thus wrote that translation is a mechanical process that can be performed by a computer and that a translator does not actually need to understand a sentence in order to translate it.[19] At the same time, many historians who work with materials in different languages may have good grounds to be skeptical about computer translation. Historians of philosophy may thus wonder, for instance, how a computer would translate Aristotle, with his departures from standard Greek. Scholarly translations of philosophical works or historical documents, for instance, are often serious research projects that computers even today—fifty years after Dummett's claim—can hardly do. Such translations cannot be reduced to the manipulation of words on the basis of grammatical rules.

A book on the philosophy of history is not a place to discuss the question of whether computers can translate. It is, however, relevant for our discussion to see the complications that arise if one assumes that translation can be done independently of *de verbis* beliefs, and to consider the difficulties that the "mechanical" model of translation, that assumes that translation can be performed by mere grammatical manipulation of dictionary contents, cannot resolve. If computers are to be able to translate competently, they need to be able to take into account the kinds of information that *de verbis* beliefs normally provide (and probably much more). It is beyond the scope of the discussion in this book to say whether and how such information can be actually fed to a computer and processed in a computer program. Some people may argue that the capacities of a computer that could process the information I describe below are so similar to human that one should in that case attribute to the computer mental states and beliefs, including *de verbis* and *de signis* beliefs. My main aim here is to illustrate how various complex situations that arise in translation can be understood in terms of *de verbis* and *de signis* beliefs.

Among the complexities that make it impossible to reduce translation to the manipulation of dictionary content according to the rules of grammar, two types of problems come to the forefront: those that pertain to homonyms and those that result from differences in information that different grammars require in order to form sentences.

A decade before Dummett's easy-going statement about translation Yehoshua Bar-Hillel noticed the problems that homonyms generate for mechanical translating.[20] His example was "The box was in the pen": the word "pen" can mean "writing utensil" but also "enclosure where children play." The full resolution of such ambiguities requires human-like understanding of reality, and the question is whether such information can be provided to the computer. Dictionary entries hardly ever recommend one-to-one translation. Most words used in any language express more than one concept, and clusters of concepts that words in different languages express do not coincide.

A different kind of problem arises in situations when the grammar of the language into which translation is made requires the inclusion of information that is not available in the original. These are the situations when the translator must provide the missing elements. The grammatically correct sentence structure in different languages often requires the speaker to include in the statement information that is unimportant in relation to the content that the speaker wants to convey. At the same time, different languages impose different requirements of this kind. A good example is the one stated by Roman Jakobsen: when translating the English sentence "she has brothers" into a language that has dual forms in addition to singular and plural, it will be necessary to convey the information whether she has two or more brothers.[21] Similarly, Jakobsen observes, when translating into Russian the English sentence "I hired a worker" it will be necessary to state whether the action (hiring) was completed or not and whether the worker was male or female. At the same time, the translation will leave it unclear whether the person has hired *a* or *the* worker. Problems of this kind are well-known nightmares of historians of philosophy. Consider a type of problem that arises in translating works of German philosophers such as Immanuel Kant's *Critique of Pure Reason*. Kant often used pronouns that refer to abstract concepts mentioned earlier in his text. The fact that the nouns that express these concepts differ in gender should have enabled his readers to establish which ones he had in mind. Nevertheless, it often happens that in the preceding text there are a number of same-gender nouns, which substantially complicates the understanding of the original text. An English translation is likely to introduce a new level of confusion if it merely translates all these pronouns with English "it" that is neuter. A translation may reveal or hide ambiguities of original sentences and the translator will have to decide to allow the ambiguities to come through or decide not to convey them in the translation. If the translator is to provide solutions for such dilemmas (and a translation cannot *not* propose a solution), he or she can do so only on the basis of his or her *de verbis* or *de signis* beliefs.

In some situations when the translator may not be able to establish the meaning of a word he or she may indeed opt for a systematic, mechanical translation that does not rely on his or her understanding of the text. For instance, experts may debate the meaning of a technical term an author used. The translator may simply want to avoid taking a position in an existing scholarly debate and may prefer to enable the readers to analyze the text themselves. Insofar as the term is systematically used in the text, the translator will be able to translate it systematically with a single term. An example is the extensive debate about the meaning of the term *lineamenta* in Leon Battista Alberti's opus. Translators of Alberti's works have typically avoided taking a position in the debate by translating the term consistently (or sometimes not quite consistently) with a single term (such as English "lineaments") whose meaning is similarly undecided.[22]

A particular kind of complication arises when the translator attempts to convey the actual *de verbis* beliefs of the author or his or her public. This is, for instance, likely to be the case when the author's use of a certain term was itself motivated by some other false beliefs and the translator thinks that a specific public may be interested to know about these beliefs. (Historians may be interested in beliefs about the use of specific terms.) Dante in his *De vulgari eloquentia* stated that in his youth he drank water from the river Sarnus, as he grew up in Florence.[23] The Sarnus, we know today, is actually a river in Campania. Dante's statement makes little sense unless we also know that he and his contemporaries heard about this river from Vergil and identified it, by mistake, with the Arno that flows through Florence. Should the translator translate Dante's statement following what Dante meant or what he actually said? Should the translation be faithful to what Dante wanted to say, or convey his false *de verbis* beliefs as well? It is hard to say that there can be a definite answer; rather, it all depends on the public that the translation is targeting and what content the translator believes they really want to know about. Translator's beliefs about his or her public and the public's expectations have to guide the translation.

NOTES

1. The distinction between understanding and interpretation presented here formalizes the important distinction made by Hirsch, *The Aims*, 79–81. See also similarly Irwin, *Intentionalist Interpretation*, 61.
2. Even when additional information about the author and its interpretative implications are known, one may decide to revert to zero author information reading. This answers Stephen Knapp's and Walter Benn Michaels's criticism (in their "Against Theory") of P. D. Juhl and E. D. Hirsch. (See also Wilson, "Again, Theory," as well as answer by Hirsch, "Against Theory?") All these authors agree that meaning is to be identified with the author's intention, but Knapp and Michaels criticize Juhl and Hirsch for postulating, at the same time, linguistic meaning parallel to the author's intention. They attribute to them the understanding that a text has multiple linguistic meanings whereby the right one is only to be chosen on the basis of the author's intention. ". . . Hirsch is imagining a moment of interpretation before intention is present. This is the moment at which the text's meaning 'remains indeterminate,' before such indeterminacy is cleared up by the addition of authorial intention. But if meaning and intention really are inseparable, then it makes no sense to think of intention as an ingredient that needs to be added; it must be present from the start. The issue of determinacy or indeterminacy is irrelevant." Knapp and Michaels, "Against Theory," 726. As a result (see Wilson, "Against Theory," 171), Knapp and Michaels seem to be forced to reject the common sense belief that English words, phrases and sentences have meanings—because they believe that this would lead them to postulate language *in abstracto*. But this is not necessarily the case. The "zero information about the author understanding" described here resolves these problems: there are certain social, linguistic, conventions of communication and authors use them to communicate. The fact that readers will understand a text on the basis of commonly shared assumptions (or the assumptions that they believe to be commonly shared) about the use of language does not mean postulating abstract meanings. These meanings are the contents of the mental states of readers.
3. See Knapp and Michaels, "Against Theory 2," 54.
4. Imagine thus a situation in which an author used a technical term without defining it, and that a survey of all cases in which he or she used the term shows that there are two possible meanings that cover, equally well, all its occurrences in a document. It is reasonable to expect that there would exist a substantial scholarly debate between the proponents of the two meanings. Now imagine that someone finds in an archive a letter written by this author in which he or she states that he had in mind one of the two meanings when he used the word. It is fair to expect that for most historians this finding would decide the debate and that few of them would still consider the alternative understanding credible.
5. Foucault, "Auteur," 84. For a summary see the opening section of Nehamas, "Author." Nehamas also denies Foucault's claim that the concept of author came about only in the Enlightenment. For a philosophical analysis of Foucault's and Barthes's theses about authorship see Lamarque, "Death." As Lamarque pointed out, "*Écriture* is in effect stipulated to be author-less, to be lacking in determinate meaning, to be free of interpretative constraints. . . . It is a non-starter—pointless if not impossible—to conceive of scientific or historical or philosophical discourse as *écriture*." Lamarque, "Death," 330–331.
6. Juhl, "Appeal," 280–281.
7. Gracia, "Can There Be," 247.
8. Roland Barthes, "La mort," 61–67.
9. Bevir, *Logic*, 54, 57.
10. Ibid., 129.
11. Ibid., 50–51.
12. Ibid., 54–55.
13. Ibid., 56.
14. A good example are general collections of introductory or research papers on the philosophy of language such as Martinich and Sosa (eds.), *Philosophy of Language*, Devitt and Hanley (eds.), *The Blackwell Guide*, or Russell and Farra (eds.), *The Routledge Companion*. These books are intended to provide their readers with a comprehensive perspective of the

contemporary philosophy of language—and they completely fail to discuss the problem of translation.

15. Unlike Swedish or Danish, Norwegian does not have standard pronunciation. There are two standard orthographies, Nynorsk and Bokmål, but no specific pronunciation is attached to them, though the former is more used in combination with south-western dialects and tends to rely on the words used in that part of the country.

16. I exclude from this the propositions that state the author believed that a certain sentence can or should be used in order to express the proposition he or she was expressing. In other words, when reading a text, we are reading sentences that express:

a) certain propositions
b) implicitly also the author's belief that these proposition should be expressed using that specific sentence.

These latter beliefs also pertain to certain propositions, and these latter propositions are normally not reproduced in a translation. However, there are exceptions: a translator may want to preserve some aspects of the original expression by retaining a technical term or using a cognate from a language into which he or she is translating.

17. For a discussion of such situations see Keenan, "Logical Problems," 171.
18. See discussion in Munday, *Introducing*, 31.
19. "In principle, we can imagine a person—or a very skillfully trained computer—able to translate between two languages without understanding either." Dummett, "What Do I Know," 98.
20. Hutchins, "Milestones."
21. Jakobsen, "Linguistic Aspects." Munday, *Introducing*.
22. See Mitrović, *Serene Greed*, 29–47 for a survey of the debate and translations.
23. Dante, *De vulgari*, 1.6.3.

Chapter Nine

Transparency

The dilemma about transparency pertains to the question of whether historical works, *as historical works* (and not merely as sets of individual sentences or propositions), can refer to the historical past and be true or false on the basis of their correspondence with it. Historical narratives consist of sentences, these sentences express propositions, and these propositions are true or false depending on the existence of historical items that meet the conditions of satisfaction of these propositions. (In what follows, I will use the term "narrative" for the set of sentences that constitute a historical text and the term "account" for the propositions that these sentences convey.) The problem is how to establish the truth or falsity of entire historical accounts and how to determine their relata. What are the relata of such historical accounts (or the narratives used to express them), and can such accounts be true or false? Historical reality, it has been pointed out by many authors, does not have the structure of a historical account or narrative. A narrative is a set of sentences that express a set of propositions; but historical reality is not pre-packed into story-like conglomerates of events that have plots and the structure of stories the way historical accounts, or narratives that express them, do.[1] In the 1930s, Maurice Mandelbaum formulated this argument by saying that the continuity and structure of historical works are different from the continuity and structure of historical events.[2] Or as David Carr put it, "Real events do not hang together in a narrative way . . . in virtue of its form any narrative account will present us with a distorted picture of the events it relates."[3] How can one then say that historical representations refer to the historical past, if the past itself has no narrative structure they could refer to? Or, to paraphrase C. Behan McCullagh, can we actually say that a historical representation bears any more resemblance to the past than a bouquet of flowers does to a garden from which it was picked?[4] This concern may be also responded to with a counter-question: why should one expect historical accounts to resemble past events in order to be true or false? Propositions about past events (or anything else) can be true or false without resembling the events they refer to—and it is not clear why a cluster of propositions, such as a historical account, cannot do the same. Similar to the arguments in favor of anti-realism in Chapter One, here too we encounter an argument that, if applied outside historical research, would invalidate many human activities: scientists in all fields describe in words the objects they study, although these objects do not look like the texts in which they are described.

One can differentiate between two views on the dilemma about the truth, reference, or meaning of historical accounts. The *transparent* view assumes that they in some way derive from the truth, reference, meaning, and so on of the totality of propositions expressed by the narrative, whereas the *opaque* view claims that they do not. The aim of this chapter is to show that the perspective on language, meaning, and mental states, as developed throughout this book, provides a consistent response to the dilemma in favor of the transparency of historical accounts.

OPACITY AND ANTI-REALISM

There exists an obvious similarity between the views of the proponents of the opacity of historical works and the anti-realist position discussed in Chapter One. Saying that historical narratives (or the accounts they express) cannot be true or false amounts to saying that they do not refer. The important difference, however, is that the proponents of opacity such as Heyden White or Keith Jenkins do not deny historical reality or the view that historians can make *individual* true statements about it.[5] The connection with past reality, in their view, is lost only when such statements are clustered into texts, historical narratives or historical representations, because other forces (rhetoric, literary style, political agendas and so on) take over—and this results in the opacity of such accounts. If they were transparent, then the relatum of a historical account (narrative) would be, in some transparent way, a function of the truth or of the relata of the totality of the propositions that make up the account.

Traditionally, the proponents of opacity took W. H. Walsh's analysis of colligatory concepts as the starting point of their arguments.[6] Walsh pointed out that historians typically encounter a large and unconnected sum of material that needs to be organized into a coherent whole. In order achieve this, a historian will have to formulate wider concepts that classify this material as items subsumable under a single concept—such as the Renaissance, the Enlightenment, or World War I. Typically, historians observe a set of events or phenomena that have certain common traits and classify them together by forming a concept that covers them all. When doing this one needs to specify, implicitly at least, the classificatory criteria of that concept: typically, such a concept refers to events that have certain characteristics and have occurred in a specific period. Walsh insisted that such colligatory concepts must be made to fit historical facts, rather than forcing facts into a straightjacket. The authenticity of colligatory concepts in his view is in their ability to cover details; for every statement that includes such concepts one must be able to produce a series of subordinate statements that support it. As he put it, "there is a point beyond which no self-respecting historian could persist with his interpretation in the face of unassimilated data."[7]

While the importance of colligatory concepts has been widely accepted among philosophers or history, some authors such as Frank Ankersmit or Jouni-Matti Kuukkanen have insisted that such concepts cannot refer and that there is nothing in historical reality that they pertain to. The claim is bound to raise eyebrows among practicing historians, since it boils down to the claim that, for instance, the Renaissance or World War I did not happen. The critics have even pointed out that "the Holocaust" is a colligatory concept and that the claim that such concepts have no reference entails the denial that the Holocaust happened as well.[8] At the same time, the claim that colligatory concepts do not refer cannot be limited to history-writing. Colligatory concepts are widely used in all fields of science and the humanities and if Ankersmit's and Kuukkanen's arguments are valid, this will have exceptionally wide consequences. "Global warming," for instance, is a colligatory concept too, and if such concepts do not refer, then there is no need to worry about it.

Here are the arguments that they state in favor of this view.[9] According to Ankersmit, it is impossible to fix the reference of colligatory concepts such as "the Renaissance" or "the French Revolution"; attempts to individuate the Renaissance in his view can at most give us necessary, but never sufficient conditions for fixing the reference of the term.[10] The reference of "Renaissance," Ankersmit observed differs in the works of various historians such as Burckhardt, Michelet, Huizinga, Wölfflin and so on.[11] Similarly, different historians had different things in mind when they wrote about the French Revolution. It is thus not clear "What exactly is this French Revolution. . . . Does it include Robespierre's having had breakfast on the morning of 20 March 1791? Even more so, does it include the kinds of things that historians in, say, 2200 AD—and thus still unknown to us—will mention in their histories of the Revolution?"[12] His next move in the argument is to ask "Can you refer to an x that is unknown to you? What does it mean to 'refer' to something that expands or shrinks with the vagaries of historical debate?"[13]

Kuukkanen's point concentrates on the observation that colligatory concepts are formed using metaphors. For instance, one talks about "Khrushchev's Thaw" in Soviet politics and public life following Stalin's death that manifested itself as the liberalization of public life, the release of political prisoners from Gulags, greater freedom in creative activities, the reestablishment of communication with countries that were regarded as hostile in the final years of Stalin's rule and similar trends and events. Such metaphors cannot be true, Kuukkanen pointed out, because the world was not literally frozen in Stalin's time.[14] The metaphor covers such a great diversity of social and political phenomena that there is "no possibility that she [the historian] would stumble upon a unifying link between phenomena in the source material itself" (117).

Both Ankersmit and Kuukkanen assume that only singular objects can be objects of reference. Reference, according to Ankersmit, picks out unique objects in the world.[15] The term "Renaissance," he explains, does not refer because there is no "unique individual thing in the past" that it could be said to refer to.[16] Similarly, according to Kuukkanen, "the Cold War" in the statement "The Cold War was dangerous" cannot refer because "reference" needs to be understood as in the case of proper names, which refer to individuals.[17] Kuukkanen says:

> The name "Barack Obama" refers to one individual only, namely to the person who is the president of the USA in 2015. What would be a *particular* to which the "Cold War" refers? Colligatory expressions do not seem to instantiate any individual—they do not seem to correspond to any singular object in the historical world.[18]

These arguments have received much attention, but it is still hard not to think that something must have gone wrong with a philosophy of history that infers that historical events, or clusters of historical events such as the Renaissance, or the French Revolution, did not happen. If Ankersmit's and Kuukkanen's arguments are valid, they will apply to many non-historical statements as well. "Global warming" does not refer to a single particular object, but should we therefore say that it is not real? "Software industry" also expresses a colligatory concept and it would follow that "software industry grows steadily" does not refer nor pertain to anything. In fact, if we statistically established that software industry grows steadily, the suggestion is that we would not be able to say it, because we would have to use a phrase that expresses a colligatory concept and consequently cannot refer to the situation we want to describe.

Ankersmit's and Kuukkanen's arguments, in fact, have straightforward responses. In the case of the first argument, the fact that various individuals use a term differently, does not mean that the term does not refer. Rather, it means that it expresses somewhat different concepts and has somewhat different relata when used by different individuals. For instance, one person says: "The chair is in the corner." Another person responds: "Not quite in the corner, but close." They disagree about what counts as "corner" but this does not mean that the room has no corners. It would be actually hard to find a word or a term in any language that was always used consistently the same way by everyone. It is normal that scholars engaged in historical research, at some point, may have to consider whether they are talking about the same things when they use certain words.[19] An architectural historian may state that the Renaissance starts with Brunelleschi's departure for Rome after he lost the competition for the door of the Baptistery of Florence; for a literary historian the crucial date may be Petrarch's ascent of Mont Ventoux. In this case, the classificatory criteria of the concept "Renaissance" may not even be different, but they happen to be satisfied for the first time by different events in different fields. In the case of Robespierre's breakfast on 20 March 1791, it is fair to say that the French Revolution was a cluster of political events and an event such as breakfast may or may not have political relevance and accordingly, count or not count as part of the Revolution. (For instance, important decisions may have been discussed or made during the breakfast.) Historians may also disagree about its political relevance and include it or exclude it from their accounts of the French Revolution.

As for the second argument, the possession of a concept requires that the person must know the criteria of its application. If the events and phenomena subsumed under the concept "Khrushchev's Thaw" really had nothing in common, we would simply not be able to identify the events or phenomena that belong under that concept.[20] In fact, it is simply false that the phenomena that are taken to belong under "Khrushchev's Thaw" have nothing in common. Here belong the liberalization of public life, the release of political prisoners, the greater freedom of press, and so on—and what they all have in common, and what constitutes the concept expressed by the phrase "Khrushchev's Thaw," is that they are all manifestations of different, more liberal attitudes of the Soviet government after Khrushchev came to power. The *phrase* "Khrushchev's Thaw" is a metaphor, but this merely means that the *phrase* used to express the concept has been chosen as a metaphor. Grasping the meaning depends on grasping the *de signis* and not only the *de verbis* beliefs of the people who use the phrase. The fact that the world was not literally frozen in the Stalin era has no effect on the nature of the concept that the phrase "Khrushchev's Thaw" expresses (at most, this can be used to criticize the choice of that specific phrase). The same applies to another example mentioned by Kuukkanen, "the Cold War." The phrase that is chosen to express the concept is metaphorical (there was no real war between the United States and the USSR at the time)—but the concept pertains to a series of phenomena and events in international politics that were real enough and can be described as the manifestations of the confrontation between two superpowers.

The third argument relies on the assumption that colligatory concepts have to refer to singular, particular objects and function as the names of individual humans, in order to have relata. It is unclear why one would expect them to do so. In fact, colligatory concepts are precisely constructed to refer to numerous historical objects, events or phenomena that share the characteristics according to which historians classify them under the same colligatory concept. In this sense "Khrushchev's Thaw" is not different from "Venetian ships in the battle of Lepanto"—the former pertains to a set of phenomena that resulted from the same attitude change of the Soviet government; the latter is a set of ships the *Serenissima* sent into the battle. In both cases, there is a set of phenomena, events or objects that has more than one element and they all satisfy the classificatory criteria of the given concept.

These considerations now clarify the use of colligatory concepts, such as "the Renaissance" in history-writing. The relata of the concept expressed by the term will be a very large set of historical items (events, trends, phenomena, beliefs and so on) that can be subsumed under certain tendencies that are characteristic of Italian life of the fifteenth and sixteenth centuries and that differentiate it from previous and subsequent centuries. These tendencies can be understood as subsidiary concepts of the wider colligatory concept "Renaissance." Here belong intensified cultural and intellectual production whose artifacts differ significantly from those of the previous centuries, intensified interest in classical antiquity that coincided with the influx of Byzantine scholars, the importation of Greek manuscripts and the ability to disseminate knowledge using the printing press, the increased independence of intellectuals from the Church and so on. The colligatory concept is not random, because Italian cultural and intellectual life of the period indeed differed from the preceding and later periods in these aspects. It was created bottom-up, in order to fit the facts: well before the term "Renaissance" came into use, it was known that Italian cultural life of the era differed that way from other periods—well before Michelet used the metaphor of rebirth, Voltaire described it in his *History of the Era of Louis XIV* while Hegel referred to it using the term "Restoration."[21] Also, it would be futile to attempt to state a single cause of the events and tendencies that made up the Renaissance, because, as mentioned in the Introduction, no event ever has a single cause. A colligatory concept such as the one expressed by the term "the Renaissance" is more comparable to the descriptions of medical syndromes, whereby one can observe a series of symptoms, signs and phenomena in the patient, that can be correlated without having a common cause—but they are still given a joint name. The fact that there exists a certain variation in the relata of the concepts that various scholars express using terms such as "Renaissance" does not mean that the concepts they express using such terms have no relata. Predominantly they do have the same relata, with some variation. This variation has to be marginal, otherwise the very field of Renaissance studies could not be constituted. In that case people simply would not know what to call "Renaissance" and how to use the word. Finally, it makes no sense to say that there is no evidence that the Renaissance happened—*not* only because the evidence is overwhelming, but because this concept was originally created in order to colligate the trends and events that were known to have happened; in Walsh's phrase, the concept was "tailored to fit the facts."[22] In other words, the concept expressed using the word "Renaissance" is a colligatory concept that includes a number of subsidiary concepts, such as "revived interest in classical antiquity," "discovery and use of perspective in paintings," "increased availability of original Greek texts" and so on. The conditions of satisfaction of these concepts are satisfied by numerous events and phenomena of Italian life of the fifteenth and sixteenth centuries in ways that differentiate it from previous and subsequent epochs. The fact that the relata of these concepts are not empty sets, means that the extension of "the Renaissance" is not an empty set, and the proposition expressed by the sentence "the Renaissance happened" is true.

It is useful to provide here an example that can illustrate this discussion. Let me use the term "Felinia" for the set of all cats that ever existed or will ever exist. It is merely the set of all cats; it is not something more, over and above that set. To be a member of Felinia, an item must be a cat. If we want to know whether an item is a member of Felinia, we need to establish whether it has all the properties that are necessary for something to be a cat. This is quite similar to the way, in the case we want to know whether Robespierre's breakfast on 20 March 1791 was part of the French Revolution, we need to consider the criteria that an event must satisfy to be part of the Revolution—for instance, the breakfast must be politically relevant and so on. It can be pointed out that the definition of a cat is not always very precise and even if we rely on cats' DNA in order to differentiate them from other creatures, it may remain unclear where to draw the boundary when it comes to Savannah cats or Bengal cats (hybrid breeds with servals and Asian leopard respectively). However, this does not mean that Felinia, as a set of all cats, does not exist. It means that its boundaries in some cases are not precise. Further on, through history, as cats evolved and moved from one continent to another, Felinia started manifesting itself in various regions at various times; in New Zealand, for instance, Felinia arrived only a couple of centuries ago. This is again similar to the way the Renaissance started manifesting itself in various fields (architecture, literature) at different times. Finally, if I metaphorically start calling cats "lions" and rename "felinia" into "leonia," cats will not stop to exist.

Chapter 9
THE PROPOSITIONS THAT A HISTORICAL TEXT CONVEYS

While the arguments proposed in favor of opacity are unsatisfactory, their refutation does not show that historical works can be transparent. Why (and how) should one expect clusters of propositions taken together to be true or false in addition to the truth-value of each individual proposition that makes up the cluster? After all, it is normally understood that it is individual propositions, and not clusters of propositions, that can be true or false, or have reference. When two propositions are combined in a syllogism, that syllogism can be valid or not, its conclusion can be true or false, but one does not talk about the truth or falsity of the syllogism itself. Similarly, concepts are not true or false. The possession of truth and falsity is really a defining characteristic of propositions. Independently of the arguments presented by the proponents of opacity, therefore, on purely definitional grounds, someone may argue that a historical narrative, or the account that it expresses, cannot be true or false in addition to the set of the individual truth-values of each sentence (proposition) that makes it up. This is an argument about terminology and it is best responded by adjusting terminology. In order to avoid confusion in what follows I will talk about the accuracy or inaccuracy of historical accounts, rather than their truth and falsity. But then, what is the relationship between the accuracy or inaccuracy of historical works and the truth or falsity of individual propositions expressed by the sentences that make them up?

In order to respond to the dilemma, it is reasonable to start by establishing the actual set of propositions that a historical narrative—the total set of all sentences of a historical work—conveys. Historical narratives normally convey more propositions than all sentences that make them up taken individually. Their truth and relata cannot be identical with the truth-values and the relata of the propositions individually expressed by the sentences that make up the narrative. Consider, for instance, what Gibbon says about Peter the Hermit:

> He was born of a gentleman's family (for we now must adopt a modern idiom), and his military service was under the neighboring counts of Boulogne, the heroes of the first crusade. But he soon relinquished the sword and the world; and if it be true that his wife, however noble, was aged and ugly, he might withdraw with the less reluctance from her bed to a convent, and at length to a hermitage. In this austere solitude his body was emaciated, his fancy was inflamed; whatever he wished, he believed; whatever he believed, he *saw* in dreams and revelations. From Jerusalem the pilgrim returned an accomplished fanatic; but as he excelled in the popular madness of the times, Pope Urban the Second received him as a prophet, applauded his grand design,

promised to support it in a general council, and encouraged him to preach the deliverance of the Holy Land.[23]

Gibbon does not say that Peter the Hermit *went to* Jerusalem. It is nevertheless enough to know that Boulogne is not in the neighborhood of Jerusalem to grasp that one could not have *returned from* Jerusalem without having gone there. He obviously expected his readers grasp this. A historical narrative or representation is not identical to the sum of individual propositions expressed by all individual sentences. It says much more—and this depends on the reader's beliefs (knowledge) as well as the beliefs (knowledge) that the author attributes to the reader. The meaning and the understanding of a historical text fundamentally depends on interpretation, including the interpretation that the historian expects the reader to be able to perform. The total sum of the propositions a historical narrative expresses also includes the propositions that are implied by the style and the rhetoric the historian uses—for instance, the author may use irony in order to reveal his or her value judgments about the events described. Ranke in *Die serbische Revolution* describes the joint activities of the Turkish and Russian fleets off the coast of Italy during the Second Coalition against Napoleon: "a joint Turkish-Russian fleet appears off the coast of Italy; the Caliph of Rum, as was the Sultan's proper title, made the efforts to re-install the Pope in Rome."[24] The sentence describes a fact: Turkish political aims behind a certain naval intervention—but the phrase "Caliph of Rum" is obviously used in order to remind the readers of the absurdity of the situation, in the wider religious and historical context that (the sentence also indicates) Ranke expects his readers to be aware of. It also conveys Ranke's own judgment of the events. There are thus a number of additional propositions conveyed by the sentence, in addition to the one that describes the activities of the Turkish fleet. Hayden White similarly analyzed a brief paragraph from A. J. P. Taylor's *The Course of German History* in order to point out that literary conventions and rhetoric support the historical explanation the paragraph provides.[25] Taylor argued that the real life of the Weimar Republic was much shorter than the period 1919–1933: the first four years were marked by the confusion that followed the war; during the last three years a temporary dictatorship "half cloaked in legality . . . reduced the republic to a sham long before it was openly overthrown." White's analysis presents a series of propositions that can be derived from the literary structure of the text and its rhetoric. However, precisely because his analysis recovers these propositions so successfully, it is much harder to follow him in his claim that the explanatory effect of Taylor's writing derives from "its appeal to certain conventions of literary characterization."[26] One would much rather say that the explanatory effect derives from the *propositions conveyed* using certain literary conventions—after all, literary conventions themselves cannot explain anything, but the propositions they convey can. Simply, a historical text conveys a set of propositions, some of which are expressed using more literary or rhetorical means than others and some may express the author's judgment. A historian who calls the political life of an era "sham" knows that he is expressing a value judgment and expects the readers to recognize the truth of the corresponding proposition ("The author thinks . . ."). But this is a proposition like any other expressed by the text—and it is not clear that (as White suggests) one should privilege the propositions conveyed by means of rhetoric or literary structure over other propositions that one can read in or otherwise infer from a text.[27]

CONTENTS OF HISTORICAL WORKS

A historical narrative is a set of sentences that taken individually express a certain set of propositions. In addition to this, further propositions can be inferred from these propositions, and still more propositions can be inferred when the propositions that have been conveyed are combined with other propositions known to the reader. Historians write historical texts with certain assumptions, conscious or unconscious, about their readers, what they know, believe, and assume. The knowledge, assumptions, and beliefs of readers, however, may be quite different from those that the authors assumed. It is not necessarily even likely that they coincide. Readers may belong to a very different social or cultural context from the one that the historians imagined. Reading Roman historians such as Suetonius or Tacitus can often be challenging because of the knowledge about Roman political institutions that they expect their readers to share with them. Also, readers will often have their assumptions about authors—what the authors assumed or could not have assumed—and this will affect the propositions the readers infer. Or they may be interested in the way the text was understood in a certain era (for instance, in the Renaissance reception of Roman historical works) and base their reading of the text on the assumptions they make about the assumptions of other readers, not on those of the authors themselves.

Unstated assumptions, as well as assumptions believed to be stated, play an immensely important role in every act of communication, not only in history-writing. In the analytic philosophy of language, there is an extensive literature about presuppositions and implicature in communication. (Presuppositions have already been mentioned in relation to *de verbis* and *de signis* beliefs.) A presupposition is a proposition that has to be assumed ("presupposed") in order to make sense of a certain linguistic act.[28] Compare "John did not meet his niece" with "John said that he met his niece." The former sentence presupposes that John has a niece, but the latter does not. Sometimes, a historian may present a line of reasoning in the form of an enthymeme, an argument in which some premises are missing, because one assumes that they are known, and a logical analysis may be necessary in order to establish the premises of the incompletely stated argument.[29] In the case of implicature, the author says one thing but implies something else and counts on the interlocutor's ability to recover the unsaid implication.[30] For example, "they are poor but honest" implies, but does not state directly, that there is a contrast between being poor and being honest. Similarly, "Paul got pneumonia and was hospitalized" does not imply the same things as "Paul was hospitalized and got pneumonia." It is also important to bear in mind that what authors imply is not quite the same as what can be inferred from what they state.[31] From a true proposition one can infer only further true propositions, whereas authors can state a true proposition and still imply something false. Also, the audience may infer from the authors' statements various facts about the authors—their envy, prejudices, narcissistic traits—but such inferable information is often not part of what the authors imply. What applies to communication in general applies to communication between historians and their readers; presuppositions and implicature play an important role in the reading of historical texts. However, in addition to these phenomena, which are extensively described and discussed by philosophers of language, there are also numerous propositions that the readers of historical texts normally infer by combining other propositions that they know or believe to be true with those that can be inferred from the historical text itself. These assumptions with which readers approach a text define the questions that they can ask of the text, as well as ultimately its interpretation and what readers get from the text.

The questions that historians themselves ask and the answers they provide decide the content and structure of the corpus of propositions that they express in a historical work. Historians do not approach the material they are writing without assumptions or interest and, as Croce pointed out, there is no disinterested writing of history.[32] A historian who attempted to collect facts randomly and present them without a question (or questions) that the collection is meant to respond to would be, to use Croce's phrase, a *raccattatore maniaco*, a collector-maniac, and it is not clear that much sense could be made from a history that was a random concoction of true sentences.[33] (Danto's ideal chronicler is then precisely an ideal collector-maniac, who collects the totality of descriptions of events, with the only limit being that they have to be stated using information available at the time when the events happened.) In the case of research papers in history, the topic—the question the author is trying to respond to—is typically clearly stated. In the case of books, many historical works strive to describe a line of events—how something happened—and such *quomodo* histories have a clear topic and a principle according to which the authors select the events. Thucydides thus described the series of events that made up the Peloponnesian War (though not quite to its end); Gibbon the long series of events that constituted the decline and the fall of the Roman Empire; Veronica Wedgewood the Thirty Years War. In all such histories, the historian selected and described a series of events whose description constitutes the response to the question "how did this happen"; the selection can be challenged or criticized for omitting or downplaying some events and overemphasizing others. Also, some descriptions of some events may be inaccurate. The greater the presence of such inaccurate descriptions, the more the text ceases to be a historical work and becomes a work of historical fiction. Conversely, works of historical fiction cannot be false in everything they describe (otherwise they would not be *historical* fiction). Since it is not easy for historical works to be accurate in all details, the boundary between historical works and historical fiction is arguably better defined by the intentions (or claims) of their authors about the category than by the actual truth or falsity of the propositions they convey.

The historian's selection of facts and events that the work describes may happen to be different from the one that the work purports to describe. This can happen inadvertently or, for instance, in order to meet the demand of a contemporary public. In some cases, one can really say that the book has a crypto-topic that one recognizes as a pattern in the selection of the facts or events that it describes. Tacitus in his *Annals* did not merely describe important events in the era he was writing about. Rather, he systematically selected and described examples of the decline of personal integrity and uprightness among the Roman aristocracy from Tiberius through Nero; the pattern of his comments suggests that a major implicit topic of his book is the moral decline of the upper strata of Roman society. Similarly, Ranke in his *Geschichten der romanischen und germanischen Völker* sought to emphasize similarities between Germanic and Romance nations in Europe (in opposition to non-Germanic-non-Romance nations) in order to assert German participation in and contribution to the Italian Renaissance. The book eventually spawned a long tradition of German historians' appropriation of the Italian Renaissance. Although the book is typically cited for Ranke's phrase "wie es eigentlich gewesen," it falls quite far from that target. In order to establish greater similarity between Romance and Germanic nations, Ranke made some quite extraordinary assertions, such as the claim that non-Germanic and non-Romance nations (such as Greeks, Hungarians, or Russians) did not develop cities or use heavy armor.[34] The use of the word "eigentlich" ("actually") introduces an essentialist claim: that Ranke is not merely describing what happened, but that-what-matters in the era, its essence (i.e., the Germanic contribution to the Italian Renaissance). This should not be confused with a profession of historical realism, the view that historians describe what happened, τὰ γενόμενα as Aristotle put it. The claim that there is such a thing as the essence of an era is subject to all the difficulties of essentialism described in Chapter Six. Such claims, one is easily tempted to think, are often made in order to enable the historian to make his or her research subservient and therefore pleasing to the political agendas of the general public or individuals in political power. Johann Gustav Droysen's *Geschichte Alexanders des Großen* systematically recast the relationship between Macedonia and small Greek city-states as equivalent to that of Prussia and small German states in the nineteenth century. The aim of condemning the opponents of German unification under Prussia by condemning the opponents of Macedonian domination of Greece can hardly be missed. Unsuccessfully concealed nationalistic agendas can seriously damage the credibility of a historical work. Even when the topic of the book is explicitly stated, historians' beliefs about the interests of their public, and the questions that they believe are of interest to the public, often determine the topic. Other works are motivated by historians' desire to challenge (what they regard as) historical misconceptions in the context in which they work. Fritz Fischer's *Griff nach der Weltmacht* was controversial in its time in Germany because it introduced a new perspective, widely denied by German scholars of the era, on German war aims in World War I and German leadership's role in the outbreak of the war. For someone who does not read Fischer's book from the perspective equivalent to that of 1960s German historians, the book's main theses can hardly be controversial. Rather, one may think that it presents a German-centric perspective about the outbreak of the war in which other powers seem to have played only a passive role. (That Fischer explicitly rejected this reading in his *Begleitwort* from 1977 merely indicates that he was aware of the possibility of such misunderstanding, and that the totality of the picture he painted invites it.[35]) Something similar could be said of A. J. P. Taylor's thesis about Adolf Hitler's passive role in the outbreak of World War II.[36] The book presented an unflattering perspective on the actions and competence of British and French diplomats and their blunders in dealing with the Third Reich; like Fischer's, it also caused a controversy when it came out. However, the book focuses on the outbreak of the war in western Europe and Poland as if the *Wehrmacht* invasions of the Soviet Union, Yugoslavia, or Greece had never happened—and it is simply impossible to attribute to Hitler a passive role in the initiation of those conflicts.[37] Taylor certainly did not overlook or ignore the fact that World War II in Europe was fought predominantly in eastern and not western Europe (the military losses of a medium-sized country such as Yugoslavia were twice as high as those of France, not to mention the size of the Soviet military effort)—but he was writing for the British public and challenging the standard view of the outbreak of the war in the area that interested them.

The explanations that historians provide and the causes they state depend on the questions that the explanation is meant to answer and the assumptions historians make about their public. The fall of the western Roman Empire can be explained differently, depending on whether one is responding to the question "Why did the western Roman Empire succumb to external invasions in the fifth century and the eastern did not?" or "Why did the western Roman Empire succumb to external invasions in the fifth century and not a century before"?[38] At the same time, the selection of the information that historians provide typically says much about the what they expect their readers to believe and know, and can even be a document about the era in which they were writing.

QUESTIONS AND ANSWERS

Historians thus approach the writing of history with their own questions, which include the question that their research was intended to answer as well as those that they think will be the questions with which the readers will approach the text. Their assumptions about the knowledge and beliefs of their readers—they may regard some of these beliefs as true, others as false—largely define the content of descriptions and explanations that they will provide. At the same time, readers approach the text with their own questions that they expect to be answered; they encounter the historians' questions and answers from their own perspectives and beliefs and ask questions derived from these perspectives and beliefs. Sometimes, but not always, readers' and historians' questions and assumptions coincide.

At the same time, as mentioned, historical works are not only about the propositions that historians directly assert, but also those that they lead readers to infer. Howard Zinn, in his *People's History of the United States*, ceaselessly lists individual cases of oppression and discrimination of members of minority groups. He avoids general statements about the oppression that a certain group suffered as a group; he always talks about individuals. But readers who read about these individual cases of oppression will doubtlessly grasp that they occurred in contexts in which they were possible. Zinn need not describe wider contexts of such events in order to make it clear that the social environment enabled oppression. His descriptions of individual cases paint a damning and comprehensive picture of their wider social environment, without talking about that environment. Similarly, Thomas G. Otte's *July Crisis* describes minute communications between diplomats during July 1914 that led to World War I. His detailed description provides the reader with the picture of interactions within a political mechanism in which participants, acting in their own contexts, had very little choice and in which, for instance, even railway mobilization schedules significantly constrained the attempts to prevent the war. Such a detailed description substantially invalidates the explanations of the outbreak of the war that refer to general or abstract entities, such as the interests of capital, imperialism, nationalism, and so on. At most, such general terms describe or qualify the motivation and acting of individuals. There are also situations in which the historian predicts the reasoning, impressions, or judgments that the readers are likely to make and adds explanatory contextual information that is strictly unrelated to the topic of the narrative, but enables readers to get a more balanced perspective. Andrew Roberts in his biography of Napoleon regularly interrupts the main course of the narrative in order to provide such information: when he talks about the madness of Tsar Paul I, he also discusses other mentally instable monarchs during the era; when he describes Napoleon's Introduction of the death penalty for smuggling, he notes that the British did the same; when he says that Napoleon did not differentiate between his personal wealth and that of France, he also points out that this was not uncommon at the time.[39] Obviously, such additional explanations are made on the basis of the questions and assumptions that historians presume their readers will make.

In such cases readers are still guided by the historian; the questions that they come to answer through their reading are those that the historian wanted them, or expected them, to ask. It is, however, not necessarily the case that historians and their readers ask the same questions, and it is even less often the case that they share the same assumptions when they ask them. Questions that readers ask may be very different from those that motivated the historian, but readers will nevertheless read the historical work in search of the answer to the questions that interest them. In the process, the propositions that historians expressed and those they intended to be inferred will be combined with those with which the readers approach the text and will be used in order to respond to the questions that they form. Sometimes only a small portion of a historical work will be relevant to a question a reader is interested in.

TRANSPARENCY

These observations answer the dilemma about the transparency or opacity of historical works. It is as responses to questions, historians, and their readers, that historical works can be accurate or inaccurate. The historian may claim to have written a work in order to answer one set of questions, implicitly actually address another set of questions, while readers may approach the work with the expectation that it will respond to a third set of questions. Similarly, when Peter Kosso points out that each statement in a historical work can be individually true, but taken together such statements "could collectively add to a misleading or inaccurate picture of the past," he is certainly right, and one should add that a picture is always a picture of something and will depend on the questions that the work is expected to answer.[40] Fischer's *Griff nach der Weltmacht* discussed above is a good example: it may be argued that it gives an accurate presentation of the German political elite's contribution to the outbreak of World War I, but that it is not accurate when it comes to (and it even plays down) the contribution of others. ("Accurate" in this case should be taken to mean that the book does not fail to present the actions of German leadership that were significant for the outbreak of the war. A person who says that the book is accurate in that sense is stating that in his or her opinion, one cannot state specific actions of the German leadership that contributed to the outbreak of the war that were left unmentioned in the book. Other distinctions, such as McCullagh's distinction between fair and misleading presentations, are also possible.[41]) A historical work thus necessarily has multiple meanings depending on the different questions it is asked to answer; it can be accurate or inaccurate depending on what we expect it to answer.

We can now also see how historical works can refer. A single proposition defines a single set of conditions that need to be satisfied for it to be true. It does not have multiple or diverse truth-values depending on the various individual readers or interpretations. At the same time, for something to be true or false, it needs to be a proposition, a truth-bearer. Even when it comes to visual representations such as pictures or maps, it is propositions about them that are true or false. A portrait or the photograph of a house, for instance, is a set of lines that can be taken to describe a specific spatial object, such as a person or a house. Many other same-looking spatial objects can also satisfy such a visual description. (In this sense, a visual image is comparable to a concept, and can indeed be part of a concept that specifies "something that looks like this image."[42]) Taken on its own, a visual image cannot be true or false (or accurate or inaccurate); what can be true or false is a proposition that asserts that a certain specific person or a building satisfies the visual description that the image provides. Something similar applies to historical works. One can derive a great variety of historical accounts (clusters of propositions) from a historical narrative: those that the author expressed in sentences, those that the author also implied, those that various readers thought was the content of the work, those that someone judges that some readers took to be the content of the work, and so on. There are also the propositions that readers infer by combining the propositions the author expressed with other propositions they believed, in relation to questions that interested them, the questions that they attributed to the author and so on. Among visual representations, such clusters are best compared to maps. For a map to be accurate, it does not have to be accurate in all aspects (and certainly not in those aspects it is not intended to represent), but only those that are an accurate response to a specific question. The map of public transportation routes in a city need not indicate the positions of kindergartens—it is supposed to answer questions pertaining to the functioning of bus- and tramlines. However, it does not answer these questions—it cannot be true or false, accurate or inaccurate—until it is asked these questions, until it is taken to respond to them. In other words, until we claim that it is a map of public transportation routes in the city. Then this claim can be true or false, and the map will consequently be accurate or inaccurate, and insofar as it is accurate it refers to the organization of public transportation that makes it true. If we do not say that it is a map of public transportation in a specific city, we may treat it as the map of public transportation of some imaginary city or as an abstract painting. It becomes pointless to discuss whether it is accurate or inaccurate, or what it refers to.

Like a map, any historical account can be read as a pure fiction if we, for instance, replace all names of historical figures, countries, cities, and so on with imaginary ones, or insofar as we do not make the claim that it is a description of something that really happened, or if we state that it represents imaginary events—in other words, until we take (assert) that it describes specific events (and other historical items) and answers historical questions. A description of the Borodino battle refers to the actual battle because the historian states that it is a description of the Borodino battle—that it is the description of the same event as the event that is called "the Borodino battle." The historical item that is being described is identified by and is the relatum of the description established on the basis of some other description such as its name (in accordance with the discussion of metalinguistic descriptivism about names in Chapter Six). Once the item referred to is identified, one can ask the question of whether the description is accurate and provides true answers to questions asked about it. Similar to a map, the account will then be accurate if it provides true answers to the questions asked. It may also happen that the truth of all propositions participating in a cluster is not sufficient for the cluster to be an accurate response to a historical question, the way an accurate map of city transportation routes may fail to include a tramline. A historical account must provide a true response to a historical question in order for it to be accurate. (Imprecision is always possible, and it may also happen that, like a map, the account is not accurate in certain respects.) The way it is the case with a map, the answer provided by a historical account is accurate because its conditions of satisfaction are satisfied by historical items of the past, such as past events. This is expected from and achieved by accurate historical accounts.

NOTES

1. As Hayden White pointed out: "The notion that sequences of real events possess the formal attributes of the stories we tell about imaginary events could only have its origin in wishes, daydreams, reveries. Does the world really present itself to perception in the form of well-made stories, with central subjects, proper beginnings, middles, and ends, and a coherence that permits us to see 'the end' in every beginning?" White, "Value of Narrativity," 24.
2. Mandelbaum, *Historical Knowledge*, 30.
3. Carr, "Narrative," 117.
4. McCullagh, "Narrative Logic," 395.
5. White, *Metahistory*, 6, note 5. Jenkins, *Re-thinking History*, 40. For a different view see Jenkins, *Refiguring History,* 5, where he claims that "historians can just never get things right." See also the discussion in McCullagh, *Truth in History*, 4.
6. Walsh, "Colligatory Concepts."
7. Ibid., 140.
8. Saari, "Postmodernist Theory," 16. See also Ankersmit's response, "Reply."
9. For a complete survey of arguments proposed by Ankersmit and Kuukkanen, see Mitrović, "Opacity" and Mitrović, "Refutation."
10. Ankersmit, *Meaning*, 145.
11. Ankersmit, *Representation*, 40. The same argument is stated in Frank Ankersmit: "Reply," 26.
12. Ibid., 26.
13. Ibid., 26.
14. Kuukanen, *Post-Narrativist*, 106.
15. Ankersmit, *Meaning*, 92.
16. Kuukanen, *Post-Narrativist*, 145.
17. Ibid., 106–107.
18. Ibid., 106–107. The same understanding of reference is in Ankersmit, *Meaning,* 65, where he explains that the operation of reference consists in "picking out uniquely," which is crucial for a description's being capable of being true or false. The argument then asserts that "As long as we cannot be sure what object in the world the statement is referring to, we cannot decide about propositional truth and falsity." Ibid., 65. "The logic of the true statement (or description) implies a specific ontology: the ontology of a world made up of identifiable unique objects, to which we can ascribe certain properties using the predicates of true statements whose subject terms refer to those objects." Ibid., 65. The obvious response is that individual objects can constitute sets and that it is possible to refer to sets of objects as well.
19. As Searle pointed out: ". . . it is a condition of a precise theory of an indeterminate phenomenon that it should precisely characterize that phenomenon as indeterminate; and a distinction is no less a distinction for allowing for a family of related, marginal diverging cases." Searle, "World," 78.
20. Kuukkanen, *Postnarrativist*, 112–113 actually addresses this problem but fails to resolve it. On the one hand, he claims that if a colligatory category is to be meaningful, there has to be a feature that applies to all subsumed entities; on the other, he also states that colligatory concepts categorize without any necessary shared features or resemblance among sub-ordinated entities. He states that "There is thus this one feature or principle that has to apply to all subsumed entities in order for the colligatory category to be meaningful." Ibid., 112. But he also claims that "Colligatory concepts (1) *organize* lower-order data into higher-order wholes; (2) categorize *without* any necessary *shared features* or resemblance among sub-ordinated entities; . . ." Ibid., 113.
21. Voltaire, *Louis XIV*, 1. Hegel, *Philosophie der Geschichte*, 488–491.
22. Walsh, "Colligatory Concepts," 139.
23. Gibbon, *Decline and Fall*, vol. 3, 418.
24. Ranke, *Die serbische Revolution*, 181.
25. He actually claims that the explanatory effect *derives* from the appeal to literary conventions. White, "Historicism," 107–114.

26. Ibid., 107. Note that White's analysis *has to* consist of the propositions that can be recovered from the text: if he could not state the propositions conveyed by literary and rhetorical means, he could not specify the relevance of the rhetorical and literary aspects that he wants to attribute them.

27. He clearly suggests that they constitute "deeper"—presumably, this is a value judgment meaning "more profound"—level: "The facts and their formal explanation or interpretation appears as the manifest or literal 'surface' of the discourse, while the figurative language used to characterize the facts points to a deep-structural meaning." Ibid., 110.

28. See Dekker, "Presupposition."
29. Kleene, *Logic*, 67–68.
30. See Horn, "Implicature" and Kent Bach, "Speech Acts."
31. See the analysis in Kent Bach, "The Top 10."
32. Croce, *Teoria*, 14–16.
33. Ibid., 120.
34. Ranke, *Geschichten*, 14. For an analysis of Ranke's bizarre claims see Mitrović, "Romantic Worldview," 13–14. For German appropriation of the Renaissance that starts with Ranke's book see Mitrović, *Rage and Denials*, 70–81.
35. He wrote in the *Begleitwort* from 1977 "Daß auch die anderen Großmächte im Zeitalter des Imperialismus expansive Politik betrieben und im Kriege ihre eigenen Kriegsziele verfolgt haben, habe ich nie in Frage gestellt." Fischer, *Griff*, 15.
36. Taylor, *Origins*.
37. If one considers how the wars with the Soviet Union and Yugoslavia broke out, Taylor's claim that Hitler "[f]ar from wanting a war, a general war was the last thing he wanted" is hardly credible (Taylor, *Origins*, xix.)
38. See discussion by Martin, "Causes."
39. Roberts, *Napoleon*, 295,
40. Kosso, "Philosophy," 14.
41. McCullagh, *Truth in History*, 57–61.
42. "Looks like" means here "generates a similar bundle of light rays that reach the eye"—see the Appendix.

Conclusion

*Materialism and Humanist Values, Or:
How Is Idealism Possible?*

The materialist perspective on human history presents historical figures as real biological creatures with genuine mental capacities that are irreducible to the influence of their social, cultural, linguistic or historical contexts. These contexts, in fact, as well as the events and phenomena that they generate, are nothing more than sets of biological humans considered together with their actions and interactions. Social or historical contexts cannot have causal capacities beyond those that they derive from participating individuals and their interactions. Discussions in this book have been largely motivated by the need to understand social phenomena in their historical contexts as ultimately biological—in other words, not to attribute them causal capacities beyond those that one can account of in physical terms. Insofar as social entities and phenomena affect the mental states of individual historical figures, this can happen only through interactions between individuals. Certain ideas can be inconceivable to individuals in certain contexts, but only because these individuals could not have acquired the knowledge necessary to form them through interactions available in the given context—and not because of top-down structured causal capacities of contexts themselves. Similarly, language is a social phenomenon, and linguistic phenomena are not to be attributed ontological status or causal capacities beyond those that can be explained in physical, biological terms. A meaning-based conception of language is credible; the one that postulates reference as an abstract force independent of human mental states is not. Determinism seems to be a particularly conspicuous aspect of the materialist perspective on the human position in the world and history. Once it is assumed that no event (including changes of mental states) can happen uncaused, and that causes and effects can only be physical, it becomes difficult to see how humans could change their minds, acquire new ideas or make decisions in ways that are not physically determined. However, determinism of this kind is little relevant for a historian: even if we could read people's mental states from their brain states, brain states of historical figures are and will forever remain inaccessible to historians. When it comes to historical research and historiography, physicalist determinism about the human mind *de facto* results in a compatibilist position that is, from a historian's point of view, indistinguishable from the attribution of free will to historical figures.

There should be no doubt that this materialist perspective on the human position in history opposes the postmodernist, anti-realist, social-constructionist and anti-foundationalist assumptions that have dominated the humanities in the final decades of the twentieth century and are still influential today. Some of the reasons are rather obvious: once it is postulated that no thing can be uncaused, it follows that some past events had to happen in order to cause the evidence that we have about them today. Similarly, once perception *simpliciter* is possible (see the Appendix), anti-foundationalism becomes impossible to sustain. In our present situation, marked by the exponential growth of the ability of natural sciences to explain the world, it is hard to challenge materialism seriously. To do this credibly, it is not enough to simply deny the inconvenient assumptions of the materialist worldview. The alternatives need to be explicated. This applies not only to postmodernist authors, but to analytic philosophers as well. In Chapter Five we have seen that Burge rejected as metaphysical the assumption that beliefs could not be different if brain states were not different.[1] Such a rejection can be stated, but it is not clear how it can be made convincing without the elaboration of the alternative metaphysical assumptions that would support it. His arthritis argument advocates the possibility that linguistic communities can affect human minds without affecting human biology, but the causal mechanisms that would enable this to happen remain undescribed. Yet, in order to make the argument credible it would be necessary to describe these causal mechanisms, and this would necessarily involve major metaphysical claims, such as the possibility of immaterial causation. Maybe materialism is wrong, maybe immaterial causation is really operational in our world, but if this is so, then one would want to know how it works and hear about some examples. At the same time, it would be hard to find, outside dilemmas related to the mind-body problem, other phenomena whose explanation could require the postulation of immaterial forces and causation. For the past century, enormous efforts have been made in the philosophy of the social sciences in order to show that this is the case, but, as we have seen, without much result.

The tendency to rely on postmodernist views in historical scholarship and the philosophy of history is nevertheless still strong today, even though the heyday of such ideas was decades ago. It is therefore useful to survey here the aspects of the materialist perspective on history, described through the book, that oppose anti-realist, social-constructionist and anti-foundationalist positions. This should place the conclusions of the book in a context well known to many readers. A reasonably comprehensive list could be stated as follows:

1. The rejection of the view that the historical past did not happen and that historians construct it on the basis of available evidence. The properties of evidence that enable such construction cannot be uncaused, and the causing events have to have happened in the past.
2. The understanding of social, cultural and linguistic items, and their causal capacities, as independent of the biological nature of human subjects and their interactions (including interactions with the physical environment) becomes unsustainable.
3. Social, cultural or linguistic entities, forces or phenomena cannot affect or predetermine the mental states of individuals, except through biologically explainable interactions between these individuals and their environment.
4. Vision (perception) *simpliciter*, independent of conceptualization, is possible. Vision (perception) can be unaffected by the social or cultural context. (See the Appendix.)
5. The impenetrability of vision precludes anti-foundationalist perspectives. (See the Appendix.)
6. Thought-contents or the meanings of linguistic items cannot exist outside human minds—that is, those of historical figures or historians. Mental phenomena—which are ultimately biological—can only be in human minds and affected in ways that are biologically possible.
7. Meanings of texts and documents are contents of mental states. Author's meaning is one legitimate form of meaning.
8. Linguistic phenomena result from mental phenomena in a way that supports meaning-based perspectives on language. The understanding of reference as an abstract, immaterial, non-mental relationship is not compatible with materialism.
9. Historical works have a transparent relationship with the historical past, otherwise they are works of fiction and not historical works. Historians can produce descriptions of past events (works that answer questions about past events) whose conditions of satisfaction are satisfied by past events.

The discussion of these topics through the book has followed the formulations and arguments presented in works of analytic philosophers. It is not articulated in relation to postmodernists' writings. The book concentrates on arguments, which makes it a study in the analytic philosophy of history. The fact that a series anti-materialist arguments from analytic philosophy discussed here align with core postmodernist perspectives certainly indicates that analytic philosophy, in some of its variations, is much closer to postmodernism than it is commonly assumed. Arguments that needed to be discussed in this book because of their anti-materialist implications were formulated by large and dominant streams of analytic philosophy over decades. They were often intended to defend views on the human position in the world and history that also coincide with postmodernist perspectives. The style of arguing may be different, idealist analytic philosophers may have insisted on logical rigor more than postmodernists, but they shared with postmodernism and continental philosophy the aim to oppose the materialist worldview and replace it with idealist perspectives. Postmodernist, anti-realist, social-constructionist and anti-foundationalist positions are therefore specific formulations of wider idealist attitudes that came to dominate the humanities, including analytic philosophy, in the second half of the twentieth century.

It is certainly proper to ask how idealism could have achieved such prominence in the humanities during the era. What is it that motivated the proliferation of anti-materialist positions in an era dominated by materialist science, and how could it happen that ideas that are in sharp contradiction with the dominant, mainstream, and increasingly successful understanding of the world could have become dominant and mainstream in the understanding of the human position in the world? An explanation that is commonly heard when it comes to postmodernism associates its rise with the French cultural influence. (Obviously this will not apply to idealism in analytic philosophy.) The explanation is not credible on a closer look, because it is hard to specify what this influence might consist in. The works of authors such as Jacques Derrida or Gilles Deleuze are largely incomprehensible even to specialists, which makes it hard to specify their ideas that actually exercised influence.[2] It may be even pointed out that although they were widely read and cited during the era, one should differentiate between genuine intellectual influence and the instrumentalization of abstruse texts in order to justify the populist relativism that was widespread in academic circles at the time and often necessary for academic promotion. While this argument against the assumption that French cultural influence played a major role in the rise of postmodernism may be valid, it is not clear that it is very relevant. Much more importantly, people do not merely get influenced by reading books accidentally; intellectual influences do not spread unwanted, the way it is the case with viral infections. Rather, people choose to be influenced and endorse ideas because these ideas provide responses to the concerns, worries, economic interests, the issues that are at stake for them. Very often, this choice can be unconscious and motivated by insecurities or self-esteem regulation, but it is hardly ever random. In order to understand such motives it is often important to consider what these widespread ideas implicitly deny, and not merely what they openly assert—in Panofsky's phrase, what their authors betray, rather than what they parade. Consider, as an example, the highly bizarre proliferation of claims about Germanic origins of the intellectual and artistic achievements of individuals from other ethnic groups that were widespread in German scholarship during the Wilhelmine and Weimar eras.[3] Here belong, for instance, the claims that the Acropolis belongs to nordic art, that Michelangelo, Copernicus and Van Gogh were Vikings, that Jesus Christ was Aryan, that Christianity is the original religion of the Aryan North about which Jesus Christ learnt while he lived in Iran, extensive studies trying to establish which Italian artists of the Renaissance were blond, claims that the Italian Renaissance did not happen or that it happened but it was a Germanic achievement.[4] Such remarkable claims were made by some of the most prominent scholars of the era and they certainly did not have detrimental effects on their reputation—on the contrary. The phenomenon is difficult to understand unless we consider what these claims deny—in which case it becomes obvious that they were meant to assuage the profound cultural insecurities that were widespread among German intelligentsia during the era.[5] Similarly, if we want to understand how perspectives on history that are in sharp contradiction with the materialist worldview could have achieved such prominence in recent decades, it is likely to be helpful to analyze what these perspectives deny.

Let us therefore consider once again the above list of the materialist views on history that oppose the postmodernist, anti-realist, social-constructionist and anti-foundationalist positions. Imagine that someone denies all items on that list. If one thus converted the list into a list of positions that assert the opposite, the common denominator of positions on that new list would be the denial of the cognitive capacities of human subjects *as human subjects* in favor of the preeminence of communal factors. In a stronger version, the claim would be not only that the cognition of reality is determined by communal factors, but that these factors construct this reality. The fact that these assumptions could have acquired such prominence during the final decades of the twentieth century, certainly says much about the intellectual life of the era, while their wide endorsement indicates that some deeper social forces—such as widely shared beliefs, insecurities or concerns—were at work.

One possible line of explanation—let me call it "theological"—has been already mentioned in the Introduction. The thesis that society, culture, history or language determines human thoughts and constructs the reality in which humans live (including physical reality) merely uses different words to repeat the views of Protestant theologians that God is not only the Creator of the world, but that He also determines the thoughts humans have and the decisions they make. As Luther put it, God foresees, gives the purpose and decides about all things by his immutable, eternal, and infallible will; everything that happens, both in the sense of the physical world and human thoughts, happens necessarily by God's will.[6] The proponents of social, cultural or linguistic constructionism reject the identification of society, culture, history, language and so on with sets of individuals, their properties (including mental states) and interactions, because such identification would not provide society, culture or language with the causal capacities to create ("construct") the world, determine physical laws or thoughts of individuals. Because of the causal capacities that they attribute to social items, they cannot rely on the individualist (materialist) understanding of these items. For the same reason they have to reject the biological understanding of human mental capacities. What they describe is a force, active in history, that has capacities equivalent to those of God in Protestant theology (but not in those Christian theologies that attribute free will and independent reasoning capacities to humans). In modern times, the word "God" has become unfashionable and people prefer to use other words, but things do not change because we name them differently. In other words: theology is often about the human position in the Universe as much as it is about God. People may believe that they have stopped being religious and that they have repudiated the religion that they have been brought up with—but, nevertheless, if they retain religion-based anthropology with the top-down conception of the world, in which there is one single cause of the physical world and human thinking, deciding and acting, they will need a name for that force. In the final decades of the twentieth century, the explanation further goes, it became fashionable to use words such as "Society," "Culture," "History," or "Language" for the purpose. The fashion affected idealist authors (not only postmodernists) in general, including analytic philosophers—as can be seen on the example of externalism about mental contents and the assumption that social or linguistic context can determine thoughts of individuals independently of their biology. This link between idealism and Protestantism can be further seen in the tendency to play down human visuality by denying visual thinking and by asserting that all thinking is verbal. It is also confirmed by the fact that postmodernism has exercised much less influence in eastern and southern Europe, where dominant religious traditions emphasized free will and the capacity of individuals to think and decide independently of God. The weakness of this explanation, however, is that it cannot explain the fact that the terms chosen to replace "God" were systematically those that normally refer to communal items, such as "society," "culture" or "language."

Another possible explanation worth considering, that can also explain this choice of words, could be called "Marxist," because it relates to the class interests of academics who endorsed idealist perspectives such as postmodernism. The explanation starts from the observation that the widespread idealist opposition to materialism was a phenomenon in the intellectual lives of wealthy North American and west-European countries. The explanation further assumes that the wealth of these countries predominantly derives from the exploitation of the Third World. Looking analytically, this wealth is generated by coordinated efforts of western governments, secret services and military institutions whose activities create exploitation-favorable political contexts, as well as business people and capitalists who organize actual exploitation. According to this analysis, the contribution of humanist scholars or social scientists (excluding economists) to the wealth of their societies is marginal or non-existent. Consequently, it becomes unclear why they should participate in the wealth thus created. Idealism in the humanities is then to be interpreted as the claim that such an analysis is not accurate. The claims that actions of a community are not reducible to the actions of individuals, that communal, supra-individual structures determine the mental processes of individuals (or even construct the reality in which they act) *de facto* assert that the exploitation of the Third World could not have happened without the collaboration of all segments of western societies. They are in that case arguments for the egalitarian division of the profits acquired through the exploitation of other countries. What the proponents of idealism are saying is that as members of their societies they also actively contribute to the exploitation of the Third World and that they should not be excluded from the division of the wealth thus created. Anti-realism about past events in this context serves as a way to deny responsibility for the oppression of peoples in other parts of the globe: one cannot be responsible for something that did not happen, and acts of oppression resulting from imperialism and colonialism could not have happened if one needs colligatory concepts to describe them. (The important point here is not in relativism about ethical norms, but in the denial of the events and acts of oppression to which these norms could possibly apply.[7]) From this point of view, postmodernist anti-realism is merely an ideology of unrestrained colonialism.[8] It should be noted that for this explanation to work, it is utterly irrelevant whether the wealth of North American and West European countries *really* derives from the exploitation of the Third World. What matters is that people believe that this is the case— if they do, idealist arguments of this kind will be necessary in order to justify the participation of scholars in the humanities and social scientists in the division of social wealth. An additional advantage of this explanation is that it explains the exceptional expansion of postmodernism (and idealist perspectives in general) in English-speaking scholarship in the aftermath of the demise of the Soviet Union. The failure of communism revealed the unviability of social systems based on egalitarian distribution of wealth. According to this explanation, the vehement promotion of postmodernist ideology by many humanist scholars in the late 1980s and the 1990s stemmed from the perceived need to assert reasons that would justify their economic welfare, and this need was certainly further emphasized at that time by the economic policies of Ronald Reagan and Margaret Thatcher.

The strength of this, latter, explanation is that it points out that by endorsing postmodernist and idealist perspectives, humanist scholars, analytic philosophers, and social scientists were acting in accordance with their economic class interests—and in such situations it is always hard to argue that they were not motivated by these interests. At the same time, it is hard not to think that actual motivation could have differed from person to person. It is, for instance, also important to bear in mind the generational context. The highest influence of postmodernism in English-speaking academia was in the late 1980s and the 1990s, the time when the student generation of 1968 achieved professorships and the positions of power in the academic world. Arguably, the peculiarities of postmodernism, such as anti-realism, the rejection of rationality, the collectivist top-down understanding of society including social-cultural determinism and constructionism, could not have become influential if they had no attraction for (or did not respond to the concerns and insecurities of) this generation. In general, we are dealing here with a phenomenon much more diverse than the germanocentric fantasies of Wilhelmine- and Weimar-era historians. It is unlikely that any single explanation may be sufficient. Most likely, in most cases, various explanations are going to be mutually compatible. Different individuals may have been drawn to idealist theoretical perspectives for different reasons, regardless of their commitment to the materialist worldview in their everyday lives. Nevertheless, counterintuitive ideas such as anti-realism, social constructionism or anti-foundationalism could not have gained wide acceptance without some deeper and widespread attitude that made them attractive.

It is an old adage that metaphysical positions cannot be repudiated, let alone refuted, without the articulation of alternative metaphysical positions. As Francis Herbart Bradley put it, even a person who asserts that metaphysics is impossible is but a brother metaphysician with an alternative theory about the first principles.[9] It is important to bear this in mind, and also be aware that one cannot get very far in theoretical considerations by endorsing contradictory positions, the way one can in everyday life. Typically, scholars who reject materialist perspectives on the humanities nevertheless rely on materialism in their everyday lives: they expect technology based on materialist science to work and they rely on it, when they get sick they rely on materialist medicine and not on spiritual healing, they decide how to vote on the basis of the assumption that the past events in which individual politicians were involved really happened. People are certainly capable of having contradictory beliefs when this suits their interests or when consistent thinking would damage their self-esteem. However, when it comes to theoretical work, the fabrication of narratives in accordance with what one wants to believe, and what one's public or peers want to hear, is in most cases not more than a document of self-deceptions. In the case such perspectives on history had wide reception in their time, they also become documents of the widespread lack of intellectual integrity during the era. The bizarre claims by early twentieth-century German historians were motivated by such self-deceptions and desires to contribute to self-esteem regulation of their readers—and, from the perspective of (almost) the third decade of the twenty-first century, the postmodernist ideas dominant in the final decades of the twentieth century are already looking hardly less awkward. Sooner or later some historians will have to write about the bizarre intellectual history of the era and try to explain it. Whatever explanation may be eventually provided, the fact that such periods of massive self-deception happen should not be taken to suggest that intellectual integrity is impossible, or that views of historians or philosophers of history are mere products of their times. Chapter Seven of this book argued precisely against this view. What we can learn, however, is that it is dangerous for a historian or a philosopher of history to make metaphysical claims in order to justify their historical or theoretical claims, without being able to explicate and independently justify these metaphysical claims. This is especially so if provisional metaphysics is constructed in order to justify sham historical claims, that are motivated by some other agenda (such as the desire to please one's peers) and not the effort to establish what happened in the past. Such provisional metaphysics can hardly achieve much more than temporary deception, because we live in one world, which is the physical world and human history is part of that world. A historian or a philosopher of history cannot easily deny the physical nature of our world—in order to be convincing, such a denial would have to cover a very wide ground and be able to compete with and provide a credible alternative to materialist science. Materialism is a metaphysical position like any other, and, as mentioned, metaphysical positions can be credibly denied only if one can present a comprehensive credible metaphysical alternative instead.

NOTES

1. Burge, "Individualism and Psychology," 17.
2. Arguably, this does not apply to Michel Foucault. The position of Foucault, and the originality of his ideas, in relation to preceding German intellectual traditions (especially authors such as Karl Lamprecht and Oswald Spengler), however, is unclear and debatable. His contribution (unlike that of Derrida or Deleuze) may well have been that of a conduit and not a source, whereby the ideas of German historicist thinkers could have reached English-speaking postmodernists directly as well.
3. See Mitrović, *Rage and Denials* for a survey of this kind of scholarship.
4. For the Acropolis, see Strzygowski, *Ahnenerbe* 17–28. For Michelangelo as a Viking, see Strzygowski's *Deutsche Nordseele*, 172. For Copernicus as a Viking, see Spengler, *Untergang*, 425. For Van Gogh as a Viking, see Pinder, *Gesammelte Aufsätze*, 212–218. For the Aryan background of Jesus Christ, see Haupt, "Die arische Abkunft Jesu." For the Germanic origin of Christianity, see Strzygowski, *Ahnenerbe*, 78. For the denial of the Renaissance, see Spengler, *Untergang*, 288. For the extensive analysis of the Germanic ethnic origin of Italian Renaissance artists, see Woltmann, *Die Germanen und die Renaissance*; he concludes that 85–90 percent of Italian genius is of Germanic origin (ibid., 145).
5. See Mitrović, "Romantic Worldview."
6. Luther, *De servo*, 615: "Est itaque hoc imprimis necessarium et salutare Christiano, nosse, quod Deus nihil praescit contigenter, sed quod omnia incommutabili et aeterna infallibilique voluntate et praevidet et proponit et faciat."
7. Roth, "What," 543–544, has tried to argue that postmodernist constructionism does not entail that it is impossible to condemn acts of oppression that have happened through history:

> Absent some further premise or premises, it simply does not follow from the statements that events are historiographical constructs to the conclusion that people did not suffer, or that their cries need go unheard. "Injustice" is indeed a normative term. And as a normative term, it requires some explicit moral theory to license applying it. Constructivists can, like anyone, employ norms as part of their account. Denying that norms are timeless is completely consistent with arguing for the embrace of certain norms in the here an now. Labeling a norm "absolute" does nothing to justify it. The label only signals a person's attitude toward the value in question.

The obvious response is that the criticism has nothing to do with the dilemma about timelessness of ethical norms. Once it is stated that past events did not happen and that they are merely constructed by historians, then there is nothing to apply norms to. If past events did not happen, then this applies to past events of oppression as well. No additional premises (except for the elementary understanding of causation) are necessary to infer that past events of oppression that did not happen and that are mere historiographical constructs could not have caused anything and therefore could not have caused suffering or injustices. And it is pointless to apply ethical norms or condemn something that did not really happen.

8. See the analyses in Mitrović, "A Refutation" and Bricmont, *Humanitarian Imperialism*.
9. Bradley, *Appearance*, 1.

Appendix

On Not Seeing-As

The "Theory"-theory of concepts discussed in Chapter Four fundamentally depends on the assumption that human perception is inseparable from the classification of its contents. During the middle decades of the twentieth century this view dominated the psychology and philosophy of perception and since the 1960s it has exercised a huge impact on the humanities. Without it, "Theory"-theory of concepts (and anti-foundationalist positions in general) simply cannot be sustained. In the meantime, however, modern research in psychology has made the position obsolete. The aim of this Appendix is to explain why the modern understanding of human (visual) perception undermines the credibility the "Theory"-theory of concepts and anti-foundationalism in general.

CLASSIFICATION AND PERCEPTION

The core dilemma pertains to the detachability of perceptual experience from its content. On the one hand is the view that all perception is inseparable from classification, commonly expressed (in the case of visual perception) by slogans such as "all seeing is seeing-as" or that "there is no innocent eye." On the other hand is the view that it is (sometimes, mostly or always) possible to see things, events, or their properties *simpliciter*—that is, independently of how one classifies them. As Allan Millar put it: imagine that Charlie Brown and his friend Jimmy go looking for pumpkins.[1] Charlie has seen pumpkins in the past and knows what they look like, but Jimmy has not and cannot recognize them. When they come across a pumpkin, do they have the same visual experience? This question could be answered, for instance, by asking both Charlie and his friend to look at the pumpkin through a piece of glass from the same angle and under the same conditions and draw what they see on the glass. Should we expect that the shape of the pumpkin they draw will be the same or not?

The possibility of seeing *simpliciter* is potentially a serious problem for the validity of the "Theory"-theory of concepts: if it is possible to see things and observe their properties (such as shapes) independently of how one classifies them, then one can classify things according to the properties one perceives in them independently of any other concepts. In this case, one will be able to further classify objects on the basis of such properties and consequently formulate concepts purely on the basis of perception and independent of other concepts one has. Such concepts will be independent of theories one believes, and consequently the "Theory"-theory will be false. The possibility of seeing *simpliciter* also affects the credibility various anti-foundationalist positions insofar as they, as Bevir summarized it, assume that "our experience of ... objects [in the world] must in part be constructed using prior theories."[2] Contrary to such anti-foundationalist views, the modern psychology of perception shows that large part of human perception is generated by hard-wired functions of the brain, and independently of any "theory" understood as something that is learnt through social interaction. The argument against the "Theory"-theory of concepts and anti-foundationalism presented here was originally formulated in an incomplete form by Jerry Fodor in 1984.[3] At the time Fodor was writing, the argument could not have been fully elaborated and it was only the subsequent developments in the psychology of perception that, as I describe below, fully confirmed and justified Fodor's insight.

It should be clarified that the discussion here does not pertain to the metaphorical use of words such as "see" or "perceive"—for instance, the way we sometimes say that it can be seen (perceived) that someone is intelligent. The discussion pertains to genuine visual experience. Also, one should not confuse perceptual contents with reports about them. When reporting what a person saw, it is necessary to classify the contents of the visual experience in order to describe them in words, but one should not confuse perception with the description that describes its contents. When stating what a person saw, it is not necessary to report that person's classifications: one can say that a person saw the wife of his dentist without being aware whom he saw.[4] In other words, perceptual contents need to be conceptualized in order to be described verbally, but this does not mean that perception *simpliciter* is impossible. One should also bear in mind that the word "observation" and the claim that observation cannot be separated from theorization can mean two things. It may suggest the understanding that perception *simpliciter* is impossible and that perception (observation) is inseparable from the conceptualization of its content, which happens in accordance with one's conceptual framework (theory). Alternatively, the background assumption may be that perception *simpliciter* is possible, that perceptual contents are subsequently conceptualized, and that the word "observation" is used to refer to such conceptualized contents. In this case, observation trivially depends on theorization. Different authors use the word "observation" differently, and it is often only through the textual analysis of their statements that one can establish what they mean. For instance, Danto uses the term to suggest the impossibility of perception *simpliciter*, whereas Tucker and Kosso do not make such a suggestion.[5]

THE IMPACT OF "NEW LOOK" PSYCHOLOGY ON THE HUMANITIES

The assumption that perception is inseparable from the classification of its contents dominated mid-twentieth-century research in psychology. The idea was known even before that. In the 1920s, Kurt Koffka, one of the early gestalt psychologists, claimed that if one looks at a diesel engine, then hears the explanation of how it works, then looks again, the engine will look different.[6] After explanation, Koffka says, one sees parts of the machine that have names, and not merely round and angular parts. As he put it, "a 'picture,' a phenomenon," becomes "better," in the sense that it can be better described in words.[7] After the end of World War II, similar views spread in American psychology as the influence of "New Look" psychology, a wave of research that sought to confirm by means of experiments the dependence of perception on classification. In a highly influential experiment, Jerome Bruner and Cecile Goodman sought to establish how socioeconomic background affects the way ten-year-old children perceive the size of coins.[8] The children were asked to adjust the size of a light circle on a screen to the size of coins placed next to the screen, by rotating a control knob. According to the interpretation of the experiment presented by Bruner and Goodman, children from less affluent families perceived the size of the quarter-dollar coin as larger by 25 percent than children from wealthy families. Psychological research in the 1950s was massively dominated by similar experiments designed to show how knowledge and expectations affect visual perception. Research literature of the era, the psychologist Ian Gordon observed,

> abounds in examples of perception being tricked in ways which reveal the involvement of knowledge, experience and familiarity. . . . Publications of the time describe oddly-shaped rooms which appear normal when viewed through peep-holes, pictures and figures which are difficult if not impossible to decipher without verbal hints, delays in recognizing briefly exposed words when these are threatening or taboo, and of course, many illusions. Showing the

malleable and vulnerable aspects of perception under laboratory conditions increased the belief that this was how perception must be all the time.[9]

The impact that "New Look" psychology has had on the historical humanities since the 1960s can hardly be overemphasized. A number of highly influential books in various fields of history and the philosophy of history published in that decade fundamentally relied on the assumption that seeing *simpliciter*, independently of how one classifies things, is impossible.

Danto, for instance, dismissed the possibility of perceiving *simpliciter* in the Introduction to *Narration and Knowledge* as "a naïve view that observation and theory can be neatly separated, that the latter can rest upon the former as its base."[10] He endorsed Norwood Russell Hanson's theory of perception that, as he summarizes it, observation is "'always already' permeated by theory to the point that observers [sic] with different theories will interpret even retinally indiscriminable observations differently."[11] The second part of this statement may still appear compatible with the possibility of perception *simpliciter* since people interpret what they see on the basis of what they believe—but the opening claim that observation is "always already" permeated with theory is certainly not. Later through the book one can see that he really means that perception is inseparable from classification. When he describes that we can still visit the house in Woolsthorpe in which Newton was born, he adds that we will see the same house as his contemporary yeoman and peasants saw, but we will see it differently, as the birth spot and dwelling of one of the greatest scientists of all ages.[12] In line with his endorsement of "New Look" psychology of perception stated in the Introduction, he thus assumes a genuine difference in visual experience between us and Newton's contemporaries. Such a theory of perception then obviously widely affects his theory of narrative sentences, since the latter depends on his assumption that events are witnessed under descriptions.[13]

Danto also accurately pointed out that Kuhn's highly influential *The Structure of Scientific Revolutions* fundamentally depended on the assumption that perception is inseparable from conceptualization (classification). Kuhn, indeed, directly stated that "paradigm changes do cause scientists to see the world of their research-engagement differently."[14] Similarly:

> Looking at a contour map, the student sees lines on paper, the cartographer a picture of a terrain. Looking at a bubble-chamber photograph, the student sees confused and broken lines, the physicist a record of familiar subnuclear events. Only after a number of such transformations of vision does the student become an inhabitant of the scientist's world.[15]

The situation with scientific perception, he also says, is different from the gestalt switch.[16] A gestalt switch in perception, he says, enables the subject to return to the original state of perception, but this is not possible in the case of learning to perceive things in accordance with another scientific paradigm. Kuhn extensively relied on another "New Look"-era psychology experiment, in which Bruner and Leo Postman exposed subjects for small parts of a second to pictures of playing cards, some of which were non-standard, such as a black three of hearts or red two of spades.[17] The experiment established that subjects needed a longer time to identify such non-standard cards. If they were given a shorter time than necessary, they reported inaccurately, or reported a compromise between what they were shown and what they expected to see, or simply failed to report what they saw. For instance, the subject exposed to a red six of spades would report "six of spades" or "purple six of spades." Bruner's and Postman's results, on one interpretation, merely establish that people need a longer time to identify objects that they have not experienced in the past. However, through the article they systematically converted "reported to have seen" into "seen" and simply erased any distinction between what subjects saw, how they classified it, and what they reported.[18] This imprecision (that a benevolent reader may take as metaphorical) enabled the article to be cited in favor of the inseparability of perception from identification. As Kuhn put it, "[o]ne would not even like to say that the subjects had seen something different from what they identified."[19]

The view that perception *simpliciter* is impossible should not be related merely to the influence of "New Look" psychology. In Germany, this view had a longer tradition due to the earlier influences of gestalt psychology. In the late 1920s, Hans Sedlmayr relied on gestalt psychology in order to criticize Alois Riegl's tendency to separate seeing from conceptualization.[20] Gadamer in his *Truth and Method* also relied on gestalt psychologists such as Wolfgang Koehler and Max Wertheimer.[21] He emphatically rejected the possibility of perception *simpliciter*: "[p]erception always includes meaning," he insisted.[22]

The impact of "New Look" psychology was particularly strong in art historiography, especially because of the influence of Ernst Gombrich's *Art and Illusion*. Gombrich insisted that "[t]o perceive is to categorize, or classify."[23] He assumed that the beliefs, expectations, and available classifications that influence one's perception result from the individual's previous experiences, but his position was soon endorsed by those authors who advocated that, rather than individual experiences, it is individuals' membership in groups such as cultures, historical contexts, or linguistic communities that organizes one's perception and reality.[24] In other words, they amended Gombrich's individualist position with a holist perspective on social ontology. Gombrich vehemently opposed such holistically motivated endorsements of his book, and this led to debates that persisted for decades. About the same time as Gombrich, the architectural theorist Christian Norberg-Schulz insisted that all perception is the recognition of things known from experience and that things are always perceived with meanings—a view that *de facto* implied the need to reduce the study of architectural history to the study of meanings associated with architectural works.[25]

Most of these books came out in the 1960s: Gadamer's *Truth and Method* and Gombrich's *Art and Illusion* in 1960; Kuhn's *The Structure of Scientific Revolutions* and Norberg-Schulz's *Intentions in Architecture* in 1962; Danto's *Analytical Philosophy of History* (which he subsequently placed in the context of "New Look" psychology in the opening of *Narration and Knowledge* that I cited above) in 1968. The influence of the view that perception *simpliciter* is impossible continued in later decades, even once "New Look" psychology lost its credibility among psychologists of perception. As late as 2015, Searle, in his philosophy of perception, endorsed the view that all seeing is "seeing-as."[26] Goldstein, in his 1986 response to Pompa, which was discussed in Chapter One, similarly stated that a biologist and a layman who look at a bacillus through a microscope will see different things.[27] His formulation closely coincides with Koffka's view that an engineer and a layman see a diesel engine differently. The claim provided an important support in the polemic with Pompa because it enabled Goldstein to claim that historians have "historical sense" that enables them to recognize historical evidence, the way a biologist can recognize a bacillus. (See the discussion in Chapter One.)

A good example of the influence of the view that (culturally determined) conceptual thinking affects perception is C. Behan McCullagh's 1998 book *The Truth in History*. McCullagh was hardly interested in promoting or defending cultural relativism in matters of perception, since this would be in contradiction with the general realist perspective of his book.[28] Nevertheless, since the view that culture affects perception was still widely present in the humanities at the time, McCullagh endorsed it and admitted that "our perceptions are influenced by our culture" and that "how they [people] see the world depends, of course, on their culture." He then endeavored to play down this cultural influence by saying that "people from different cultures see the world slightly differently" and that "cultural variation of people's perception of the everyday world is not great."[29] McCullagh's positioning thus reflects the fact that at the time he was writing, the influence of "New Look" psychology in the humanities, which started in the 1960s, was still strongly felt. (Admittedly, by that time, psychologists of perception would have regarded the forty-year-old experiments and the views of "New Look" psychology as very dated.) A year after McCullagh published his book, in a highly influential article Zenon Pylyshyn addressed the issue directly and argued that the functioning of the human visual module is impenetrable for conceptual thinking (and consequently cultural influences).[30] But before discussing the current views of psychologists of perception, it is useful to survey the relevant philosophical arguments in order to get a clearer picture of the dilemma.

Appendix

POSITIONS IN FAVOR AND AGAINST PERCEPTION *SIMPLICITER*

The claim that perception is *always* dependent on conceptualizations is crucial for the "Theory"-theory of concepts. Such a theory would become pointless if some concepts were generalizations from perceptual experiences that can be formed independently of the concepts one already has—that is, independently of one's pre-existing beliefs, expectations, or available theoretical frameworks. If such perceptual experience were (even sometimes) possible, the "Theory"-theory of concepts would be easy to reject. The question that needs to be considered here is thus whether our visual experience is *detachable* from the ways we classify its content. Can perception provide the atheoretical rock-bottom of the human experience of the world?

Writing in the late 1960s, Fred Dretske insisted that humans and animals share some elementary contents of visual experience.[31] As he put it, seeing a bug does not involve any more conceptual content than stepping on the bug inadvertently, and X-ray tubes can be seen by four-year-olds, regardless of what they know.[32] ("Why should they not see them? Are they invisible?"[33]) Contrary to then-dominant "New Look" psychology, Dretske claimed that "[t]here is then no reason to think that how things appear must be constrained by what concepts the perceiver has."[34] Much closer to our time, José Luis Bermúdez expressed the view that even if we assume that a child and an ecclesiastic confronting a religious painting will have different perceptual experiences, one may attribute to them the same basic perceptions at the level of non-conceptual content and place the differences in what they see at the level of conceptual content.[35] Other authors have similarly stated that if two perceivers are presented with the same shape, one perceiver may think of it as a rectangle and another as a straight-sided figure, but this difference in their thoughts need not prevent them from seeing it in exactly the same way.[36] If two persons perceive the Cyrillic script, and one of them can read it while the other cannot, it has been claimed that they nevertheless perceive the same shapes in the same positions.[37] In the case of tactile perception, those authors who advocate the detachability of perceptual contents from conceptual thinking state that one can feel something smooth and silky when running a hand over a sheepskin rug without having the concept of a sheepskin rug.[38]

The proponents of the opposing view, aligned with "New Look" psychology, however, have insisted that one can see things only if one can identify them: "Anyone who can see things *must* be able to identify them in a number of circumstances. Otherwise we should not allow them the claim to see things at all."[39] Another participant in the debate put it: "if a person sees something at all, it must look like something to him."[40] In the case of feeling something smooth and silky when running a hand over a sheepskin rug, it has been claimed that the knowledge that one's hand is running over a sheepskin rug might totally transform the experience: "if one had no concepts of smoothness and silkiness what on earth would the experience be like?"[41] John Searle expressed the same view by saying that a change in intentionality can result in a change in phenomenology, although he does not think that this is always the case.[42] According to Searle, if a person perceived two identical cars and he or she owns one of them, the two cars would be perceived differently, even though the optical stimulus is the same.[43]

The proponents of the "Theory"-theory of concepts have to defend the strong claim that *all* contents of visual perception are inseparable from classification—that "all seeing is seeing-as." If they accept that some properties of objects can be perceived independently of how these objects are conceptualized, then their opponents can argue that perceived objects can be classified according to such properties and consequently that new concepts, based on such classifications, can be created independently of the concepts that a person already has. If people can perceive some properties of objects independently of how they classify (identify) these objects and properties, then they can classify objects according to these properties. They will thus introduce new classifications and generate new concepts independently of other concepts they already operate with, which would defeat the "Theory"-theory of concepts. Such empirical concepts, derived purely by generalizing the properties of objects perceived non-conceptually, are then a solid foundation for the generation of new concepts, independent of those that one already has.

It needs to be pointed out that the dilemma about the detachability of the contents of visual experience from their classification should not be confused with the long-standing philosophical debate about the non-conceptual content of perception, originally initiated by Gareth Evans and John McDowell. The differences are as follows:

(a) The capacity to classify is a necessary but not sufficient condition for concept-attribution. The debate about detachability pertains to seeing without classifying. The debate about the non-conceptual content of perception has concentrated on a more robust notion of concept-possession that includes the capacity to form propositions and inferences.[44] The participants in the debate about non-conceptual content have been interested mainly in the way concepts participate in beliefs, propositions, and inferences.[45] The debate was motivated by the need to explain the way beliefs can be justified by perceptual experience.[46] As a result, the discussion about non-conceptual contents in human perception does not necessarily pertain to mere absence of classification; content could be non-conceptual but still derive from classifications.

(b) Classifications discussed here are mental processes, whereas the concepts discussed by the proponents and opponents of non-conceptual content are (often) conceived of as abstract entities.[47]

(c) The dilemma about detachability pertains to the question of whether (what) one can perceive without classifying what one sees, whereas the problem of non-conceptual content pertains to the question of whether one can possess concepts for everything one can see.[48]

PHILOSOPHICAL ARGUMENTS IN FAVOR OF PERCEPTION *SIMPLICITER*

There are a number of philosophical arguments against the view that *all* perception is predetermined by classification:

(a) Assume that I perceive two cubes, one red and one blue. If all perception is inseparable from classification, then it is wrong to say that I perceive the two cubes as different because I perceive one cube as red and another as blue and then classify one of them as red and another as blue. Rather, the point is that in order to perceive the cubes as different in color, I have to classify them first (or at the same time) as red or blue. But then, if I ask *why* I classify these cubes as red or blue, the response can be either that classification is random, or that it is based on some properties that these objects possess (e.g., objects reflect light of a certain frequency, which one perceives as color). However, if one classified objects in a certain way because they possessed certain properties, one would somehow have to know independently of (previously to) that classification that they have these properties. The only way to achieve this would be to perceive them *independently of* classification. This is precisely what the thesis that "all seeing is seeing-as" denies. At the same time, if our classifications (which are necessary for our perceptions, according to the thesis) are not based on the properties of objects, they are random, and there is no correlation between objects in the world and the way we perceive-cum-classify them. It may be pointed out, however, that this is not really an argument against the view that all perception depends on classification, but merely shows the anti-realist implications of this view. This response is accurate: for someone who accepts that perception does not provide us with information about an independently existing material world, the argument merely states the obvious.

(b) Long before "New Look" psychology, Edmund Husserl pointed out that the view that all seeing depends on classification ends up in an infinite regress.[49] Husserl argued against the view that when one perceives an object with a certain property, one does not perceive the specific occurrence of that property in the object, but rather its similarity with other occurrences of the same property on other objects that have that same property (i.e., its classifiability together with other occurrences). For instance, this would be as if someone argued that when perceiving a red cube, one does not perceive its color and shape, but its similarity with other red and cubic things. (In other words, there is no perception without classification, according to the formulation stated above: "if a person sees something at all, it must look like something to him.") This view leads to an infinite regress, Husserl pointed out—for one can then ask, what it is to perceive such similarities, and the answer will have to be their similarity to other similarities, and to perceive these similarities one needs to perceive their similarity to other similarities, and so on *ad infinitum*.

(c) It is pointed out that our capacities for perceptual discrimination by far exceed our capacities for recognition. This is the argument about the fine-gradedness of perceptual experience. For instance, one can perceive the curved line of a distant mountain range without having ever perceived such a curve earlier. As Gareth Evans pointed out, "Do we really understand the proposal that we have as many color concepts as there are shades of color that we can sensibly discriminate?"[50]

(d) Another group of arguments in favor of the detachability of perception pertains to the fact that our perception is not always in accordance with our beliefs and knowledge. In the case of optical illusions, we perceive them even after we have realized that they are illusions. Modern developments in the digital technology of visual representation further confirm the view that perception is independent of conceptual contents we associate with it. Virtual reality devices today make it possible to imitate the possible experience of architectural environments (e.g., interiors of buildings) by exposing the eye to bundles of light rays identical to those that the observer's eyes would receive in the real environment. The observer can move in space, his or her movements are registered by sensors and the computer adjusts accordingly the bundles of light rays the headset exposes the eyes to. (Instead of "brain in the vat" we have a "eye with a headset" situation with an equivalent result.) Although the observer is aware that he or she is not perceiving reality, this awareness does not affect the visual experience.

SEEING *SIMPLICITER*

For psychologists, "New Look" theories of vision belong to the history of their discipline.[51] Today, they widely agree that perceptual discrimination surpasses by far the visual memory and exceeds the capacities for visual identification and classification that depend on it.[52] As Diana Raffman stated, "It is a truism of perceptual psychology and psychophysics that, with rare exceptions, discrimination along perceptual dimensions surpasses identification"[53]—and if this is so, then much of our perception has to be independent of how we classify the objects and properties we perceive. For our discussion here, it is particularly important that the thesis about the detachability of visual experience is in line with the modern understanding of human visuality in the psychology of perception as manifested in the psychological debate about the impenetrability of visual perception. This debate pertains to the question of whether *sometimes* and in *some* cases our beliefs, knowledge, expectations, and so on can affect our visual experience. (The idea that this is *always* the case—which is necessary in order to sustain the "Theory"-theory of concepts—is simply not even discussed.) The dominant view in contemporary psychology, as Alva Noë and Evan Thompson put it, is that "perception is thought independent," whereby "the beliefs and expectations of the perceiver are thought to have no influence on the character of the subpersonal computations that constitute perception."[54] In 1999, Zenon Pylyshyn forcefully argued that (at least the early stages of) visual perception were impenetrable by top-down influences deriving from higher-level thought processes.[55] At the same time, an extensive production of empirical research strives to find and experimentally confirm individual cases of the top-down impact of higher cognitive processes on human vision.[56] Very recently, in 2016, Chaz Firestone and Brian Scholl surveyed a large number of these studies and argued that their findings are generated by a small number of methodological pitfalls that they describe in their paper.[57] The question of whether the processes that generate human vision are *sometimes* accessible to and affected by the influences that derive from higher-level cognitive processes is thus unresolved among psychologists. As Firestone and Scholl point out, if such effects of cognition on perception were discovered, this would revolutionize the scientific understanding of the organization of the mind. But "maybe sometimes" is a far cry from the "always already" that we have seen Danto and his contemporaries insisted on. Psychologists today debate whether our cognition can in *some* situations affect perception; the idea that *all* perception is inseparable from classification is simply not the topic of discussion, and whatever the outcome of the existing debate, it cannot justify the claim that "all seeing is seeing-as." Even if the proponents of penetrability showed that in some cases perception is affected by cognition (knowledge, expectations, desires, and so on), this would not be enough to save the "Theory"-theory of concepts or anti-foundationalism, since, as we have seen, they must rely on a much stronger claim that *all* perception is conceptually pre-determined.

NOTES

1. Millar, *Reasons*, 32.
2. Bevir, "Anti-Foundationalism," 53.
3. Fodor, "Observation." The problem Fodor struggled with pertained to the so-called ambiguity argument that seemed to confirm the view that our perception is always dependent on what we believe, know and expect—in other words, on our previous (social and cultural) experience and the theory of the world with which we come to see things. Our visual experience is generated from the retinal picture—while every possible retinal picture can always be a projection of an infinite number of different dispositions of objects in space. A single line, for example, is projected on the retina as a single line, but a single line on the retina could also be a projection of any number of disconnected smaller lines in space. At the time Fodor was writing, the only available explanation was that the brain resolved such problems and constructed our perception on the basis of beliefs it already had—which suggested that perception was through and through dependent on conceptual thinking. Fodor opposed this view by pointing out that in the case of visual illusions we know that we are dealing with the illusion but we still see them. From this he deduced that in some cases, perception must be impenetrable for beliefs, what one knows, expects and so on. Within a decade, developments in the psychology of perception provided a different explanation of the ambiguity problem: our brain does not rely on beliefs or previous experiences, but on specific hard-wired rules or constraints when interpreting a two-dimensional image three-dimensionally. (Hoffman, *Visual Intelligence* surveys these "rules," as he calls them. For a summary see Pylyshyn, *Seeing and Visualizing*, 107.) Following these constraints the brain always interprets a straight line in an image as a three-dimensional straight line, even though it may actually consist of a number of disconnected lines that only appear to be in continuation of each other. Similarly, if the tips of two lines coincide in a retinal image, the brain will assume that they coincide three-dimensionally. These interpretative procedures that construct our visual experience are assumed to be hard-wired, impenetrable for conceptual thinking, theories, cultural influences or similar.
4. This point is regularly repeated in the literature. ". . . a specification of the content of perception can be sensitive to how an organism perceptually represents its environment even though it utilizes concepts the organism need not possess." Bermúdez and Arnon, "Nonconceptual Mental Content." Similarly, Dretske, *Seeing and Knowing*, 10, points out that it is not logically inconsistent to say of someone that he saw a candlestick holder without believing himself visually aware of anything. Stalnaker, "Nonconceptual," 105, points out that the ascriptions of informational content are external in that the concepts used to ascribe them are not thereby attributed to the subject. In such ascriptions one may or may not use concepts that the subject shares with the person reporting.
5. Kosso, "Observation," 21, for instance, talks about observation "in terms of the acquisition of information through interaction with the world," and for perception to become such information it obviously needs to be conceptualized. Similarly Tucker, *Our Knowledge*, 95, talks about "[p]roblems in differentiating observation from theoretical sentences" and the examples he states, such as the need to interpret eyewitness accounts—clearly indicate that by "observation" he does not mean perception taken on its own, but perception that is conceptualized in order to be interpreted. In both cases their statements do not suggest that they presuppose the impossibility of perception *simpliciter*. For Danto, see the discussion later in the text.
6. ". . . sieht er anders aus," Koffka, "Zur Theorie," 393.
7. Note the use of scare quotes: ". . . jetzt wird durch Begriffe, die das Funktionieren eines Gegenstandes betreffen ein 'Bild,' ein Phenomen von dem Gegenstand 'besser,' ich kann jetzt besser beschreiben." Ibid., 393. It is not clear whether the use of scare quotes for "Bild" may mean that the word is used figuratively and does not pertain to the perception of shapes and colors.
8. Bruner and Goodman, "Value and Need."
9. Gordon, "Gombrich," 63.
10. Danto, *Narration and Knowledge*, xi.
11. Ibid., xi.
12. Ibid., 158.

13. See esp. Ibid., 151.
14. Kuhn, *Scientific Revolutions*, 111.
15. Ibid., 111.
16. Ibid., 114.
17. Ibid., 62–63. Bruner and Postman, "Perception of Incongruity."
18. Their typical formulations are "one subject saw the red five of hearts" (ibid., 214), "another saw the red ace of hearts" (ibid., 214), "[t]he subjects perceived color . . ." (ibid., 215) and so on.
19. Kuhn, *Scientific Revolutions*, 63.
20. Sedlmayr, "Quintessenz," 38. See also Mitrović, *Rage and Denials*, 115–117.
21. For his reference to gestalt psychologists see Gadamer, *Wahrheit und Methode*, 96.
22. "Das bloße Sehen, das bloße Hören sind dogmatische Abstraktionen, die die Phänomene künstlich reduzieren. Wahrnehmung erfaßt immer Bedeutung." Gadamer, *Wahrheit und Methode*, 97.
23. A systematic survey of Gombrich's statements can reveal that for him these theses meant that no object can be perceived without being classified as an object of a specific kind, see Mitrović, "A Defence of Light," 23–25.
24. For the history of the debate see Mitrović, "A Defence of Light."
25. Norberg-Schulz, *Intentions*, 37 and 168.
26. Searle, *Seeing*, 37.
27. Goldstein, *The What and the Why*, 215.
28. As he puts it, "True descriptions tell us about the state of the world. They are not merely reports of rational consensus." McCullagh, *Truth in History*, 54.
29. McCullagh, *Truth in History*, 17, 18, 24, 26–27, 52.
30. Pylyshyn, "Is Vision Continuous."
31. Dretske, *Seeing and Knowing*, 4–77.
32. Ibid., 6, 37.
33. Ibid., 37.
34. Martin, "Perception," 246.
35. Bermúdez, "Peacocke's Argument," 294.
36. Peacocke, "Perception," 245.
37. Peacocke, "Scenarios," 123.
38. Millar, "Concepts," 496.
39. Hamlyn, *Psychology*, 71, cited in Dretske, *Seeing and Knowing*, 16.
40. Vesey, "Seeing as Seeing-As," 114.
41. Hamlyn, "Nonconceptual Content," 257.
42. Searle, *Seeing*, 37. He actually endorses the phrase "all seeing is seeing-as" but then drops the claim that this is always the case.
43. Searle, *Seeing*, 37. Searle's views about seeing *simpliciter* are inconsistent. He says that one does not "typically" see shapes and colors, one sees a black car. This would allow that sometimes (atypically) one does see *simpliciter*. However, he also insists that "all seeing is seeing-as" and denies that two people with normal visual neurobiological equipment confronted with the same stimuli would see pretty much the same thing. Ibid., 74, 70. But he also allows that one may know nothing about the object of perception except that it caused perception (ibid., 108)—which contradicts the thesis that "all seeing is seeing-as."
44. See Crowther, "Two Conceptions" for the view that the possession of the concept F requires that one is able to make the inference from the judgment that a is F, to the judgment that a is G, where being G is an analytic (or more broadly "conceptual") consequence of some thing's being F.
45. Clark, "Constructionism," 173, says that Evans's Generality Constraint insists "that to truly possess a concept a you must be able to think a in all the (semantically sensible) combinations which it could enter into with other concepts you possess. Thus if you can really think Fa, and really think Gb, you must (as a matter of stipulation) be able to think Fb and Ga." Peacocke, "Perception," 243, says that by "conceptual" he means the content of a kind that can be the content of judgment and belief. Concepts are constituents of those intentional contents which can be the complete, truth-evaluable, contents of judgment and belief.

46. See Kelly, "Demonstrative Concepts," 402, for a summary of this motivation.

47. This was at least McDowell's position—see his statements such as McDowell, *Mind and World*, 26: "although reality is independent of our thinking, it is not to be pictured as outside an outer boundary that encloses the conceptual sphere." Similarly: "Impressions made by our senses already have conceptual content." Ibid., 46.

48. See Cleve, "Defining," 411, who cites a series of definitions by various authors who all insist on the possession of concepts. Characteristically, Raftopoulos, "Cognitive impenetrability," 609, who is concerned with the relation between impenetrability and nonconceptuality, says that a person's state S with content p has nonconceptual content if and only if the person need not possess or apply the concepts used to characterize p.

49. Husserl, *Logische Untersuchungen*, 197–207, esp. 200–201.

50. Evans, *Varieties* , 229.

51. See for instance Pylyshyn, "Is Vision Continuous," 342–343.

52. Raffman, "Persistence." Dokic, and Pacherie, "Shades and Concepts," 198.

53. Raffman, "Persistence," 294. See similarly Dokic and Pacherie, "Shades and Concepts."

54. Noë and Thompson, eds, *Vision*, 2, 3.

55. Pylyshyn, "Is Vision Continuous." See also Raftopoulos, *Cognition* and Raftopoulos: "Impenetrability."

56. For a list of 182 such papers published since 1995 see Firestone, "Reference."

57. Firestone, Scholl, "Cognition."

Bibliography

Achinstein, Peter. "On the Meaning of Scientific Terms." *The Journal of Philosophy* 61 (1964): 497–509.
Albertini, Luigi. *Le origini della guerra del 1914*. Gorizia: Libreria Editrice Goriziana, 2010.
Ankersmit, Frank. *Historical Representation*. Stanford, CA: Stanford University Press, 2001.
———. "Reply to Professor Saari." *Rethinking History* 9 (2005): 23–33.
———. *Meaning, Truth, and Reference in Historical Representation*. Ithaca, NY: Cornell University Press, 2012.
Arrian. *Anabasis of Alexander*. Cambridge, MA: Harvard University Press, 1976.
Ast, Friedrich. *Grundlinien der Grammatik, Hermeneutik und Kritik*. Landshut: Jos. Thomann, 1808.
Augustine, Aurelius. *De civitate Dei: The City of God against the Pagans*. Cambridge, MA: Harvard University Press, 1957.
Ayer, Alfred Jules. *Language Truth and Logic*. London: Victor Golancz, 1962.
Bach, Kent. "What's In a Name." *Australasian Journal of Philosophy* 59 (1981): 371–386.
———. *Thought and Reference*. Oxford: Clarendon, 1987.
———. "Giorgione Was So-Called Because of His Name." *Philosophical Perspectives* 16 (2002): 73–103.
———. "Speech Acts and Pragmatics." In *The Blackwell Guide to the Philosophy of Language*, edited by Michael Davitt and Richard Hanley, 147–167. Malden, MA: Blackwell, 2006.
———. "The Top 10 Misconceptions about Implicature." In *Drawing the Boundaries of Meaning*, edited by Betty Birner and Gregory Ward, 21–30. Amsterdam: John Benjamins, 2006.
Bal, Mieke. *Travelling Concepts in the Humanities*. Toronto: University of Toronto Press, 2002.
Barber, Alex. "The Pleonasticity of Talk about Concepts." *Philosophical Studies: An International Journal for Philosophy in the Analytic Tradition* 89 (1998): 53–86.
Barthes, Roland. "La mort de l'auteur." In Roland Barthes, *Essais Critiques IV. Le Bruissement de la Langue*, 61–66. Paris: Éditions du Seuil, 1984.
Beckermann, Ansgar, Hans Flohr, and Jaegwon Kim, eds. *Emergence or Reduction? Essays on the Prospects or Nonreductive Physicalism*. Berlin: Walter de Gryter, 1992.
Below, Georg von. "Die neue historische Methode." *Historische Zeitschrift* 81 (1898): 193–273.
Bermúdez, José Luis, and Arnon Cahen. "Nonconceptual Mental Content." Accessed December 19, 2019. http://plato.stanford.edu/archives/fall2015/entries/content-nonconceptual/.
Bermúdez, José Luis. *Thinking without Words*. Oxford: Oxford University Press, 2003.

———. "Peacocke's Argument against the Autonomy of Nonconceptual Representational Content (1994)." In *Essays on Nonconceptual Content*, edited by York Gunther, 293–308. Cambridge, MA: The MIT Press, 2003.
Bevir, Mark. *The Logic of the History of Ideas*. Cambridge: Cambridge University Press, 1999.
———. "Anti-Foundationalism." In *Encyclopedia of Political Theory*, edited by Mark Bevir, 53–57. London: Sage, 2010.
Bhargava, Rajeev. *Individualism in Social Science: Forms and Limits of a Methodology*. Oxford: Clarendon Press, 1992.
Bicchieri, Cristina. *The Grammar of Society*. Cambridge: Cambridge University Press, 2012.
Block, Ned. "Anti-Reductionism Slaps Back." *Noûs* 31 (1997) (Supplement 11, *Mind, Causation, and World*): 107–132.
Bock, Hilary. "Freedom and Practical Reason." In *Free Will*, edited by Gary Watson, 130–166. Oxford: Oxford University Press, 2011.
BonJour, Laurence. "The Dialectic of Foundationalism and Coherentism." In *The Blackwell Guide to Epistemology*, edited by John Greco and Ernest Sosa, 117–142. Oxford: Blackwell, 1999.
Bradley, Francis Herbert. *Appearance and Reality*. Oxford: Clarendon Press, 1930.
Bratman, Michael. "Shared Cooperative Activity." *The Philosophical Review* 101 (1992): 327–341.
Braun, David. "Extension, Intension, Character and Beyond." In *The Routledge Companion to Philosophy of Language*, edited by Gillian Russell and Delia Graff Fara, 9–18. New York: Routledge, 2012.
Bricmont, Jean, and Alan Sokal. "Defense of a Modest Scientific Realism." Accessed April 7, 2019. https://physics.nyu.edu/sokal/bielefeld_final_rev.pdf.
Bricmont, Jean. *Humanitarian Imperialism: Using Human Rights to Sell War*. New York: Monthly Review Press, 2006.
Brownson, C. D. "Euclid's *Optics* and Its Compatibility with Linear Perspective." *Archive for History of Exact Sciences* 24 (1981): 165–194.
Bruner, Jerome, and Cecile Goodman. "Value and Need as Organizing Factors in Perception." *Journal of Abnormal and Social Psychology* 42 (1947): 33–44.
Bruner, Jerome, and Leo Postman. "On the Perception of Incongruity: A Paradigm." *Journal of Personality* 18 (1949): 206–223.
Brush, Kathryn. "The Cultural Historian Karl Lamprecht: Practitioner and Progenitor of Art History." *Central European History* 26 (1993): 139–164.
Bryce, Trevor. *The Kingdom of the Hittites*. Oxford: Clarendon Press, 1998.
Bryson, Norman. *Vision and Painting: The Logic of the Gaze*. London: Macmillan, 1985.
Bunge, Mario. "Ten Modes of Individualism—None of Which Works—And Their Alternatives." *Philosophy of Social Sciences* 30 (2000): 384–406.
Burge Tyler. "Reference and Proper Names." *The Journal of Philosophy* 70 (1973): 425–439.
———. "Individualism and the Mental." *Midwest Studies in Philosophy* 4 (1979): 73–122.
———. "Individualism and Psychology." *The Philosophical Review* 95 (1986): 3–45.
———. "Epiphenomenalism: Reply to Dretske." In *Reflections and Replies: Essays on the Philosophy of Tyler Burge*, edited by Martin Hahn and Bjørn Ramberg, 397–403. Cambridge, MA: The MIT Press, 2003.
Burgess, Alexis. "Metalinguistic Descriptivism for Millians." *Australasian Journal of Philosophy* 91 (2013): 443–457.
Burr, Vivien. *Social Constructionism*. London: Routledge, 1995.
Carr, David. "Narrative and the Real World: An Argument for Continuity." *History and Theory* 25 (1986): 117–131.
Carroll, Lewis. *Alice through the Looking Glass*. Accessed December 13, 2019. http://birrell.org/andrew/alice/lGlass.pdf.
Carruthers, Peter. *Language, Thought and Consciousness*. Cambridge: Cambridge University Press, 1996.
Cat, Jordi. "The Unity of Science." Accessed May 17, 2019. https://plato.stanford.edu/archives/fall2017/entries/scientific-unity.

Bibliography

Chant, Sarah Rachel, Frank Hindriks and Gerhard Preyer. "Introduction." In *From Individual to Collective Intentionality New Essays*, edited by Sarah Rachel Chant, Frank Hindriks and Gerhard Preyer, 1–12. Oxford: Oxford University Press, 2014.
Chickering, Roger. *Karl Lamprecht: A German Academic Life (1856–1915)*. Atlantic Highlands, NJ: Humanities Press, 1993.
Chomsky, Noam. *Knowledge of Language: Its Nature, Origin and Use*. New York: Praeger, 1986.
———. "Internalist Explorations." In *Reflections and Replies: Essays on the Philosophy of Tyler Burge*, edited by Martin Hahn and Bjørn Ramberg, 259–288. Cambridge, MA: The MIT Press, 2003.
Cicero, Marcus Tullius. *De oratore: On the Orator*. Cambridge, MA: Harvard University Press, 1948.
Clark, Andy. "Constructionism and Cognitive Flexibility." In *Essays on Nonconceptual Content*, edited by York Gunther, 165–182. Cambridge, MA: The MIT Press, 2003.
Churchill, Winston. *The World in Crisis*. London: Macmillan, 1942.
Churchland, Paul. "The Logical Character of Action-Explanations." *The Philosophical Review* 79 (1970): 214–236.
Cleve, James, van. "Defining and Defending Nonconceptual Contents." *Philosophical Perspectives* 26 (2012): 411–430.
———. "Why Coherence Is Not Enough: Defending Moderate Foundationalism." In *Contemporary Debates in Epistemology*, edited by Matthias Steup and Ernest Sosa, 168–180. Malden, MA: Blackwell Publishing, 2005.
Coffman, E. J. "Warrant without Truth?" *Synthese* 162 (2008): 173–194.
Cohen, Mendel. "Causation in History." *Philosophy* 62 (1987): 341–360.
Cohen, Morris. "Causation and Its Application to History." *Journal of the History of Ideas* 3 (1942): 12–29.
Colebourn, R. *Latin Sentence and Idiom*. Bristol: Bristol, Classical Press, 2003.
Collingwood, Robin George. *The Idea of History*. New York: Oxford University Press, 1956.
———. *Autobiography*. Oxford: Oxford University Press, 2017.
Crane, Tim. "All the Difference in the World." *The Philosophical Quarterly* 41 (1991): 1–25.
———. *The Objects of Thought*. Oxford: Oxford University Press, 2013.
———. *Aspects of Psychologism*. Cambridge, MA: Harvard University Press, 2014.
Croce, Benedetto. *Teoria e storia della storiografia*. Milano: Adelphi, 2011.
Crowther, T. M. "Two Conceptions of Conceptualism and Nonconceptualism." *Erkenntnis* 65 (2006): 245–276.
Dante, Alighieri. *De vulgari eloquentia*. Milan: Garzanti, 1991.
Danto, Arthur. *Narration and Knowledge*. New York: Columbia University Press, 1985.
Davidson, Donald. "On the Very Idea of a Conceptual Scheme." In Donald Davidson, *Inquiries into Truth and Interpretation*, 183–199. Oxford: Clarendon Press, 2001.
———. "Thought and Talk." In Donald Davidson, *Inquiries into Truth and Interpretation*, 155–170. Oxford: Clarendon Press, 2001.
———. "The Structure and Content of Truth." *The Journal of Philosophy* 87 (1990): 279–328.
Davis, Martin. "Foundational Issues in the Philosophy of Language." In *The Blackwell Guide to the Philosophy of Language*, edited by Michael Davitt and Richard Hanley, 19–40. Malden, MA: Blackwell, 2006.
Dedijer, Vladimir. *The Road to Sarajevo*. New York: Simon & Schuster, 1966.
Dekker, Paul. "Presupposition." In *The Routledge Companion to Philosophy of Language*, edited by Gillian Russell and Delia Graff Fara, 42–52. New York: Routledge, 2012.
Devitt, Michael. "Brian Loar on Singular Terms." *Philosophical Studies: An International Journal for Philosophy in the Analytic Tradition* 37 (1980): 271–280.
Devitt, Michael, and Richard Hanley, eds. *The Blackwell Guide to the Philosophy of Language*. Malden, MA: Blackwell, 2006.
Dilthey, Wilhelm. *Der Aufbau der geschichtlichen Welt in den Geisteswissenschaften*. Frankfurt am Main: Suhrkamp 1981.
Dokic, Jérôme, and Élisabeth Pacherie. "Shades and Concepts." *Analysis* 61 (2001): 193–202.

Donnellan, Keith. "Reference and Definite Descriptions." *The Philosophical Review* 75 (1966): 281–304.
Dray, William. *Laws and Explanations in History*. London: Oxford University Press, 1970.
Dretske, Fred. *Seeing and Knowing*. Chicago: The University of Chicago Press, 1969.
———. "Burge on Mentalistic Explanations Or Why I am Still Epiphobic." In *Reflections and Replies: Essays on the Philosophy of Tyler Burge*, edited by Martin Hahn and Bjørn Ramberg, 153–164. Cambridge, MA: The MIT Press, 2003.
Dreyfus, Herbert, and Paul Rabinow. *Michel Foucault: Beyond Structuralism and Hermeneutics*. Chicago: The University of Chicago Press, 1982.
Droysen, Johann Gustav. *Geschichte Alexanders des Großen*. Gotha: Fridrich Andreas Perthes, 1880.
———. *Historik*. Stuttgart: Frommann-Holzboog, 1977.
Dummett, Michael. "The Reality of the Past." *Proceedings of the Aristotelian Society* 69 (1968–1969): 239–258.
———. "What Do I Know When I Know a Language." In Michael Dummett, *The Seas of Language*, 94–105. Oxford: Oxford University Press, 2003.
———. "Language and Communication." In Michael Dummett, *The Seas of Language*, 166–187. Oxford: Oxford University Press, 2003.
———. *Truth and the Past*. New York: Columbia University Press, 2004.
Dumont, Louis. *From Mandeville to Marx*. Chicago: The University of Chicago Press, 1977.
Dvořák, Max. *Kunstgeschichte als Geistesgeschichte*. Berlin: Mann, 1995.
Elder-Vass, Dave. *The Reality of Social Construction*. Cambridge: Cambridge University Press, 2012.
Elgin, Catherine. "Non-Foundationalist Epistemology: Holism, Coherence and Tenability." In *Contemporary Debates in Epistemology*, edited by Matthias Steup and Ernest Sosa, 156–167. Malden, MA: Blackwell Publishing, 2005.
Elster, Jon. *Nuts and Bolts for the Social Sciences*. Cambridge: Cambridge University Press, 1992.
———. *Making Sense of Marx*. Cambridge: Cambridge University Press, 1985.
———. "A Case for Methodological Individualism." *Theory and Society* 11 (1982): 453–482.
Epstein, Brian. "Ontological Individualism Reconsidered." *Synthese* 166 (2009): 187–213.
———. "What Is Individualism in Social Ontology? Ontological Individualism vs. Anchor Individualism." In *Rethinking the Individualism-Holism Debate*, edited by Julie Zahle and Fin Collin, 17–38. Cham: Springer, 2014.
———. *The Ant Trap*. Oxford: Oxford University Press, 2015.
Evans, Gareth. "The Causal Theory of Names." In *The Philosophy of Language*, edited by Aloysius Martinich and David Sosa, 74–85. Oxford: Oxford University Press, 2013.
———. *The Varieties of Reference*. Oxford: Oxford University Press, 1982.
Fara, Delia. "Literal Uses of Proper Names." In *On Reference*, edited by Andrea Bianchi, 251–279. Oxford: Oxford University Press, 2015, 251–279.
Fay, Brian. *Social Theory and Political Practice*. London: George Allen & Unwin, 1975.
———. *Contemporary Philosophy of Social Science*. Malden, MA: Blackwell, 1996.
Fermia, Joseph. "An Historicist Critique of 'Revisionist' Methods for Studying the History of Ideas." In *Meaning and Context: Quentin Skinner and His Critics*, edited by James Tully, 156–175. Princeton, NJ: Princeton University Press, 1988.
Field, G. C. *Some Problems of the Philosophy of History. Annual Philosophical Lecture Henriette Hertz Trust British Academy*. London: Humphrey Milford Amen House, 1938.
Firestone, Chaz, and Brian Scholl. "Cognition Does Not Affect Perception: Evaluating the Evidence for 'Top-Down' Effects." *Behavioral and Brain Sciences* 39 (2016): 1–77.
Firestone, Chaz. "Reference Guide: Top-Down Effects of Cognition of Perception." Accessed December 19, 2019. http://perception.yale.edu/Brian/refGuides/TopDown.html.
Fodor, Jerry. "Special Sciences (or: the Disunity of Science as a Working Hypothesis)." *Synthese* 28 (1974): 97–115.
———. *The Language of Thought*. Cambridge, MA: Harvard University Press, 1975.
———. *Representations: Essays on the Foundations of Cognitive Science*. Cambridge, MA: MIT Press, 1979.

———. "Methodological Solipsism Considered as a Research Strategy in Cognitive Psychology." *Behavioral and Brain Sciences* 3 (1980): 63–109.
———. "Observation Reconsidered." *Philosophy of Science* 51 (1984): 23–43.
———. *Psychosemantics: The Problem of Meaning Is the Philosophy of Mind*. Cambridge, MA: The MIT Press, 1987.
———. "Concepts: A Potboiler." *Philosophical Issues* 6 (1995): 1–24.
———. "A Modal Argument for Narrow Content." In *The Twin Earth Chronicles: Twenty Years of Reflection on Hilary Putnam's "The Meaning of Meaning,"* edited by Andrew Pessin and Sanford Goldberg, 264–283. Armonk, NY: M. E. Sharpe, 1996.
———. "Special Sciences: Still Autonomous After All These Years." *Philosophical Perspectives* 11 (1997): 149–163.
———. "Do We Think in Mentalse." In Jerry Fodor, *In Critical Condition: Polemical Essays on Cognitive Science and the Philosophy of Mind*, 63–75. Cambridge, MA: MIT Press, 1998.
———. *Concepts: Where Cognitive Science Went Wrong*. Oxford: Clarendon Press, 1998.
Fodor, J. A., M. F. Garrett, E. C. Walker and C. H. Parkes. "Against Definitions." *Cognition* 8 (1980): 263–367.
Føllesdal, Dagfinn. "Hermeneutics and Hypothetico-Deductive Method." *Dialectica* 33 (1979): 319–336.
Førland, Tor Egil. *Values, Objectivity and Explanation in Historiography*. New York: Routledge, 2017.
Foucault, Michel. *Les mots et les choses*. Paris: Gallimard, 1976.
———. *The Order of Things: An Archaeology of Human Sciences, with a Foreword to the English Edition*. The name of the translator not stated. New York: Vintage Books, 1994.
———. *The Archaeology of Knowledge and the Discourse on Language*. Translated by A. M. Sheridan Smith. New York: Pantheon Books, 1972.
———. "Qu'est-ce Qu'un Auteur." *Bulletin de la Société Francais de Philosophie*, 63 (1969): 75–95.
———. "What Is an Author." Translated by Josué V. Harari. In *The Foucault Reader*, edited by Paul Rabinow, 101–120. New York: Pantheon Books, 1984.
Frege, Gottlob. "Der Gedanke. Eine logische Untersuchung." *Beiträge zur Philosophie des deutschen Idealismus* 2 (1918–1919): 58–77.
———. "Über Sinn und Bedeuting." In *Funktion-Begriff-Bedeuting*, edited by Mark Textor, 23–46. Göttingen: Vandenhoeck & Ruprecht, 2007.
Frey, Dagobert. *Englisches Wesen im Spiegel seiner Kunst*. Stuttgart: Kohlhammer, 1942.
Fritz, Kurt von. *The Theory of Mixed Constitution in Antiquity*. New York: Arno Press, 1975.
Gadamer, Hans Georg. *Wahrheit und Methode*. Tübingen: Mohr 1990.
Gardiner, Patrick, ed. *Theories of History*. Glencoe: The Free Press, 1959.
———. *The Philosophy of History*. Oxford: Oxford University Press, 1978.
Gardiner, Patrick. *The Nature of Historical Explanation*. Oxford: Oxford University Press, 1971.
Gates, Gary. "Physicalism, Empiricism and Positivism." In *Physicalism and Its Discontents*, edited by Carl Gillet and Barry Loewer, 251–267. Cambridge: Cambridge University Press, 2001.
Gauker, Christopher. *Thinking Out Loud*. Princeton, NJ: Princeton University Press, 1994.
———. "Semantics and Pragmatics." In *The Routledge Companion to Philosophy of Language*, edited by Gillian Russell and Delia Graff Fara, 18–28. New York: Routledge, 2012.
Gerring, John. "Ideology: A Definitional Analysis." *Political Research Quarterly* 50 (1997): 957–994.
———. "What Makes a Concept Good? A Criterial Framework for Understanding Concept Formation in the Social Sciences." *Polity* 31 (1999): 357–393.
Gettier, Edmund. "Is Justified True Belief Knowledge?" *Analysis* 23 (1963): 121–123.
Geurts, Bart. "Good News about the Description Theory of Names." *Journal of Semantics* 14 (1997): 319–348.
Gibbon, Edward. *The Decline and Fall of the Roman Empire*. New York: Random House. The year of publication not stated.

Giddens, Anthony. *Central Problems in Social Theory: Action, Structure and Contradiction in Social Analysis*. London: The Macmillan Press, 1979.
Gilbert, Margaret. "Shared Intention and Personal Intention." *The Philosophical Studies* 144 (2009): 167–187.
Ginzburg, Carlo. "Checking the Evidence: The Judge and the Historian." *Critical Inquiry* 18 (1991): 79–92.
Goldstein, Leon. *Historical Knowing*. Austin: University of Texas Press, 1976.
———. "History and the Primacy of Knowing." *History and Theory* 16 (1977): 29–52.
———. *The What and the Why*. Leiden: Brill, 1996.
Gombrich, Ernst. *Art and Illusion: A Study of Psychology of Pictorial Representation*. London: Phaidon 1960.
———. "Representation and Misrepresentation." *Critical Inquiry* 11 (1984): 195–201.
———. "Image and Code: Scope and Limits of Conventionalism in Pictorial Representation." In Ernst Gombrich, *The Image and the Eye: Further Studies in the Psychology of Pictorial Representation*, 278–297. London: Phaidon, 1981.
Goodman, Nelson. *Languages of Art: An Approach to a Theory of Symbols*. Indianapolis: Hackett Publishing Company, 1976.
Gordon, Ian. "Gombrich and the Psychology of Visual Perception." In *Gombrich on Art and Psychology*, edited by Richard Woodfield, 60–77. Manchester: Manchester University Press, 1996.
Gracia, Jorge. "Can There Be Texts Without Historical Authors?" *American Philosophical Quarterly* 31 (1994): 248–253.
Grafton, Anthony. "Preface." In Cecily Wedgwood, *The Thirty Years War*, vii–xi. New York: New York Review Books, 2005.
Gray, Aidan. "Name-Bearing, Reference and Circularity." *Philosophical Studies* 171 (2014): 207–231.
Hamlyn, D. W. *The Psychology of Perception*. London: Routledge, 1957.
———. "Perception, Sensation and Nonconceptual Content." In *Essays on Nonconceptual Content*, edited by York Gunther, 251–262. Cambridge, MA: The MIT Press, 2003.
Harman, Gilbert. "Language: Thought and Communication." In Gilbert Harman, *Reasoning, Meaning and Mind*, 166–182. Oxford: Clarendon Press, 2005.
———. "Language Learning." In Gilbert Harman, *Reasoning, Meaning and Mind*, 183–191. Oxford: Clarendon Press, 2005.
Haupt, Paul. "Die arische Abkunft Jesu und Seiner Jünger." *Orientalische Litteratur-Zeitung* 11 (1908): 237–240.
Hedicke, Robert. *Methodenlehre der Kunstgeschichte. Ein Handbuch für Studierende*. Strassburg: Heitz, 1924.
Hegel, Georg Friedrich Wilhelm. *Vorlesungen über die Philosophie der Geschichte*. Frankfurt am Main: Suhrkamp, 1986.
Hemming, John. *The Conquest of the Incas*. Harmondsworth: Penguin, 1983.
Hempel, Carl. "The Function of General Laws in History." *The Journal of Philosophy* 39 (1942): 35–48.
———. "Reasons and Covering Laws in Historical Explanation." In *The Philosophy of History*, edited by Patrick Gardiner, 90–105. Oxford: Oxford University Press, 1978.
———. "Comments on Goodman's Ways of Worldmaking." *Synthese* 45 (1980): 193–200.
Herodotus. *The Persian Wars*. Cambridge, MA: Harvard University Press, 1920.
Herder, Johann Gottfried. *Abhandlung über den Ursprung der Sprache*. Stuttgart: Phillip Reclam, 1966.
Hetherington, Stephen. "Gettier Problems." Accessed January 4, 2018. http://www.iep.utm.edu/gettier.
Hirsch, E. D. *Validity in Interpretation*. New Haven, CT: Yale University Press, 1967.
———. *The Aims of Interpretation*. Chicago: Chicago University Press, 1976.
———. "Against Theory?" *Critical Inquiry* 9 (1983): 743–747.
Hodgson, Geoffrey. "Meanings of Methodological Individualism." *Journal of Economic Methodology* 14 (2007): 211–226.
Hoffman, Donald. *Visual Intelligence*. New York: Norton, 2000.

Hon, Giora, and Bernard R. Goldstein. *From Summetria to Symmetry: The Making of a Revolutionary Scientific Concept*. New York: Springer, 2008.
Horn, Laurence. "Implicature." In *The Routledge Companion to Philosophy of Language*, edited by Gillian Russell and Delia Graff Fara, 53–66. New York: Routledge, 2012.
Howard-Snyder, Daniel, and Frances Howard-Snyder. "Infallibilism and Gettier's Legacy." *Philosophy and Phenomenological Research* 66 (2003): 304–327.
Husserl, Edmund. *Logische Untersuchungen*. The Hague: Martinus Nijhoff, 1984.
Hutchins, John. "Milestones in Machine Translation: Bar-Hillel and the Nonfeasibility of FAHQT." Accessed March 5, 2019. https://www.infoamerica.org/documentos_pdf/bar04.pdf.
Ichikawa, Jonathan Jenkins and Steup, Matthias. "The Analysis of Knowledge." Accessed January 4, 2018. https://plato.stanford.edu/archives/fall2017/entries/knowledge-analysis/.
Irwin, Willam. *Intentionalist Interpretation: A Philosophical Explanation and Defense*. Westport, CT: Greenwood Press, 1999.
Iseminger, Gary, ed. *Intention and Interpretation*. Philadelphia: Temple University Press, 24–40.
Israel, Joachim. "The Principle of Methodological Individualism and Marxian Epistemology." *Acta Sociologica* 14 (1971): 145–150.
Jakobsen, Roman. "On Linguistic Aspects of Translation." In *Theories of Translation*, edited by Rainar Schulte and John Biguenet, 144–153. Chicago: The University of Chicago Press, 1992.
Jay, Martin. "Historical Explanation and the Event." *New Literary History* 42 (2011): 557–571.
Jenkins, Keith. *Re-thinking History*. London: Routledge, 1991.
———. *Refiguring History: New Thoughts on an Old Discipline*. London: Routledge, 2004.
Jones, Howard Mumford. "Ideas, History, Technology." *Technology and Culture* 1 (1959): 20–27.
Jones, Tod. "Methodological Individualism in Proper Perspective." *Behavior and Philosophy* 24 (1996): 119–128.
Juhl, P. D. "The Appeal to the Text: What Are We Appealing To?" *Journal of Aesthetics and Art Criticism* 36 (1978): 277–287.
Justice, John. "On Sense and Reflexivity." *The Journal of Philosophy* 98 (2001): 351–364.
Kane, Robert. *A Contemporary Introduction to Free Will*. Oxford: Oxford University Press, 2005.
Kant, Immanuel. *Kritik der reinen Vernunft*. Leipzig: Reclam, 1980.
———. *The Oxford Handbook of Free Will*. Oxford: Oxford University Press, 2011.
Karttuunen, Lauri. "Presuppositions of Compound Sentences." *Linguistic Inquiry* 4 (1973): 169–193.
———. "Presuppositions: What Went Wrong." *Proceedings of SALT* 26 (2016): 705–731.
Katz, Jerrold. *Language & Other Abstract Objects*. Totowa, NJ: Rowman & Littlefield, 1981.
———. "Names Without Bearers." *The Philosophical Review* 103 (1994): 1–39.
Keenan, Edward. "Some Logical Problems of Translation." In *Meaning and Translation: Philosophical and Linguistic Approaches*, edited by Franz Guenther and M. Guether-Reutter, 157–189. London: Duckworth, 1978.
Kelly, Sean Dorrance. "Demonstrative Concepts and Experience." *The Philosophical Review* 110 (2001): 397–420.
Kim, Jaegwon. *Physicalism, Or Something Near Enough*. Princeton, NJ: Princeton University Press, 2005.
———. *Philosophy of Mind*. Boulder, CO: Westview Press, 2011.
Kincaid, Harold. *Individualism and the Unity of Science: Essays on Reduction Explanation and the Special Sciences*. Lanham, MD: Rowman & Littlefield, 1997.
Kleene, Stephen Cole. *Mathematical Logic*. Mineola, NY: Dover, 1967.
Knapp, Stephen, and Walter Benn Michaels. "Against Theory." *Critical Inquiry* 8 (1982): 723–742.
———. "Against Theory 2: Hermeneutics and Deconstruction." *Critical Inquiry* 14 (1987): 49–68.

Koffka, Kurt. "Zur Theorie der Erlebnis-Wahrnehmung." *Annalen der Philosophie* 3 (1923): 375–399.
Koselleck, Reinhart. "Die Geschichte der Begriffe und Begriffe der Geschichte." In Reinhart Koselleck, *Begriffgeschichten*, 56–76. Frankfurt am Main: Suhrkamp, 2006.
———. "Hinweise auf die temporalen Strukturen begriffgeschichtlichen Wandels." In Reinhart Koselleck, *Begriffgeschichten*, 86–98. Frankfurt am Main: Suhrkamp, 2006.
Kosso, Peter. "Observation of the Past." *History and Theory* 31 (1992): 21–35.
———. "Philosophy and Historiography." In *A Companion to the Philosophy of History and Historiography*, edited by Aviezer Tucker, 9–25. Chichester: Wiley-Blackwell, 2011.
Koyré, Alexandre. "Galileo's Treatise *De motu gravium*: The Use and Abuse of Imaginary Experiment." In Alexandre Koyré, *Metaphysics and Measurement*, 44–88. London: Chapman & Hall, 1968.
Krieger, Murray. "The Ambiguities of Representation and Illusion: An E. H. Gombrich Retrospective." *Critical Inquiry* 11 (1984): 181–195.
Kripke, Saul. *Naming and Necessity*. Malden, MA: Blackwell, 1981.
Kuhn, Thomas. *The Structure of Scientific Revolutions*. Chicago: The University of Chicago Press, 1996.
Kumar, Chandra. "A Pragmatist Spin on Analytical Marxism and Methodological Individualism." *Philosophical Papers* 37 (2008): 185–211.
Kuukkanen, Jouni-Matti. "Making Sense of Conceptual Change." *History and Theory* 47 (2008): 351–372.
———. *Postnarrativist Philosophy of Historiography*. Houndmills: Palgrave Macmillan, 2015.
———. "The Future of Philosophy of Historiography: Reviving or Reinventing." In *Towards a Revival of Analytical Philosophy of History: Around Paul A. Roth's Vision of Historical Sciences*, edited by Krzystof Brzechczyn, 73–94. Leiden: Brill/Rodopi, 2018.
Lamarque, Peter. "The Death of the Author: An Analytical Autopsy." *British Journal of Aesthetics* 30 (1990): 319–331.
Lamprecht, Karl. "Was ist Kulturgeschichte? Beitrag zu einer empirischen Historik." *Deutsche Zeitschrift für Geschichtswissenschaft* 7 (1896–1897): 75–145.
———. *Einführung in das historische Denken*. Leipzig: Voigtländer 1912.
Latour, Bruno. "On the Partial Existence of Existing and Nonexisting Objects." In *Biographies of Scientific Objects*, edited by Lorraine Daston, 247–269. Chicago: The University of Chicago Press, 1999.
Laudan, Larry. "Demystifying Underdetermination." *Minnesota Studies in the Philosophy of Science* 14 (1990): 267–297.
Levine, Andrew, Elliott Sober, and Erik Olin Wright. "Marxism and Methodological Individualism." *New Left Review* (1987): 67–84.
Lewis, David. "Causation." In David Lewis, *Philosophical Papers*, vol. 2, 159–171. Oxford: Oxford University Press, 1986.
———. "Causal Explanation." In David Lewis, *Philosophical Papers*, vol. 2, 214–240. Oxford: Oxford University Press, 1986.
List, Christian, and Kai Spiekermann. "Methodological Individualism and Holism in Political Science." *American Political Science Review* 107 (2013): 629–643.
Loar, Brian. "The Semantics of Singular Terms." *The Philosophical Studies* 30 (1976): 353–377.
———. "Names and Descriptions: A Reply to Michael Devitt." *The Philosophical Studies* 38 (1980): 85–89.
———. "Social Content and Psychological Content." In *The Twin Earth Chronicles: Twenty Years of Reflection on Hilary Putnam's "The Meaning of Meaning,"* edited by Andrew Pessin and Sanford Goldberg, 180–192. Armonk, NY: M. E. Sharpe, 1996.
Locke, John. *An Essay Concerning Human Understanding*. Amherst, NY: Prometheus Books, 1995.
Loewer, Barry. "From Physics to Physicalism." In *Physicalism and Its Discontents*, edited by Carl Gillett and Barry Loewer, 37–56. Cambridge: Cambridge University Press, 2001.

Lorenz, Chris. "Historical Knowledge and Historical Reality: A Plea for 'Internal Realism.'" In *History and Theory Contemporary Readings*, edited by Brian Fay, Philip Pomper, and Richard Vann, 342–376. Malden, MA: Blackwell, 1998.

Losonsky, Michael. *Linguistic Turns in Modern Philosophy*. Cambridge: Cambridge University Press, 2006.

Lucretius. *De natura: On the Nature of Things*. Cambridge, MA: Harvard University Press, 1924.

Lukes, Steven. "Methodological Individualism Reconsidered." *The British Journal of Sociology* 19 (1968): 119–129.

Luther, Martin. *De servo arbitrio*. Weimar: Hermann Böhlaus Nachfolger, 1908.

Lycan, William. *Philosophy of Language*. New York: Routledge, 2008.

Maar, Alexander. "Applying D. K. Lewis's Counterfactual Theory of Causation to the Philosophy of Historiography." *Journal of the Philosophy of History* 10 (2016): 349–369.

Mandelbaum, Maurice. "Societal Facts." In *Modes of Individualism and Collectivism*, edited by John O'Neill, 221–234. London: Heinemann 1973.

———. *The Problem of Historical Knowledge*. New York: Harper & Row, 1967.

———. "The Problem of 'Covering Laws.'" In *The Philosophy of History*, edited by Patrick Gardiner, 51–65. Oxford: Oxford University Press, 1978.

Margolis, Eric, and Stephen Laurence. "Concepts and Cognitive Science." In *Concepts*, edited by Eric Margolis and Stephen Laurence, 3–83. Cambridge, MA: MIT Press, 1999.

———. "The Ontology of Concepts—Abstract Objects or Mental Representations?" *Nous*, 41 (2007): 561–593.

———. "Concepts." Accessed February 22, 2017. https://plato.stanford.edu/entries/concepts/.

Martin, Michael. "Perception, Concepts and Memory." In *Essays on Nonconceptual Content*, edited by York Gunther, 237–250. Cambridge, MA: The MIT Press, 2003.

Martin, Raymond. "Causes, Conditions and Causal Importance." *History and Theory* 21 (1982): 53–74.

Martinich, Aloysius, and David Sosa, eds. *The Philosophy of Language*. Oxford: Oxford University Press, 2013.

Marwick, Arthur. *The Nature of History*. London: Macmillan, 1993.

Marx, Karl. *Der 18te Brumaire des Louis Napoleon*. In Karl Marx and Friedrich Engels, *Werke*, vol. 8, 115–207. Berlin: Dietz, 1957–1968.

Marx, Karl, and Friedrich Engels. *Die deutsche Ideologie*. In Karl Marx and Friedrich Engels, *Werke*, vol. 3, 10–607. Berlin: Dietz, 1957–1968.

———. *Die heilige Familie*. In Karl Marx and Friedrich Engels, *Werke*, vol. 2, 7–223. Berlin: Dietz, 1957–1968.

McCullagh, Behan, C. "Narrative Logic: A Semantic Analysis of the Historian's Language." *History and Theory* 23 (1984): 394–403.

———. *The Truth in History*. London: Routledge, 1998.

McDonald, Fritz. "Linguistics, Psychology and the Ontology of Language." *Croatian Journal of Philosophy* 27 (2009): 291–301.

McDowell, John. *Mind and World*. Cambridge, MA: Harvard University Press, 1994.

McLaughlin, Brian. "The Rise and Fall of British Emergentism." In *Emergence or Reduction?*, edited by Ansgar Beckermann, Hans Flohr, and Jaegwon Kim, 49–93. Berlin: Walter de Gryter, 1992.

Meiland, Jack. *Scepticism and Historical Knowledge*. New York: Random House, 1965.

Mellor, David Hugh. "The Reduction of Society." *Philosophy* 57 (1982): 51–75.

———. "Natural Kinds." In *The Twin Earth Chronicles: Twenty Years of Reflection on Hilary Putnam's "The Meaning of Meaning,"* edited by Andrew Pessin and Sanford Goldberg, 69–80. Armonk, NY: M. E. Sharpe, 1996.

Merricks, Trenton: "Warrant Entails Truth." *Philosophy and Phenomenological Research* 55 (1995): 841–855.

———. "More on Warrant's Entailing Truth." *Philosophy and Phenomenological Research* 57 (1997): 627–631.

Millar, Alan. *Reasons and Experience*. Oxford: Clarendon Press.

———. "Concepts, Experience and Inference." *Mind* 100 (1991): 495–505.

Mink, Louis. "Change and Causality in the History of Ideas." *Eighteenth-Century Studies* 2 (1968): 7–25.

———. "Is Speculative Philosophy of History Possible." In Louis Mink, *Historical Understanding*, 147–162. Ithaca, NY: Cornell University Press, 1990.

Mitrović, Branko. "Leon Battista Alberti and the Homogeneity of Space." *Journal of the Society of Architectural Historians* 63 (2004): 424–440.

———. *Serene Greed of the Eye: Leon Battista Alberti and the Philosophical Foundations of Renaissance Architectural Theory*. Berlin: Deutscher Kunstverlag, 2005.

———. "Intellectual History, Inconceivability and Methodological Holism." *History and Theory* 46 (2007): 29–47.

———. "Humanist Art History and Its Enemies: Erwin Panofsky on the Individualism-Collectivism Debate." *Konsthistorisk Tidskrift* 78 (2009): 57–76.

———. "Intentionalism, Intentionality and Reporting Beliefs." *History and Theory* 48 (2009): 180–198.

———. "A Defence of Light: Ernst Gombrich on the Individualism-Collectivism Debate." *Journal of Art Historiography* 3 (2010): 3BM/2.

———. "*From Summetria to Symmetry: The Making of a Revolutionary Scientific Concept*, by Giora Hon and Bernard R. Goldstein. Dordrecht: Springer, 2008." [Book review.] *Journal of the Society of Architectural Historians* 68 (2009): 576–577.

———. "Attribution of Concepts and Problems with Anachronism." *History and Theory* 50 (2011): 303–327.

———. "Opacity and Transparency in Historical Representations. Review of *Meaning, Truth and Reference in Historical Representation* by Frank Ankersmit. Ithaca, NY: Cornell University Press, 2012." [Book review.] *History and Theory* 53 (2014): 277–294.

———. "Historical Understanding and Historical Interpretation as Contextualization." *History and Theory* 54 (2015): 311–332.

———. *Rage and Denials: Collectivist Philosophy, Politics and Art Historiography 1890–1947*. University Park: Pennsylvania State University Press, 2015.

———. "Visuality, Intentionality and Architecture." Review of *Seeing Things as They Are* by John Searle. Oxford: Oxford University Press, 2016." [Book review.] *Journal of Art Historiography* 15 (2016): 15/BM1.

———. "Is Multiple Realizability a Valid Argument Against Methodological Individualism?" *Philosophy of the Social Sciences* 47 (2017): 28–43.

Mondolfo, Rodolfo. *L'infinito nel pensiero dei Greci*. Florence: Le Monnier, 1934.

Moon, Andrew. "Warrant *Does* Entail Truth." *Synthese* 184 (2012): 287–297.

Munday, Jeremy. *Introducing Translation Studies*. London: Routledge, 2001.

Murphey, Murray. *Our Knowledge of the Historical Past*. Indianapolis: The Bobb-Merrill Company, 1973.

———. *Truth and History*. Albany, NY: SUNY Press, 2009.

———. "Realism about the Past." In *A Companion to the Philosophy of History and Historiography*, edited by Aviezer Tucker, 181–189. Chichester: Wiley-Blackwell, 2011.

Nagel, Ernest. "Some Issues in the Logic of Historical Analysis." *The Scientific Monthly* 74 (1952): 162–169.

———. "Determinism in History." In *The Philosophy of History*, edited by Patrick Gardiner, 186–215. Oxford: Oxford University Press, 1978.

Nay, Alyssa. "Defining Physicalism." *Philosophy Compass* 3 (2008): 1033–1048.

Neander, Karen. "Naturalistic Theories of Reference." In *The Blackwell Guide to the Philosophy of Language*, edited by Michael Davitt and Richard Hanley, 374–391. Malden, MA: Blackwell, 2006.

Nehamas, Alexander. "What an Author Is." *The Journal of Philosophy* 83 (1986): 685–691.

Nersessian, Nancy. *Faraday to Einstein: Constructing Meaning in Scientific Theories*. Dordrecht: Martinus Nijhoff Publishers, 1984.

———. "The Method to 'Meaning': A Reply to Leplin." *Philosophy of Science* 58 (1991): 678–686.

Noë, Alva, and Evan Thompson, eds. *Vision and Mind*. Cambridge, MA: MIT Press, 2002.

Norberg-Schulz, Christian. *Intentions in Architecture*. Oslo: Universitetsforlaget, 1963.

———. *Mellom jord og himmel*. Oslo: Pax Ferlag, 1992.
Nowell-Smith, Patrick Horace. "The Constructionism Theory of History." *History and Theory* 16 (1977): 1–28.
Oakeshott, Michael. *Experience and Its Modes*. Cambridge: Cambridge University Press 1966.
O'Connor, Timothy. "Agent Causation." In *Free Will*, edited by Gary Watson, 255–284. Oxford: Oxford University Press, 2011.
Osherson, Daniel N., and Edward E. Smith. "On the Adequacy of the Prototype Theory of Concepts." In *Concepts*, edited by Eric Margolis and Stephen Laurence, 261–278. Cambridge, MA: The MIT Press, 1999.
Otte, Thomas G. *July Crisis*. Cambridge: Cambridge University Press, 2014.
Panofsky, Erwin. "History of Art as a Humanistic Discipline." In Erwin Panofsky, *Meaning in the Visual Arts*, 1–25. Chicago: The University of Chicago Press, 1955.
———. "Die Perspektive als 'symbolische Form.'" In Erwin Panofsky, *Deutschsprachige Aufsätze*, vol. 2, 664–757. Berlin: Akademie Verlag, 1998.
———. "Der Begriff des Kunstwollens." In Erwin Panofsky, *Deutschsprachige Aufsätze*, vol. 2, 1019–1034. Berlin: Akademie Verlag, 1998.
Papineau, David. "The Rise of Physicalism." In *Physicalism and Its Discontents*, edited by Carl Gillett and Barry Loewer, 3–36. Cambridge: Cambridge University Press, 2001.
Pateman, Trevor. *Language in Mind and Language in Society*. Oxford: Clarendon Press, 1987.
Pataut, Fabrice. "Anti-Realism about the Past." In *A Companion to the Philosophy of History and Historiography*, edited by Aviezer Tucker, 190–197. Chichester: Wiley-Blackwell, 2011.
Paul, L. A., and Edward Hall. *Causation: A User's Guide*. Oxford: Oxford University Press, 2013.
Peacocke, Christopher. *A Study of Concepts*. Cambridge, MA: The MIT Press, 1992.
———. "Does Perception Have a Nonconceptual Content?" *The Journal of Philosophy* 98 (2001): 239–264.
———. "Scenarios, Concepts and Perception." In *Essays on Nonconceptual Content*, edited by York Gunther, 107–133. Cambridge, MA: The MIT Press, 2003.
———. "Rationale and Maxims in the Study of Concepts." *Nous* 39 (2005): 167–178.
Pérez-Gomez, Alberto. "The Myth of Dedalus: On the Architect's *Metier*." In Alberto Pérez-Gomez, *Timely Meditations*, vol. 1, 2–21. Montreal: Right Angle International, 2016.
———. "Abstraction in Modern Architecture: The Gnostic Dimension." In Alberto Pérez-Gomez, *Timely Meditations*, vol. 2, 37–60. Montreal: Right Angle International, 2016.
———. "Place Is Not a Post-Card: The Problem of Context in Contemporary Architecture." In Alberto Pérez-Gomez, *Timely Meditations*, vol. 2, 127–141. Montreal: Right Angle International, 2016.
Pinder, Wilhelm. *Das Problem der Generation in der Kunstgeschichte Europas*. Berlin: Frankfurter Verlags-Anstalt, 1926.
———. *Gesammelte Aufsätze aus den Jahren 1907–1935*. Leipzig: Verlag E. A. Seemann, 1938.
Pirenne, Maurice Henri Léonard. *Optics, Painting & Photography*. Cambridge: Cambridge University Press 1970.
Plato. *Statesman. Philebus. Ion.* Cambridge, MA: Harvard University Press, 1995.
———. *Theaetetus. Sophist.* Cambridge, MA: Harvard University Press, 2002.
Polybius. *The Histories*. Cambridge, MA: Harvard University Press, 2012.
Pompa, Leon. "Truth and Fact in History." In *Substance and Form in History*, edited by Leon Pompa and William Herbert Dray, 171–186. Edinburgh: Edinburgh University Press, 1981.
Pontano, Giovanni. *De fortuna. La fortuna*. Naples: La scuola di Pitagora, 2012.
Prudovsky, Gad. "Can We Ascribe to Past Thinkers Concepts They Had No Linguistic Means to Express?" *History and Theory* 36 (1997): 15–31
Ptolemy. *Tetrabiblos*. Cambridge, MA: Harvard University Press, 1940.
Putnam, Hilary. "Meaning and Reference." *The Journal of Philosophy* 70 (1973): 699–711.
———. "Introduction." In *The Twin Earth Chronicles: Twenty Years of Reflection on Hilary Putnam's "The Meaning of Meaning,"* edited by Andrew Pessin and Sanford Goldberg, xv–xxii. Armonk, NY: M. E. Sharpe, 1996.

———. "The Meaning of 'Meaning.'" In *The Twin Earth Chronicles: Twenty Years of Reflection on Hilary Putnam's "The Meaning of Meaning,"* edited by Andrew Pessin and Sanford Goldberg, 3–51. Armonk, NY: M. E. Sharpe, 1996.

———. *Reason, Truth and History*. Cambridge: Cambridge University Press, 1981.

———. "Is Semantics Possible?" In *Concepts*, edited by Eric Margolis and Stephen Laurence, 178–187. Cambridge, MA: The MIT Press, 1999.

Pylyshyn, Zenon. "Is Vision Continuous with Cognition? The Case for Cognitive Impenetrability of Visual Perception." *Behavioral and Brain Sciences* 22 (1999): 341–423.

———. *Seeing and Visualizing: It's Not What You Think*. Cambridge, MA: The MIT Press, 2006.

Quine, Willard van Orman. "On What There Is." In Willard van Orman Quine, *From a Logical Point of View*, 1–19. New York: Harper and Row, 1961.

———. "Two Dogmas of Empiricism." In Willard van Orman Quine, *From a Logical Point of View*, 20–46. New York: Harper and Row, 1961.

———. "Meaning in Linguistics." In Willard van Orman Quine, *From a Logical Point of View*, 47–64. New York: Harper and Row, 1961.

Raffman, Diana. "On the Persistence of Phenomenology." In *Conscious Experience*, edited by Thomas Metzinger, 293–308. Paderborn: Schoningh Verlag, 1995.

Raftopoulos, Athanassios. *Cognition and Perception: How Do Psychology and Neural Science Inform Philosophy?* Cambridge, MA: The MIT Press, 2009.

———. "The Cognitive Impenetrability of the Content of Early Vision Is a Necessary and Sufficient Condition for Purely Nonconceptual Content." *Philosophical Psychology* 27 (2014): 601–620.

Railton, Peter. *Explaining Explanation: A Realist Account of Scientific Explanation and Understanding*." PhD diss., Princeton University, 1980.

Ranke, Leopold von. *Die serbische Revolution*. Berlin: Duncker und Humblot, 1844.

———. *Geschichten der romanischen und germanischen Völker von 1494–1514*. Hamburg: Standard Verlag, 1957.

Rey, Georges. "Concepts and Stereotypes." In *Concepts*, edited by Eric Margolis and Stephen Laurence, 279–299. Cambridge, MA: The MIT Press, 1999.

Roberts, Andrew. *Napoleon the Great*. Harmondsworth: Penguin, 2015.

Roberts, Clayton. *The Logic of Historical Explanation*. University Park: Pennsylvania State University Press, 1996.

Robinson, Teresa. "Reference." In *The Routledge Companion to Philosophy of Language*, edited by Gillian Russell and Delia Graff Fara, 189–198. New York: Routledge, 2012.

Rockmore, Tom. "Introduction." In *Anti-Foundationalism Old and New*, edited by Tom Rockmore and Beth J. Singer, 1–12. Philadelphia: Temple University Press, 1992.

Rosenauer, Artur. "Max Dvořák—Kunstgeschichte als Geistesgeschichte." In Max Dvořák, *Kunstgeschichte als Geistesgeschichte*, 277–283. Berlin: Mann, 1995.

Rosh, Eleanor. "Principles of Categorization." In *Concepts*, edited by Eric Margolis and Stephen Laurence, 189–206. Cambridge, MA: The MIT Press, 1999.

Roth, Paul. "What Is to Be Done." In "Globalizing Hayden White," edited by Ewa Domańska and María Inés La Greca, 540–546. *Rethinking History* 23 (2019): 533–581.

Ruben, David-Hillel. "The Existence of Social Entities." *The Philosophical Quarterly* 32 (1982): 295–310.

Russell, Bertrand. "On Denoting." *Mind* 14 (1905): 479–493.

———. *Analysis of Mind*. London: Allen and Unwin, 1921.

———. "Descriptions." In *The Philosophy of Language*, edited by Aloysius Martinich and David Sosa, 114–120. Oxford: Oxford University Press, 2013.

Russell, Gillian, and Delia Graff Fara, eds. *The Routledge Companion to Philosophy of Language*. New York: Routledge, 2012.

Saari, Heikki. "On Frank Ankersmit's Postmodernist Theory of Historical Narrativity." *Rethinking History* 9 (2005): 5–21.

Saussure, Ferdinand, de. *Course in General Linguistics*. Translated by Wade Baskin. New York: Columbia University Press, 2011.

Sawyer, Keith. "Nonreductive Individualism: Part I—Supervenience and Wild Disjunction." *Philosophy of the Social Sciences*, 32 (2002): 537–559.
———. "Nonreductive Individualism: Part II—Social Causation." 33 (2003): 203–224.
———. *Social Emergence. Societies as Complex Systems*. Cambridge: Cambridge University Press, 2005.
Schleier, Hans. "Der Kulturhistoriker Karl Lamprecht, der 'Methodenstreit' und die Folgen." In *Alternative zu Ranke*, edited by Lothar Reher, 7–45. Leipzig: Reclam, 1988.
Schleiermacher, Friedrich. *Hermeneutik und Kritik mit besonderer Beziehung auf das Neue Testament*. Frankfurt am Main: Suhrkamp, 1999.
Schultz, Heiner. "Begriffsgeschichte und Argumentationsgeschichte." In *Historische Semantik und Begriffsgeschichte*, edited by Reinhart Koselleck, 43–74. Stuttgart: Klett-Cotta, 1979.
Schwartz, Stephen. "General Terms and Mass Terms." In *The Blackwell Guide to the Philosophy of Language*, edited by Michael Davitt and Richard Hanley, 274–287. Malden, MA: Blackwell, 2006.
Schweikard, David P., and Schmid, Hans Bernhard. "Collective Intentionality." Accessed November 20, 2016. http://plato.stanford.edu/archives/sum2013/entries/collective-intentionality/.
Scriven, Michael. "Causation as Explanation." *Noûs* 9 (1975): 3–16.
Searle, John. "Proper Names." *Mind* 67 (1958): 166–173.
———. "Intentionality and the Use of Language." In *Meaning and Use*, edited by Avishai Margalit, 181–197. Dordrecht: Reidel, 1979.
———. "The World Turned Upside Down." *The New York Review of Books* 27 (1983): 74–79.
———. *Intentionality*. Cambridge: Cambridge University Press, 1983.
———. "Indeterminacy, Empiricism and the First Person." *Journal of Philosophy* 84 (1987): 123–147.
———. "Collective Intentions and Actions." In *Intentions in Communication*, edited by P. Cohen, J. Morgan, and M. E. Pollack, 401–415. Cambridge, MA: Bradford Books, 1990.
———. "Animal Minds." *Midwest Studies in Philosophy* 19 (1994): 206–219.
———. *The Rediscovery of Mind*. Cambridge, MA: The MIT Press, 1994.
———. *The Construction of Social Reality*. London: Penguin, 1995.
———. "Intentionality 1." In *A Companion to the Philosophy of Mind*, edited by Samuel Gutenplan, 379–386. Oxford: Blackwell, 1998.
———. *Making the Social World: The Structure of Human Civilization*. Oxford: Oxford University Press, 2010.
———. *Seeing Things As They Are*. Oxford: Oxford University Press, 2015.
Sedlmayr, Hans. "Die Quintessenz der Lehren Riegls." In Hans Sedlmayr, *Kunst und Wahrheit*, 32–48. Mittenwald: Mäander, 1978.
Seeba, Hinrich. "Ansätze einer vergleichenden Kulturkritik bei Karl Lamprecht und in der Exil-Germanistik." *German Studies Review* 16 (1993): 1–17.
Seifert, Friedrich. *Der Streit um K. Lamprechts Geschichtsphilosophie*. Augsburg: Benno Filser Verlag, 1925.
Simmel, Georg. *Soziologie. Untersuchungen über die Formen der Vergeselschaftlichung*. Berlin: Duncker & Humboldt, 1908.
———. *Grundfragen der Soziologie (Individuum und Gesellschaft)*. Berlin: Göschen'sche Verlagshandlung, 1917.
Skinner, Quentin. "Meaning and Understanding." In *Meaning and Context: Quentin Skinner and His Critics*, edited by James Tully, 29–67. Princeton, NJ: Princeton University Press, 1988.
———. "Language and Social Change." In *Meaning and Context: Quentin Skinner and His Critics*, edited by James Tully, 118–132. Princeton, NJ: Princeton University Press, 1988.
Smith, Barry, ed. *John Searle*. Cambridge: Cambridge University Press, 2003.
Smith, Barry, and Klein, Gunnar O. "Concept Systems and Ontologies." *Transactions of the Japanese Society for Artificial Intelligence* 25 (2010): 433–441.
Smith, Edward, and Douglas Medin. "Exemplar View." In *Concepts*, edited by Eric Margolis and Stephen Laurence, 207–222. Cambridge, MA: The MIT Press, 1999.

Spengler, Oswald. *Der Untergang des Abendlandes. Umrisse einer Morphologie der Welgeschichte*. Munich: DTV 2003.

Spreizer, Christa. "The Old Guard and the Avant-Guard: Karl Lamprecht, Kurt Pinthus, and Literary Expressionism." *German Studies Review* 24 (2001): 283–301.

Srbik, Heinrich Ritter von. *Geist und Geschichte vom deutschen Humanismus bis zur Gegenwart*. Munich: Verlag F. Bruckmann, 1950.

Stainton, Robert, J. "The Deflation of Belief Contents." *Crítica: Revista Hispanoamericana de Filosofía 28* (1996): 63–82.

Stalnaker, Robert. "Presuppositions." *Journal of Philosophical Logic* 2 (1973): 447–457.

———. *Context and Content: Essays on Intentionality in Speech and Thought*. Oxford: Oxford University Press, 1999.

———. "What Might Non-Conceptual Content Be?" In *Essays on Nonconceptual Content*, edited by York Gunther, 95–106. Cambridge, MA: The MIT Press, 2003.

Steel, Daniel. "Methodological Individualism, Explanation and Invariance." *Philosophy of Social Sciences* 36 (2006): 440–463.

Sterelny, Kim. "Natural-Kind Terms." In *The Twin Earth Chronicles: Twenty Years of Reflection on Hilary Putnam's "The Meaning of Meaning,"* edited by Andrew Pessin and Sanford Goldberg, 98–114. Armonk, NY: M. E. Sharpe, 1996.

Stern, Joseph. "Figurative Language." In *The Blackwell Guide to the Philosophy of Language*, edited by Michael Davitt, and Richard Hanley, 168–185. Malden, MA: Blackwell, 2006.

Stoljar, Daniel. "Physicalism." Accessed December 27, 2018. https://plato.stanford.edu/entries/physicalism/.

———. *Physicalism*. London: Routledge, 2010.

Strzygowski, Josef. *Das indogermanische Ahnenerbe des deutschen Volkes und die Kunstgeschichte der Zukunft*. Vienna: Deutscher Verlag für Jugend und Volk, 1941.

Sturgeon, Scott. "The Gettier Problem." *Analysis* 53 (1993): 156–164.

———. *Die Deutsche Nordseele. Das Bekenntnis eines Kunstforschers*. Vienna: Adolf Luser Verlag, 1940.

Suetonius, Caius Tranquillius. "Gaius Caligula." In Caius Tranquillius Suetonius, *De vita caesarum*, vol. 1, 418–507. Cambridge, MA: Harvard University Press, 1998.

Tacitus, Publius Cornelius. *Historiae. Histories.* Cambridge, MA: Harvard University Press, 1925.

———. *Annales. Annals.* Cambridge, MA: Harvard University Press, 1931.

Tarrit, Fabien. "A Brief History, Scope and Peculiarities of 'Analytic Marxism.'" *Review of Radical Political Economics* 38 (2006): 595–618.

Taylor, A. J. P. *The Habsburg Monarchy 1809–1918*. Chicago: The University of Chicago Press, 1976.

———. *The Course of German History*. London: Hamish Hamilton, 1962.

———. *The Origins of the Second World War*. New York: Simon & Schuster Paperbooks, 2005.

Taylor, Charles. "Rationality." In *Rationality and Relativism*, edited by Martin Hollis and Steven Lukes, 87–105. Cambridge, MA: The MIT Press, 1982.

Thagard, Paul. *Conceptual Revolutions*. Princeton, NJ: Princeton University Press, 1992.

Thomas, Hugh. *The Conquest of Mexico*. London: Pimlico, 1993.

Thucydides. *History of the Peloponnesian War*. Cambridge, MA: Harvard University Press, 1919.

Todhunter, I. *History of the Theories of Attraction and the Figure of the Earth*. New York: Dover, 1962.

Tollefsen, Deborah. "Collective Intentionality." Accessed November 20, 2016. http://www.iep.utm.edu/coll-int/.

Troeltsch, Ernst. *Der Historismus und seine Probleme*. Tübingen: Mohr, 1922.

———. "Das Wesen des modernen Geistes." In Ernst Troeltsch, *Lesebuch*, 124–167, Tübingen: Mohr, 2003.

Tucker, Aviezer. "Historical Truth." In *Forms of Truth and the Unity of Knowledge*, edited by Vittorio Hoesle, 232–259. South Bend, IN: Notre Dame University Press, 2014.

———. *Our Knowledge of the Past: A Philosophy of Historiography*. Cambridge: Cambridge University Press, 2004.

———. "Historiographical Counterfactuals and the Philosophy of Historiography: A Introduction." Accessed on May 1, 2019. https://www.academia.edu/30424554/Historiographic_Counterfactuals_and_the_Philosophy_of_Historiography_An_Introduction.

Tucker, Aviezir, ed. *A Companion to the Philosophy of History and Historiography*. Chichester: Wiley-Blackwell, 2011.

Tuomela, Raimo, and Kaarlo Miller. "We-Intentions." *Philosophical Studies* 53 (1988): 367–89.

Tuomela, Raimo. "We-Intentions Revisited." *Philosophical Studies* 125 (2005): 327–369.

Udehn, Lars. *Methodological Individualism*. London: Routledge, 2001.

Ulam, Adam. *Stalin The Man and His Era*. London: Tauris, 2007.

Uzquiano, Gabriel. "The Supreme Court and the Supreme Court Justices: A Metaphysical Puzzle." *Nous* 38 (2004): 135–153.

Vesey, G. N. A. "Seeing and Seeing As." *Proceedings of the Aristotelian Society* (New Series) 56 (1955–1956): 109–124.

Voltaire, François-Marie Arouet. *The Age of Louis XIV*. Translated by Martyn P. Pollack. London: Everyman's Library, 1969.

Walsh, W. H. "Colligatory Concepts in History." In *The Philosophy of History*, edited by Patrick Gardiner, 127–144. Oxford: Oxford University Press, 1978.

Watkins, J. W. N. "Methodological Individualism: A Reply." *Philosophy of Science* 22 (1955): 58–62.

Watson, Gary, ed. *Free Will*. Oxford: Oxford University Press, 2011.

Weldes, Jutta, "Marxism and Methodological Individualism: A Critique." *Theory and Society* 18 (1989): 353–386.

Wheeler, S. C. "Indeterminacy of Radical Inerpretation and the Causal Theory of Reference." In *Meaning and Translation: Philosophical and Linguistic Approaches*, edited by Franz Guenther and M. Guether-Reutter, 83–94. London: Duckworth, 1978.

White, Hayden. *Metahistory: Historical Imagination in Nineteenth-Century Europe*. Baltimore, MD: Johns Hopkins University Press, 1973.

———. "Historicism, History and the Figurative Imagination." In Hayden White, *Tropics of Discourse: Essays in Cultural Criticism*, 101–120. Baltimore, MD: Johns Hopkins University Press, 1978.

———. "The Value of Narrativity in the Representation of Reality." In Hayden White, *The Content of the Form: Narrative Discourse and Historical Representation*, 1–25. Baltimore, MD: Johns Hopkins University Press, 1987.

White, Morton. *Foundations of Historical Knowledge*. New York: Harper & Row, 1965.

Wilson, George. "Again, Theory: On Speaker's Meaning, Linguistic Meaning and the Meaning of a Text." *Critical Inquiry* 19 (1992): 164–185.

Wittmer, Gene. "Sufficiency Claims and Physicalism: A Formulation." In *Physicalism and Its Discontents*, edited by Carl Gillett and Barry Loewer, 57–73. Cambridge: Cambridge University Press, 2001.

Wittgenstein, Ludwig. *Philosophical Investigations*. Oxford: Blackwell, 1953.

Wolff, Robert. "Methodological Individualism and Marx: Some Remarks on Jon Elster, Game Theory and Other Things." *Canadian Journal of Philosophy* 20 (1990): 469–486.

Woltmann, Ludwig. *Die Germanen und die Renaissance*. Leipzig: Thüringische Verlagsanstalt, 1905.

Worringer, Wilhelm. *Formprobleme der Gotik*. Munich: R. Piper, 1920.

Zagzebski, Linda. "The Inescapability of Gettier Problems." *Philosophical Quarterly* 44 (1994): 65–73.

Zemach, Eddy. "Putnam's Theory of the Reference of Substance Terms." *The Journal of Philosophy* 73 (1976): 116–127.

Zinn, Howard. *A People's History of the United States*. New York: Harper, 2015.

Index

accuracy of historical works, 198–200, 204–205
Achinstein, Peter, 102n37
action: judgement and, 72; rationality and, 72–74
Alberti, Leon Battista, 185
Albertini, Luigi, 52
Anabasis of Alexander (Arrian), 29
anachronism, 121, 136; essentialism and, 130, 132–134
analytic philosophy, 19–21
Ankersmit, Frank, 24, 36–37, 191–195, 206n18
answers, about transparency and historical documents, 202–203
anti-foundationalism, 2, 27n52, 99, 210, 220, 228
anti-mentalism, language and, 105–107
Antiquity, 166
anti-realism, 29–43, 189–195, 214–216; coherentism and, 29, 34–35, 39–40; inaccessibility of past and, 31–33; incommensurability of concepts and, 97; materialism and, 38–40; opacity and, 190–195; "Theory"-theory and, 97–99
Ant Trap (Epstein), 64n23
Archimedes, 132–134, 148
Aristarchus, 86–87
Aristotle, 40, 89, 111, 135, 137, 175; essentialism and, 128–129

Arrian, of *Anabasis of Alexander*, 29
Art and Illusion (Gombrich), 96, 223
arthritis argument, 116, 119–120, 146
Ast, Friedrich, 166
astrology, 66
astronomy, 86–87, 99–101, 129–130, 134–136, 161–164
Der Aufbau der geschichtlichen Welt (Dilthey), 157–158
Augustine, Aurelius, 65–66
Authorship, 175–178; *de verbis* and *de signis* beliefs and, 109; inconceivability and, 144–151; meaning and, 174–178, 187n4; zero external author information understanding and, 174–175
Ayer, Alfred Jules, 86

Bach, Kent, 142n21
Barber, Alex, 141n2
Bar-Hillel, Yehoshua, 184
Barthes, Roland, 5
Begriffsgeschichte, 89, 122
beliefs: *de signis*, 108–112, 174–175; language and, 107–115; meaning and, 107; mental states and, 109; novel properties and, 151–152; shared rationality and, 161, 164; translation and, 179–183, 184–187; words and, 110. See also *de verbis* beliefs
Bermúdez, José Luis, 225

Bevir, Mark, 154, 170n24, 181, 220; antifoundationalism and, 27n52; *The Logic of the History of Ideas* by, 27n52, 166–167, 177–179; materialism and, 21, 27n52; procedural individualism and, 51; weak intentionalism and, 177–179
bias, 43–45
Bicchieri, Cristina, 74
biology, 8–9
biological phenomena, 3–4, 8–11; mental states and, 9, 16–17, 79, 116–117
Bismarck argument, 58–59
bivalent logic, 33, 45n19
Black Hand officers, 75, 75–76, 81n33
Bonaparte, Napoleon, 49, 78–79
Bonitz, Herman, 111
Bradley, Francis Herbart, 216
brain: language and, 114, 116–118; mental states and, 9, 16–17, 78–79, 90–92, 116–118; neurobiology and, 16–17, 78–81, 114
Braun, David, 101n6
Brunelleschi, Filippo, 151–152, 193
Bruner, Jerome, 221, 223
Bryson, Norman, 5
Burge, Tyler, 23, 115; arthritis argument by, 116, 119–120, 146; *de verbis* beliefs and, as response to, 118–121

Caesar, Julius, 110
Carnap, Rudolf, 26n29
Carr, David, 189
Carrol, Lewis, 108
Cartesian dualism, 16, 18
causal closure: assumption of, 12–13; formulations, 26n33; mental states and, 17
causal inference, 37–38
causation: assumptions about, 11–13; coherence and, 38–40; constructionism, materialism, and, 36–38; explanation and, 13–14; Foucault on, 25n15; historical evidence and, 37–38, 39, 40; imaginary items and, 12–13; immaterial, 4–6, 66; physical items and, 11–13; questions pertaining to, 14; realism and, 36–40
causation by omission, 12–13

change, conceptual, 89–84, 101n22
chemistry, 8–9, 89, 122
Chomsky, Noam, 10–11, 112–113, 180
Churchill, Winston, 76
Churchland, Paul, 72–73, 81n27
Cicero, Marcus Tullius, 66, 81n7
Clark, Andy, 231n45
classical theory concepts, 83–85, 87–88, 101n1
classification: concepts, propositions, and, 84–87, 93; perception and, 99, 219–221, 227–228; perception *simpliciter* and, 219–221, 228–230
Cleve, James van, 232n48
coherence, 38–40
coherence-based truth, 33, 34–35
coherentism: advantages of, 34–36; antirealism and, 29, 39–40; realism and, 34–36, 39–40
Cold War, 192
collective entities, 47–61
colligatory concepts, 189–195, 206n20
Collingwood, Robin George, 71–72, 133–134, 162
colonialism, 214–216
Columbus, Christopher, 94
compatibilism, 77–79
computer translation, 183–184
concepts: in anti-realism, 97; classical theory, 83–85, 87–89, 98–99, 101n1; classification, propositions, and, 84–87; definitions and terminology of, 84–87, 141n1; essentialism and, 127–136; facts and, 93–95; incommensurability and, 96–97, 98–101; meaning and, 88–90, 93, 101n13, 101n14; mental state and, 83, 85; propositions, words, and, 87–90, 93; propositions and, as mental representations, 90–92; relata of, 93–94; theories and, 95–98, 102n37; thought-contents and, 90–92. *See also* "Theory"-theory concepts
conceptual change, 89–90, 101n22
conceptual conjunctions and disjunctions, 134–136
consciousness, 16–17; realism about, 25n25
constructionism, 29–40; causation, materialism, and, 36–38; methodology

and, 35–36; opponents of, 33; postmodernism and, 6, 30
contents of historical works, 198–205
contextualization, 157–167; authorship and, 171n66; *de verbis* and *de signis* beliefs and, 167; holist understanding of, 164–166; inconceivability and, 144–151; individualism and, 157–158, 166–169; novel properties and, 151–152; reflexive argument and, 157–167; shared rationality and, 160–163
continuity argument in the social sciences, 56
Copernicus, Nicolaus, 86–87, 97, 136, 146, 150–151
The Course of German History (Taylor, A. J. P.), 197
Crane, Tim, 117
Critique of Pure Reason (Kant), 185
Croce, Benedetto, 30, 199

Dante, Alighieri, 185–187
Danto, Arthur, 11, 86, 93, 146–147, 154, 170n24, 222, 224
Darwin's theory of evolution, 144–146
Davidson, Donald, 124n5, 153, 170n17
De architectura (Vitruvius), 162
death of the author thesis, 5
decisions, 72–77
Decline of the West (Spengler), 144–146, 169n6
Descartes, René, 43–45, 117
descriptivism, 138–141, 141n19, 142n20. See also metalinguistic descriptivism
de signis beliefs, 108–112, 174–175. See also beliefs
detachability of perceptual contents, 219–221, 225, 226–228
determinism, 9, 209–210; on free will, 77–81; hard, 78–81; materialism and, 78
de verbis beliefs: *de signis* beliefs and, 108–112, 174–175; externalism and, 118–123; language and, 108–114, 118–123; metalinguistic descriptivism and, 139–141; as response to Burge, 118–121; as response to Putnam, 121–123; translation and, 111, 179–185

Dilthey, Wilhelm, 157–158, 159, 169
Donnellan, Keith, 108–109
Dray, William, 72
Dretske, Fred, 225
Droysen, Johann Gustav, 201
Dummett, Michael, 32, 153–154, 170n22, 179, 183–184
Durkheim, Émil, 63
Dvořák, Max, 66

Einstein, Albert, 97, 129–130
emergence, 17, 50, 78
Engels, Friedrich, 7, 51
épistémè, 146
Epstein, Brian, 64n23
Erasmus, Desiderius, 72
essentialism, 22; anachronism and, 130–134; Aristotle and, 128–129; concepts and, 127–136; conceptual conjunctions and disjunctions in, 134–136; historical research and, 127–136; language and, 131–134, 136–141; materialism and, 127–128; naming and, 137–141; thought-contents and, 136–141
ethnic prejudice, 146
Euclid, 130, 178
Evans, Gareth, 226–227, 228, 231n45
explanation: causation and, 13–14; free will and historical explanations, 69–72; *quomodo*, 66–69, 76, 79, 152
externalism about mental contents, 115–123

facts: definition, 95; reference and, 93–95
fallibility (of evidence), 41–42
fallibility and frailty (according to Erasmus), 69
falsehood, 93–95, 196
"Felinia" (the colligatory concept of all cats), 195
Fermia, Joseph, 158–159
Field, G. C., 86
Firestone, Chaz, 230
Fischer, Fritz, 201, 203–204
Fodor, Jerry, 9, 87–88, 117–118, 153, 220, 230n3
Foucault, Michel, 25n15, 146, 149, 151, 169n6, 169n9, 175–176, 187n5, 218n2

Index

free will, 3–4, 65–66; compatibilism on, 77–79; decisions and, 72–77; determinism on, 77–81; historical explanations and, 69–72; libertarianism on, 77–78; materialist historiography and, 77–81; mental states and, 78; motivation and, 74–77, 79–81; neurobiology and, 78–81; *quomodo* explanations on, 66–69, 76–77, 79; rationality and, 72–77
Frege, Gottlob, 90–92, 93, 102n33
French Revolution, 191, 192, 193, 195
Frey, Dagobert, 71

Gadamer, Hans Georg, 158, 169, 171n38, 223–224
Galilei, Galileo, 129, 135–136, 142n20, 148, 161–162
Gauker, Christopher, 111
Gavrilo Princip, 67, 69
Geist (Spirit), 66, 70–71, 166
geometry, 42, 141n3, 169n3; Pythagoras's theorems and, 90–92
German Ideology (Marx), 51
Gerring, John, 141n3
Gettier, Edmund, 41
Gibbon, Edward, 196–197, 199–200
Giddens, Anthony, 63n18
Ginzburg, Carlo, 30
God, 136, 141, 213–214
gold, 128, 131, 132–134
Goldstein, Leon, 34–35, 39, 45n20, 96, 224
Gombrich, Ernst, 96, 223–224, 231n23
Goodman, Cecile, 221
Gordon, Ian, 221–222
grammar, 184–185
Grundlinien (Ast), 166
Gumplowicz, Ludwig, 63

Hanson, Norwood Russell, 222
Hapsburg, dynasty, 108
Hapsburg, Maximilian I, 4
hard determinism, 78–81
Harman, Gilbert, 169n15
Hedicke, Robert, 70–71
Heidegger, Martin, 113
Hempel, Carl: Hempel's dilemma, 10–11, 22; Panofsky and, 70; historical explanations and, 67–69; historical laws and, 67–69; on rationality, 72
Herder, Johann Gottfried, 152–153
hermeneutic circle, 169
hermeneutic meaning, 177–178, 181, 183
Herodotus, 12
Herschel, William, 129–130
Hirsch, E. D., 158, 187n2
historical documents, 39, 41, 171n56; assumptions about, 198–203
historical entities, 22
historical evidence, 22; causation and, 37–38, 39, 40
historical figures, 22–23, 65–66; as historians, 24; Nowell-Smith on, 39; social ontology and, 50–52. *See also* mental states
historical items, 11
historical knowledge: assumptions and, 42, 51–52, 54, 198–203; reliability of, 41–45; fallibility of, 41–42; infallibilism of, 41, 46n39; observability and, 37; warrants and, 46n39
historical laws: historical explanations and, 69–72; *quomodo* explanations and, 67–69
historical reality, 30
historical research: essentialism and, 129–130; materialism and, 3–4, 9–11, 18–21, 209–211; methodological problems in, 20, 35; Goldstein on methodology of, 35, 39
historical-social environment, 65; individualism and, 48–50; materialism and, 48–50
historiography: materialist, 77–81; postmodernist, 5–6, 210–211, 212; historical works; contents of historical works, 198–202; opacity of, 190–195; propositions that historical text conveys, 196–198; questions and answers about, 202–203; shared rationality and, 162–164; translation of, 179–187; transparency of, 189–205; understanding of, 173–179
Der Historismus und seine Probleme (Troeltsch), 158
history: causation in, 11–96; contextualization and, 143–167;

philosophy of, 2–7
Hitler, Adolf, 201
Hohenzollern, Wilhelm, 66
holism: inconceivability and, 148–151; individualism-holism debate, 50–54, 61–63; methodological, 49–50; ontological, 49, 52, 61–63
homonyms, 154–156
humanities: materialism and, 212–218; "New Look" psychology's impact on, 221–224; perception *simpliciter* and, 221–224
Husserl, Edmund, 227–228

idealism, 212, 216
imaginary causation, 12–13
imaginary immaterial entities, 1–2
immaterial causation, 4–5
impenetrability of vision, 230, 232n48
imperialism, 214–216
incommensurability, 96–99
inconceivability, 144–152; contextualization and, 144–151; dilemma between weak and strong, 146–151; holism and, 148–151; novel properties and, 151–152
Index aristotelicus (Bonitz), 111
individualism, 47–61; coincidence arguments against, 56–57; contextualization and, 166–169; continuity argument against, 56; individualism-holism debate, 47–61; individuals' interactions and, 54–59; materialism and, 47–50; mental states and, 60–61; methodological, 49, 52; modal statements about collective entities and, 58–59; ontological, 49–50; procedural, 21, 51; social ontology and, 48, 50–52; social rules, regulations, and roles relating to, 60–63; straw-man arguments against, 54–57
inertial mass, 129–130
infallibilism, 41, 46n39
intentionalism, 177–179
intentionality, 102n24
interpretation: defining, 174; meaning and, 24, 173–179; translation and, 183–185; understanding and, 173–176, 187n1
irrationality, 73–74

Jakobsen, Roman, 184–185
Jay, Martin, 158–159
Jenkins, Keith, 190
Jesus Christ, 213, 218n4
Juhl, P. D., 187n2
July 1914 crisis, 52, 75–76, 202

Kant, Immanuel, 162, 185
Katz, Jerrold, 112–113
"Khrushchev's Thaw," 193
Kim, Jaegwon, 42
Kincaid, Harold, 26n28
Knapp, Stephen, 187n2
knowledge: definition of, 41–42. *See also* historical knowledge
Koch's bacillus, 116
Koffka, Kurt, 221
Koselleck, Reinhart, 89, 122
Kosso, Peter, 31, 32, 203, 230n5
Koyré, Alexandre, 129
Kripke, Saul, 49, 122, 127, 141n7, 142n21; *Naming and Necessity* by, 130–134, 137–141
Kuhn, Thomas, 11, 96, 102n39, 103n42, 222–223, 224
Kunstwollen concept, 4, 146
Kuukkanen, Jouni-Matti, 24, 101n22, 191–195, 206n20

Lamprecht, Karl, 4, 70, 165
language: anti-mentalism and, 105–107; beliefs and, 107–115; brain and, 114, 116–118; constructionism and, 65; *de signis* beliefs and, 108–112; *de verbis* beliefs and, 108–114, 118–123; essentialism and, 131–134, 136–141; externalism and, 115–123; homonyms and, 154–156; linguistic meaning and, 181; materialism and, 108–112; meaning and, 105–107, 112–113; mental states and, 105–107, 116–118, 152–154; naming and, 130–134; ontological considerations, 112–115, 124n10; postmodernists and, 4–6, 25n13; presuppositions and, 124n7. *See also* translation
Latin, 1–2
Latour, Bruno, 84–85, 87, 116, 134
Laurence, Stephen, 101n1, 102n37

Lavoisier, Antoine, 129
Lewis, David, 14
libarum arbitrium, 72
libertarianism: on free will, 77–78; political, 53
linguistic meaning, 181
Loewer, Barry, 26n29
The Logic of the History of Ideas (Bevir), 27n52, 166–167, 177–179
Lorenz, Chris, 45n5
Lorraine, Franz Ferdinand: July 1914 crisis and, 75–76; World War I and, 12–13, 36–37, 67
Lorraine, Franz Joseph, 73
Luther, Martin, 213–214

Maar, Alexander, 14
Mandelbaum, Maurice, 189
Mao Tse-Dung, 109
Margolis, Eric, 101n1, 102n37
Marwick, Arthur, 122–123
Marx, Karl, 7–8, 51
Marxism, 214–216
materialism: analytic philosophy and, 19–21; anti-realism and, 40; Bevir and, 21, 27n52; causation, constructionism, and, 36–38; definition of, 7–9; determinism and, 78; essentialism and, 127–128; historical research and, 3–4, 9–11, 209–211; historical-social environment and, 48–50; humanities and, 212–218; individualism and, 47–50; language and, 108–112; mind-body problem and, 16–18; philosophy of history and, 2–7; physicalism and, 7–11; postmodernism and, 6–7; realism and, 29–38; term usage, 2. *See also specific topics*
materialist historiography, 77–81
McCullagh, C. Behan, 32, 74, 189, 204, 224
McDowell, John, 226–227, 232n47
meaning: authorship and, 174–176, 187n4; concepts and, 88–90, 101n13, 101n14; hermeneutic, 177–178, 181, 183; interpretation and, 173–179; language and, 105–107, 112–113; linguistic, 181; mental states and, 187n2; ontology and, 176; semantic, 112–113, 177; thought-contents and, 114, 154, 170n24, 175–176; translation and, 179–187; of words, 93, 101n13, 106
Meiland, Jack, 43
Mellor, D. H., 122
mental states: assumptions about, 16–18; beliefs and, 109; biological states and, 9, 16–17, 116–117; brain and, 9, 47, 78–79, 116–118; causal closure and, 17; concepts and, 83, 85, 90–92; externalism and, 115–118; individualism and, 60–61; language and, 105–107, 116–118, 152–154; mind-body problem and, 16–18, 116–118; nervous system and, 9, 16–17, 116–118; propositions and, 85–86; propositions and concepts, as mental representations, 90–92; social institutions and, 17, 60–61; social sciences and, 47, 60–61; verbal thinking and, 152–154
metalinguistic descriptivism, 138–141, 141n19, 142n20
metaphysics, 5, 7, 30, 129–131, 137, 148, 158, 216
Methodenlehre der Kunstgeschichte (Hedicke), 70–71
methodological holism, 49
methodological individualism, 49, 52
methodology, 20, 35–36
Michaels, Walter Benn, 187n2
Millar, Allan, 219–220
mind-body problem, 16–18
modal argument against individualism, 58–59
Moses, 137, 139
motivation, 74–75, 77, 79–81
Murphey, Murray, 32, 37

Nagel, Ernest, 46n43
naming, 142n21; essentialism and, 130–134, 137–141; language and, 130–134; metalinguistic descriptivism and, 138–141, 141n19, 142n20; theories of names and, 130–134, 137–141, 142n20
Naming and Necessity (Kripke), 130–134, 137–141
Narration and Knowledge (Danto), 86

naturalism, 2, 7–11
nature, 26n29
nervous system, 9, 16–17
Neurath, Otto, 26n29
neurobiology: brain and, 78–81, 114; free will and, 78–81
"New Look" psychology, 87, 101, 221–225
Newtonian physics, 97, 123
Nixon, Richard, 131, 137–138, 142n21
Noë, Alva, 230
non-conceptual content, 225–227, 226–227
Norberg-Schulz, Christian, 113, 223–224
novel properties: beliefs and, 151–152; holist perspective and, 151–152
Nowell-Smith, Patrick Horace, 39

Oakeshott, Michael, 30
observability: historical evidence and, 37; realism and, 31–32; science and, 32
observation, 222, 230n5
ontological holism, 52, 61–63
ontological individualism, 49–50. *See also* individualism
ontology: meaning and, 176; social, 48, 50–52
opacity of historical works, 190–195
oppression, 202, 214–216, 218n7
Otte, T. G., 52, 202

painting, 87–88
Panofsky, Erwin, 22, 25n10, 69–72, 72, 73, 144
Parthenon idea, 170n21
Pašić, Nikola, 75, 81n33
Pasteur, Louis, 84
perception, 219–228; classification and, 86–87, 99, 219–221, 227–228; Fodor on, 220, 230n3; "New Look" psychology and, 87, 101, 221–225; non-conceptual content of, 225–227; observation and, 222, 230n5; seeing and, 101; "Theory"-theory concepts and, 219
perception *simpliciter*, 210, 225–228; classification and, 219–221, 228–230; detachability of perceptual contents and, 219, 225, 226–227, 228; humanities and, 221–224; non-conceptual content and, 225–227; philosophical arguments in favor of, 227–228; positions in favor of and against, 225–227; seeing, 228–230, 231n43; "Theory"-theory concepts and, 220–221, 226
Pérez-Gómez, Alberto, 5
Peter the Hermit, 196–197
petitio principii, 54
Petrarch, Francesco, 146–147, 193
philosophers, 20–21, 22; postmodernist, 6
philosophy: analytic, 19–21; of history, 2–7; of social sciences, 47–50, 53–54
Philosophy of Mind (Kim), 42
physical event, 26n33
physicalism, 26n29; definition of, 9–11; Hempel's dilemma and, 10–11; materialism and, 7–11
physical items, 11–13
physics, 7, 8–9, 10–11, 148. *See also* metaphysics
Pinder, Wilhelm, 71
Pizarro, Francisco, 128
Plato, 5, 41, 146
political libertarianism, 53
politics, 53
Polybius, 4, 89–90
Postman, Leo, 223
postmodernism: constructionism and, 6, 30; materialism and, 6–7, 210–216
postmodernist historiography, 5–6, 190–195, 210–211, 212
postmodernist philosophers, 6
Pouchet, Félix Alèxandre, 84
presuppositions, 198; language and, 124n7; Princip, Gavrilo, 67, 69
Pristley, Joseph, 129
procedural individualism, 21, 27n52, 50, 166
properties: artifacts and, 148–151; novel, 151–152
propositions: classifications, and, 84–87; concepts, and, 87–89; as mental representations, 90–92; mental state and, 85–86; reference, and, 93–94; that historical text conveys, 196–198; truth and falsehood in, 93–95, 102n33
Protestantism, 213–214
Prudovsky, Gad, 170n24

Ptolemy, 66, 97, 99–101, 136, 164
Putnam, Hilary, 23, 115–122, 124n19, 132–134
Pylyshyn, Zenon, 230
Pythagoras's theorem, 90–92

questions that historical works answer, 202–203
Quine, Willard van Orman, 97–98, 103n50, 179
quomodo explanations: on free will, 66–69, 76–77, 79; novel properties and, 152

Raffman, Diana, 228–230
Ranke, Leopold, 4, 40, 197, 200
rationality: action and, 72–74; decisions and, 72–77; free will and, 72–77; Hempel on, 72; irrationality and, 73–74; shared, 160–164
realism: causation and, 36–40; coherentism and, 34–36, 39–40; consciousness and, 25n25; facts and, 30; historical knowledge reliability and, 41–45; historical reality and, 29–30, 31; materialism and, 29–38; observability and, 31–32; straw-man arguments and, 31–33. *See also* anti-realism
reality: language and, 5–6; metaphysics and, 30
Red Army, 14
reducibility, 9, 49–50
reductionism, 8–9
reference, 93–92, 106; reflexive argument, 24, 157–159
relata, 93–94, 194
religious perspectives on history, 4–7, 42, 65, 213–214; Renaissance, 85, 144, 146–147, 162, 191, 193, 194–195, 200; denial of, 36–37, 136–137
Riegl, Alois, 4, 70, 223
Roberts, Clayton, 67, 72–73, 81n7
Russell, Bertrand, 137, 141n19
Russia, 78–79

Sarajevo assassination, 73, 75–76, 81n33
Saussure, Ferdinand de, 152–153
Sawyer, Keith, 26n28
Scheele, Carl Wilhelm, 129
Schleiermacher, Friedrich, 169

Scholl, Brian, 230
Schwartz, Stephen, 122
Searle, John, 7, 16–17, 50, 117, 137, 206n19, 231n43; on intentionality, 102n24, 226
Sedlmayr, Hans, 66, 71, 223
semantic meaning, 112–113, 177
Serbia, 73–74, 75–76
shared rationality, 160–164
Simmel, Georg, 54, 63n19
skepticism, 43; bias and, 43; Nagel on, 46n43
Skinner, Quentin, 154, 159, 170n24
social institutions, 17, 54–61
social interactions, 54–59; social ontology, 48, 50–52
social programs, 53
social sciences: historical-social environment and, 48–50; individualism-holism debate in, 50–54, 61–63; mental states and, 47, 60–61; philosophy of, 47–50, 53–54; politics and, 53; social interactions and, 54–57, 60–63; social rules, regulations, and roles, 60–63
Spengler, Oswald, 4, 25n15, 71, 144–146, 159–160, 169n6
Spinoza, Baruch, 71
Spirit (*Geist*), 66, 70–71, 166
Stalin, Joseph Vissarionovich, 114–115, 118, 191–192
Stalingrad, 14
Sterelny, Kim, 122
strong inconceivability, 146–151
Supreme Court of the USA (Uzquiano's argument), 56–57, 60–61, 64n24

Tacitus, Publius Cornelius, 4, 25n3, 35, 66, 110
Taylor, A. J. P., 74, 197, 201
Taylor, Charles, 161–162
teacher-pupil relationship (Bevir), 166–167
Thatcher, Margaret, 53
theology, 213–214
"Theory"-theory concepts, 95–98; incommensurability and, 98–101; perception and, 99, 220, 226; The Thirty Years War, 86–87, 101n9
Thomas Aquinas, 85, 156–157

Thompson, Evan, 230
Thucydides, 4
Total Consciousness (Troeltsch), 158
translation, 154–156, 179–185; computer translation, 183–184; *de verbis* beliefs and, 111–112, 179–183, 184; grammar and, 184–185; of historical documents, 179–187; homonyms and, 154–156; legitimacy of, 181–182; meaning and, 179–187; problems with, 154–157; understanding and, 179–187; for whom?, 179–183
transparency of historical workd, 189–205;
Troeltsch, Ernst, 51–52, 66, 158
Truth, correspondence versus coherence-based theories of, 32–33; *The Truth in History* (McCullagh), 74, 224
Tucker, Aviezer, 38, 48, 123, 230n5
Twin Earth argument, 115–119, 121–122
"Two Dogmas of Empiricism" (Quine), 97–98

underdetermination thesis, 97–98
understanding, 173–176; defining, 173–174; of historical documents, 173–179; interpretation and, 173–176, 187n1; translation and, 179–187; zero external author information, 174–175

Uzquiano, Gabriel, 56, 64n24

verbal thinking, 152–154
visual imagination, 153–154
Vitruvius, Marcus Pollio, 162
Volga river, 14

Wahrheit und Methode (Gadamer), 158
Walsh, W. H., 53–54, 190–191
warrants, 46n39
Washington, George, 37
weak inconceivability, 146–151
weak intentionalism, 177–179
White, Hayden, 190, 197, 206n1, 207n26
White, Morton, 20
Witmer, Gene, 26n29, 26n30
Wittgenstein, Ludwig, 87–88
words: beliefs and, 110; concepts, propositions, and, 87–90, 93; meaning of, 93, 101n13, 106
World War I, 73–74, 191, 201, 202, 203–204; World War II, 201, 221
Worringer, Wilhelm, 71
writing history, 21, 52

zero external author information understanding, 174–175
Zinn, Howard, 52, 202

About the Author

Branko Mitrović received PhDs in architectural history and philosophy and is currently employed as a professor at NTNU (*Norges Teknisk-Naturvitenskapelige Universitet*), Trondheim, Norway. He is the author (or co-author) of seven other books and has been the recipient of the Humboldt Research Award.

www.ingramcontent.com/pod-product-compliance
Lightning Source LLC
Chambersburg PA
CBHW050901300426
44111CB00010B/1329